Austin Climbing

Sport Routes • Deep Water Solos

john hogge

Austin Climbing

Sport Routes • Deep Water Solos

John Hogge
Copyright © 2012 Gnarly Press

Gnarly Press
1010 Bee Creek Road
Spicewood, TX 78669
AustinClimbing@pobox.com
www.AustinClimbingBook.com

FIRST EDITION

First Printing (2012)

Photography: John Hogge unless otherwise credited.
Cover Photo: Pete Bishop on Lip-o-suction (5.12a), Reimers Ranch
Back Photo: Jan Salinas, Trip Lucas, Laura Yero, David Phillips at Hueco Wall, Pace Bend
Page 3 Ad Photo: Scott Harris, BITD
Adobe Consultant: Britta Kakacek
Graphics: John Hogge and Britta Kakacek

International Standard Book Number: ISBN 978-0-9850300-0-1

Printed in the United States of America at Ginny's Printing, Austin, Texas
Published by Gnarly Press in Spicewood, Texas.

WARNING: Rock climbing is inherently dangerous. YOU MIGHT DIE. You might be severely injured. Don't rock climb. Don't do it. Don't re this guidebook. GET OUT WHILE YOU CAN, MANG!!!!!!!!!!!!! If you choose to climb, do so at your own risk, seek proper instruction, b off when you need to, and don't trust anything in this guidebook. It has subjective opinions, and errors may exist. Some routes are labe PG/R/X risky, but really every route is X (guaranteed death) if a hold breaks while you're clipping high, or if you pull up tons of unnecess rope and pump out, or if your belayer drips unnecessary slack towards the ground or lead-belays while sitting, or if any of a numbe things go wrong. And your belayer could be injured or die from rock fall or you falling on them. It's your decision to climb or not cli

Always presume this guide is inaccurate, out-of-date and its information subjective to each climber. Use your judgment, not guide, when climbing and belaying. Expect bad luck to strike, due to rock fall, hold breaks, and bad belays. Expect hold breaks all areas, not just the new ones. Expect fixed protection to be missing, damaged, unsafe, and innacurately described her

THE AUTHOR AND PUBLISHER EXPRESSLY DISCLAIM ALL REPRESENTATIONS AND WARRANTIES REGARDING THIS BOO THE ACCURACY OR RELIABILITY OF ITS INFORMATION, AND THE RESULTS OF YOUR USE OF ITS INFORMATION. TH MAKE NO REPRESENTATIONS OR WARRANTIES, EXPRESSED OR IMPLIED, OF ANY KIND REGARDING THE ACCURA OR RELIABILITY OF THIS BOOK'S INFORMATION. THEY MAKE NO WARRANTIES OF MERCHANTABILITY OR FITNESS F A PARTICULAR PURPOSE. THE USER OF THIS BOOK ASSUMES ALL RISK ASSOCIATED WITH THE USE OF THIS BO

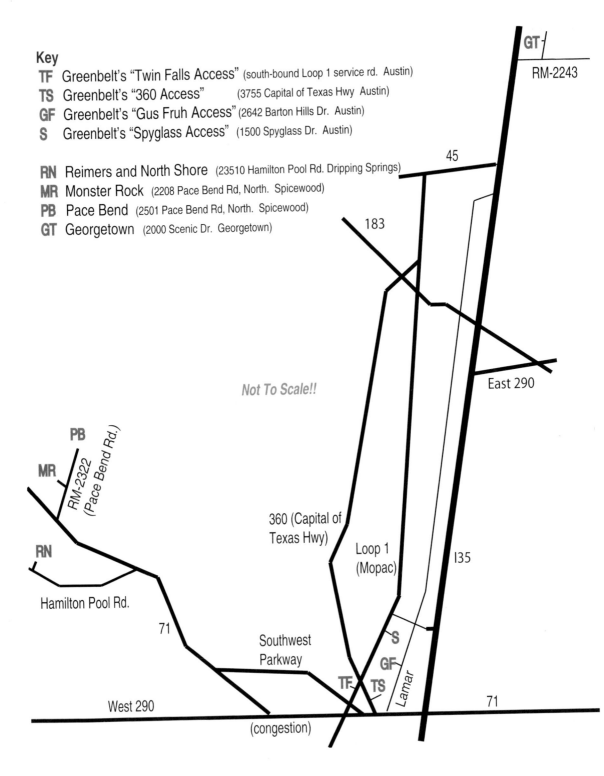

Table of Contents

Introduction

This guidebook covers 584 sweet sport routes, an awesome 800 problem Deep Water Soloing (DWS) park, and 40 new boulder problems, all within 35 minutes of a great little city, Austin, Texas. Rock & Ice once reported Austin as one of the best urban climbing areas. It's even better now, with over 200 routes added since then. Austin has a wealth of convenient climbing, and friendly locals to help out newbs and out-of-towners.

We detail six excellent limestone climbing areas in downtown Austin and nearby: Barton Creek Greenbelt (downtown), Reimers Ranch, North Shore (a new extension of Reimers Ranch), Monster Rock, Georgetown, and Pace Bend (for DWS). Appendix B points to information on other Texas climbing areas.

Bouldering

Previous area guidebooks covered a mix of lead climbing and bouldering. Then Jeff Jackson published Texas Limestone Bouldering to

cover just the bouldering areas, an act of organizational genius for which Jeff deserves fat royalty checks. It let us cover sport routes uncluttered with bouldering. Climbers may appreciate grabbing a rope and a book full of sport routes, or grabbing a pad and Jeff's book full of boulder problems.

This guidebook only covers Monster Rock bouldering and a couple new Reimers problems. It locates undeveloped bouldering spots at North Shore. It gives a sales pitch and logistics for Duende Cove at Pace Bend, and for potential development of Choss Cave in the Greenbelt.

Daniel Ezell 📷   Ben Edwards

Water

We're excited to feature Pace Bend's fabulous deep water soloing, a huge, popular area that has never received extensive coverage. Many sport climbers turn to Pace Bend as a hot weather alternative. Pace Bend is not easy to cover, with roughly 800 problems appearing and disappearing as the water level changes. In the beginning, we figured that if we just mentioned every climbable cove and provided some parking beta, it would be a public service rivaling affordable healthcare. Then we became addicted to exploring and detailing Pace Bend every day for about two months. Mang, two months isn't enough, but it's a start.

Rock

All areas in this guidebook are lime "stone" climbing. Nearby, Enchanted Rock offers actual *rock* climbing...on granite. This book is about *sponge* climbing, on what used to be mud, carved by ancient organisms and hardened into sort-of-rock. It takes bolts, but it doesn't dependably take gear. Gear tends to blow it to smithereens on a lead fall. Followed by the deadly, vindictive wrath of a mob of stick-clip-waving sport climbers, led by whoever bolted that route and whoever was projecting that route. They usually form an assault wedge, like what the ancient Vikings used to freak out their enemies. Go to nearby Enchanted Rock to use your gear.

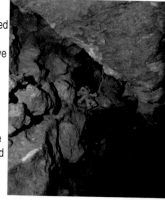

Most of Texas limestone climbing is short (25-50'), powerful, and interesting. Lynn Hill visited, back in the day, and said these routes are short, but they're *on* you the whole way. Come here for the fun party city and the interesting climbs downtown and just west of town. If you are used to taller routes, just treat this as excellent roped bouldering. For out-of-state visitors, Austin is also a fun stop on the way to Hueco Tanks or El Potrero Chico.

Priorities

Back when the last two Austin-area sport climbing guidebooks were published, 5.15 had not been sent. A contributor to the first book, Mr. X, joked about climbers evolving to where they could send 5.15 and logarithms at the same time. We've since learned that Mr. X was wrong: 5.15 isn't actually climbable, and most pro climbers realize 5.14d is as hard as humans will *ever* send. The few claimed 5.15 sends are a sham, and the pros are in cahoots with each other via a Facebook-organized conspiracy, to perpetuate the sham and keep the sponsorship dollars rolling their way as fast as usual. Money and fame are their priorities.

Climbing is a wiser priority, and Austin climbing is so convenient that one can easily prioritize it high vs. work and other responsibilities. So, buy this guide, move to Austin, and join the fun. Wait, what did we just say? Uh, buy this guide, visit Austin *just this once*, then clear off of our projects and go away. We have an afternoon appointment we need to get to, and we have time for one more send attempt if you're not on our project. Thanks.

Our priorities for this guidebook have been:

1. Positive cash flow.

2. 110% clarity, through detailed text and topos.

3. 110% accuracy on route names, locations, bolt counts, and FAs.

4. Discovery of useful variations that provide warmups or fill gaps in a wall's mix of route difficulty.

5. Icons describing each route's steepness, character, stick-clip recommendation, and "premium" moves.

6. Revised route grades at a whopping 89% accuracy!

7. Stories about the bolters and FAs. Why list these old guys unless we get to know them? The stories have been hard to collect. Please send us more for 2nd edition!

8. Edgy humor, no doubt followed one day by writer's remorse and apologies.

Values

John Sherman was proven wrong, when Chris Sharma broke into 5.15b and realized it *really is* all about the numbers. Therefore, one focus of this guidebook project was to investigate previously published route grades.

Over the years, holds break and polish out, and established grades go bad. And some were bad from the start, since grading is difficult.[1] The public conducts an ongoing debate about the routes they climb, and guidebook authors weigh the evidence and pass judgment. Some climbers are mavericks and stick their neck out in suggesting grade revisions. Many climbers are conservative, siding with established grades or whatever grade you feed them on a new route.

In an accidental social experiment, Prototype was first entered as 10c at www.rockclimbing.com. Climbers subsequently entered their grade opinions: 12 for 5.10c and 3 for 5.10d. Then, Prototype was reentered as 10d. Magically, subsequent opinions went 3 for 5.10c and a whopping 15 for 5.10d. Conclusion: most people don't want to be disagreeable. But our job is to seek the truth and express it. We've no doubt made mistakes in grading, but we've worked hard to climb routes, read online comments, interview others, and publish route grades that are, as a whole, less inaccurate.

Apologies

"Everybody is a critic." –Mr. X

The old guidebook and climber's tome of wisdom, Texas Limestone II, had an ominous Apologies section that claimed Texas climbers are cantankerous. The author expected to catch hell for sandbagging, grade-inflating, inaccuracies, etc. Given the wit of that apology and the rest of the book, few probably complained about it in its early years. Later, new routes went in, grades were bitched about, and a common complaint was voiced by all: "Where's edition 3? My route's awesome, and it needs to be listed, Jefe!"

---

[1] Grade opinions are like certain body parts. Everybody has them, and they all stink.

Sean O'Grady then stepped up, wrote the much-needed Austin Rock, and caught criticism for missing topos, errors, and confusing parts. But Sean's book was invaluable, covering roughly 124 new routes in Reimers alone, and converting most from Jefesque 5.10-/5.10/5.10+ grades to the national standard 5.10a/b/c/d letter grades. Within a month of publication, arrests for assault dropped off at Prototype Wall. With four smaller increments per number grade instead of three, debates were more frequent but less heated, and letter grades kept most ornery Texan grade debates from degrading into slugfests. Sean hopefully laughed all the way to the bank. This guidebook is built on his and Jeff's shoulders. Without Sean's book, we'd likely have a hundred Reimers routes blandly named "Unnamed Route", that few want to climb. (Climber one: "Hey man, I just sent Unnamed Route 5.11c/d! Finally!" Climber two: "Whatever.")

Texas climbers are a dichotomy, with big beautiful friend-groups, newb-fosterers and angels for the most part, and cliques, elitists, rumormongers and online-haters occupying a minority position. Visitors from out-of-state rarely see our dark side. They leave Texas with compliments to the angels, such as the following email:

Hello Austin Climbers,

I am heading back to France after a fantastic week in Austin. I am so impressed by the friendliness and hospitality of the group. The quality of climbing is awesome. In just a few days, I have been to six different walls in Greenbelt and Reimers and appreciated the great passionate discussions with you around beers, tacos…Thank you!

Please come and visit Montpellier, which is the second best place to live & climb on earth after Austin ;-) with places like Thaurac, St-Guilhem-le-Desert, Seynes, Caroux, Gorges du Verdon, Calanques de Marseille, and many more.

Cheers,
Pierre

Jeff Jackson on Pink Wall (5.12c) © Chris Hunter / www.Hunterimagery.com

May the Angels of Good overcome Evil, and may we all get the most enjoyment we can out of this powerful, interesting, limestone.

Become a part of the friendly, Austin climbing community on these online forums:

www.erockonline.com Lively discussions about Austin limestone, Enchanted Rock, gear, road trips, choss, all well organized into separate forums.

www.groups.yahoo.com/group/austin_climbers An active forum for saying what time, between about 2pm and 4pm, people will show up at the Greenbelt's "New Wall" every freakin Tuesday and Thursday, and at Reimers' "Prototype Wall" every goddang Saturday and Sunday. You don't need a partner in Austin; just show up. This group spends most of the session on 5.11's and hits some 5.12's.

www.groups.yahoo.com/group/ClimbingBuddies An active forum for planning outings mostly below 5.11, usually Wednesday evenings at various Greenbelt Walls (with flood-lit night climbing in the winter). Occasionally the troops get called out on weekends at Reimers' Dead Cats Wall. Very newb & visitor friendly.

www.facebook.com Many local climbers use this thing to coordinate plans, spray sends, and post countless butt-shots. Fan pages are sprouting; check out Central Texas Mountaineers, Reimers Ranch & North Shore, Monster Rock, Pace Bend Park, and San Antonio Rock Climbers.

GLAM Climb of Texas: a Facebook group of Gay/Lesbian/And More (all inclusive) climbers favoring mildly sexually inappropriate humor and unusual styles of ascent.

www.groups.yahoo.com/group/sheclimbs Girls rule.

www.groups.yahoo.com/group/onegreenbottle A clique we like the sounds of, described online as "Top-roped 5.10 hang-dogging fans of Jodie Foster with dreams of flashing 5.13 trad at altitude."

www.ctmrocks.com Read up about Central Texas Mountaineers, a non-profit which handles hardware replacement, applications for new bolted routes, and Austin's two fun climbing comp/festivals.

www.climbsa.org, a non-profit for securing existing climbing areas and opening new ones in and near San Antonio.
www.rockclimbing.com Read and write reviews of routes in Austin and dang near everywhere.
www.mountainproject.com for additional route information.

Promises

North Shore will likely see 60 more lines bolted. Our Pace Bend coverage is just a start; it will need corrections and more details. Reimers and the Greenbelt still have some valuable lines unbolted. North Shore's upper 5.11 (and tougher) routes have seen little traffic, and their grades will need adjustment. We promise to publish uploads and/or future editions to stay current as areas change. Please help us by sending corrections, new route information, and old stories to AustinClimbing@pobox.com. To keep your copy of this book current, look for downloads on www.AustinClimbingBook.com. Thanks!

Tacos

The Austin taco hierarchy, low to high, according to Joel Schopp:
"Taco Bell < Taco Cabana < Taco Shack < Taco Real < El Mercado < Chuy's < Taco Deli < Torchy's < Chapala."

Dogs

Dogs must stay on leash at all times at The Greenbelt, Reimers, North Shore, and Pace Bend. While the leash law is selectively enforced in the Greenbelt, the fine is $180 or a "Responsible Dog Owner" class. Monster Rock prohibits dogs, due to ladder access and crowded space in the pit. Georgetown does not prohibit dogs, but bring a leash to deal with traffic in the hospital parking lots and to keep your dog away from patients and their stressed-out visitors.

Lynn Hill once visited Reimers and said, "What's with all the dogs?" Back then, they were allowed to run loose, steal lunches, lie on rope bags, and track human/animal waste onto gear. They still do all that, as climbers disobey Reimers policy. Should your dog get off leash and be bitten by a rattlesnake, on a Sunday, your options might be limited to AM/PM Animal Hospital (2239 S. Lamar). If it gets a mouth full of 150 or so porcupine needles, they can deal with that too…for about $600. No kidding — ask Chris Barton.

In the Greenbelt, running dog packs occasionally bump belayers, and communication between climbing parties competes against barking dogs and their owners' scolding. ATX climbers generally support the presence of crag dogs, but they want to see more responsibility by the owners.

Pace Bend is hot up top where dogs will have to stay, and tree shade is spotty. Pick spots where you will top out a lot to make sure your dog has water. Some folks bring rafts to keep their dogs on the water.

Ethics / Rules

Pack-in/pack-out, including cigarette butts and doggy doogie.

Do not copy this guidebook. That's against the law. And, we've rented The Curse of the Guidebook Pirate from the authors of The Enchanted Tower Pockets Full O' Fun guidebook. If you copy this guidebook, you become cursed and will "pump out early, fall off inches from the anchors, or your foot (will pop) off at a critical moment."

Central Texas Mountaineers makes the following comment on **found-gear ethics**:

These are urban climbing areas. Draws get hung on projects and used every week until their owners remove them. Consequently, most Austin climbers see quick draws on a route as someone's project and not "booty".

Bail biners and forgotten gear get left on routes. A single carabiner left on the crux bolt is usually an indication that a climber just wanted off the route and sacrificed that piece of gear. If you need someone's worst piece of gear, then you can probably get up there and add it to your rack. Otherwise leave it. If it is in the way of you being able to clip the bolt, you are welcome to remove it. These "bail biners" are often used by many others. Many area climbers would like to see all such gear left for the owner to recover, while some still hold to "found booty" ethics.

If you find gear on the ground, please bring it to the lost-and-found at Reimers/North Shore, or leave it on the ground at Monster Rock. Gear left on the ground at the Greenbelt is exposed to a lot more hiker/biker/climber traffic. As there is no lost-and-found there, most climbers take the gear and post up to Austin_Climbers and ClimbingBuddies.

Some routes have **cheat stacks**. Overzealous types occasionally cast them far into the bushes. They are invariably reconstructed. Some routes were designed to start on cheat stacks, and many are better with them, eliminating starting cruxes. Jade's stones are there only for dealing with wet ground. If you want to climb without the stack and it's in your way, dismantle it but leave it nearby.

Many of the routes in this guidebook have sport anchors. Most locals just set topropes on the anchors, and their ropes gradually saw away the metal. Consider adopting a practice that is essential at tall crags: **set draws on the anchors**, TR off your draws, and the last partner cleans quickly by just moving the rope onto the anchors. While lowering from tall routes, rope friction saws quickly through these expensive anchors. You'll be called a douche if you do that out-of-state, and in Colorado you'll be beaten up since you're a Texan. Around Austin, it's appreciated but frankly not practiced much — routes are short (minimizing the heat), and anchors are lasting over 5 years on the most travelled routes.

Some routes are now equipped with **permadraws**. The leader is often too occupied to **inspect this hardware**. And boy does it need inspecting. *Rock & Ice* reported a rope slice and decking due to an "I-beam" shaped biner that was worn sharp. Sometimes biner gates stick open. (Try some spit and movement to free them up.) We suggest that one person on the team (whoever's seconding or not going for a redpoint), look at each piece of fixed hardware, including the anchors. Permadraws can be great on certain routes, but we each need to treat them like they are our personal gear.

All routes marked "**Project**" are open projects with estimated grades. (Email us at AustinClimbing@pobox.com if you send any of these, for a possible First Ascent listing in 2nd edition.) **Red tags** on new routes are allowed (at Reimers and North Shore) for three months, during which you should stay off the route, upon pain of death. Don't steal an FA; instead, go develop your own route. You can easily find a mentor with a drill, likely with gray hair and messed up shoulders.

The sport climbing hardware is maintained by Central Texas Mountaineers (CTM). All new bolted routes go through an approval process managed CTM. Help us maintain our good relationships with the County and City — contact CTM at www.ctmrocks.com to apply to bolt a route or to **report hardware problems**. The following will guide you in deciding what to report:

- Bolts that wiggle or pull partially out are extremely dangerous.
- Bolts that feel solid but that have exposed shafts need attention.
- Rust is probably ok on washers but is a concern on bolts.
- Ropes gradually saw through sport anchors. CTM's policy is to replace them when the grooves are halfway through the metal.
- Ropes also saw permadraws. Pay special attention for sharp edges created from sawing of "I-beam" shaped carabiners.
- Spinning hangers are a common occurrence and not a problem in most cases.
- Bent hangers are dangerous.

Acknowledgements

This book is dedicated to Milton and Joy Reimers, who opened their land to climbing, kept us happy for decades, and kept us happy into the future, by preserving their ranch as a public park. It's also dedicated to partners David Phillips, Pete Gutierrez, Brett Schuchert, and Jan Capps, whose influence got me immersed in the sport and the Austin climbing areas.

Scott Harris: thank you for initiating this guidebook project. In early 2010, I saw Scott at North Shore, stretching a several-hundred-foot spooled tape measure along the cliff. He was using it to draw topos accurately to scale. I was impressed — from the start he set the goals of completeness and accuracy. Later he invited me to write the text. When we first met to discuss the book's direction, I said, "What kind of route descriptions do you want?" and he replied, "Be creative." I asked how he felt about route grading, and he replied, "I want them to be accurate." Those were the goals of the project.

My wife Judy Hogge, for providing so much support as I spent a lot of time at the crags.

Jeff Jackson (with Kevin Gallagher and Rebecca Gonzales), and Sean O'Grady: thanks for publishing previous guidebooks covering Austin's limestone climbing.

Andy Klier for his website www.bloodyflapper.com: thanks for your vision and service. Without you, the Pace Bend chapter would not have been conceived.

Thanks for route descriptions, history, and stories about the developers: Brian Derrig, Rupesh Chhagan, Dave Phillips, Luke Stolling, Todd McCray, Tommy Blackwell, Scott Hudson, Karl Vochatzer, Scott Isgitt, Tony Faucett, David Cardosa, Mike Klein, Long Ta, Brenton Buxton, Scott Harris, Tom Suhler, Jeff Olson, James Fierbaugh, Pete Bishop, Thu Doan, Matt Twyman, Joe Sulak, Greg Brooks, Taylor Reilly, John Garcia, Shawn Treadaway, Rick Watson, Stephen Shortnacy, James Crump, Jeff Jackson, Keith Guillory, Joel Schopp, Ralph Vega, Luke Bowman, Scott Harris, Chris Barton, Roni Beer, Clayton Reagan, Eric Patrick, Dave Teykl, Duane Raleigh, Jordan DeLong, Bill Horton, Anthony Stevens, *Rock & Ice* issues June 2005, July 2007, and December 2008, and anyone we forgot to list.

Partners who devoted time to climb every route we could, no matter how ugly: primarily Rona "Tygress" Distenfeld and Dave Phillips. Also Karl & Annette, Britta Kakacek, Neil Higa, Colette Salyk, Blaine Burris, Chris Barton, Lori Bergeron, Lucas Johnson, Queanh Gip, Roger Hurtado, Mike Mayer, Frank Curry, Ryan Hartford, Nancy Nichols, and anyone we forgot.

Editing: Rona Distenfeld. Proof-reading: David Cardosa, David Phillips, and Greg Brooks.

www.rockclimbing.com, www.mountainproject.com, and the local climbers who populated the ATX sections of these databases. We appreciated having multiple sources of information on route variations, descriptions, grades, and history.

www.facebook.com for making it easy to find route developers and get their stories and route information.

Kareem al-Bassam and Ben Gaylor for stepping up to cover Austin high-tech style.

Many thanks go to all the bolters of these routes, for their time and money spent on hardware. Many thanks also go to folks who maintain that hardware, replacing anchors and thousands of bolts as needed. Through 2000-2005, Central Texas Mountaineers (CTM) records show hardware replacement work

Tommy Blackwell & Luke Bowman, "Hastur's"

by Scott Melcer, Scott Steiner, John Myrick, Tim Stich, Scott Isgitt, Valery Milner, Karl Guthrie and Eric Patrick. There were other contributors, no doubt.

In 2001, Scott Steiner initiated a full review of the haphazard rebolting efforts that had started in 1996 in the Greenbelt and in 2001 at Reimers. Tommy Blackwell took on the management of rebolting, and by 2006, he, Luke Bowman, Evan Jackson, and many other great volunteers, had replaced 300 aging bolts, funded by CTM. To date, that number is in the thousands. That's a lot of time, pulling old bolts and installing new ones!

Since 2006, CTM has put over $3,000 into hardware at Reimers. Please become a member at CTMRocks.com and donate your time and money to CTM.

A debt of gratitude goes to all the climbers who pioneered and shaped Central Texas climbing and climbing areas, largely on the granite at Enchanted Rock, but also at Bull Creek, the Greenbelt, Pace Bend, and assorted bouldering areas around Austin. Keith Guillory, Jim Blanford, and Mike Holbart established the early 5.9's and 5.10's at Enchanted Rock in the 1970's. Then this wild guy took the bull by the horns...

James "Kracken" Crump

James Crump was a prolific climber, first ascensionist, guidebook writer (authoring Stranger Than Friction and The Dome Drivers Manual covering Enchanted Rock) and guide/instructor (Yahoo Mountaineering), teaching others who later led the sport in Austin. He wrote the DDM while the park was closed to climbing, in hopes that access would be re-gained. And, he was instrumental in regaining access. His writing style tends towards wild flights of trippy poetic fantasy. You should sell this book and use the proceeds to buy a copy of the DDM on EBay.

Of the many colorful phrases he wrote, one of our favorites is that a route is a "gravitational equation." James joined some of the early climbers in scientific analysis of the sport. At age 17, he did calculations to solve the protection for Fear of Flying, after Keith Guillory decked on it. James concluded that a higher belay (for less rope stretch) and the use of a chest harness would still result in feet hitting the ground, but the upper body wouldn't. Equipped with this plan, he then sent the route.

James put up scores of routes, on lead, without a power drill, in EBs (poor early climbing shoes), many of which are extremely bold (e.g. 30-40' slab runouts), and built a huge legacy at Enchanted Rock. He made the first ascents of almost half the routes at Erock. He was hard to beat, with super skills, 6'2" tall, and a 6' 9" wingspan.

James loved the spotlight. While partner John Sanders sought to go in and do routes without anyone knowing, James would pre-announce what they were going to attempt and muster a crowd to watch. Many fondly remember Crump's loud, ritual greeting to all at Enchanted Rock; whenever he reached the top of Echo Canyon, he'd bellow, "V-D-uh-Mean-a-Bee!!" to which the proper response was, "uh-Bee-Eye!!"

Karen Ghiselli 📷   James Crump, "Texas Rodeo" FA

James was one of the pioneers of the climbing committee concept that provided stable access and bolting management at Erock. He also got the City of Austin to recognize climbing as a legitimate recreational activity, stabilizing access in the Greenbelt and Bull Creek, and he negotiated the Memorandum of Understanding that governs management of hardware. He wrote legislation that the city enacted in a bond election to fund the purchases of the Bull Creek greenbelt and an extension of the Barton Creek greenbelt.

Scott Harris said, "James is simply the most influential climber to ever come out of central Texas." And, he likely coined the phrase "Serious Margs." His shoulder ruined for climbing, James remains an active intellectual, practical, political, and spiritual guide to the community as it continues to develop and maintain climbing at Erock.

Chapter: Battle Plan for Out-of-Towners

A favorite pastime during our years in Dallas was road-tripping to Austin for climbing and Mexican food. Once you start, you will move here, during the next economic boom, and then become too busy at work to climb anywhere but the Greenbelt. That's a good thing; it will leave all of our projects west of Austin free of traffic.

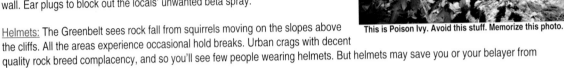

This is Poison Ivy. Avoid this stuff. Memorize this photo.

Gear: a 35 meter rope works for 99.9% of the routes. This guide hopefully mentions all the routes that require more than that. Eight quickdraws will get you up almost all routes, and five up most of them. Some routes and variations call for long draws or 24" runners. Pace Bend's DWS is safer and more fun with the equipment suggested under that chapter. Your most crucial equipment is drinking water. 3-4 liters when the Texas heat and humidity is kicking asses. A GPS unit could help you locate each wall. Ear plugs to block out the locals' unwanted beta spray.

Helmets: The Greenbelt sees rock fall from squirrels moving on the slopes above the cliffs. All the areas experience occasional hold breaks. Urban crags with decent quality rock breed complacency, and so you'll see few people wearing helmets. But helmets may save you or your belayer from rockfall, inverted falls, and deckings.

Anchors: a mix of sport anchors and chain. Monster Rock is 100% sport. North Shore is 98% sport. Reimers has mostly sport anchors at Dead Cats Wall, Serpent's Wall, Dr. Seuss Wall, Prototype Wall, War on Rugs Wall, and the classics at other walls. The Greenbelt has mostly sport anchors at Seismic Wall and New Wall. Occasionally sport anchors get stolen; always bring up two extra draws.

Temperatures rarely shut down Austin climbing. Heat and humidity bother some more than others; when it's manky out, check out the chapter on Pace Bend. Once in a while, temperatures freeze out the climbing in January or February, but then we usually catch a couple freak 80 degree winter days too.

Camping is available at Pace Bend and McKinney Falls State Park. If you are also climbing Enchanted Rock during your stay, camping options are available in that area and the park itself.

Cell phone reception is good at the Greenbelt, Pace Bend, and Monster Rock, spotty at North Shore, and poor at Reimers. Reception drops off along Hamilton Pool Road on the way in.

Approaches are all trivial. Drive times are 5-35 minutes from downtown, and hikes range between 95 seconds and 18 minutes. And all hikes are down hill, into creek or river valleys. None of that *hell hike* bullshit found in other states. Texas climbing is all about climbing, not hiking. If we wanted to hike, we'd pack a lunch and hike. This makes Austin climbers stronger than all others — we spend energy getting strong, not developing huge leg muscles. We get bored with hiking. The beta is dull: left, right, left, right…

Rainy day climbing is not plentiful, but we include suggested walls and routes below, in case you really want to sample some routes in the rain. If it's been raining heavily for many days, drips can ruin even these routes. Topouts may be wet; bring bail biners or "stick unclip". A stick clip is essential to deal with wet starts.

The best rain beta is that Reimers has a *Sacred Halo of Dryness* over it. It can be pouring on your drive from Dallas all the way through Waco and Temple; but keep coming, because it's often dry enough to climb Reimers. Rain can hit downtown Austin, Monster Rock, and Pace Bend, while Reimers stays dry. Failing that…www.austinrockgym.com. Or, Main Event with its auto-belay climbing.

After the rain stops, the limestone tends to dry out fast; we've sometimes camped out for a couple hours, watching rock dry up and become climbable. Winds, humidity, and sunshine all determine the speed of drying.

Lone Traveler Advice

Austin is one of the easiest places to find partners. (See the Introduction for online forums Austin_Climbers, ClimbingBuddies, and ErockOnline.) Climbing has been a partner-centric sport, where the loss of a partner through injury, feuding, divorce, or undependability often meant personal tragedy and a long search for a replacement partner.[2] For a long time, Austin was very much partner-centric, and

---

[2] My first mentor, Jan Capps, once identified her next climbing partner by the duct tape holding together his ripped up climbing shoes, and by their blown out toes. She knew he'd always be up for climbing.

even crowded walls such as New Wall saw pairs or groups of partners taking turns putting up routes, TRing them, and pulling ropes to clear out for the next pair. Then one day, Pete Bishop, Matt Hall, and Ralph Showalter were putting up TR's for each other, and other parties were waiting for them to finish and pull the ropes, maintaining protocol. Suddenly, Dave Phillips *snapped*, "This is stupid. We've all climbed these routes a hundred times. Why don't we all just leave our ropes up and TR each other's ropes?!?!?" This cranky seed was planted, it grew, and Austin climbing transformed from partner-dependence to a friendly pickup game.

Show up, nonchalantly look around at everyone, and you'll soon discern the energetic vibe shimmering through the moldy humid pollinated air, invisibly organizing the waiting climbers into small queues leading to each TR. Merge your personal aura into the paranormal route queue of your choice, and you're in line. The best spots for this are Reimers' Dead Cats Wall and Prototype Wall on the weekends, the Greenbelt's New Wall on Tuesday/Thursday afternoons, and the Greenbelt's Seismic Wall every day of the week.

Day Plans for Traveling Groups

While a lone traveler will seek crowds for a cheap belay, traveling groups will want to avoid them. The following plans are aimed at route quality and quantity at your level, and for avoiding crowded areas.

Climbers 5.12 and up

Day 1: Reimers. Hike in past Sex Cave, Sex Canyon, and the King Bee Memorial Buttress, spotting routes you want to try later. These areas have only one warmup (High Anxiety), so go to Serpent's Wall and/or Dead Cats Wall for a longer warmup session. Return to Sex Canyon and Sex Cave.

Day2: Reimers. Warm up on Prototype Wall and run its classic face climbs, then head to nearby Dr. Seuss Wall or to hard walls to the south (Insect Wall and House of Pain).

Day 3: North Shore, once it's open to the public, has a dozen 5.12 routes.

Day 4: Head for the Greenbelt for convenient downtown climbing.

Day 5: Reimers. Tick a bunch of hard 5.11 onsights at Tit For Tom Wall. Do the harder routes spread across the north band (particularly at T-Roofic Wall and Rhetorick Wall).

Day 6: The above areas will keep you plenty busy for many more days. Or if you want a change of scenery, visit Monster Rock and hit its few, bouldery, core intensive high 5.12's and low 5.13's, and its long stellar traverses. Or go water soloing at Pace Bend.

Rain Days: Reimers' Sex Cave and Sex Canyon. The Sex Cave has some bouldering to kill more time.

5.11 Climbers

Weekday 1: Reimers. Warm up at Shortcake Wall, Dr. Seuss Wall, or Prototype Wall and do Prototype Wall's climbs while the weekend crowds aren't all over it. (If you are at Prototype Wall on the weekends, just ask to jump on peoples' topropes, or to pull their rope, tow it on lead, and reset their TR.)

Weekday 2: Reimers. War on Rugs Wall and Crankenstein Wall.

Monday/Wednesday/Friday: New Wall and Great Wall, or Gus Fruh and Kingdom of Ging, all at the Greenbelt downtown. Or if you want beta and crowds, hit New Wall on Tuesday/Thursday afternoons. (However, read about recent hazards, under New Wall.)

Weekend Day 1: Reimers. Warm up at Serpent's Wall and/or Dead Cats. Head north to visit to Arbor Wall, dial it down on T-Roofic Wall's 10d, and then dial it up at Tit For Tom Wall.

Weekend Day 2: Arrange time at Monster Rock for some fun 5.11's and two of Austin's longest traverses (5.11a-b). And/or water solo at nearby Pace Bend.

Weekend Day 3: North Shore (once it's open to the public) has dozens of great 5.11's. If you liked Prototype Wall at Reimers, try Mossy Wall. If you like roof pulls, try Insanity Wall. If you like wild, semi-steep routes, try Undead Cats Wall.

Weekend Day 4: Reimers. Landfill Wall has good warmups and grades for everyone, in a shady breezy spot.

Any day: Georgetown offers half a dozen 5.11's and plenty of 5.10's.

Rain Days: The Greenbelt's Great Wall. North Shore (Insanity Wall right side; possibly Undead Cats Wall), Reimers (Sex Canyon; Sex Cave bouldering, and most of Lip-o-suction is sub-5.12 climbing).

5.10 Climbers

Weekday Day1: Reimers. Start at Serpent's Wall and/or Dead Cats Wall. Hike further to do T-Roofic's 10d.

Weekday Day 2: Reimers. Warm up at Shortcake Wall and Dr. Seuss Wall's 5.9, or on "8 Flake" and "Clone Call" at Prototype Wall. Climb Prototype (stellar 10c/10d). Perhaps traverse from it to set TR and hangdog the stellar 11a's. Then visit the 5.10 routes south from there on Mai Tai Wall, War on Rugs Wall and Crankenstein Wall.

Weekday Day 3: Seismic Wall at the Greenbelt downtown.

Weekday Day 4: Gus Fruh and Kingdom of Ging at the Greenbelt downtown. Or start on Hank's (at Random Walls), do the two 5.10's at The Terrace, and Cedar Fever at Geritol Wall. New Wall was in a state of collapse as of this writing. It may yield new 5.9/5.10 material, or not, but definitely visit Wowie Zowie (5.10d).

Weekend Day 1: Reimers. Avoid the Dead Cats crowd by warming up on anything easy and open as you pass Serpent's Wall, Dead Cats Wall, and Rhetorick Wall's "Talk it Up (5.8)". (Or hike in at the Arbor Wall access and warm up on "8 it Grand".) Then pick your challenges among Arbor Wall's 10's, T-Roofic's 10d, then chill and project various 10's at Hand Beyond Wall's short but fun routes.

Weekend Day 2: Arrange time at Monster Rock for one or two days.

Weekend Day 3: Water soloing at Pace Bend.

Weekend Day 4: Reimers' Landfill Wall has a steady progression of grades up to 5.10d.

Any Day: Reimers' Hand Beyond Wall for short but interesting climbing and solitude, unless you encounter other solituders. Finish by hiking south to Millennium Wall for the epic Millennium Traverse (which needs a 50-meter rope).

Any Day: North Shore (once it's open to the public) has a lot of routes in this range.

Any Day: Georgetown offers half a dozen 5.10's.

Rain Days: The Greenbelt's Seismic Wall roof routes. North Shore (More Fun Than Bubble Rap; The Airing of Grievances). But, it's probably preferable to party and not climb these. One option is the 5.10c roof and tufa sections of Lip-O-Suction (5.12a), at Reimers. You'll need a stick clip. It's only one route, but it's wild.

5.8- 5.9 Climbers

Weekday: Reimers. Climb Serpent's Wall, Dead Cats Wall, and Rhetorick Wall's "Talk it Up (5.8)". Dead Cats is bolted fairly sporty and gets very crowded on the weekends.

Weekday: Seismic Wall or Guide's Wall toprope area, at the Greenbelt downtown.

Weekend: Once it's open to the public, climb North Shore, which could take quite a few days to climb out. Reimers also offers good climbs on Mai Tai Wall.

Weekend: Water solo at Pace Bend. A lot of the climbing is challenging, but there are 5.8's and 5.9's, at the right spot, at the right water levels.

The following areas are appropriate for total newbs and small children:

Greenbelt
Seismic Wall right end: 8 routes under 5.9 (crowded on the weekends)
Guide's Wall: 5 TR routes under 5.9. Two 5.9's and 3 10a's. Seismic is taller, but we like how technical these are.
5.8 Sanctuary: 3 TR routes on a short wall with cool caves: 5.7/5.8, 5.8+, and 5.9+.

Reimers
Zoey's Wall: 6 short routes under 5.9, often empty. Avoid this wall if your newbs will be disappointed at the shortness.
Dead Cats Wall, left side: 5 routes under 5.9, four generally empty.
Serpent's Wall: 4 routes under 5.9

Arbor Wall: a short but overhung 5.8 ("8 it Grand") makes a great 1st time real-rock lead, if your newb has led some mild overhangs in the gym and is comfortable clipping.

North Shore
The Dude Wall: 4 routes under 5.9
Philosophy Wall: 9 toprope routes under 5.9. Bring 24" slings, multiple short ropes (at least 50' each), and biners.

Middle Earth Wall: 7 routes under 5.9.

Gypsy Wall: 3 routes under 5.9
Little Guide's Wall: some time after this book's publication, this wall will probably have 7-8 routes under 5.9.

Cheap Beer Wall: 2 sweet 5.7 routes.

Georgetown
The Pulpit has two tricky 5.6's. There's also easy slab bouldering, some of it with toprope anchors.

See the next chapter for additional information on planning your trip.

Chapter: Comparing the Climbing Areas

This chapter may help out-of-towners decide how they want to allocate time on their road trip to Austin.

The no-brainer priority is **Pace Bend** (for DWS), if water levels and temperatures are right. The Pace Bend chapter has water level and temperature beta.

The Greenbelt is a good choice for short "semi-rest days", since it's just downtown, near the fun on South Congress, South Lamar, 6th Street, Barton Springs (both the street and the cold spring water swimming area), and Colorado Street. A lone traveler invests much less time finding partners there than traveling to Reimers — fish for partners at Seismic Wall any time (even weekdays), or read up on "Tuesday/Thursday" under New Wall. The Greenbelt has classics at all grades, but it's also more polished than the other climbing areas. (Monster Rock, North Shore, and Georgetown are crisp; Reimers is mostly in good shape but has polish here and there.) The Greenbelt is a great workout, with a lot of on-route mantle moves onto ledges or over blocks (at Seismic and Gus Fruh).

Monster Rock is worth considering for one or two days of your road trip, especially if it's hot out. Most folks love their first outing, and repeat visits depend on taste. The 5.9-5.10 range is good, the 5.11's are stellar, and the 5.12-5.13's are bouldery and core-intensive. There are routes under 5.9, but the other areas are better for that. Monster Rock complements the other climbing areas with these unique features:

- 24 of the routes are in a narrow canyon, a unique climbing environment. On hot afternoons, the canyon's temperature is cooler than the outside air. The canyon routes range 30'-50'.

- Close bolting (to protect the canyon's unusual fall hazards) leaves most routes safer than usual for beginning leaders, as long as your belayer minimizes slack.

- Hard routes are right next to or near easy routes, a convenience when a group varies a lot in strength.

- Long, stellar traverses and variations (including Austin's longest route, a 16-permadraw pumpfest).

- Minutes from Pace Bend, offering lead climbing followed by Pace Bend's DWS and camping.

- No dogs.

Georgetown is worth considering if your party does not care about urban feel and traffic noise. The pretty cliff makes up for it, and you have a good chance of being the only party there. The routes are on the tricky side, challenging to onsight. Friction quality is high.

Enchanted Rock (not covered in this book) offers trad, mixed, sport, slab, face, and bouldering on a granite dome and boulders. The sport routes are runout more than the routes in this guidebook. Erock is taller than most area limestone but shorter than many trad areas. You start more routes, and so you're exposed to ground fall more of the day.

Reimers and North Shore deserve a lot of your time. Here's what to consider in dividing time between them:

- North Shore is not open to the public as of this writing, but it seems likely to open this year. Ask the person at the fee booth at Reimers whether North Shore is open.

- North Shore catches afternoon sun at the tops of routes. It escapes total sun exposure that hits Reimers' popular walls. But air flow is poorer, so Reimers is better on hot mornings with no wind. North Shore's best wall for airflow is Mossy Wall.

- Austin's occasional long periods of rain and humidity shut down North Shore due to copious drips. Reimers dries faster, and it's rarely shut down for more than a day.

- Reimers' route mix for 5.7-5.10 is smaller and crowded primarily into one area (Dead Cats). North Shore has more routes in this range, at multiple areas (The Dude Wall, Philosophy Wall TR's, Insanity Wall left end, Middle Earth Wall, Gypsy Wall, and Cheech & Chong Wall).

- Reimers has 36 5.13's and a few 5.14's; North Shore has none (yet).

- North Shore has a dozen 5.12's; Reimers has a lot more.

- For mixed-strength parties, North Shore is better situated for 5.11/5.12 climbing right next to 5.10-and-under climbing. (See Mossy Wall, Middle Earth Wall, and Insanity Wall.) Most of Reimers' hard areas are separated from its easier areas.

Heights: Amongst all the short Austin routes are some tall ones in each area. There are also tall-looking walls that are actually short, once you climb up the starting ledges (e.g. Prototype Wall, parts of Insanity Wall). There are short walls with intricate routes full of moves. There are many ugly routes that are stellar. Ignore what it looks like and climb everything. However, the tallest routes are at:

Seismic Wall's slabby right end (Greenbelt)
Urban Assault (Greenbelt)
Beehive Wall (Greenbelt)
T-Roofic (Reimers)
Curious George and Millennium traverses (long and continual exposure) (Reimers)
Insect Wall (Reimers)
House of Pain (Reimers)
Insanity Wall mid-section (North Shore)
Mossy Wall (North Shore)
Carnival Wall (North Shore)
D&D Wall's right end (Monster Rock)

How to Use the Route Descriptions

Each route description includes:

- Route name and grade. The grades are power plus endurance, ignoring technique and trickiness. Slash grades (e.g. 5.11d/5.12b) usually express tall/short ratings. Ranges (e.g. 5.11d-5.12a) indicate current uncertainty about the grade.

- PG/R/X rating for leading. "X" appears to be a grounder death fall, "R" suggests serious injury, and "PG" suggests minor injury. If a fall seems very unlikely, we reduce the rating severity. High first bolts don't impact a rating, due to assumed stick-clipping. Caveat: all rock climbing routes are dangerous!

- Star ratings. Routes have 3 stars if a visitor should do them. We like a lot of routes. Most routes have their fans, tastes differ, and so we give out a lot of single stars. We don't know how to give out two stars. Using this "good or great" star system, you will climb all routes, stay enthused, and never get bored with a routine.

- Bolt count. The anchor bolts are excluded from the count. Routes without anchors are marked "NO ANCHORS". We count "double bolts" (two non-anchor bolts inches away from each other) as one bolt. These occur where it was difficult to remove a bolt, or where both bolts were in suspect rock. When in doubt, clip both. "+" marks routes that are under consideration for retrobolting (the addition and/or moving of bolts).

- Permadraw count, though these counts are subject to change, as old routes occasionally get permadraws.

- Credits for first-ascents (FAs) and route construction. The FA is usually listed first, and bolter(s) last. "bb" (bolted by) prefaces bolters who didn't send the route.

- The year it was bolted, if known.

- Icons describing the route's character. Use them to find similar or dissimilar projects, or to avoid routes that have a characteristic you hate. Or, ignore them and just start on the left, hitting every Austin area route until you're finished on the right. Our icons comprise beta, albeit vague beta. If you desire pure onsights, don't look at them.

Wall Angles and Shapes:

◢ = slab   ◣ = slabby (near vertical)   ▮ = vertical   ◥ = mild overhang (4-10°)   ◤ = overhang (11-30°)

= severe overhang (31-60°)   = roof[3] (61-90°)   = mini-roof or low starting roof[4]

⚓ = arête   ⼤ = dihedral   = bulge   = wave   = severe wave   = crack   = starting ledge or ledge-on-route

Tiny arrows show transitions to a different wall angle and/or shape. Examples:

= climbs a vertical face to a bulge to an overhang to a ledge.

= climbs a vertical arête to a (vertical) dihedral, to a mildly overhanging dihedral.

= accessed scrambling up a ledge or boulder. Starts on a vertical arête and transitions to a vertical face.

= starts with feet under a mini-roof. Climbs an overhanging dihedral with a crack.

Appearances:

= eye candy. The route looks cooler than most routes in the area.

= quirky. Quirky, unique, or memorable holds or wall shapes.

---

[3] A big roof with handholds.
[4] A small roof with 0-1 handhold. Also used to describe route starts where feet are under a roof and hands are over it.

Holds:

🪨 = mixture of hold types.   🏛 = tufa/stalactite present[5]   ⣿ = hueco(s) present

🍺 = jug intensive   🐙 = pocket intensive   🤏 = pinch intensive

🖐 = sloper intensive   ✂ = edge intensive (2 finger pads)   🦅 = crimp intensive (1 pad or less)

🚶 = thin holds. Some small or non-positive "bad" holds.

🗿 = choss on some of the route.[6]

🍴 = manufactured hold(s). The route has drilled or glued on hold(s).[7]

▦▦ = cement reinforced hold(s). The route has hold(s) reinforced with cement or glue (usually caulked inside cracks around the hold; sometimes coating a chossy surface).

Readability:

$E=mc^2$ = complex beta. Much of the route requires non-obvious beta or options suiting different types of climbers.

🧩 = puzzle. The crux is puzzling, due to unapparent or exotic beta.

〰 = sea of holds. Section(s) where the best holds are hidden among many.

〰 = sea of bad holds. Section(s) having a bunch of holds and they all suck.

😬 = hidden hold(s). One or more holds are out of view or disguised.

🔀 = trap(s). The route's path is hard to read with fork(s) leading nowhere

⇥ = divide-and-conquer. The route's easiest ascent involves downclimbing after a clip to a rest or the ground.

Emotions

😨 = intimidating. Runouts, traverses around arêtes, stepping off ledges, wrecking ball falls, crux clips, etc. PG/R/X routes usually sport this icon (redundantly), but "G" rated routes sometimes have it also (to their credit).

☕ = caffeinated. A hold or section that feels like it energizes you, even though it's not a rest. A good example is the traverse section on Blood of the Dead.

🔢 = gear-shift. The route's character changes dramatically after a long span.

🥫 = painful[8]. Sharp holds or Crozlies (those tiny limestone needles) causing skin or connective tissue pain.

📷 = exposed. That feeling of being high in the air…in Central Texas. Nothing is really exposed here. Despite that, everything really is bigger in Texas. Routes with this icon have more exposure than other routes in this guidebook. Two routes of the same height may not both feel exposed, due to ledges or other things drawing your attention away from the height.

---

5   No matter what size. Even if all you do is step on it. Even if you don't touch it at all. We have a tufa fetish. (Who doesn't?)

6   A well-known Austin climber, route developer, writer, editor, yogameister, and yurt-ilator, Jeff Jackson, wrote the classic Tao of Choss for *Rock & Ice* on why he likes choss routes. Jeff bolted much of Bull Creek, providing bygone fun for many while the bolts were solid, and a legacy of "WTF is THIS" from the rare explorers who see all the rusted bolts and suspect rock. Jeff also gave us solid Reimers routes (Body Wax, Let Them Eat Flake, House of Pain) and classics in the Greenbelt. Jeff's Tunnel Vision is so great that others sent and recorded a whopping *seven* variations going from it, to it, or from-it-and-to-it.

7   We don't particularly care – any bolted route is manufactured via vegetation removal, dirt-cleaning, hold-stressing/breaking, and installation of expansion bolts. Our gear is highly manufactured. But maybe some people care about which routes are…pure? Our mentor once said, the purest form of the sport is free-solo onsighting, naked, no pads, no spotter, no chalk, on dirty choss, while escaping a pack of wild dogs, at night, in the rain. Nevertheless, we've opted to mark routes with manufactured holds (many of them classics) because some folks like to avoid such routes, while others might be interested in seeing if they go naturally. For instance, check out Symbiosis at House of Pain.

8   Pain depends on the climber's pain-threshold, weight, and the way they attack the holds. (Mas Cerveza is considered painful, and it hurt us a few times early on, but it stopped hurting us.) We fear including Pain because it may keep people off great routes such as Mas. Get on them, prepared to avoid or accept some pain.

Υ = stick clip recommended

Physical Challenges

$\dot{\mathcal{K}}$ = endurance. Difficulty is sustained enough that the route's grade is higher than the grade of the hardest move (e.g. Jade).

$\sim\!\!\mathcal{D}$ = bouldery. The crux is 1-3 moves that are much harder than the rest of the route.

$\mathcal{P}\mathcal{D}$ = crux or cruxy clip(s)

$\overline{\underline{\mathbf{A}}}$ = balancy.

$\mathcal{H}$ = on-the-edge; low percentage moves such as precision dynos and blind throws.

Premium Moves

Much of a route's character is the moves that solve it. We picked 11 pleasing or interesting moves to include in the route descriptions. If you love knee bars, put on the jeans and skim the pages for the knee bar icon. Not all climbers will use these moves on a given route, and not all of them solve cruxes.

$\boxed{\uparrow}$ = deadpoint $\overset{\circ}{\mathcal{K}}$ = dyno $\overset{GD}{UT!}$ = campus $\overline{\mathcal{D}}$ = knee bar $\uparrow$ = bat hang $\boxed{JAM}$ = hand/foot/arm jam

$\mathbb{I}$ = hard or interesting match $\Longleftrightarrow$ = rock onto foot $\mathbf{V}$ = drop knee $\overset{*}{\mathfrak{Y}}$ = rose move $\mathcal{C}$ = heel/toe/elbow/chin hook

$\overset{*}{\cancel{\lambda}}$ = traverse sections, ranging from a few moves to entire routes. We usually mix it into the wall angle icons. For example,

$\overset{\blacktriangleleft}{\mathbb{I}}\overset{*}{\lambda}\overset{*}{\lambda}\overset{*}{\lambda}\mathbb{I}\overset{*}{\lambda}\mathcal{C}$ signifies a route that starts up a severe overhang, traverses a long ways on a mild overhang, traverses shortly on a face, then goes up a bulge.

Unknown Character

$?$ = the route's character isn't fully known to us.

These icons comprise an experiment in guidebooking that's probably way overboard. [9] After a year of surveying the routes in this manner, we're freaking tired of it! But we sincerely hope you find some of the icons useful. We'll collect feedback and figure out whether to keep, revise, or flush these in a later edition.

What's a route?

Most walls have lead routes and just a few variations or toprope routes. But New Wall has 9 main routes and 15 variations! For clarity we present each type of route differently. **Main routes** own most or all of their bolts and anchors, though sometimes two main routes share bolts, branching apart or merging together. **Variations** are lead routes that use nothing but existing bolts of main routes. **Bolted Variations** use bolts of other routes, supplemented with one or two of their own bolts to traverse between the main routes they exploit.

We've structured the text to help the main routes stand out as your eyes move between text, topos, and the wall you're looking at. They are numbered and presented prominently along the left margin. A variation or bolted variation is indented under the description of the one of the main routes it uses. **Toprope** routes are prefaced with toprope. When they lack independent anchors, they are organized under the route whose anchors they use.

---

[9] Part way into this "innovative" surveying, we cracked open an old copy of Dorset by Pete Oxley, a printed version of one area on www.rockfax.com. There they are. Nine icons summarizing route character: Powerful, Technical, Fluttery Climbing with a Big Fall Potential, Sustained, Fingery Climbing with Sharp Holds, A Long Reach May Be Required, Rounded Holds, Dyno, and the cryptic "A Graunchy Route – Not Specifically For Hand and Fist Jams." Later we spotted icons in several other books, including the famous Ten Sleep guidebook, whose icons include porn stars (for stellar routes) and African dictators for reasons beyond comprehension.

Trees

Trees die. We try to use permanent (wall feature) landmarks, but trees are irresistible in some route descriptions. When a 36" wide tree sits against a cliff left of a route, it's probably more confusing to *not* mention the tree. But please take all tree references with a grain of salt. Look for stumps. We often include a tree's species so you can differentiate when multiple trees are along the same wall:

Persimmon: a small skinny tree/bush with gray paper-bark resembling a crape myrtle. Often in clumps. Non-evergreen.

Post Oak: an always straight-growing, non-evergreen tree. Most Texas trees don't grow straight and tall like this.

Spanish Oak (aka. Red Oak): another non-evergreen tree, with maple-leaf shaped leaves.

Live Oak: a very common tree with small football-shaped leaves. The dark-brown trunks rarely grow straight up. While considered an evergreen, it sheds its leaves for a couple months before regrowth in early spring.

Cedar[10]: a true evergreen with Christmas-tree type needle-shaped leaves and medium brown, peel-able bark. They grow nasty branches everywhere, clutter up views, steal water from all other forms of life, and grow uncontrolled in Central Texas due to the suppression of wild fires. Ranchers hate them, but they provide an evergreen canopy along local roadways. Back in the day, many people made a hard living chopping these to clear ranchland. These badasses were called…yes, you guessed it… Cedar Choppers. There were cedar chopping contests, in which the best could somehow fell, limb, and stack a 20-30' cedar in minutes…with a freaking axe. This takes us about 30 minutes with a $530 Stihl chainsaw.

Hackberry: the ugliest tree possible, with chewed up leaves, and light gray non-bark, usually with little dark bumps on it. Non-evergreen. Disgustingly common. Fast growing, and (thankfully) fast-dying. Many consider removal of hackberries as weed control and trail work.

Pecan: a tree with rough bark running in deep vertical grooves. The leaves are arranged symmetrically, fern-like.

Topo-Photos

Key: "X" = bolt.
       "P" = permadraw
       "XX" or "AA" = anchors
       (X) (P) (XX) (AA) = bolts/anchors hidden from view in the photo by a tree, rock, or climber.
       "+" = the route might be considered for retrobolting (the addition and/or moving of bolts).

Colored lines usually just connect the bolts of the route, rather than give the path of the climb. In a few cases where the boltline misleads everyone, we use the line to indicate the path. In cases where that path goes away from a bolt clip, the line will "reach over" and back to show an off-center clip.

The topo-photos are often shot with a wide angle lens that distorts perspective near the photo edges. Rely on the rock features in the photos, and take the bolt positions and route angles with a grain of salt.

Some routes are intentionally left out of the mix of photos. Their photographed neighbors and route descriptions should make them easy to locate.

GPS Points

Some of the GPS points will be off the mark. We shot them on a rusty old Garmin with messed up screen that made "8" look like "3", usually on cloudy days. We spot-checked the points on satellite maps. Units are provided in "GPS" degrees/minutes/seconds, followed by Digital Degrees.

---

[10] The common name, in Texas, for Mountain Juniper. This bitchy bush is ok for rustic wood fences, and its berries are a key ingredient in gin, the worst of all liquors.

Greenbelt Trail Map

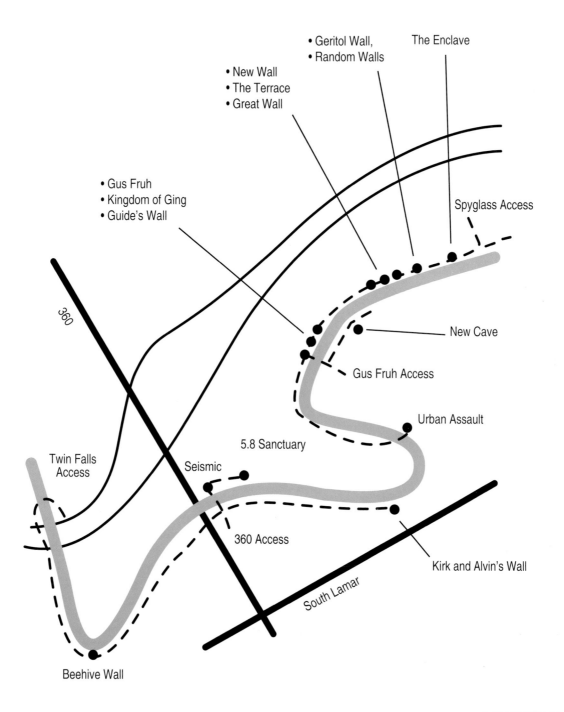

- Geritol Wall,
- Random Walls

The Enclave

- New Wall
- The Terrace
- Great Wall

- Gus Fruh
- Kingdom of Ging
- Guide's Wall

Spyglass Access

360

New Cave

Gus Fruh Access

Urban Assault

5.8 Sanctuary

Twin Falls
Access

Seismic

360 Access

Kirk and Alvin's Wall

South Lamar

Beehive Wall

Barton Creek

Climbing Area: The Greenbelt of Downtown Austin

The Barton Creek Greenbelt is a City of Austin park in the creek's valley. The valley lies north-south, located east of Loop 1 (aka. Mopac) and west of South Lamar. It has four access points to the various climbing walls, and trails connect the walls. The creek is seasonal and runs north, meandering along some wide bends.

The Greenbelt boasts interesting routes with roofs, ledges, and blockiness. Ledges force bouldery topout moves en route, for a great workout. Unfortunately, the convenience of crags so close to home created an endless clomping of sticky rubber against the defenseless limestone, pounding it like medieval soldiers across a muddy battlefield. The popular walls are *way* polished now. After years of climbing unpolished limestone west of town, our primary route review team totally had our asses handed to us on some slick, tricky routes at Seismic.

Many of the routes were bolted and graded in the 1980's, the era of shitty disco and pop, redeemed only by The Police, U2, and the maturing Indie bands. They went up before the other areas covered in this guidebook, before some grade inflation hit the sport. Thus, some grades are tougher here than at the other areas in this guidebook. It's possible we should sync them up, but who blinks first? Reimers or Greenbelt? We keep the Greenbelt grades stiff, making only the most obvious adjustments.

Charisa Bridwell 📷
charisaBphotography

Lars Remsen, "Cutting Cards for a Poke"

Access Points

There are four access points, each serving different walls. All four access points see their share of car break-ins. Not often enough to stay away, but do not leave any valuables in the car.

Joseph Williams, "Dirty Rotten Whore"

1.   **Twin Falls Access** (on the west bank). This access serves **Beehive Wall** fastest, with a side-dish of cool scenery. Use it only when the creek is dry. Otherwise, read about "Beehive Wall" below, under 360 Access. From Loop 1 (aka. Mopac), exit at 360 and take the Loop 1 south-bound service road. Park before the guardrail. Hike right of the guardrail 40 paces, walk right into a grove of trees and find the (currently) fallen-down chain link fence. Go over the fence and head downhill and left on a steep trail with severe drop-offs. At the bottom, turn right and immediately drop down over a high-water creek bank. Walk left to the bridge and cross the rest of the creekbed. At the far bank, take the trail left. Walk 200 paces to fun looking rope swings, then 150 paces to cross a feeder creek. 100 more paces to the gnar black/gray/white overhanging cliff mentioned under Beehive Wall; then you're almost at the routes. There are no restrooms at this access.

2.   **360 Access** (on the east bank). This access serves Seismic Wall (directly across the creek), Beehive Wall (same side, 18 minutes to the left), 5.8 Sanctuary (across the creek and 2 minutes right), and Kirk and Alvin's Wall (same side, 16 minutes to the right). Conveniently situated near Barton Creek Mall and various restaurants at South Lamar/290/360. There is a bad smelling outhouse at the trail head.

Directions: Set your GPS for 3755 Capital of Texas Highway, an office building, and get there. Turn left immediately to pass in front of this building. Head straight through the parking area to a big green sign that says "Barton Creek Greenbelt." Old school directions: from I-35 south of downtown, take exit #230 (West 290/71). Exit 360 (Capital of Texas Highway). Before Mopac, turn right at the light, which enters the office park. The directions from Loop 1 (Mopac): exit Loop 360 South and take the first left into the office park.

Hike the wooded trail into the creek valley and cross the (usually dry) creek to get to **Seismic Wall**. (Or, if the water is rushing, head left, use the bridge to cross, and come back on the far bank. Find the water levels before heading out at http://waterdata.usgs.gov/tx/nwis/uv. Enter site number 08155300, the rain gauge for Barton Creek near Seismic Wall.) **5.8 Sanctuary** is a short hike to the right.

Lori Bergeron, "Gros Ventre"

To get to **Beehive Wall**, don't cross the creek. Instead, cut left (upstream). Stay on trails near the creek most of the way. Hike to and under the 360 bridge. Go through the v-gate and hike 650 paces to another v-gate and later a wood bridge. Continue, passing a cool roof over a big sharp gnarly ledge, then the path splits (but rejoins) at a right leaning dihedral boulder, the start of taller cliffs. Soon you'll find the trad route and low bouldering traverse listed in the section for Beehive Wall. Continue to the chain handrail that leads to the route "Honey Dripper".

To get to **Kirk and Alvin's Wall**, don't cross the creek. Instead, cut right (downstream), staying near the creek, for 540 paces to a wooden bridge. Cross it and continue 255 paces until a short left branch of the trail runs into the creek (no creek bank to drop over), at GPS N30°14.582' W097°47.639' (30.243033 -97.793983). Directions are difficult to give from this point, especially if the creek is running. When the creek is dry, hike the main creek (ignoring tributaries, slanting left across them to track the main channel) 250 rocky paces till you see a pair of big blocky boulders against each other. Further downstream, you'll see several more boulders, one triangular and usually sporting bouldering chalk marks. Continue past it in the creek 45 paces to a little trail out of the creek, leading straight up to Airman's Cave (two side-by-side small cave openings, right of the routes) at GPS N30°14.505' W097°47.467' (30.24175 -97.791117). (When the water is high, get there via trails near the creek, crossing several tributaries along the way.)

3.   **Gus Fruh Access** (on the east bank and further north) serves Gus Fruh (across the creek), Kingdom of Ging (further right), and Guide's Wall (further right, still). In the other direction, it serves Urban Assault. Conveniently situated near Torchy's Tacos. There is no outhouse, but in 10 minutes you can hike out of Gus Fruh (or Ging or Guide's) and drive to the corner stores at South Lamar. When the creek is running, the only dry access is to Choss Cave and Urban Assault.

Directions: Set your GPS for 2642 Barton Hills Drive, a small park entrance, and get there. Old school directions: from H71/290, go North on Lamar and turn left onto Barton Skyway. (From Barton Creek, 6th Street, or anywhere else up there in town, go south on South Lamar and turn right onto Barton Skyway.) At the dead end, turn left on Barton Hills Drive. Drive 0.8 miles, past two road stubs and two full roads. The park's sign isn't very visible; look for a rustic wood fence, about 8 car-lengths long, on the right.

Hike down the trail and take the first spur trail on your right. (It's windier but easier hiking and just as fast.) Snake down the switchbacks, bear right at the fork, and dogleg left near the creek. Cross it to Whipping Post boulder and Rock Retard at **Gus Fruh**. (When the water is high, hike upstream to cross over the cobblestone dam left of Gus Fruh. When it's *really* high, approach from Spyglass Access and hike about 20 minutes total.) Further right of Gus Fruh is **Kingdom of Ging** and **Guide's Wall**.

News Flash!! **Choss Cave** just popped out of the ground, sporting some new, steep bouldering. Instead of crossing the creek, cut right and hike 390 paces to a well-trod spur trail cutting right. It's a short hike to the cave, and in winter the cave is visible from the main trail.

To reach **Urban Assault**, skip that first right spur trail, stay straight, and cross the creek a little upstream from Gus Fruh wall. (But if the water is high, skip the creek crossings and hike the poorer trail on the east bank.) Turn left, take the left fork and hike roughly 900 paces on a trail that stays close to the creek. After a while it forks again, but the left fork along the creek is a sucker trail. Take the right fork away from the creek. When it opens up across a meadow, you're close. 900 paces isn't

Jen Knowles, "Thumb Dance"

the most exacting measure, so look for a short trail left to the creek's edge to view the most majestic expanse of choss in ATX. Hike a little further, to and through a turnstile and look for a very faint overgrown trail that comes out across from Urban Assault (route). Cross the creek.

Gus Fruh Access is conveniently close to **Sunken Gardens**. If your partner doesn't show up or you want an extra burn, head to Sunken Gardens for way-long traversing on limestone masonry. No need for a sketch pad or spotter. SG is an old-school training ground. It's been closed a long time for restoration. When it re-opens: from Gus Fruh Access, take a U-turn to head North on Barton Hills Drive, go left when it ends at Robert E Lee Road, and turn left into the nearby park. Park at the baseball diamond nearest the road and look for concentric walls in a sunken area.

4. **Spyglass Access** (on the west bank) serves the following spots, all on the west bank: Enclave bouldering, Random Walls, Geritol Wall, Great Wall, The Terrace, and New Wall, in that order with New Wall being furthest from the trailhead. Spyglass Access also serves a great lunch strategy at the awesome Taco Deli and a passable beer strategy at the convenience store.

Directions: Set your guidance system for 1500 Spyglass Drive (which is Taco Deli). Old school directions: from H71/290, go north on Loop 1 (Mopac). (From Barton Creek, 6th Street, or north roads such as 45 or Parmer, go South on Loop 1.) Exit Barton Skyway, and cross east over Loop 1. (If you've read the Gus Fruh Access, note that both use a road called Barton Skyway. But that road is cut in half by the entire Greenbelt valley! Gus Fruh uses the section east of the valley; Spyglass Access uses the section west of the valley.) As Barton Skyway is about to dead-end, look for parking. If there's none, turn left or right for more parking. The "Spyglass" park entrance is at this intersection, as are the Taco Deli and the convenience store.

Hike the trail downhill. There's a composting outhouse off trail to the right that's often nasty and always unthinkably odorous. (Use the convenience store instead.) Turn right at the "T" in the trail at GPS N30°15.466' W097°47.238' (30.257767 -97.7873). Hike a while[11], 400 paces to a manhole right of the trail. Continue another 225 paces to a small (usually dry) creek crossing at GPS N30°15.297' W097°47.480' (30.25495 -97.791333). You can cut right up that feeder creek, 140 rugged paces, to reach **The Enclave** bouldering area. Or cross the feeder creek and continue 200 paces to the wood v-gate that blocks bikes from a section of hiking trail.

Squeeze through the fencing and hike 108 paces to the route **Hank's (5.9)** at **Random Walls**, a decent warmup for the nearby walls. Spot **Hank's** and **Save a bolt for me!** near the trail at two stone ledges leading to three more stone ledges, forming steps to the routes. The cliff is tall, with a large shallow tan bowl above a big base of gray limestone and also topped with a little gray limestone near the two route's anchors. (GPS N30°15.264' W097°47.613') **Geritol Wall** is a little further left.

From Hank's, hike 92 paces to **Through the Looking Glass (5.11a)** at **Great Wall** (GPS N30°15.249' W097°47.659' / 30.25415 -97.794317). Go 43 more paces to the gnarly leaning live oak 6' from the cliff, separating **New Wall** from **The Terrace**. Go down the stone steps to New Wall.

If you continue hiking the creek trail for 10 minutes, you'd reach **Guide's Wall**, **Kingdom of Ging**, and **Gus Fruh**, though those are also accessible via "Gus Fruh Access".

Greenbelt: **Bouldering**

The Greenbelt is blessed with quality bouldering right near or next to the sport routes, much of it covered in Texas Limestone Bouldering. We mention a little of it where it might complement an outing at particular sport climbing walls. Also check out the section on "Choss Cave."

Jeremy Barnes 📷   Lyndee McKinley, New Wall

---

[11] Only 10 minutes from the "T" to New Wall, this trail runs flat but rocky. It feels twice as long as it really is. Bring an interesting partner. The rockiness pounds our hip joints hard! When the creek isn't running, we recommend using the Gus Fruh Access, hiking right of Guide's Wall to New Wall. It takes about the same amount of time.

Greenbelt (west bank): **Seismic Wall (aka. Maggie's Wall)**

Sun conditions: All day sun with some limited tree shade. Cliff shade a couple hours before sunset.
Approach: 3 minutes via the "360 Access."
GPS @ Diving for Rocks: GPS N30˚14.727' W097˚48.002' (30.24545 -97.800033)

A big tan wall capped with a high roof. Route grades are relatively low, and this wall gets buku traffic. Lines for routes on the weekend are long enough for Austin to successfully sell tickets. The consequent rock polish is severe on certain routes. But the location and fast approach are compelling, it's easy to find belays, and route quality is high. Reach this wall via the directions for "360 Access" at the start of this chapter.

Seismic Wall was named for the crashing of a huge block climbers pried off a ledge next to Over Easy. Upon impact, ripples were seen rolling across the sand. Seismic Wall's other name (Maggie's Wall) was all about Tom Suhler's great crag dog, Maggy. Many of the route names reference her.

Seismic has been home-base for regular Wednesday (and winter-months night climbing) outings posted on ClimbingBuddies, a Yahoo group started by Joel Schopp and Brenton Buxton. Check out the Greenbelt history section to learn how night climbing came about.

Tree with forking branch 3' up, growing out of a boulder. (The tree is partly shown at the photo's left edge.)

1. **Man Hands**[12] (5.10c/5.11a)* 4 bolts, Roni Beer, David Cardosa, Scott Harris, Kareem al-Bassam. The slash grade is for small fingers / big fingers. Human-stick-clip Bolt 1 from the tree and boulder, but start the route without using them. Climbs to Capt. Morgan's anchors. '09.

---

[12] A famous Seinfeld eposide.

2. **Capt. Morgan** (5.10c)* 4 bolts, Scott Harris, David Cardosa, Kareem Al-Bassam. Use anything available except Man Hands' horn and crescent finishing holds; stay right of them. Shares anchors with Man Hands. '09

3. **Mr. Blister** (5.10d)*** 2 bolts, David Cardosa, Scott Harris, Ralph Vega. About 12' right of Capt. Morgan. *Beta.*[13]

4. **Short People** (5.9 PG)* 2 bolts. Runout to Bolt 2 on a slab fall. Polished, and it's as awkward as the opening lecture in Proctology 101.

9" Post Oak against the cliff, at a right-leaning blobby crack.

5. **Hoover Head**[14] (5.9)*** 3 bolts, Tom Suhler, Bruce Becker[15]. Starts 6' right of the 9" post oak. '93

    a. toprope: **Hoovering** (5.9 TR)* separate TR anchors, Tom Suhler, Bruce Becker. To set the TR, lead Hoover Head, traverse right to the clifftop jug, and reach to clip the anchors. Climb right of Hoover Head's bolts. Touch the mini-roof under the anchors and call that much 5.9. Maybe there's a 5.11 move to touch the anchors? Hoovering got squeezed by the (worthy) new route Torpedo's Away, but it somehow still pulls unique moves on the starting slab while using holds of Hoover Head and Torpedo's Away.

Wide mini-roof over the next three routes.

6. **Torpedo's Away** (5.9)*** 4 bolts, Karl Vochatzer. Try the sit start (5.10a) to include the nice hueco.[16] '08

    toprope: **Torpedo** (5.11 TR)* Tom Suhler, Bruce Becker. Start right of the hueco that's 5' off the ground and climb to Torpedo's Away's anchors. This TR route preceded Torpedo's Away by many years.

7. **Angel of Poets** (5.10b)*** 3 bolts, Ross Robertson, Ehren Siegenthaler, Srin Surapanani. Cool black rock spots at the anchors. A lot of moves in a small space. '04

    toprope: **Raining Skyward** (Unrated). Set TR on Angel of Poets or Matter of Honor. Climb between the lead routes. The two lead routes kicked off a renaissance at Seismic. (See the Greenbelt History section.)

8. **Matter of Honor** (5.10a)*** 3 bolts, Ross Robertson, Ehren Siegenthaler, Srin Surapanani. '04

9. **Lick the Window**[17] (5.10c)*** 4 bolts, Tom Suhler, Bruce Becker. High first bolt, ever since a flood removed a starting boulder. The anchors are at the right end of the roof. '93

    variation: (5.11a)* Start right of the little starting ramp.

Cody Rushing, "Angel of Poets"

---

[13] There's a crazy body position mantle involved. Karl Vochatzer jokes that the mantle almost gave him a hernia.

[14] Named for Maggy's fast vacuuming of any food that hit the floor.

[15] Back then, Bruce was a NASA contractor. His favorite response to any question was, "What do you think I am — a rocket scientist?"

[16] Austin sport routes are mostly short. A guilty pleasure of ours is making a few of them longer via sit starts on cool holds.

[17] Maggy would ride in the back of a truck and attempt to get in the cab by licking the rear window.

10. **Luminaire Noir** (5.11b-c)* 4 bolts, Ralph Vega, Karl Vochatzer. Aka. "Whimper." The direct route through pockets is 5.11b-c; going to the cave and traversing left is 5.11a.

toprope: **Seismic Step** (5.7 TR)*** anchors only, Keith Guillory. Set TR from the surrounding lead routes. Climbs the dihedral crack up and left. The start is close to 5.8. Good teaching spots for liebacks and easy mantles.

Left-leaning lumpy dihedral.

11. **ACK!**[18] (5.11b)* 4 bolts, Tom Suhler, Bruce Becker. Feet get anything, but hands stay out of the Seismic Step crackline and the low left-hand "wallet shaped" finger jug. The exact original definition of the route is forgotten, but we liked this interpretation and the below variation. '93

variation: (5.10d)* 4 bolts. Hands get anything right of the Seismic Step crackline, including the left-hand "wallet shaped" finger jug.

12. **She's No Dog; She's My Wife** (5.11b)*** 4 bolts, Tom Suhler, Bruce Becker. Soft belay over Bolt 1 to prevent wrecking onto the face bulge.

Left end of the big clifftop roof.

13. **Nose Print on the Windshield** (5.11c)*** 4 bolts, Tom Suhler, Bruce Becker. Stay off the crack, jug and ledge on the right. '93

variation: (5.11a)*** 4 bolts. Use the crack to the jug and ledge.

14. **Just for Fun** (5.9-5.10a)* 5 bolts, Tommy "Ambassador" Blackwell[19], Luke Bowman, Evan Jackson. After Bolt 2, traverse up and left the rest of the climb, to a large crack in the roof. The grade is reach-dependent and assumes you clip the anchors without pulling the whole roof.[20] If you fail on the roof, fief into Bolt 5 and stretch to clip the anchors. '07

extension: (5.10c)***. Clip Bolt 5 and then use the crack and/or surrounding holds to pull the roof, the short headwall above the roof, and then clip the anchors. This extension is pretty interesting and a relatively low grade, in these parts, for a roof problem.

toprope: **Rock Dog** (5.11c-d TR)*, Tom Suhler, Bruce Becker. This former lead route got chopped, except for one high bolt. Now it's a TR off of Just for Fun's anchors. Start just to the left of the steepest part of the low roof and the high lone bolt.

toprope: **Right Dog** (5.11d-5.12a TR)*. Start right of Rock Dog and the most prominent piece of the overhang, on two finger jugs just to the right of two thin cracks.

15. **Magster** (5.10a)*** 4 bolts, Tom Suhler, Bruce Becker. Bolt 3 is at 1 o'clock. Bolt 4 is invisible, atop a ledge. '93

The trail head on the opposite side of the creek is centered about here.

---

[18] Maggy would eat anything available, even wood and stone. When they wouldn't go down, she'd Ack them back up.

[19] Ralph S was called the Mayor of the Greenbelt, while Tommy was called the Ambassador of the Greenbelt. Tommy is remarkable in being able to climb 5.12a at age 58, and also in what he can't onsight. His hardest onsight is 5.10a.

[20] On diagonal routes like this, a common mistake is made when the second climber removes all the draws on the way up and hands a third climber the rope to toprope it. NO third climber, DON'T do it. You'll fall, swing on a huge arc and deck or club against those trees off left. Or you'll not fall, but your potential swing will totally brand you as a newb with no understanding of basic physics. The second climber should have pulled the rope and re-led it. Or, he could TR the route and then reclip the rope through most or all the draws on the way down, to provide you "directionals" that greatly reduce potential swing falls.

Cavason Sutton, "Cutting Cards for a Poke"

16. **Diving For Rocks**[21] (5.10b/d)*** 4 bolts, Tom Suhler, Bruce Becker. Bolt 4 is hidden on top of a ledge. Joel Schopp says "it's probably the coolest route at Seismic." The slash grade is complicated — few routes are as popular while receiving so much grade debate. (See comments in Appendix A.) The crux is done probably eight different ways. '93

variation: (5.11b-c)* instead of using the famous pockets, go right with both hands into and/or right of the crack.

a. extension: **Lonesome Dove** (5.11a)*** additional permadraw & anchors, Steve Brothers, Tommy Blackwell, Evan Jackson, Luke Bowman. Continue past Diving's anchors on one roof permadraw to anchors above the roof. Steve Brothers sent without any gear, tearing down roof choss on the way. Tommy et. al. bolted it in '04.

b. extended extension: **Do It For Shane** (5.12a)* Kenley Baraban. Topout over the anchors of Lonesome Dove. Many project the topout, but few succeed, since there's barely any rock available to climb.

c. extension: **Cutting Cards for a Poke** (5.12a)*** additional 3 permadraws and anchors, Derek McAlister, Russell Mayes. Climb Diving For Rocks, clip the permadraw of Lonesome Dove, then traverse right on 3 additional roof permadraws, to separate anchors. Cutting Cards may feel a little short, so go for Undertow. '08

[21] Maggy would dive 3-4' under water for rocks. One day at Reimers, Maggy was having fun fetching rocks out of the river, when someone was irritated and told Tom she was the stupidest dog they'd ever seen. Right about then, Maggy dropped a big rock on the guy's foot.

d. <u>extended extension:</u> **Undertow** (5.12b)*** Jesse Ryan. Climb Cutting Cards and top out.'09

17. **Ice Cubes, Popcorn, and Popsicles (aka. Slimy Crack)** (5.9)*** 3 bolts, Tom Suhler, Bruce Becker. The boltline and especially the anchors angle to the right. Popular despite the slime. Climb the wide slimy crack. '93

<u>toprope:</u> (5.9+)*. Set TR on Ice Cubes. Climb the face right of the boltline and left of Maggy Needs New Shoes' crack.

<u>toprope:</u> **Maggy Needs New Shoes** (5.9 TR)***, Tom Suhler, Bruce Becker. Set TR on Ice Cubes and climb the crack slightly right of the anchors.

18. **Birddog** (5.8)*** 3 bolts, Chris "Birddog" Keistler, David Cardosa. The bolts are to the right of the ugliest fractured crack/flake formation ever. Great warmup. David spotted the line on his return (after 10 years) to climbing. That's a sharp eye, spotting a good line in the middle of a super-trafficked old wall. Chris bolted it on lead and took a fall when a hook popped off. '07

<u>toprope:</u> **Birddog Bulge** (5.10a or 5.9)*. Climb the face of the bulge left of Bolt 2 (5.10a) with some lively beta, or the right edge of the bulge with less-lively beta (5.9). *Beta.*[22]

<u>variation:</u> **Birddog Arête** (5.8)*. Start the crack to the ledge. Climb the little arête right of Bolt 2, pull right of Bolt 3, and traverse the ledge back to make the steep anchor clip.

The rest of the routes are all on gray rock, just right of the big clifftop roof.

19. **Over Easy** (5.9)*** 5 bolts. The boltline is under the right end of the big clifftop roof. Go up the steep slabby face, then go left to Bolt 4 to pull the mini-roof. Bolt 4 looks strangely placed, to protect the contrived fun of pulling the mini-roof and staying out of the easier looking dihedral to the right. When toproping, leave a directional to avoid the swing. Bolt 5 is up and right.

<u>variation:</u> **Over Easy Direct** (5.9+)*. Stick-clip Bolt 2 and climb the thin holds directly under it.

20. **It's a Wiggle Butt** (5.8+ PG)*** 4 bolts, Tom Suhler, Bruce Becker. Easily identified by having the highest anchors among the routes right of the big clifftop roof. Runout to Bolt 4 on a slab fall. Aka Jiggle Butt. '93

21. **Butt Scratch**[23] (5.7)*** 3 bolts, Tom Suhler, Bruce Becker. Good warmup. The anchors are invisible from the ground and from the route, until Bolt 3. At Bolt 3, cut right slightly, though the anchors are at 11 o'clock from there, up and right of a left facing block. '93

22. **Roo Dog**[24] (5.8)* 4 bolts, Tom Suhler, Bruce Becker. Aka. "Maggy's Best Friend." If you stick-clip Bolt 1, the route might feel 5.7. '93

23. **Hollywood** (5.7)* 4 bolts, Ralph Showalter. Originally a TR-only route. Climb the slabby dishy dihedral.

6" Tree against the cliff.

24. **The Mongrel** (5.9 PG)*** 3 bolts, Karl Vochatzer, Annette Pelletier. Grounder runout to Bolt 3 on super easy terrain. The PG rating is about making the second clip. Stick-clip it or take the risk and its pick-your-poison beta. '09

---

[22] The bulge's 5.10a face is solved by a fun sequence of right heel hook, left toe hook, then possibly another right heel hook. The bulge's 5.9 right edge is pulled on two obvious underclings.

[23] When Maggy's partners were climbing, she focused on them and their return, distracted only by an occasional butt scratch. When they returned, she would excitedly do a big full-body-and-tail wag (a Wiggle-Butt).

[24] Roo Dog was Maggy's best friend, a black lab that was a little stiff, resembling a torpedo. They both liked ice cubes, popcorn, and popsicles.

Sarah Newman, "Butt Scratch"

e. <u>variation:</u> **Dogtailing** (5.8 PG)*** 7 bolts, Karl Vochatzer. Longest route on the wall. Climb Bolts 1-2 of The Mongrel, traverse left on Hollywood's Bolt 2, easy runout to Roo Dog's Bolt 3, go up to its Bolt 4 and left anchor, traverse left to Butt Scratch's left anchor, and end on the anchors of It's a Wiggle Butt.

?

Mini-roof 7' up, under a wide black rock ledge headwall.

25. **Die Easy** (5.6)*** 4 bolts, Tommy Blackwell, Luke Bowman, Evan Jackson, Stefanie Petermichl. Bolts are right of the dihedral end of the low black rock headwall. Use the stump, or start just right of it. '07

26. **Black Slabbath** (5.7)* 3 bolts, Ralph Vega, Rick Rivera. Starts between a skinny tree on the left and a fat tree on the right. '09

<u>toprope:</u> (5.8 and/or 5.9). Start 2-3' left of Bolt 1 for 5.8. Pull the bulge right of Bolt 3 for a 5.9.

Turn right and hike 333 paces to reach 5.8 Sanctuary, or 273 paces to the path to set topropes on 5.8 Sanctuary. That trail also provides a shortcut to Gus Fruh (total 10 minutes). The shortcut cuts across the creek's peninsula between Seismic and Gus Fruh. We've not taken it, and a likely better shortcut is to just drive to Gus Fruh Access. However, the following might work out: follow the trail and stay headed North. Intersect with an old power line right-of-way. Head downhill (East) for about 200 feet and find a trail on the left in a cactus patch. Follow it downhill to the main trail just upstream from Gus Fruh. Walk 300' to the route Fern Bar.

Greenbelt (west bank): **5.8 Sanctuary**

Sun conditions: tree shade
Approach: 5 minutes via the "360 Access;" 2 minutes from Seismic Wall.
GPS @ Face Off: N30˚14.708' W097˚47.847' (30.245133 -97.79745)

A short wall with one lone lead route and two cool looking low caves. The lead route's anchors serve five routes and variations. The wall also has a 5.4 trad/solo route, and one of the TR's can be led trad. Despite the short height (comparable to the left side of Hand Beyond Wall at Reimers), the routes pack plenty of moves. A fun way to finish a session at Seismic, but leave some gas for it!

See directions for the 360 Access. This wall is 333 paces to the right (downstream) of Seismic Wall. Keep an eye out for two low caves, because there are only two bolts and anchors to spot. 60 paces left of this wall is a trail accessing the top, an option for setting better (no swing fall) anchors on several of the routes.

1. <u>trad or toprope:</u> **Fist Crack** (5.8)* no bolts no anchors, Keith Guillory. A wide overhanging crack in the dihedral. Use large gear, or TR it from Face Off's anchors. Climb the crack all the way to the clifftop. On TR, you face a safe but exciting swing fall, until you traverse hands across the ledge to the anchors.

   a. <u>variation:</u> **Abandon the Crack** (5.7)***. Leave the crack and traverse right onto Face Off until your right hand is on the best hold of Swordfish, then go up to the anchors. This will not feel 5.7 unless your selection of handholds and footholds is stellar.

2. **Face Off**[25] (5.9+)* 2 bolts. Pulls the middle/right of the cave roof below Bolt 1, working the feet up the diagonal edge of the cave. Since the start is high on the cave, it's a tiny looking route...full of moves.

   b. <u>variation:</u> **Face On** (5.10c)*. Start slightly left of Face Off, right-hand on a positive 3-finger pocket. Pull over the cave and then climb left of the bolts. Beta[26].

   c. <u>trad or toprope:</u> **Swordfish** (5.8+ TR)***, Tom Halicki. Start between the caves and climb the shallow left-leaning finger crack to Face Off's anchors. Lead with small to medium stoppers, or set a TR on Face Off and ideally sling vegetation up top for a directional. Without a directional, you risk swinging hard into the ground. And, higher up, you risk swinging hard onto the big block out left. As a safer alternative, just Start Face Off and immediately traverse right onto the finger crack.

3. <u>trad/solo:</u> **Pointless Wonder** (5.4)* no bolts, no anchors. A crack in the dihedral 10 paces right of Swordfish. It sure looks like an easy solo! But add dirt, a couple fractured-looking handholds, and falls bouncing down the slab, and you have the sensation of risking your ass. And possibly you are.

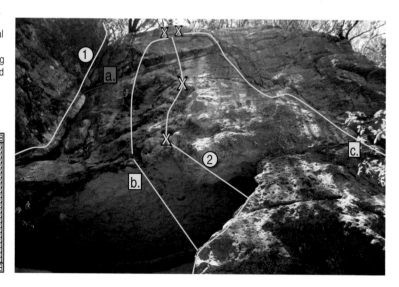

> Solo's are a personal choice, a choice I have had the pleasure of doing many times before the birth of my daughter. One I will never persue again. Her well being comes 1st now.
> *Kirk Holladay*

---

[25] Keith named it after the good ol' leper-hockey joke. Face Off was the original name of Fist Crack, but it somehow migrated to the lead route. "Heard about the lepers playing a hockey game? Ended with a face-off in the corner."

[26] Set hands just over the roof. Feet cut; left foot smears far left cave edge, right foot sets a stem on the right cave edge. (Maybe you pull up and lock off before the right foot goes up; we don't remember.) If you're not tall enough to set this wide stem, we're interested in what the grade is for you. (11a?)

Barton Creek

Greenbelt (east bank): **Beehive Wall**

Sun conditions: sun around 2pm; lots of it, with tree shade on Suhler Route and on the bottom halves of the toughest routes
Approach: 11 minutes (via the Twin Falls access when the creek is dry); 18 minutes via the 360 Access.
GPS @ creekbed in front of Honey Dripper: N30˚14.388' W97˚48.537' (30.2398 -97.80895)

Check it out! A tall, steep wall that's home to one of the best 5.12a's in the park. 5.11 climbers should ignore the set of grades and use the following recipe to have a full outing. After the (new) 5.9 and (old) 5.10 warmups, the two rough 5.12's right of Dirty Rotten Whore have really fun 5.11 starts and low sections. Lead them to the cruxes; download or stick-unclip to clean. Start with Super Yummy (5.11a low section), then Champagne n' Reefer (5.11c to Bolt 3). Then, Honey Dripper is the style of route a lot of ATX climbers like. Climb most of it (stout 5.11a), as far as the bees allow you, and lower on the available bail biners below the hive. Then hit Dirty Rotten Whore or Hedonistic Urges (which has plenty of climbing until the 12c crux, and it can be downled to clean).

Some of the holds were reinforced here by a semi-slick glue,[27] on excellent routes. Shun them only if you shun indoor climbing gyms. Three routes have no glue on them, and two have only a couple reinforced holds.

The wall is a pretty setting on a bend in the creek. When the water is up, it's a great swimming hole, especially up river where there are rope swings. Hikers are very active in front of Honey Dripper and Dirty Rotten Whore, where the trail is narrow. Please place your stuff away from there, pile the rope off the trail, and congregate out of the way. We do not want to risk the city decommissioning the two routes, due to hiker complaints.

trad: **Meat and Potatoes** (5.10a)* no bolts, no anchors. This short, well-formed left-facing crack angles left, then right, then left again. There are some potential routes nearby.

Ryan Hartford, "Honey Dripper"

100 paces.

bouldering: Long low ledge 3' off the deck. It transitions to 5-6' for a cool, dirty traverse. (Bring a fat brush.) It is 38 paces wide.

110 paces.
Slab cliff with a lone hard-to-spot route and some more route potential (4-6 easy routes?).

1. **Sucker Sipper** (5.11b) 3 bolts, no anchors, Eddie Pain, Alvino Pon. Sling a big tree up-and-left for anchors. The route climbs obviously easy slabs most of the way up to a short crux face. Skip this one. Such venom was spewed by our test-climbing party that I didn't even get on it. Bolt 1 is high at mid cliff, above a tree on a ledge, and slightly right from under a large cedar at clifftop. Low anchors might make this a nice 5.6.

15 paces to a chain handrail across a ledge.
Bee Hive near the clifftop. It's wild!

2. **Honey Dripper** (5.11c or 5.11a)*** 8 bolts, Kirk Holladay, Alvino Pon. Bolts 1-4 are on the face, 6' left of the blocky arête. Bolt 5 is a big ring on the roof. Bolt 7 is just under the hive. Bolt 8 is left of the hive. Climb to the current bail-biner on Bolt 6. Or, possibly to the biner on Bolt 7 if the bees are inactive in cold weather; have an epipen/Benadryl at the ready.[28] The "or" grade reflects whether you topout or bail early.

    a. variation: **Big Dipper** (5.11a)* Kirk Holladay, Alvino Pon. Cut left (probably around the arête) for an easier finish that goes less close to the hive.

Blocky Arête 25' tall, over the left end of a wide, steep low overhang. Some mysterious spectra comes out of the right face of the arête, held by a nail.

3. **Dirty Rotten Whore** (5.12a)*** 6 bolts, Kirk Holladay, Alvino Pon. Bolts 1-5 angle right. Several locals say this is the best 5.12a in the park; another says it's the hardest! This route appeared to have gone unclimbed for over a decade after the FA.

    b. variation: **Prickly Heat** (5.11d-5.12a)* Kirk Holladay, Alvino Pon. Goes left at Bolt 5 of Dirty Rotten Whore to separate anchors. This path might be blocked now by the big cactus patch, or it runs right of it. We have a call into Alvino.

---

[27] We prefer Sika Anchor-Set for such work, producing a rough cement texture. A thinly brushed coat of Sika would improve the glue-jobs.
[28] Long before the world's bee population began dying off, Alvino killed off the bees here, twice, but they came back. He also kept bees at his place. Making him a sort of Bee Lord. (The Lord giveth, and the Lord taketh away.)

4. **Champagne n' Reefer** (5.13a)*** 7 eye bolts. For 5.11c fun, climb the first 3 bolts. After that are a lot of fracture crimps reinforced by semi-slick glue.

5. **Super Yummy** (5.12c)*** 6 bolts. Bolt 1 is on light gray rock under the left end of a left-tilting ledge. For 5.11a fun, climb the starting section.

6. **Hedonistic Urges** (5.12b)*** 5 bolts, Eddie Pain. A hard-to-spot boltline 12' right of Super Yummy. Bolt 1 is low but somehow nearly invisible, 12" right of an abandoned bolt hole, on a gray spot under the roof. Bolt 2 is on the roof, also next to an abandoned hole. Easy runout to Bolt 3. The remaining bolts slant slightly right.

7. **Moammar No Amore** (5.12a)*** 6 bolts, Matt Twyman, Erin Murdock. Exactly 35' tall. '11

8. toprope: **Unfinished Route** (5.??? TR)*** 3 bolts up high & anchors, Alvino Pon. The bolts are hard to spot. They're under a precarious-looking protruding left-pointing boulder at clifftop. Alvino intends to finish this old, city-approved project. J.W. and others worked part of it and found wild moves. Set TR anchors easily from route #7.

Right end of a wide, steep low overhang.

9. **Suhler Route**[29] (5.10b)*** 4 bolts, Tom Suhler, David Cardosa. Bolt 1 is high, just below a ledge to the right of the wide, steep low overhang.

10. **Erin's Route** (5.9+ PG)*** 5 bolts, Matt Twyman, Erin Murdock, Brian Tickle, Massim Kammah. Bolt 4 is at 11 o'clock. Mild runouts over ledges for the PG rating. '11

Cavason Sutton, "Dirty Rotten Whore"

David Phillips, Undeveloped Bouldering on Gnarly Wall #1

bouldering: a long traverse on the right side of the wall.

Gnarly Wall #1: Not far upstream is this curved overhung gray and black wall with white speckles and wild blocks. 35' tall, 60 paces wide. Low traverses, highball potential, and route potential. The rock shapes are cool, but various blocks are suspect. Maybe it would clean up nicely.

Gnarly Wall #2: Not far further upstream is a similar, low-overhung blocky black/white/gray rock wall.

Far upstream lies the Loop 1 (Mopac) bridge, home of Urban Surprise, discussed in Appendix C.

---

[29] Previously published as Cardosa Route without asking the FA's. Tom and David talked in 2011 and named it Suhler Route.

Greenbelt (east bank): **Kirk and Alvin's Wall**

Sun conditions: All day shade. The cave under Skank Hole provides belayer air-conditioning on hot afternoons.
Approach: 16 minutes via the "360 Access."
GPS @ creek bank below Airman's Cave: GPS N30°14.505' W097°47.467' (30.24175 -97.791117)

Named after Kirk Holladay (now deceased) and his bolting buddy Alvino Pon. "Monfy" (swallow the "n") is missed by many. More is written about him under North Shore, his last area of concentrated route development. (See Holladay Wall, page 142.) The routes here are shaded and relatively tall (35'), on a wall that is strangely both ugly and beautiful. The slopey tops accumulate some dirt, but the rock is unpolished and the routes are worth doing. This wall is disdained by many, but it rightly has its fans. We like it and suspect many got a bad impression of the routes from hugely sandbagged grades, rather than the actual climbing. Our updated grades are still a little sandbagged, in keeping with the tradition of Greenbelt sandbaggery. The Puss Crack variation improves the wall with a warmup climb, and there's some bouldering in both directions that could round out an outing. This wall could be improved by some gardening up top, to make it easy to set X-Rated Negro and other unestablished toprope routes over a cool, overhanging cliff section.

For directions, see the "360 Access" and its section about this wall at the start of this chapter.

bouldering: a boulder stack forms an "A" frame cave visible from the feeder creek. A couple of problems.

60 paces, crossing a feeder creek. The creek is small but was running water in the middle of the drought.

bouldering: Pull a 10' tall bulge under a short 45 degree roof. Walk off under the roof. Looks like 5-8 problems.

84 paces between bouldering and Bloody Butt.

1. **Bloody Butt**[30] (5.10d)*** 3 bolts, Kirk Holladay, Alvino Pon. Bolt 1 is on the left face of a little dihedral. Bolt 2 is right of a scar. Anchors are at 11 o'clock from Bolt 3, out of sight over the top. Watch for rock fall. The crack on the right is "on" for clipping Bolt 2.

   a. variation: **Puss Crack** (5.10c lead / 5.9TR)***, John Hogge, David Phillips. Stick-clip the second bolt of Bloody Butt. Start left of its first bolt, at the dihedral and crack. Climb the features left of Bloody Butt's boltline, clipping its third bolt and anchors. Your hands won't need any holds right of the boltline until the fin above the last bolt, near the anchors. Watch for rock fall. A good warmup if you use the beta[31].

2. **Skank Hole** (5.10d)*** 2 bolts, Kirk Holladay, Alvino Pon. Bolt 1 is high and right of the crack. Bolt 2 is at 11 o'clock.

   b. variation: (5.12)* Stay right of the crack and pull the bulge.

3. **Pay Dirt** (5.11d-5.12a PG)*** 4 bolts, Kirk Holladay, Alvino Pon. Stick-clip Bolt 2 to remove the PG rating. Suspect rock made leading to it pretty creepy. We love fun beta on bolt clips.[32] Air runout to the anchors, out of sight, among top vegetation. This route has elements a lot of people like. If cleaned up towards the top and the grade better determined, it could become a cult classic.

   c. variation: **Pay the Skank** (5.11a-b)* 4 bolts. Climb Pay Dirt through four bolts, then cut left to Skank Hole's anchors. A good way to skip Pay Dirt's crux section and to clean the gear.

---

[30] The route name reminds us of the term *butthurt* originated by Kirky and used occasionally on www.erockonline.com during heated political discussions. *Butthurt* means hurt feelings. It has cheered many in the wake of childish online harshness. But this route name occurred because Kirk took a huge whipper and cut his ass. He cut his ass so badly that it almost needed stitches.

[31] The clips are hard, making the TR only a 5.9. Its anchor clip is so difficult (for the 5.10c grade) that, for warm up purposes, we recommend grabbing the chains to clip. If you're going for a redpoint, rock onto your left foot to set an unlikely left kneebar left of Bolt 3 for a near full rest before the anchors. Work the crimps to a right-hand gaston on the fin for a hard first anchor clip, then left-hand thumb-down pinch just above the right hand, right hand pinch the dirty shelf above the anchors, and clip the other anchor. The last hold isn't better; it just provides a little relief from that gaston.

[32] Set a left kneebar to clip Bolt 3.

20' space between Pay Dirt bolts and the toprope route

<u>toprope:</u> **X-Rated Negro** (5.10b TR)* No Anchors, Jeff Jackson. Set a TR slinging trees about 20' right of Pay Dirt. From Bloody Butt, hike 34 paces, hugging the cliff edge, to an easy scramble up and right to set topropes. There's more TR potential than just one route. Bring gardening tools and safety rope so you can work safely. If you do this work, let us know, because we can find guys who like this wall and would maintain your work.

40 Paces between Pay Dirt and Airman's Cave

Airman's Cave (two small cave openings, side by side).

<u>caving:</u> **Airman's Cave** (5.10 C)***. A spelunking destination known for a long intimidating squeeze tube and, deep in, dioramas using toy soldiers and the like. The cave goes deep for many hours with branches; don't wing a trip in there. Get training, experience, and beta. The cave entrance was barred and locked recently to reduce the city's hassles rescuing the clueless. Call the city for permission to cave here.

Trailhead below Airman's Cave

<u>bouldering:</u> the triangular boulder in the creek.

<u>bouldering:</u> on the trail just right of Airman's Cave, you'll find a cool looking chossy potential bouldering wall, dirty with fine dust, but it felt pretty solid.

David Phillips, "Bloody Butt"

> Our business isn't about the money and never has been, it's about teaching what we love to do & promoting our sport in the safest manner possible.
> *Kirk Holladay*

Barton Creek

Greenbelt (west bank): **Gus Fruh**

Sun conditions: sun roughly 10am to 2pm with partial tree shade; cliff shade after that.
Approach: 5 minutes via the "Gus Fruh Access" described at the start of this chapter.
GPS @ Running Man: N30°14.915' W097°47.819' (30.248583 -97.796983)

This popular wall is full of tricky cruxes, often involving powerful, balancy, exotic moves. It has tricky warmups with hotly-contested grades. For a warmup, try the 5.8/5.9 Aid variation to Iranian Arms Deal. For directions, see "Gus Fruh Access" at the start of this chapter. Some of these routes could use more cleaning by the general public. Dirt is often ignored deep in pockets you don't use, but "off route" cleaning is good to do, particularly here, where insects sometimes burrow and produce a slick powder on the holds you need.

It's a 10-minute hike downstream to New Wall. It's a 25-minute hike upstream to the right of Seismic Wall (22 minutes from 5.8 Sanctuary), but there's a shortcut across the peninsula, out of the creek valley, reducing this to 10 minutes. (See its description at the end of the section on Seismic Wall.)

> bouldering: **Green Mile Traverse** (V5). A short right-to-left traverse just left of Running Man's alcove.

Fern-dotted alcove.

1. **Running Man** (5.12a)*** 5 bolts, Scott Harris, David Cardosa[33]. Bolt 1 is left of the start on an edge forming a "V", at the V's upper left corner. Bolt 2 is 2' up. Bolt 3 is at 11 o'clock, Bolt 4 at 1pm. '87

Sloping ledge sprayed with pockets low to the ground.

The next two routes share Bolt 1, way up above the sloping ledge formation.

Evening Galvin, "Running Man"

2. **Reefer Madness** (5.11c)* 5 bolts, Scott Harris. Scramble up the sloping ledge to the high first bolt. Use long runners to cut the rope drag. The anchors are out of sight, above the roof. It's common to do the 5.11a variation to set TR on Running Man.

> variation: (5.11a)*** 4 bolts. Climb bolts 1-4, then walk the ledge left to clip Running Man's anchors.

> bouldering: **The Big Traverse** (V3)***. 400' big! Climb sections of this for a great warmup. Start at Reefer Madness and traverse right to the cave at Kingdom of Ging. Lap it. Use it when your partner stands you up.

3. **Cyborg** (5.11b)*** 6 bolts, Scott Harris. Uses Reefer Madness' Bolt 1. Start Reefer Madness, then go right after Bolt 1. Anchors are out of sight, above the roof. Use long draws on bolts 1 and 6 to cut the rope drag. The route's pretty close to 11c.

Elegant right-facing curved crack.

---

[33] Knowing the manufacturing of pockets would draw the wrath of Ralph Schowalter and other old-schoolers, they thought about it a lot, then decided to do it since they were about to split town for Colorado ☺. In 2011, Matt Twymann and David accomplished the Austin area's first-ever "pure rebolting" in limestone, extracting all of the 23-year old bolts (starting with some ideas out of the Red and some new tools and techniques) and re-using the bolt holes with Wave Glue-Ins. A common practice in granite, this can be tough in limestone.

4. **Birdland** (5.10d R)*** 4 bolts, Jeff Jackson[34]. Climb the crack to the ledge and Bolt 1, which is too high for most stick-clips. Bolt 2 is at 11 o'clock. Bolt 3 is in the roof. On toprope, a lot of people avoid dirty holds (instead of cleaning them!) by walking the ledge right and climbing up the left part of the column onto the roof. '87 ⌁

5. **Iranian Arms Deal** (5.10d)*** 4 bolts, Keith Guillory, David Renburg. Start just left of Fern Bar's ramp. '87 ⌁

Evening Galvin, "Fern Bar"

⑤ ⑥ ⑦

variation: (5.8/5.9 Aid)***, 4 bolts. Best warmup on the wall, the brainchild of DP. Hang a fat draw on Bolt 1 and pull on it to gain the ledge.

variation: (5.8 R / 5.8 trad)*. "R" rating is for leading it as a sport route (no gear). Start Birdland and hang a long draw on its bolt above the ledge. Walk the ledge right to Iranian Arms Deal's bulge. Rehearse these moves on TR beforehand, as you're poorly protected. Climb right and up the bulge to reach Bolt 2 on its right side. Finish Iranian Arms Deal.

the original version: (5.9)*. Start on Fern Bar and traverse left after its first bolt to Iranian Arms Deal. IAD's first bolt wasn't there originally.

toprope: (5.10d TR)*. Climb the right-facing flake on the face right of Birdland's crack. ⌁

6' tall diagonal ramp

6. **Fern Bar** (5.9)*** 1 piton and 3 bolts, Keith Guillory[35]. Bolt 1 is over the diagonal ramp. Bolt 3 is at 1 o'clock. This was the first route on the wall. Easy runouts, with one balancy runout. Beta[36]. ⌁

7. **Gros Ventre** (5.10d/5.11a)*** 4 bolts, David Cardosa, Adam Hurst. Height-dependent grade. The crux is a super hard-to-read 3-ring circus. Beta.[37] ⌁

20 Paces to a pretty, wide, offwidth flake/crack.
toprope & trad: **Wyoming Women** (5.8)*** George "Hap" Hazzard[38]. Set TR from Heir Apparent and climb the pretty offwidth flake/crack. ⌁

---

[34] Jeff developed much of the bouldering at the Greenbelt, Reimers, and the harder problems at Rogers Park. He bolted lines all over the world. He wrote a lot of fun stuff over the years, including Texas Limestone II. It is a great read, and word has it that it will enter the public domain, online, for your enjoyment. Jeff's been the editor of *Rock & Ice* magazine for years, writing delightful editorials. He's not at the top of the sport, but his writing is at the top of all fun writing, full of supremely creative, wacky, off-the-wall similes. With Texas Limestone II, Jeff set the bar for gonzo-guidebook-journalism.

[35] Keith Guillory, Jim Blanford, and Mike Holbart established the early 5.9's and 5.10's at Enchanted Rock in the 1970's. While progressing up the slab climbs of Erock's backside, Keith actually perfected *falling* on Texas Radio before he mastered the crux. His controlled fall strategy was an unconventional turn *away* from the rope and last pro, then a run down the slab, and a swing back to the by-then-belayer-tightened rope. Usually the last move of the fall was a hop over the taught rope as he swung to a stop. Slab climbing: true gnar.

[36] The standard crux footwork has become very polished. Try to set a super high right foot and rock on.

[37] From the ramp top, left-hand to the long crimp sidepull. Left foot stretches way high to toe the mini-ledge up and left of the previous left-hand pocket. Slowly rock onto it while alternatively bumping left hand higher to the high sweetspot of the long crimp sidepull, working the right foot up, and picking the right balance point to right-hand mantle. Out of all Dave's routes, unlocking this crux and the joy it brought was one of his most precious moments.

[38] Back in the 80's George climbed in a Euro hot pink body suit, of all things. George used to set out pink flamingos at the base of routes he and Scott Harris were on, for style.

Barton Creek

variation: **Wandering Women** (5.8). Start Wyoming Women and traverse right, very very far, walking across the ledge system, clip one of the anchors on Chicken Supreme, go up to an anchor of Rock Retard, and finish on Thumbdance. Several people say don't bother. One said, "The traverse was just a dirty 4th class walk."

8. **Heir Apparent** (5.9)*** 4 bolts.

variation: **Limestone Cowboy** (5.10d/5.11a)*. Climb Heir Apparent, but pull the center of the roof left of Bolt 1, hands and feet staying left of the bolt. Best done as a TR.

9. **Chicken Supreme** (5.9+ / 5.10b)* 3 bolts, Ralph Showalter (FA prior to bolts). Start to the right of the bulge. Beta[39].

toprope: **Betwixt** (5.11b TR)*** Ralph Showalter. Start just left of the roof's big slot on the thin face right of Chicken Supreme. Use a chicken head on the lip of the roof, a sidepull up and left, and the flat area on the right. Climb the upper bulge to the anchors.

toprope: **Egg Salad Sandwich** (5.10a TR)*. Aka "Old #9". Start 5' right of Betwixt. Climb the right end of the roof. (One can keep hands off the flat area used by Betwixt, using crimps above and right of the roof.) Finish right of the bulge.

10. **Rock Retard** (5.11a PG)*** 4 bolts, Scott Harris[40], Randy Spears, Mike "The Profit" Head. Bolt 2 is at 10 o'clock; Bolt 3 is at 11 o'clock. Use long draws on bolts 2 and 3 to reduce rope drag. Pull the roof right of Bolt 3. '87

a. toprope: **Trash Can Man** (5.11b TR)*** Hank Caylor. "Rock Retard direct." Go up the shallow dihedral left of Rock Retard's Bolt 1. Pull the gap in the roof left of Rock Retard's Bolt 3. Climb to Rock Retard's anchors. Boldly led on the FA in 1987, the first 5.11 at Gus Fruh.

b. toprope: **Apostrophe** (5.11 TR)*, Rick Watson (trad FA[41]). Set TR on Rock Retard. Start to its right, under a tan and black bulge below the karst layer. Climb to and above the bulge to the ledge, up the dihedral, up the face, and traverse left to the anchors. The original trad line stayed left of Thumb Dance's Bolt 2 and went to Thumb Dance's anchors.

11. **Thumb Dance** (5.10b R)*** two pitches: 2 bolts, 1 old piton, 1st anchors, 2 more bolts, 2nd anchors, "Goomba" John Sanders[42]. Super (close to decking) runout to the first anchors. Clip the old piton just under the anchors. Bolts 1 and 2 are next to original pitons. A 35meter rope is barely enough for both pitches; however, the meat of the climb is the first pitch's headgame runout. My belayer was ready to *take* and run left — probably the best plan. The 2nd pitch is interesting. It has a little suspect rock and a lot of loose gravel to dodge, with a bad ledge fall to the last bolt. That last bolt is on the left side of the final chimney, whereas the anchors are above clifftop on the right. Tons of rock fell off the top, making the second pitch less classic.

c. toprope: **Blind Date** (5.10c TR)*** David Cardosa (trad FA, X-rated). If you prefer a well-bolted 11a to super-runout 10b, set this TR by leading Rock Retard and traversing right (on runout, balancy, 5.5 pebble-dodging) to Thumb Dance's 1st anchors. Start a few feet right of Thumb Dance, climbing a well defined diagonal seam parallel to Thumb Dance's seam. Blind Date's seam is over a big black oval karst stone imbedded in the wall. Pull a bulge 5 ½ feet right of Thumb Dance's Bolt 2 and finish on Thumb Dance's anchors.

---

[39] KV's beta is a left footjam in the cubby-hole, leaning off right and reaching lefthand high. Ours was a high right foot, rock-on.

[40] Scott is the founding father of Mountain Madness climbing school and one of the most accomplished route developers at Enchanted Rock and the Greenbelt. He coauthored the beloved climbing guide Dome Driver's Manual. He's an architect, music producer, audio engineer (www.big-bang-music.com), and singer-song-writer.

[41] A bold, poorly-protected ascent that drew the comment, "You're an idiot" from onlooker Scott Harris.

[42] Goomba John and Lauren Clayton were some of the earliest climbers active in Austin. They did much of the early exploring in the Greenbelt and "pointed the way" at Gus Fruh with Thumb Dance. Due to an argument with his partner at the time, John got a total newb to belay him on the FA. He used one piece above Bolt 2 to cut the runout. John named the wall The Cherry Hole, but the parks department's name (Gus Fruh) stuck.

d. <u>toprope:</u> **Praying Mantle** (5.11a TR)*** Ralph Showalter. Start 2' right of Blind Date. [43] Climb to the little rounded dihedral under a very small mini-roof, then pull the big right-facing edge sidepull above the miniroof's right side. Pull the bulge risking a big swing, and head for Thumb Dance's anchors.

e. <u>toprope:</u> **Rent a Pig** (5.10? TR)* Ralph Showalter. A bolt with no hanger marks the route. It goes straight up and over a thin section right of Praying Mantel. The swing fall is big but safe. 5.10? We got on it briefly, and blankness pushed us onto Praying Mantle. Either we missed something, or it's harder than Praying Mantle.

<u>bouldering:</u> In addition to the big traverse from Reefer Madness, the Whipping Post Boulder (near the creek in front of Thumb Dance) has several dozen problems documented in Texas Limestone Bouldering.

45 paces to Kingdom of Ging routes.

> Sometimes the best gear for a climb is a good excuse.
>
> *John Sherman*

---

[43] When we saw we had to review these squeeze jobs, it made our eyes roll and we prepared to hate it like we hated sorting out Betwixt from Egg Salad Sandwich. But Dave and Ralph found great routes here, on all-unique holds despite the squeeze. Bravo!

Barton Creek

Greenbelt (west bank): **Kingdom of Ging**

Sun conditions: sun roughly 10am to 2pm (summer); shaded after that.
Approach: 6 minutes via the "Gus Fruh Access" described at the start of this chapter.
GPS @ Charlie Don't Surf: N30°14.954' W097°47.818' (30.249233 -97.796967)

This wall is just right of Gus Fruh and just left of Guide's Wall. A huge cave spans the start of all the routes. Good boulder problems are under the roof, described in Texas Limestone Bouldering by Jeff Jackson (page 135 — Kingdom of Ging was left out of the index). The right three routes are well-justified squeeze jobs. Purists would probably have omitted King of Ging/Sex Dwarfs. Except for Charlie Don't Surf, the routes meander and get a handhold on another route's foothold. Read the route path comments, or you'll start up a route, find another route's bolt near your face and wonder if you're off-route.

For directions, see "Gus Fruh Access" at the start of this chapter.

Liang Wu, "King of Ging"

1. **Charlie Don't Surf** (5.10d)*** 4 bolts, Scott Harris, David Cardosa. Starts (obviously) with a dyno to the ledge. This route was the first rap-bolted route on the Greenbelt. '87

2. **Jerry's Kids** (5.11b)*** 5 bolts, Mike Head[44], Scott Harris, Randy Spears, Larry Spears[45]. Another obvious dyno-to-the-ledge start. Folks who can't do it often start on Charlie Don't Surf or King of Ging, and traverse the low roof over before pulling up. Bolt 5 is at 2 o'clock, and the anchors

---

[44] With this route, the four guys did the Greenbelt's last hard-man hand-drilled bolted-on-lead hanging-on-hooks style route installation. Mike Head was one of the great early climbers, who put up routes on lead but also transitioned into hard sport route development. He was a big influence on the Stupid Brothers and David Cardosa. David said Mike's influence is why there is a New Wall, and that he was and is the Man! Mike and others put up the first routes at Hueco Tanks in the late 1970's.

[45] Randy, his brother Larry, Scott Harris, and Scott's brother were locally famous and influential as the Stoopid Brothers for their parties, crazy antics and hard climbing. Both sets of brothers lived and vacationed together, started businesses together, and held long summer freakouts in Boulder.

are out-of-sight, directly above it. Onsight attempts are ridiculous without the following path beta.[46] '87

3. **King of Ging** (5.10b)*** 5 bolts, Hank Caylor[47]. Starts on Gray Streak (under its 1st bolt). Climb straight up for 4 bolts, then traverse left to Bolt 5 and the anchors. Nicely seasoned with polish. '86

   a. <u>bolted variation:</u> **Sex Dwarfs** (5.11c)* 5 bolts, David Cardosa, Scott Harris. Climb Kingdom of Ging for three bolts, then traverse left and slightly up to this route's lone bolt (on the bulge), then straight up to rejoin Ging at its last bolt and anchors. While Kingdom of Ging also traverses left, its traverse is higher, from its fourth bolt.

4. **Gray Streak** (5.10c PG)*** 4 bolts, Tony Faucett, Rene Payne. Starts under Bolt 1. Runout to Bolt 4 and the anchors. Never abandon your belay![48] Beta.[49]

30 paces to Guide's Wall, if you hug the cliff.

> Trouble was, we'd been experiencing a spell of bad weather: It would rain for a couple of days, look like clearing, then rain some more. We lived in fear of the dreaded Royal Robbins appearing to take over the climb. Worse, we were in danger of becoming "overtrained." All summer we'd trained hard—eating, drinking, loafing. Now, as we waited out the bad weather, the excitement of the impending climb precipitated almost constant partying.
>
> *Warren Harding, in Downward*

---

[46] After high-clipping Bolt 4, traverse right about 3' near the next route, then up. On the next rebolting, please move Bolt 4 right a little as a guide.

[47] Hank has likely mellowed a little from his crazy-man days as an urban BASE jumper and soloist…he now chills as a wildlife fire fighter! Hank is best known for a downtown Denver sky scraper BASE jump where winds blew him back into the building, through a window. He picked himself up and bled his way down the elevator and out of the building. The cops followed his blood trail and busted him. He received 150 stitches and an acquittal. Hank excelled at X-rated routes, with a tendency for sketching out and screaming obscenities, and falling/decking once in a while, whereas his peers on these types of routes were about calm control and never falling. His primary motivation: he likes to be scared. At age 16 he fell 60-70' on Gravatron at Erock, hit his head, vomited, got back on and sent the route. Hank owned Austin's first climbing gym, Pseudo Rock, a tasty, old-school short-wall pea-gravel-padded un-air-conditioned space where climbers trained and dogs broke their house training.

When asked for stories about Hank, most people say "Geeze, where do we start?" One time Ralph Showalter was climbing a route and dropped a piece at a critical placement. Hank grabbed it, soloed up and handed it to him. One hung-over New Years Day, after the first day of sinking bolts at New Wall, Hank soloed up an easy spot near Walk the Dog. Then he cut left onto sketchier uncleaned terrain, and fought a belly-flop inch by inch over a topout, during which David Cardosa was sure Hank was going to die.

[48] One day, Joey Phillips was clipping the anchors when a large block fell off, the belayer fled, and Joey plummeted onto a tree stump near the belay. Joey wasn't seriously hurt, perhaps because he was a paratrooper and blackbelt badass.

[49] Try a stem (left knee down) to mellow out the start.

Greenbelt (west bank): **Guide's Wall**

Sun conditions: extensive tree shade.
Approach: 6 minutes via the "Gus Fruh Access" described at the start of this chapter.
GPS @ rightmost route: N30˚14.970' W097˚47.816' (30.2495 -97.796933)

This wall is just right of Kingdom of Ging and 10 minutes left of New Wall. For directions, see "Gus Fruh Access" at the start of this chapter. It's a great wall for beginners, guiding and climbing instruction, with crack climbing and a lot of technical moves for lower grade routes. Great routes, with a tragic lack of lead bolts. Since it's all toprope, you can invent a lot of variations.

Anchors: The anchors are all above topouts, not visible from the ground. From right-to-left when facing the cliff, the anchors are: a pair of chain anchors, a big cedar tree with smaller backup brush, a set of three hangers (no chain), and another pair of chain anchors.

Minimum Gear to Bring: Seven routes and variations can be done setting only two ropes via Anchoring steps #3 and #4 listed below, skipping the two classic routes on the right end of the wall. Two ropes, four quickdraws, and enough webbing or quickdraw chains to back up the single anchors described in step #3. The quickdraws minimize wear on chain anchors, plus there is some missing chain (just hangers), as of this writing.

Maximal Gear: To set up all the routes, bring up 8 quickdraws, 4 ropes and whatever gear you want to set an anchor on one thick cedar tree, backed up to small trees about 6' away (e.g. 2 36" slings connected with one locking biner, two biners to attach the rope, and maybe 10' of webbing backup to the biners). 4 ropes will cover all routes, but not every route will be climbable at the same time. If you are guiding a lot of people, bring maybe 7 ropes and extra slings to connect anchors as backup, so each rope can hang off one anchor.

Accessing the Anchors: We found three ways up. None of them are perfect:

    1. The Unnamed 5.6 access solo left of the routes (described below). This is the most likely to get you freaked out, especially when weighted down with gear and rope. If you use this, tote a rope to haul up your gear and other ropes after topping out.

    2. A trail to the right of the wall, running up and right, with a left short-cut up a short cliff, stemming a large tree. We didn't trust the holds. It's probably 5.7 and might be the safest path when carrying gear and ropes.

    3. As with #2, but continue away from the routes on the trail, until it reaches a short bit of 5.6 climbing, topping out on a balancy slab of dirt, with no trees to grab. (A fixed line would be nice and out-of-sight from the ground.) From there, hike left 40 paces to a down-trail that comes out at the anchors for Touch of Class. We don't like topping out on tilted dirt, but this is our favorite of the 3 access methods.

Anchoring is described right-to-left (when facing toward the anchors, away from the cliff):

    1. The approach trail drops down at chain anchors set 3' back from the cliff, serving Worm, Touch of Class and Steep Bulge.

    2. Next, find the big Cedar Tree 9' from the previous anchors, serving April Fool and Early Bird. Set your main anchor on this tree, backing it up on small trees 6' uphill.

    3. Hike down a small drop and look right for three hangers bolted to a little cliff above the topout area you're hiking, set 5' apart from each other. Set draws on the left and right hangers. Run a rope through both. Run the rightside rope (when facing the anchors) right of the quadruple-trunk

Spanish oak; it serves Flash Crack. Run the leftside rope 5' from it to serve Stand Off, or run it left a few feet, over a boulder, to serve Thin Crack. (Or, from the ground, you can just flick the rope left to serve Thin Crack.) If you have a big group, instead set two ropes on these three anchors. Set each rope on the outside hangers, then back up those hangers from the middle hanger. One could instead set two routes on the three anchors in a "W" pattern, but we did not like the rope positions as well.

4. Leftmost anchors: Angle the left end of the rope leftward and position it to stay over the arête, held by a curve at the cliff's edge. The left end serves routes Arête, Bulge Lite and Bulge. The right end serves Bulge Right and Bulge Middle.

5. To keep the ropes separated as described in #3 and #4, rap down from the Touch of Class or April Fool (tree) anchors.

All the main routes and Early Bird were put up trad or solo. Previously unpublished variations "Arête," "Bulge Lite," "Bulge Middle," and "Bulge Right" came about by climbing this area without much route information.

> I miss the Greenbelt climbing, never appreciated how accessible it was until I left it. Mountains are great, but each one is a project and a (welcome) disruption of schedules.
>
> *Ralph Showalter*

access solo: (5.6). 12' left of the wall's arête is a left facing short crack to a ledge. Walk up and right to a wide crack near the clifftop. One could trust the rock and stay out of the crack for elegance, or play it safe, body jamming and thrashing slowly upward like we did. *Beta*: the topout involves finding the feet while jammed, then a decent lefthand sloper ball, righthand pinch, and high righthand sloper. If you fall, we're not sure if the ledge will save you.

Arête starting half way up the cliff, right of a big ledge.
Big black shallow cave/bowl at clifftop, over a leaning mini-roof.

1. **Bulge** (5.10b TR)*** John "Goomba" Sanders[50], Lauren Clayton. Climb to ledges below the leaning mini-roof. Pull the roof to the cave/bowl, then pull the topout right of the arête, roughly centered over the cave/bowl. *Beta[51]*. If the toprope slips to the right, you can easily flick it to land in the curve just left of the cave/bowl.

 a. variation: **Arête** (5.7 TR)***. Start Bulge. Go up and left under the roof and onto the big party ledge left of the arête. Finish up the arête.

 b. variation: **Bulge Lite** (5.10a TR)***. Start Bulge. Pull the leaning mini-roof to reach the cave/bowl, but skip the hard topout by traversing left out of the cave, onto the arête, and up from there. We like this for gifted beginners, as it gets them on a crux crimp and cool surfaces (the bowl and the high arête). *Beta[52]*

2. **Bulge Right** (5.10d TR)*. Climb the thinner crack left of Thin Crack, the little arête over the right end of the mid-cliff roof, the black cave/ bowl, and top out over the right edge of the black cave/bowl.
 c. variation: **Bulge Middle** (5.10c TR)*. Top out smack-dab over the middle of the bulge that overhangs the cave/bowl.

3. **Thin Crack** (5.6 TR)*** John Sanders, Lauren Clayton. Thin Crack is confusing to find, because its crack isn't as thin as that of Bulge Right. Start on the big right-facing rounded flake under a thin crack that leads briefly to a triangular block/shield. Gain the ledge, then exit up the dihedral. The toprope for this climb will generally slide its way far to the right. Just flick it left to catch in the middle of the topout-dihedral before climbing.

---

[50] John is one of the first people to have done topo-photos for Enchanted Rock. He still has photo proofs with pasted-on route markers. Back then, guidebooks were difficult to do, without word processing and digital photography. Guidebook projects would get passed on to successions of people over the years. John collaborated with another guy on a book, until they had a falling-out. The other guy would not return John's materials, so John took matters into his own hands and seized them. (In contrast, mild-mannered Warren Harding just rolled over when his El Cap partner, Dean Caldwell, refused to send Harding his share of the valuable, historic ascent photo slides.) Don't mess with Goomba!
[51] To top out, find the lefthand edge sidepull amongst the sea of bad choices, and lean right on it to begin a nice beached whale struggle.
[52] To pull past the roof and up into the black cave/bowl, find a high left-hand crimp just over the left part of the roof.

Barton Creek

At mid-cliff, over the mini-roof, two crack lines facing each other come together.

4. **Stand Off** (5.8 TR)* Ralph Showalter. Start up the slab 6' right of Thin Crack's start. Over the mini-roof are cracks forming the outline of a baby carriage or a cartoon ghost. Climb the right end of the "ghost's arm" crack up and left to the column right of the dihedral. Go up the column. ▟ ⌐•⌐⌐ ⁑•⌐ ⥇◐⇌ ❤︎ ≋

5. **Flash Crack** (5.7 TR)*** John Sanders, Lauren Clayton. Climbs a slab for 10', reaching a thin left-facing crack and continuing straight up. Very technical for the grade. ▟•⌐⌐•⌐•⌐ ⌐•⌐ ⥈❤︎⊃ 🗑

Wide gap between routes, due to a small tree growing half way up and vegetation near the top. The tree and vegetation have displaced a former 5.10. Boo!

6. **April Fool** (5.10a TR)*** Ralph Showalter. Start at the lower left end of a diagonal little crack left of Touch of Class. Climb assorted features on a steep dome to a higher crack that angles right to the cave. Climb into the cave. (The original 5.9 trad route stopped there, with a walking exit left.) Top out over the left edge of the cave. Spectacular crux. Beta[53]. ▟•⌐ ▟⌐•⥈❤︎⌇ 🧍⊖ 🗑⊿🗑

d. variation: **Early Birds** (5.9+ TR)*** David Phillips. Start April Fool and climb into the cave. Exit right of the cave roof. '91-92 ▟•⌐ ▟⌐•⥈❤︎⌇ 🧍⊖ 🗑

7. **Worm** (5.9+ TR)*. Start up the little hand-dihedral just left of Touch of Class. Rock onto the ledge left of the dihedral top. Climb to the wide diagonal undercling flake not used by any of these other routes, stay out of the cave and exit right of the cave. 🏃•⌐▟•⌐ ⌐⥈❤︎⌇ 🛶

8. **Touch of Class** (5.7 TR)*** John Sanders. Climb the wide right-facing crack on the right end of the wall. The crack goes all the way up to a diagonal roof. Pull over the roof and finish left of the big point. Extremely technical for a 5.7. ⌐•⌐•⌐ ⌐⊿ $E=mc^3$ ❤︎ ≋ 🗑⊿🗑

9. **Steep Bulge** (5.10a TR)*. Start 7' right of Touch of Class. Pull the mini-roof and bulge, using holds spread widely atop the bulge. Go to the ledge, pull up and left over the high mini-roof, and finish on Touch of Class. The low moves are a great place to teach double kneebars, not for resting here but for scoping holds. 🏃•⌐•⌐⌐•⌐ ⥈❤︎⌇ 🦟⊖⌇⟩ 🗑

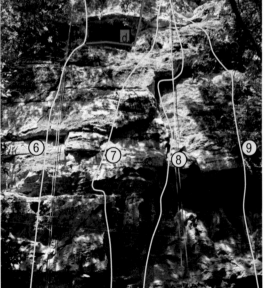

bouldering: **Guide's Wall Traverse** (V2+). Traverse the ledge either direction. Bad falls on the slab. ？卒

---

[53] 5.11 technique and flexibility solve a 5.10a power move. To pull over the mini-roof, set left-hand big sidepull and right hand half-moon crimp. Right foot up and right; rock onto it. Left hand mantle the little sloper shelf, 12" below and left of the right foot. Stretch to match left foot on that sloper shelf and stand up.

Greenbelt (east bank): **Choss Cave**

Sun conditions: all day shade
Approach: 5-8 minutes via the "Gus Fruh Access" described at the start of
this chapter.
GPS: N30˚15.088' W097˚47.774' (30.2495 -97.796933)

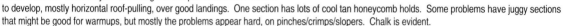

Take the Gus Fruh Access and its switch-back trail to the creek-side trail.
Turn right and hike 390 paces. The first half of the trail is flat, then it gets
somewhat rough, and (as of this writing) you stoop under branches several
times. Pass a sucker mini-roof along the way. You'll reach a well trod spur
trail cutting a short hike to the cave. In winter time, without foliage, you can
see the cave easily from the main trail.

The cave is 40' wide and 10-12' tall, with problems starting as deep as 18'
inside the cave. It has maybe 15-20 long low-ball problems and variations
to develop, mostly horizontal roof-pulling, over good landings. One section has lots of cool tan honeycomb holds. Some problems have juggy sections
that might be good for warmups, but mostly the problems appear hard, on pinches/crimps/slopers. Chalk is evident.

Despite wild holds and cush landings, this cave somehow escaped bouldering development until 2011, when some work started. The good news is
it's a pretty cave with cool holds, long steep problems, and, dependent on drips, it might be good climbing during rain. The bad news is there is some
graffiti, and few holds can be trusted 100%. One old timer suggested that he himself and other Chris Barton types should stay away and let the small
people have the fun, while the holds last. We think it might be more solid than that implies. Long term it looks like it will clean up to produce good
problems, and it looks worth the effort.

As problems go up, please contact us at AustinClimbing@pobox.com. We'll publish them in the next edition and on-line (at www.AustinClimbingBook.
com). Travis Johnson reports the only known problems so far are:
>   Colbsters Revenge (V7)***.

>   Warmups 1, 2, and 3 on the far right side.

Greenbelt (east bank): **Urban Assault**

Approach: 11 minutes via the Gus Fruh Access described at the start of this chapter.
GPS: No point was shot, but off a map, it will be near N30°14.915' W097°47.819' (30.246686 -97.790079)
Sun conditions: Scorching. Climb in 50 degree weather — even then, you'll be peeling layers off on the way up Urban Assault (route).

Jeff Jackson says, "The Urban Assault routes require a little love (i.e. brushing) but they offer the best long-route experience in A-town." The cliff is about 90 feet tall and by far the prettiest one in this book. With choss issues, dust, and extreme sun exposure, it's rarely climbed, but people do like the multi pitch route Urban Assault, and some locals have annual cold weather outings on it. We've not climbed here yet. Tommy Blackwell provided the following beta. Starfish is in good shape, and he always climbs three routes: Buzzard's Breath, Cell Block, and Urban Assault, all of which got hardware replacements in 2005. Medicine Man and Mah Jong got new first bolts, while the rest of the bolts looked good, as they stay out of the weather.

Rock quality appears solid on the bolt placements but sketchy for trusting handholds. Sean O'Grady had a particularly "seismic" outing here on Manchild, sending down huge blocks, and so his book Austin Rock may have overstated the loose rock situation regarding the other routes.

Urban Assault was the setting of the ultimate Texas good-old-fashion ethical debate. Jeff Jackson, Paul Clark and others were into free climbing at the upper end of the scale of the day (13b-c), back when there were no climbing gyms. They sought tall, difficult climbs at Bull Creek and Urban Assault, manufactured holds on blank sections to make them go, and viewed them as climbing gyms. Other locals were putting up the occasional Aid route (pounding in pins and bolts to create ladders), while focusing on trad and mixed routes. The two camps were not on the same page, and a clash of styles played out in Austin, and in many parts of the world.

Locally, it played out very quickly. Paul was a Mesquite, Texas policeman with tattoos, gargantuan lats, and overall musculature as cut as diamond. He and Jeff headed to Urban Assault one day and found a group of guys talking about chopping the bolts due to the manufacturing. Paul said, "If you chop my bolts, I'll kick your ass." Thus ended, bloodlessly, the good-old-fashioned ethical debate.

At the time, Jeff didn't think manufactured holds were that big a deal, because they are so easy to fill in. And chipping seemed not so stylistically different than pounding in pins. Today, Jeff supports the filling in of any of his manufactured holds, if the community wants that.

1. **Buzzard's Breath** (5.9)* 4 bolts, No Anchors. Climbs a discontinuous crack. After Bolt 4, keep climbing up and out of the face to the tree. The move is worth it. Top out and walk off, or down-lead it. Bad rock prohibited setting anchors.

2. **Ladrone** (5.11)* 4 pitons, Paul Clark.

3. **Masada** (5.12)* 7 bolts, Paul Clark.

4. **Femme** (5.13)* 7 bolts, Kevin Gallagher.

5. **Starfish** (5.12c)*** 9 bolts, Jeff Jackson. Mild rope drag. Fantastic moves. *Beta.*[54]

6. **Cell Block** (5.11b/c)*** 4 bolts, Russell Rand. Shares Bolt 1 with Mah Jong, then branches left. Cuts back right to its anchors. Height dependent grade.

   2nd pitch: **Medicine Man** (5.12)* 5 bolts, Jeff Jackson. At Cell Block's anchors, continue up and then right (traversing under the roof, over Mah Jong's anchors) to finish on Plate Techtonics.

---

[54] Jeff wrote, "The lip encounter where you lead with your foot is so unique and fun."

7. **Mah Jong** (5.12)* 4 bolts, Karen Rand. Uses Bolt 1 of Cell Block and branches right.

[Erased route: Plate Techtonics (5.13b-d)*** formerly 7 bolts, Jeff Jackson. As of 2005, hangers were missing. Jeff recommends it be restored, as the best, most historical route at the wall. He rated it 13b; Hank thought c or d. Rick Watson says the face below the roof is solid rock, disgustingly hard, and the roof moves are fantastic. He says "Folks are really missing out" with the hangers missing.]

8. **Spelioantics** (5.12d)* 5 bolts.

9. **Urban Assault** (5.10b A0)*** pitch1: 3 bolts. pitch 2: 3 bolts. pitch 3: 5 bolts, 1 piton. Anchors at each pitch. FA James Crump. 60-meter rope minimum. Bring long slings for pitch 3 to facilitate the aid climbing. Pitch 1: Start on the dihedral, climb to the chains in the cave (belay station). The cave is 75' long, 2.5' tall, and goes nowhere. Pitch 2 (5.10): Climber goes out of sight of belayer around a corner, on a clean-fall runout. Pitch 3 (5.10 A0). The pitch probably has never gone free, due to hard moves on dirty rock over the first two bolts. Climb through the remaining 3 bolts to the anchors. Sun exposure makes it a bad idea to climb this when it's warm out. The very top has an extra bolt to bring up the 2nd climber, and just for fun, there's a PVC container with an ascent log. Get a good swing going on the rappel down to stay out of the water, or else cool off aggressively like Tommy does.

[Erased route: Deep Flow (5.13a) formerly 2 bolts, Jeff Jackson. Climb through the low roof. As of 2005, the hangers were gone.]

10. **Mandibles** (5.12b/c)* 3 bolts, Rick Watson. High first bolt. Climb to the right of the triangular roof, then left above it to follow a thin crack to the anchors. Rick imagines Mandibles has never been repeated.

11. **Lydesaid** (A1)* Tom Lyde[55].

12. **Manchild** (5.12 R)* 7 bolts, No Anchors, Jeff Jackson. 30-40' right of Mandibles. Huge rock falls off this route have occurred.

Boulder 200 yards to the right

13. **Unknown Route** (5.10?), 4 bolts. Bandit-bolted in this no-more-bolt zone. A low (5th) bolt is missing its hanger.

Luke Bowman

Tommy Blackwell, "Urban Assault"

[55] Tom started Flatland Mountain Works, a company that eventually would make all of Black Diamond's harnesses. Starting off sleeping in his company storage space in South Austin, he built the business and set new standards in the industry. He and Robert Price put up the FA of the remote 12-pitch mixed route, Book of Saturday (5.11a) , at Notch Peak. He also made FA's in the Santa Elena Canyon of Big Bend. He died rapping off the ends of his ropes.

Greenbelt (west bank): **New Wall**

Sun conditions: Good tree shade throughout the day, but heavy sun roughly 10 am to 3pm. Cliff shade about 3 hours before sunset.
Approach: 13 minutes via the Spy Glass Access or by Gus Fruh Access, described at the start of this chapter. Gus Fruh has a milder, prettier hike.
GPS @ Meet the Flintstones: N30°15.247' W097°47.686' (30.254109 -97.794762)

A tall, popular wall full of classics. The wall was always ugly and scary looking with its many fractured plates, but they held up well until Feb. 2012, when the huge crack/flake system comprising Schoolboys Indirect shifted wider and rotated left, threatening the future of routes 1-4. Tremors occurred about the same time, 100 miles away. A week later, the crack had widened even more. The City closed the routes and began looking for a contractor to topple the formation. Meanwhile, we were getting this book ready to print. Check www.AustinClimbingBook.com for updates that will include whatever reworked routes might replace the original left four routes. What's documented below is for your pleasant memories.

The seven most-trafficked routes are (were?) so good that they spawned 13 variations — then one of those spawned its *own* variation. The variations provide some really long routes, or skip some cruxes, or traverse horizontal features that would otherwise go unused. The big traverses are best done when you find the wall empty. The developers of New Wall devised most of the variations during a five month span when they didn't have anything else to climb. These variations could become more important if the left four routes end up sucking.

The New Wall bolt schemes are a little complicated; start by locating Hysteria, which has the lowest anchors and likely survived the above events.

Prior to Mother Nature's wrath, the wall was crowded on Tuesday and Thursday afternoons but kept well organized, with folks routinely jumping on each other's topropes. The spiritual and cyber leader of New Wall is Pete Bishop, who started a Yahoo group called Austin_Climbers to call out the troops here every Tues/Thurs, and to Reimers on weekends. (Search Austin_Climbers under www.yahoo.groups.com.) He, Ralph Showalter, and Matt Hall founded "Tuesday/Thursday."[56] Depending on how the routes evolve, this group will either return to New Wall or shift its time to Great Wall or Gus Fruh.

Random 5.8 (5.8)* 3 bolts. This line is usually wet or dirty. Anchors are out of view. It is located well left of New Wall's routes, slightly upstream from the turnstile. Though not on New Wall, it needs a home. CTM will talk to Parks about adding some easy routes near it, to make it a useful destination.

bouldering: In the cave left of the routes (described at rockclimbing.com under New Wall Bouldering), and further south (described in Texas Limestone Bouldering).

1. **Vertical Ditch** (5.7 TR/ 5.7 trad X)*** anchors, Ralph Showalter. Climb the crack that Flintstones starts. The anchors are high and left of Flintstones' anchors. Trad placements (horn-slinging and cams) are thin and unreliable. An alternative way to set the TR is to lead Flintstones, walk/climb/stretch left maybe 15', draping the rope on a horn, and avoiding kicking down loose rocks. It's a great route for first-time climbers, with huge exposure.

    a. toprope: **Superman** (5.7 TR)*** Clayton Norman. Set TR on Vertical Ditch. Up high, jump from the huge ledge to the roof. Stick it for 5.7. Pull the roof from there at 5.10.

2. **Meet the Flintstones** (5.9)*** 5 bolts, David Cardosa[57], Greg Brooks, Scott Harris. Tall and polished. Bolt 1 was added long after the FA; the route used to be "R" and injury-prone. Bolt 1 is on the arête to the right of the wall's left slabby section. The arête is under a big table-roof way up.

    b. variation: **Gladly, The Cross I'd Bare** (5.11c)*. 60-meter rope minimum. A long traverse using Flintstones bolts 1-3, Mr. Slate's Bolt 4, then lay the rope on the big horn, then Yabba Dabba Do's Bolt 3, Schoolboy Fantasy's Bolt 3, Cloud Nine's Bolt 4, Hysteria's Bolt 4, and Mandingo's Bolts 3, 4, and anchors.

3. **Mr. Slate / Mrs. Slate** (5.11a)*** 6 bolts, Greg Brooks, David Cardosa, Scott Harris. Bolt 1 is on a small arête that sharpens to a point. The start climbs to the dihedral left of Bolt 1. The original route (Mr. Slate) finished on Meet the Flintstones' last two bolts and anchors. To help alleviate traffic, two upper bolts and anchors were installed right of that (Mrs. Slate).

    c. bolted variation: **Yabba Dabba Do** (5.11b)*** 4 bolts, Greg Brooks, David Cardosa, Scott Harris. Starts just right of Mr. Slate's first bolt, to a left-facing rounded flake, clips Mr. Slate's Bolt 1, then cuts up and right over the roof and a bowl/dihedral on two of its own bolts,

---

[56] Prior to that, Pete did ten years (!) of Tuesday/Thursdays at Planet of the Apes Wall, Malibu State Park.

[57] David is one of a handful of prolific bolters around Austin. What's unique was his pace. In only 18 months time, he learned to climb, developed a lot of routes, and brought his game up to 8a (5.13b). At 14 months he was onsighting 5.12b/c regularly. Almost every day at the crag, he worked on new routes. Then he moved to Dallas for ten years and brokered stocks, or did whatever the hell climbers do in Dallas. Now he's back and bolting again.

Cavason Sutton, "Mrs Slate"

Barton Creek

without using the crack on the right (used on Schoolboy Fantasies) until the highest possible hold on that crack. (Skip that hold for a higher grade.) Run it out to the last bolt of Schoolboy Fantasies and finish on its anchors. However, with the new Mrs. Slate bolt and anchors, many cut up and left to finish on them.

d. <u>variation:</u> **Schoolboys Indirect** (5.9+)*** 5 bolts, Greg Brooks, Robert Middleton. A long, hugely popular variation, with summer-time air conditioning floating out of the big flake system. Start on Mr. Slate and clip its Bolt 1, then traverse right under the roof, clipping Yabba Dabba Do's bolt (with a 24" runner) and Schoolboy Fantasies' Bolt 2 (also with a 24" runner). Finish straight up the crack system and Schoolboy Fantasies' last bolt and anchors. If you do not have runners, long draws will catch some acceptable rope drag.

e. <u>variation on a variation:</u> **Chain Gang** (5.9+)*** 5 bolts. Minimum 50m rope. Climb Schoolboys Indirect for four bolts (reaching Schoolboy Fantasies' third bolt). At the flake, go up and right to Hysteria's anchors, then continue up and right to Mandingo's last bolt and anchors.

4. **Schoolboy Fantasies** (5.11a)*** 4 bolts, Greg Brooks, Robert Middleton. Bolt 1 is 6' right of Mr. Slate's Bolt 1. Bolts 2-3 are right of an ugly right-facing flake system. Humidity's effects on the crux hold can bring this route up to 5.12a. '88.

f. <u>toprope:</u> **James' Cheap FA** (5.12c TR)***, James Fierbaugh. Start and climb Cloud Nine through its crux. At its Bolt 3, traverse left on the obvious ledge till you're right of the flake. The flake is off route. Dyno from there to the next ledge.

g. <u>toprope:</u> **Pebble's First Day at School** (5.11c-d TR)* Nathaniel Biggs. A super long training circuit. Set toprope on Schoolboy Fantasies. Climb up Meet the Flintstones to the shelf. Downclimb Mr. Slate to right under the roof. Traverse right to Yabba Dabba Do. Go up to the shelf. Downclimb Schoolboy Fantasies to the ground.

Next two routes share Bolt 1, Bolt 2, and anchors.

5. **Cloud Nine** (5.11d)*** 4 bolts, Adam Hurst[58]. Shares bolts 1-2 and anchors with Hysteria. Goes up and left, solving the acute dihedral, then right to the anchors.

6. **Hysteria** (5.11b)*** 4 bolts, Adam Hurst, Scott Harris, David Cardosa, Hank Caylor. The shortest route on the wall, but it's full of moves and the "must do" 5.11 here. Bolt 1 is at 7 o'clock from a left-facing chalked-up ear. Bolts 2 and 3 are up and right. Bolt 2 is hated by all of Austin.[59] '88

---

[58] Adam was killed by lightning, rappelling off The Naked Edge, Eldorado. He and partner Randal Jett could not see the nearby storm. Sadly, lightning can travel horizontally 4 miles. It hit Adam directly, travelled the rope to Randal, went through his chest, and fused wires and carabiners together. Randal plunged off the end of his rope (having skipped tying a safety knot) and fell onto a knife's edge formation. The formation pinched his rap device, holding him while he was stunned. Randal survived. David Cardosa said, "Adam was one of the kindest and most warm hearted souls to ever grace the walls of the Greenbelt." In the mid 90's, in his memory, Adam was added to the developers list of Cloud Nine and Hysteria.

[59] Even a member of the FA list hates the high placement. Clipping a draw on this bolt is as stiff as an ugly Viagra salesman at a cheap Nevada brothel. Tommy Blackwell even built a long-reach draw using PVC over a runner for clipping this bolt, locally known as the Tommy Draw. Despite all this, Hysteria is classic. If you don't prehang the draw, Hysteria is bouldery and pressing towards 11c. With a prehang draw, it's a great endurance route.

Ryan Hartford, "Gunning for the Buddha"

h. variation: **Lots of People** (5.11a)* 5 bolts, Rick Watson, Tony Faucett. Climb Hysteria's Bolts 1-3, then climb the short vertical seam right of Bolt 3, then up and right to Mandigo's Bolt 3, finishing on Mandingo.

7. **Mandingo** (5.11d)*** 4 bolts, Scott Harris, David Cardosa, Hank Caylor. Starts up an easy (class 2) slab. Bolt 1 is on a bulge above and slightly left of the slab's high point. Bolt 2 is up and left of Bolt 1; the other bolts slant slightly right. Runout to Bolt 3. Exciting, reasonable start without the stick-clip. '88

i. toprope: **Eraser Head** (5.12a-b TR)*** Scott Harris, David Cardosa, Hank Caylor. Set TR on Mandingo. Start up the center of the wide block between Hysteria Bolt 2 and Mandingo Bolt 1, on a broken axe head. Move slightly right and finish Mandingo. David corrected the definition published in Austin Rock, which took the line to Hysteria instead of Mandingo. Not knowing the correct definition, locals worked up **Dingohead** as a 3 bolt lead route (stick-clipping Mandingo's Bolt 2). Paul McFarlin adds that both start by pulling right-handed on the broken axe head, or left-handed for 5.11. (From Hysteria, move right 5-6 feet to midway under the overhang. Roughly in the middle of that roof is the axe head, fitting 4 fingers and a thumb-lock.) Meanwhile, we risk much umbrage by writing six lines about this toprope.

k. variation: **Girly Man** (5.11b R)*** **4 bolts**. Usually toproped, since the traverse risks a grounder. Start Mandingo. Under its Bolt 2, traverse left to Hysteria, go up under the center of the roof, traverse right under the roof, then up and right to finish on Mandingo's Bolts 3, 4, and anchors. Safe, intimidating swing potential. Pete says it's a nice long finger pump, and we liked it a lot.

l. variation: **Rest and Relaxation** (5.11b)*. Lead Mandingo Bolts 1 and 2, traverse left to Hysteria Bolt 3, and finish on Cloud Nine bolts 3, 4, and anchors. Expect rope drag.

m. toprope: **Hut Rabbit**[60] (5.11c TR)***. Set TR on Mandingo's anchors. Climb Girly Man through the right traverse under roof, then traverse right along the horizontal ledge/seam all the way to Buddha's Bolt 3, topout Buddha, and jog up and left to Mandingo's anchors.[61]

n. toprope: **Cross-Eyed Dog** (5.11d TR)*. Set TR on Mandingo's anchors. Start Mandingo. Before its Bolt 3, cross right to Buddha's Bolt 3, finish Buddha, then climb up and left to Mandingo's anchors.

8. **Gunning for the Buddha** (5.12a)*** **4 bolts & 1 piton**, Jeff Jackson, Greg Brooks. Bolt 1 is in a little "V" centered on the bottom of the bulge. Shares anchors with Walk the Dog and Wowie Zowie. Some folks skip the piton. Rub the Buddha's belly for good luck. '88

o. bolted variation:[62] **Walk the Dog** (5.11b)*** **4 bolts & 1 piton**, Hank Caylor, David Cardosa, Scott Harris. Climb Wowie Zowie's bolts 1-2. Traverse left to Buddha's Bolt 3 over the shelf and finish on Buddha. '88

p. variation: **Rabbit Hut** (5.11c)* **8 bolts**, Rick Watson. 60-meter rope minimum. Climb Walk the Dog bolts 1-3, keep traversing left on Mandingo Bolt 3, continue traversing under Hysteria's roof and clip Hysteria Bolt 4, Schoolboy Fantasies Bolt 4, and Flintstones' Bolt 5 and anchors. However, this variation was done before Slate got its new upper bolts, so you'll find one more potential pro.

9. **Wowie Zowie** (5.10d)*** **4 bolts + 1 piton**, Hank Caylor[63]. Starts on an easy slab to a ledge, adorned with a permanently installed cheat stone. Shares anchors with Gunning for the Buddha. Pull the small dihedral right of the cave to Bolt 1. Bolt 2 is up and left. The piton is the 5th protection, off right. People are often tempted to skip clipping Bolt 1, and then several have taken 15' falls before clipping Bolt 2. It is extra fun and (with proper beta) safe without the stick clip.

Huge leaning live oak and rock steps lead up and right to The Terrace.

So was Iranian Arms Deal the first Rapp and Tap on the Green Belt? I think it may have been. If not, it sure was one of the first. I know when Charlie Don't Surf on the Ging wall went in, Scooter and I rapp & tapped that… It's kind of funny now but I recall we were always looking over our shoulder for the ethics police.   *David Cardosa*

---

[60] aka. ManHysteriaDingoDogForTheBuddha.

[61] This path is very different from that published in Austin Rock; the correction is courtesy Pete Bishop.

[62] Walk the Dog was bolted first and is technically the primary line. Buddha and Wowie Zowie are *its* variations. Only for consistency/clarity do we format Walk the Dog as a bolted variation linking two main routes.

[63] Hank is a legend among BASE jumpers. About that sport, Hank once said, "I sense that it must take an incredible amount of Faith in oneself and the Universe, if you will, to make a leap into dead air. That one must reconcile themselves that they will either fly, i.e., float via canopy to safety, or enter a world beyond this one and that's okay." He took to it quickly, completing 100 jumps in his first year. But the first jump was interesting. Wayne Crill and he used a 1000' antennae tower in Austin for their self-taught first jumps. Wayne broke his foot. They returned a week later, and Hank broke his also.

Greenbelt (west bank): **The Terrace**

Sun conditions: Heavy sun roughly 11am to 3pm
Approach: 13 minutes via the Spy Glass Access described at the start of this chapter.
GPS: ????

This wall is just right of New Wall (but up on a raised landing) and just left of Great Wall.

10. **Crystal New Persuasion** (5.10c)*** 4 bolts, Calvin Hiser, Hank Caylor. Zigzag boltline. Mild runout. At Bolt 4, pull straight up the bulge for 10c. '88

> variation: **CNP Left**: (5.10a)*. Climb just left of the upper bulge for an easier finish. We're not sure about this being any easier than 10c, but we're trusting Joel.

> variation: **CNP Lefter**: (5.9)*. Climb even further left of the upper bulge for an easier finish.

Two low bolts (same level, 4' apart) offer two leadable starts to the next route. The left is now considered Cactus Patch's 1st bolt; the right is for leading Cactus Patch Direct.

11. **Cactus Patch** (5.10a)*** 5 bolts, Tony Faucett. Start under the left of the two low bolts; climb up and right to Bolt 2. Bolt 5 is out of sight over the upper ledge. Mild runout. The topropes and variations described below are listed in the order of their starts (left-to-right).

> toprope: **Crystal Patch** (5.8/5.9 TR, PG)*** Start Crystal New Persuasion, traverse right to Bolt 1 of Cactus Patch (mildly risking a swing fall contacting the ground), and continue up Cactus Patch. A nice sustained height-dependent grade. Set Cactus Patch and then get your newbs on this toprope.

> bolted variation: **Cactus Patch Direct** (5.11b)* 5 bolts. Start under the right of the two low bolts.

> toprope: **Evan's Gate** (5.11a TR)* Evan Jackson. Set TR on Cactus Patch and lower, clipping the piton above and right of Bolt 2 for a directional. Stand on the right of two big boulders, slightly right of the line under the piton. Use a right foot triangular credit-card-width hold and a right sidepull pinch or gaston.

> Oh god Dave, that route is such a heap of shit. Please don't say "It's one sweet line" ever again.... come to colorado and stay on my couch for a week man! We can recalibrate.
>
> *Hank Caylor*

Greenbelt (west bank): **Great Wall**

Sun conditions: All day shade on the lower 2/3rds of the left-side routes; heavy sun on topouts roughly 11am to 3pm
Approach: 12 minutes via the Spy Glass Access described at the start of this chapter.
GPS @ Through the Looking Glass: N30°15.249' W097°47.659' (30.25415 -97.794317)

This wall is just right of The Terrace and just left of Geritol Wall. See "Spyglass Access" for directions. It has five classic routes ranging 5.11a to 5.12a, three harder classic climbs, and a lot of variations. Heaven's Gate and Peewee's Big Adventure traverse cool features right, and five other routes/ variations share portions of them, branching up or left at different spots. These two complex route sets flank Disneyland and Iron Man, which are straight-up climbs.

To sort out this complexity, grok the following: 1. Identify the horizontal ledge spanning the entire wall. All the routes start and pull immediately to this ledge. Also identify the big dihedral under a big triangular roof. These two features are referenced in the route descriptions. 2. Heaven's Gate and Hug Thy Mother cross each other. Heaven's Gate starts left of Hug Thy Mother, but finishes right of it. 3. Find the low bolts of Heaven's Gate, which traverse up and right. Then find the low bolts of Disneyland, then Bolt 1 of Iron Man (shared with Peewee's Big Adventure). Through the Looking Glass is easy to identify from its description, and so the routes right of it are easy to identify.

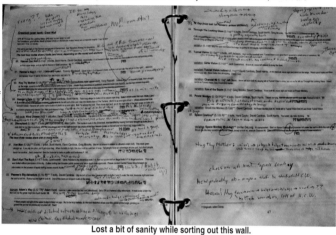

Lost a bit of sanity while sorting out this wall.

The next four routes share 3 bolts (and more, depending on the route) and anchors:

1. **Heaven's Gate** (5.11b)*** 7 (optionally 8) bolts, David Cardosa, Scott Harris. Take long slings for Bolts 3-4 to reduce drag. Bolt 1 is 4' right of the left end of the roof, near the slabby face of The Terrace. Bolt 2 is up and right. Bolt 3 is straight up. Traverse right under the roof on Bolts

57

4-5. An optional bolt (part of Hug Thy Mother) is over the roof up and right, but it makes the route harder. Ignore it and stay low on a runout right-traverse to this route's real Bolt 6 up on the bulge. Bolt 7 and anchors are straight up.

a. bolted variation: **Heaven's Hug** (5.11b R)* 3 bolts and 1 piton, Tommy Blackwell. Climb bolts 1-3 of Heaven's Gate, pull the roof (not well protected) and run it out to the old piton up and right (Bolt 8 of Heaven Can Wait). Finish on Heaven's Gate anchors.

b. bolted variation: **Heaven Can Wait** (5.11a)* 8 bolts, Scott Harris, David Cardosa. Climb Bolts 1-5 of Heaven's Gate and Bolt 5 of Hug Thy Mother to pull the upper roof. Cut left to two independent bolts (the last being an old piton), then up and right to Heaven's Gate anchors. '88

2. **Hug Thy Mother** (5.12c PG)*** 6 bolts (3 of them permadraws), Tony Faucett. Bolt 1 is on a block on the left face of the big dihedral described below. Bolts 2-3 angle left with permadraws. (Bolt 3 is in the mini-roof.) Pull up and right to Heaven's Gate Bolt 5 (a permadraw), then up and slightly right to this route's independent bolt over the upper roof (the one described as an optional bolt for Heaven's Gate). Pull the left-leaning arête/bulge straight up and runout to our last bolt, then up and slightly right to Heaven's Gate anchors.

The center of a big dihedral under a triangular roof. The dihedral sits just above the long low ledge spanning the wall.

aid route: **Wind Chimes** (A2) 1 old piton, David Cardosa, Greg Brooks. This aid route climbs the center of the big dihedral and pulls the roof. A piton with a sling for aiding is in one of the cracks on this route. The FAs advise against doing this route.

3. **Disneyland** (5.13b)*** 5 bolts, Alex Catlin[64]. The hardest route in the Greenbelt. Bolt 1 is on the right side of the pretty little side-by-side dihedral/arête triangles, over the long low ledge. Bolt 2 is hard to spot, straight up. Bolt 3 is in the roof, at the right end of the big dihedral. After Bolt 5, go up and right to Iron Man's anchors.

8' gap between first bolts of Disneyland and Iron Man/Peewee's.
The next three routes share one or more low bolts:

4. **Iron Man** (5.12a)*** 5 bolts, Scott Harris, Dave Cardosa, Greg Brooks. Start 2' left of Bolt 1. Bolt 2 is up and left. When humidity is high, the crux hold is a wet bar of soap. Tall people have an advantage on one part, but short people have it on another…that's awesome! See the footnote for a little path beta.[65] '88

c. bolted variation: **Fook Yu**[66] (5.11c X or TR)*** 5 bolts, Loren Graham, Randal Morris. (The 3 star rating assumes toproping.) Climb Peewee's Big Adventure Bolts 1-3, clip this route's first independent bolt just above the roof (left of Peewee's Bolt 4), then run it out to Bolt 5 — falling is almost a grounder with a good belay. Bolt 5 is on the left face of the big triangular roof. Tommy topropes the route by leading Bolts 1-5 of Peewee's, cutting left to the anchors, pulling the rope and clipping the top two bolts (for directionals) while lowering. The route could use an additional bolt or long Bolt 5 permadraw on the bare section, though that idea blew up in controversy.[67] '00

[64] Alex discovered El Potrero Chico for climbers, in 1988. Jeff Jackson showed up a few days later, and they estimated the walls were about 300' tall. (They're 3000'!) Alex's high point was the FA of Greed (5.14c) in Thailand. He put up hundreds of routes in Mexico and has about 1,000 first ascents. On top of that, he can read Sanskrit.
[65] Most people cut right of the upper bulge to finish on jugs. But to be truly badass, do the hard beached whale over the center of the bulge, grinding on gravel bits you've not previously brushed off. Yeah!
[66] The name is a play on the Austin Powers movie "Goldmember" and a plea at that time to locals to chill out over the route's controversy and back off. Austin Rock published the name as "Don't Hurt the Rock," on a false rumor that a hiker said that to the bolter.
[67] One early weekday morning in 2000, the youngsters bolted this line to have something new to climb in this area. No one saw them, the bolts weren't visible from the ground, and, for a while, no one noticed the route. Later, others would claim they bolted it, to the amusement of the youngsters. Years later, someone added a long visible chain to protect the bare section, and all hell broke loose. It was thought the route was recent, bolted without CTM and city approval. Many prior routes had gone up without approval. In the mid-90's CTM got the city to grant a blanket approval of all existing routes and to move forward with an approval process for each new route. Now this one route brought heat on CTM from the city. The bolters weren't aware of the approval requirements back in 2000 and never wanted to cause any problems with the city. They thought about removing the bolts and were surprised others didn't. Since outlaw bolting can threaten public access and future legal route approvals, please contact Central Texas Mountaineers for information on the process for legally bolting routes around Austin.

5. **Peewee's Big Adventure** (5.11c R)*** 7 bolts, David Cardosa. Start on Iron Man and its Bolt 1, traverse right on Bolts 2 and 3 under the roof, traverse right and over the roof to Bolt 4. (There are two choices nearby for this clip; use the right bolt.) Runout up and right to Bolt 5. One of the best and longest routes in the area.

    d. <u>toprope</u>: **Adam's Way** (5.13a-b TR)* Adam Hurst. Set a TR on Peewee's Big Adventure, using long slings to reduce rope drag. Use the low piton under the first roof for directional. A hold broke under the first roof, turning a 5.12 into a V7. '88

33' Gap between starting bolts of Ironman/Peewee's and Through the Looking Glass. In the middle of this gap, 12' up, is a piton under a thin roof crack.

6. **Through The Looking Glass** (5.11a)*** 5 bolts, David Cardosa, Scott Harris, Greg Brooks. Over the start is a small tree stump wedged in the rock. The start is at the upper right edge of a bowl-shaped drop in the landing. The route has two competing paths, equally hard. It also has a sit-start. '88

<u>variation</u>: **Through the Tunnel**
(5.11b)***, Tommy Blackwell. Climb Bolts 1-4, then traverse right to Bolt 4 of Tunnel Vision and finish it. This variation adds an upper crux for 11b, and it's a great way to practice Tunnel Vision's upper crux. The traverse section can be lively.

<u>variation</u>: (5.11b)*. Skip the cave rest below the bulge, by going up and slightly right of the boltline.

<u>toprope</u>: **Unnecessary Dyno** (5.11a TR)*. Once hands are on the triangular ledge below Bolt 3, dyno to the ledge below Bolt 4.

<u>epic variation</u>: **Lefthand Path** (5.11b R)*, Ralph Vega. This route starts on a toprope and finishes on lead. Ralph would like to bolt this for total lead. Until that happens, use the following two-rope belay. Set a rope on Peewee's Bolt 5. Start Through the Looking Glass and clip Bolt 1 to prevent later swing falls, attaching to that rope via a carabiner (not tied in). Under Bolt 1, hand-traverse the shelf left and up to Peewee's Bolt 5, unclipping from the swing-protection rope as you get close. Continue traversing across Fook Yu to Iron Man, clipping bolts on runouts to Disneyland. Finish Disneyland. Making something new on a bunch of old, this route skips cruxes and runs a nice section between Looking Glass and Peewee's.

Nathaniel Biggs,
"Through the Looking Glass"

7. **Tunnel Vision** (5.12a)*** 4 bolts, Jeff Jackson. Start on one move to a baseball hold. Bolt 2 is at 1 o'clock from Bolt 1. Bolt 4 and anchors are at 11 o'clock. It's hard to second the route, as the rope is always in the way. Tunnel Vision is so good that it spawned a small army of variations. It also has a sit-start. '88

variation: **Channel 5 (aka. Five Dynos)** (5.12a)*. Climb Tunnel Vision, using five unnecessary dynos.

variation: **Girlie Vision** (5.11c)*** Jack Lawrence. At Bolt 2, move left instead of doing the dyno.

variation: **Tunnel Vision Indirect** (5.11c)*** David Cardosa, Scott Harris. At the last bolt, move right and stand on the ledge. Reach good holds and then move back left.

variation: **Channel 99** (5.12a)* Jeff Olson. Move left from Bolt 4, staying left of Tunnel Vision's crimp, but not as far left as Through the Looking Glass. Rated the same as Tunnel Vision, but harder.

variation: **Eye of the Storm** (5.11c)*** David Cardosa, Greg Brooks. From Bolt 2, move right on a semi-mild runout to Power Monkey's Bolt 3 and finish on Power Monkey. The traverse section is cool, the last section is interesting, and which way will you go? Classic linkup.

8. **Power Monkey** (5.12d PG)*** 4 bolts, David Cardosa, Scott Harris. Tweak warning. Bolt 2 is at 11 o'clock, on the left face of the small arête. Bolt 3 is at 1 o'clock. Mild runout to Bolt 4. '88

variation: **Shock the Monkey** (5.12d)*** David Cardosa. At Power Monkey Bolt 2, move left to Tunnel Vision Bolt 3 and finish Tunnel Vision.

13' Gap between low bolts of Power Monkey and Space Cowboy.

9. **Space Cowboy**[68] (5.12b R)*** 5 bolts, David Cardosa, Scott Harris. The Bolt 2 clip risks decking. '88

variation: **Space Monkey 99** (5.12d)*** Jordan DeLong. It's complicated. Start on Space Cowboy and traverse left under the roof to climb the rest of Shock the Monkey, except at Bolt 4, execute Channel 99.

> Rock climbers have been recognized by park officials in many natural areas as the most environmentally conscious user group, surpassing both hikers and bikers in minimizing their impact on resources. At Miller Springs in Belton, Texas, opening the cliffs to rock climbing has eliminated the partying and spray painting that once occurred every weekend.
>
> *from Texas Limestone II, by Jeff Jackson*

---

[68] Originally called Zebop.

Greenbelt (west bank): **Geritol Wall**

Sun conditions: Heavy sun roughly 11am to 3pm
Approach: 12 minutes via the Spy Glass Access described at the start of this chapter.
GPS @ <route name>: N30˚15.266' W097˚47.651' (30.254433 -97.794183)

See "Spyglass Access" for directions to get you close. This wall is just right of Great Wall. Great Wall's high concentration of routes is easier to spot than these. Find Great Wall's rightmost routes, then scramble down its raised platform and hike 12 paces right to Cedar Fever. The wall name comes from David having felt "they were *done* already." As in *retired*. David had moved to Dallas and wasn't climbing, when he came back to work these routes with Scott.

1. **Sunshine Boys** (5.11c)*** 5 bolts, Scott Harris, David Cardosa.

2. **Rock and Roll High School** (5.11b)*** 6 bolts, Scott Harris, David Cardosa. Bolt 1 is 3' left of Cedar Fever's Bolt 1. Bolt 4 is up and slightly left. The grade feels harder than 11b or even 11d for a lot of people, but not if the crux's style suits you.

    a. variation: (5.11a PG)***. Climb the fun low section (Bolts 1-3), then avoid the upper crux by cutting up and right to Cedar Fever's Bolt 4. Finish Cedar Fever.

3. **Cedar Fever** (5.10d PG)*** 5 bolts, Scott Harris, David Cardosa. Falls are bad at the clips for Bolts 4 and 5.

Gap of 25 paces along a slightly overgrown trail hugging the cliff. Gunsmoke starts on a 7' high ledge.

4. **Gunsmoke** (5.10b/d)* 4 bolts, Christina Jackson. The start is on a 7' high ledge. Height dependent grade. This route is chawesome. But it also has a lot of bullet-gray rock, and you can easily dodge most of the choss. Scramble up some dirt and choss to a narrow belay ledge edged with Mountain Laurels holding a boulder. Bolt 1 is 20' up on easy climbing. Watch for rock fall; belayer needs a helmet. The crux is lively, on a cool wall shape.

From Cedar Fever, drop down to the main trail and hike 75 paces to Random Walls.

Tommy Blackwell,
"Cedar Fever"

Greenbelt (west bank): **Random Walls**

Sun conditions: Heavy sun roughly 11am to 3pm
Approach: 12 minutes via the Spy Glass Access described at the start of this chapter.
GPS @ Hank's 5.10: N30°15.264' W097°47.613' (30.2544 -97.79355)

The routes are on a tall wall with a big orange shallow bowl in the middle, over a gray-rock base and topped with a short gray band where the two routes' anchors sit. From the trail, you'll see two rock ledges, a gap, and three more rock ledges, forming natural stairs to the routes. This spot is 108 paces from the "hikers only" wood turnstile on the Spy Glass Access, and 75 paces to the right of Geritol Wall.

1. **Save a bolt for me!** (5.10d)*** 5 bolts, Ralph Vega, David Cardosa[69]. Bolt 1 is way up on easy slabbing. Bolts 4 and 5 are 2' apart; Bolt 5 is at 11 o'clock from Bolt 4. Some will be able to pull the crux with a lot fewer moves (and fewer "stars" on the route), but they'll be pulling harder than 10d. '11

2. **Hank's** (5.9)*** 4 bolts, Hank Caylor. Bolt 1 is way up, at the top of the gray base of the wall. Stick-clip unless you dominate 5.6 slab. Bolt 2 is hidden over the ledge. Bolt 3 is on the right side of a small dihedral. The route looks bad from the ground, but it's plenty long up there above the slab. Good warmup alternative to Meet the Flintstones (at New Wall).

solo: **Tiddlywinks** (5.9 solo, X)* Jeff Jackson. It's hidden in the trees, somewhere, supposedly climbing a 25' tall stack of ledges.

Greenbelt (west bank): **The Enclave (bouldering)**

Sun conditions: Shaded
Approach: 10 minutes via the Spy Glass Access described at the start of this chapter.
GPS: N30°15.321' W097°47.548' (30.25535 -97.792467)

Sadly, the Enclave is often a camp for homeless gentlemen with poor sanitary habits. As of winter 2012, it was pretty clean.

Greenbelt: **History**

The Greenbelt is the centerpiece that makes Austin a great urban climbing town. The Greenbelt and Bull Creek were the first limestone climbing areas around Austin. The first technical rock climbing was likely Campbell's Hole (see Appendix C), around 1970, on the slab boulder problems Father Clem used to teach climbing techniques to some Whole Earth employees. Or it was during Sierra Club classes taught by Lehman Holden. Then Keith Guillory hit the steep faces of Campbell's Hole in 1973, and interest grew. Bill Gooch pioneered downtown bulldering and bouldering.

John "Goomba" Sanders and friends first toproped at Rappeller's Wall in 1978. At age 16, he started Hard Rock Climbing School, possibly the first individually owned guide service in Austin. YMCA, Boy Scouts, and the Sierra Club also were guiding. Goomba advertised at Whole Earth and Wilderness Whitewater and had steady business every weekend. Goomba pioneered Sunken Gardens, which became quite the popular training ground. He and Lauren Clayton kicked off Gus Fruh and Guide's Wall.

Michael Bradley 📷   Keith Guillory, hills just North East of Austin

Ralph Showalter and others sent early routes in the Greenbelt on trad gear. Ralph was the "Mayor of the Greenbelt" and "The Guru of Gus Fruh." When Enchanted Rock closed to climbing, boredom and frustration kicked in, and climbers shifted to the Greenbelt. The early bolted routes were installed on lead, since rap bolting (bolting on rappel) was not considered ethical at the time. Development on lead entails hanging on dicey aid, risking falls, weighted down with drill, hardware, and equipment, and often encountering all sorts of technical problems. Keith Guillory wrote about putting up Fern Bar, ground-up style:

---

[69] Both were waiting for Scott Harris to show up so they could all bolt the route. Scott sent a text saying he'd be late and "save a bolt for me." It became scorching hot, he never showed, and so they didn't.

It took me two different attempts to bust through the horizontal lines of ferns that draped the route and finish with the current crux move at the top. And, of course, we were trying to put it in from the ground up. (Boy, did we have a lot to learn.)

Originally the first piece was an angle piton driven into a solution pocket in the chert level just off the ground. It eventually was replaced as the flinty crystals kept breaking, casting doubt on its worthiness as pro. The current bolt is an appreciated bit above the piton placement. Especially nice now that the move past the bolt became more difficult as the flint footholds broke. (Boy, did we have a lot to learn.)

To gain the next ledge I looped a sling over a horn and then mantled onto the horn while holding the sling in place with my hand. It helped to have a long sling around the afore-mentioned sapling to keep the rope from lifting the sling off the horn. A lot of people don't care for the mantle and have other beta for this section. (Boy, did we have a lot to learn.)

I looped the pine off to the right and went up for a look at the crux. Somewhere up there I drilled a 1/4" button head but reconsidered after trying to pop the move above. I sidled back to the pine and escaped up and right. (Boy, did we have a lot to learn.)

Came back later after a couple of top rope runs off the anchors and rap drilled a pin into the crux protection scheme and finished the route as expected if not as intended originally. (Boy, did we have a lot to learn.)

Sherry Sanders 📷 John Sanders, "Ka ne nes Bane"

The current protection scheme went in as Dave Rehberg aided up the direct start on the left and then up the Fern Bar line drilling from hooks and such. We had coordinated on the new placements so it was all cool and we ended up with a more typical limestone kind of route = adequate gear. (Boy, did we have a lot to learn.)

The first bolted lines were Tit Scratch Fever (at Balrog Wall), then Thumbdance (at Gus Fruh), then Urban Assault. James Crump worked to get the city to sanction climbing throughout the Greenbelt and to expand the Greenbelt itself to new areas.

New Wall was spotted by Bill Gooch and attracted the interest of the group that ended up bolting the routes there. They saw it as an opportunity to climb routes that were harder than what was then available in the Greenbelt. New Wall was where Austin first saw rap bolting.

At some point the city banned all new bolts in the Greenbelt. Alvino Pon had developed routes in Colorado that required applications and approvals, so he sold the city on the concept and provided them an application form requiring the location of the proposed route, the type of hardware to be used, and the reason the bolts were needed (generally answered by saying a lack of natural protection made the route unsafe to climb otherwise). The first wall to see this application process in action was Beehive Wall. This type of application is still in use in the Greenbelt, Reimers, and North Shore.

Back in the day, an honorific arose called the "Sombrero man", awarded to those who sent every route at the Greenbelt plus a bizarre variation of the long Sunken Gardens traverse, involving 360's (feet over head) and some climbing with back to the wall. The original Sombrero Man was Eric Haarms.

David Cardosa, "Space Cowboy", BITD
Bill Sandlin 📷

Malgorzata Peszynskal 📷   Ralph Showalter.

Within the city limits, trad routes and later sport routes started on what's now obscure, and finished on what's now crowded! The rough sequence ran: Bull Creek (starting with James Crump's "Bedtime for Bonzo"), Wasp Wall, Balrog Wall, Campbell's Hole, and Urban Assault. Later came New Wall (which saw the transition from ground-up bolting ethics to rap-bolting) and Gus Fruh, then Tom Suhler and Bruce Becker's routes at Seismic. (Seismic had two older routes before their work: Over Easy and Short People.) Then Beehive Wall. This list is spotty and incomplete. Sean O'Grady once started a timeline of route installs, but not much is remembered. He found: 1986: King of Ging & Woofin' Hooters. 1987: Birdland, Trash Can Man, Rock Retard, Blind Date, Charlie Don't Surf, Road Pizza. 1988: the main lines at New Wall, Crystal New Persuasion, Heaven Can Wait, Heaven's

Gate, Iron Man, Adam's Way, Through the Looking Glass, Tunnel Vision, Power Monkey, and Space Cowboy. Jeff Jackson dates Thumb Dance (originally "Biner Talk") at 1978.

When Tom Suhler and Bruce Becker bolted routes at Seismic, a lot of climbers were critical, and one well-known climber chopped the bolts. (That climber later relented and restored some of them.) Some felt the routes were too easy to bother bolting. One school of thought, back then, was to minimize the development of easy routes to avoid future crowding at climbing areas. They were likely viewed by some as bagging easy lines for glory. Actually, as Luke Bowman reports, Tom was giving back to the community, making a climbing area that would help people get into the sport. Luke believes Tom was one of the first community-minded climbers in the area.

Seismic eventually became crowded, and so Ross Robertson began exploring three lines left of Lick the Window. He wanted to name them after his three sons, who began climbing at the same time Ross did. Seismic had been closed to new routes for a long time, but Ross negotiated with the parks department, and after three years, got two of the routes approved. Matter of Honor is named after Ross' oldest son (Ehren, which means "honor" in German). Angel of Poets and the toprope between them (Raining Skyward) are references to the other sons. Ross thought it would be fun to leave the routes unrated. Ross's three-year effort with the city paved the way for all the new routes at Seismic which followed.

Tom Suhler, chilling in Tamarindo

Recent Greenbelt history includes regular winter night climbing organized on ClimbingBuddies Yahoo group. Joel Schopp writes:

> Night climbing got started because some of us like to get out after our day jobs to climb and hated to waste our good Texas winter weather because of a little thing like darkness. The first time out, Frank Curry, Karl Vochatzer and I brought literally anything that made light which we could carry. Coleman lanterns, maglites, candles, bike lights, glow sticks, a car battery, an inverter, and various light bulbs. It quickly became apparent that the car battery with the inverter powering a florescent flood light was the only thing of use we had brought.

> ### All of us will be drawn to the lights like moths to the flame.
> *Joel Schopp*

After that, Joel and Karl began discussing power options, including gas powered generators, Coleman lamps, 1000 foot extension cord, etc. But Frank's battery and inverter was a good enough proof of concept, at 45 minutes of light, and so they both bought power packs.

Heather Thornton 📷   Greg Brooks at Gus Fruh

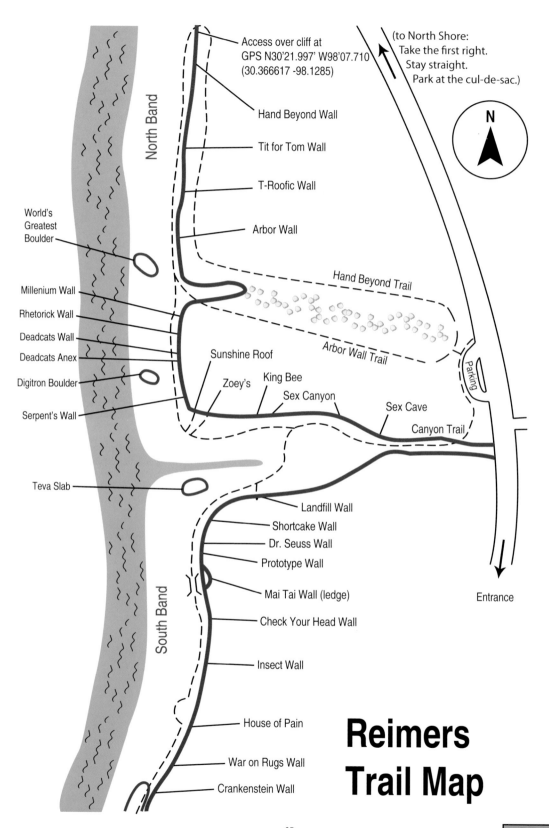

North Band

Access over cliff at
GPS N30'21.997' W98'07.710
(30.366617 -98.1285)

Hand Beyond Wall

Tit for Tom Wall

T-Roofic Wall

Arbor Wall

(to North Shore:
Take the first right.
Stay straight.
Park at the cul-de-sac.)

N

World's
Greatest
Boulder

Hand Beyond Trail

Millenium Wall

Rhetorick Wall

Deadcats Wall

Deadcats Anex

Digitron Boulder

Serpent's Wall

Sunshine Roof

Zoey's

King Bee

Sex Canyon

Sex Cave

Canyon Trail

Arbor Wall Trail

Parking

Teva Slab

Landfill Wall

Shortcake Wall

Dr. Seuss Wall

Prototype Wall

Mai Tai Wall (ledge)

Check Your Head Wall

South Band

Insect Wall

House of Pain

War on Rugs Wall

Crankenstein Wall

Entrance

Reimers
Trail Map

Reimers

Climbing Area: Reimers Ranch

Milton Reimers Ranch Park is a Travis County park roughly 40 minutes west of Austin. Set your GPS to 23610 Hamilton Pool Road, Dripping Springs, TX 78620. Old school directions: From I-35, take 290 west and exit Southwest Parkway. (Or from Loop 1 aka. Mopac, take the Southwest Parkway exit.) Southwest Parkway starts at Mopac, goes west and dead-ends into H71. Go right (west) on 71. Pass the town of Bee Cave and turn left onto FM 3238 (Hamilton Pool Road). Travel 12 miles to the Park entrance, on your right. The latest access information is at www.co.travis.tx.us/tnr/parks/reimers_ranch.asp. As of this writing:

> Hours of operation: 8am to twilight.
>
> Fees: $10 per vehicle day pass, or $100 annual pass into Reimers, Pace Bend, Hamilton Pool, and all other Travis County parks. The $10 day fee lets you visit all of the parks on the same day.
>
> Rules: No glass containers, no fires, no conspicuous consumption of alcohol, no camping.

Activities besides climbing include 18 miles of mountain bike trails, hiking, fishing[70], and swimming. Hiking is allowed off trail, and there's over 2,400 acres of it! After climbing, a nice treat is to continue further down Hamilton Pool Rd. to swim the spring waters in the huge blue hole at the County's Hamilton Pool park. Hamilton Pool is frequently closed, so call ahead, at 264-2740. (See www.co.travis.tx.us/tnr/parks/hamilton_pool.asp.) Or take a tour of Jester King Craft Brewery, a climber-owned awesome brewery close to Reimers, on Fitzhugh Road in Dripping Springs. They have a Facebook fanpage.

Access Points

Reimers is accessed via three trails.

Scott Smith, "Scorpion Child"

<u>Canyon Trail</u>: (10 minutes to Prototype Wall, 6 minutes to Serpent's Wall, 7 minutes to Dead Cats Wall). Newcomers should always take this trail to check out its incredible beauty (and routes). Limestone rimmed cypress-tree creeks and blue holes are the gems of Texas. Park on the left end of the first parking lot on the left at GPS N30°21.827' W98°07.403' (30.363783 -98.123383), near the bathroom and pavilion. Hike left on a trail, down into the small creek bed at GPS N30°21.790' W98°07.379' (30.363167 -98.122983). Hike the creek. It soon opens up into a large canyon at the Sex Cave climbing area. Stay right of the water channel but left of a lower ledge (which accesses the stalactite roof start of Lip-o-suction and other routes). Go down the steep section, then right, into and through the cave. Work high and right out of the cave, instead of dipping down into the brushy trail. This high path will take you along the Sex Canyon and King Bee Memorial Buttress routes.

The various walls at Reimers are pretty easy to find from here. As you leave the King Bee Memorial Buttress routes, a side trail cuts left to access the south band (Prototype Wall, etc.), while the main trail continues on and bends right to the north band (Serpent's Wall, Dead Cats Wall, etc.). Spur trails from both of those trails branch off to walls such as Landfill Wall, Zoey's Wall, Serpent's Wall, but the main trails pass close to most of the walls.

Jason Miars, "Head"

<u>Arbor Wall Trail</u>: (5 minutes to Arbor Wall, 6 minutes to Dead Cats Wall, 7 minutes to Tit For Tom Wall.) This trail is fastest to start the day at Dead Cats Wall, Arbor Wall, T-Roofic Wall, or Tit For Tom Wall. Park on the right end of the first parking lot on the left at GPS N30°21.894' W98°07.460' (30.3649 -98.124333). A crushed granite trail runs in front of the parking lot. Walk the short (16 paces) trail connecting it to another crushed granite trail that bends around a very mild dip in the land (the subtle start of a dry creek). Hike it left and it will bend away from parking and come to a masonry wall near the clifftop. Hike right on a dirt trail down into a usually dry creek. Walk to the right of the big Sycamore tree growing out of the creek bed's drop-off at GPS N30°21.876' W98°07.567' (30.3646 -98.126117). Scramble down to a ledge. Then pick your poison: go down again (kind of hard with backpacks), or turn right and stoop for 30' under a roof to reach 8 lt Grand (5.8). Both ways get you near the main trail that

---

[70] Fishing is especially popular around March (for white bass). Catch some and fix yerself some Pedernales Lobster: Use a scallop scoop on the bass to get 1-2" cubes. Cook it in Crab Boil (a spice mix used to flavor crab or other shellfish) for 30-60 seconds. Put it on a bed of rice, and dip it in a bowl of warm garlic butter. Truly cheap and delicious!

accesses all of Reimers' north walls. Go right (facing the river) to the main Arbor Wall routes or left to Millennium Wall, Rhetorick Wall, Dead Cats Wall, and Serpent's Wall.

Hand Beyond Trail: (9 minutes to Hand Beyond Wall.) This access is fastest to start the day at Hand Beyond Wall. Park and hike the 16-paces trail described under Arbor Wall Trail above, and turn right to take the trail along the right side of the mild dip (dry creek). It bends along the clifftop briefly, then bends right away from it. At that point, veer left on a dirt trail and continue along the cliff edge to a very small seasonal creek. Continue 55 more paces. The cliff shortens to 3' tall at GPS N30°21.997' W98°07.710' (30.366617 -98.1285) Hike down and left about 120 semi-rugged paces until you reach the leftmost bolted routes of Hand Beyond Wall.

Reimers: **Bouldering**

Reimers' ample bouldering is covered well in Texas Limestone Bouldering by Jeff Jackson, Rock Hound Publishing (2007), available at www.erockonline.com. We just add Butt Traverse at Arbor Wall (don't get too excited) and Calories at Shortcake Wall (get excited!). Also, at Landfill Wall, Garbage and Tufafest are basically roped boulder problems.

Reimers: **Sport Routes**

Past guidebooks listed the north band of Reimers right-to-left, mirror images of the topos' route labels. That really messed with our dyslexia. They probably did it assuming climbers would always access these routes from the right, via the Canyon Trail. But Arbor Wall Trail enters the middle of the north band, and it's now the fastest trail to Dead Cats. So we simply list all Reimers walls and routes left-to-right. Whenever you happen to be hiking right-to-left, turn back pages to the end of the next wall's description to see if there are comments about spacing between it and the wall you're currently at.

If you hike in via the canyon trail, **turn to page 99 for Sex Cave**. If you hike in via Arbor Wall trail, **turn to page 77 for Arbor Wall**. If you hike in via Hand Beyond trail, turn to the next page.

Queanh Gip on her 1st send of "Crankenstein"

We hope you enjoy the dozen new routes at: Dead Cats Wall, T-Roofic Wall, Rhetorick Wall, Serpent's Wall, Dr. Seuss Wall, and the left end of Crankenstein Wall (now called War on Rugs Wall). More are on the way at Arbor Wall; see our notes there, and a couple might go in next to Bastard in the Brothel (House of Pain wall).

It will also be fun to enjoy the obscure routes and walls that were incompletely covered in the past: Hand Beyond Wall, Tit For Tom Wall's right side, Zoey's Wall, the left end of Sex Canyon (now called The King Bee Memorial Buttress by Limestoner and this book), Sex Cave (routes Mud Lip and Roman Orgy if it gets restored), Landfill Wall, Mai Tai Wall, Check Your Head Wall, Insect Wall and Crankenstein Wall. Crankenstein Wall isn't just for Crankenstein anymore! Bride and Cotton Mouth are just as fun. And throughout the park, check out the variations we've learned of or invented.

The harder climbers usually spend their time in the canyon and south band. However the north band offers a nice circuit of routes over 5.11 to check out: Rhetorick (5.12a), Summon (5.13a), Incredible Journey (5.12a), Curious George (5.12b), Rust Never Seeps (5.12c), T-Roofic's Big Brother (5.12c), Flea Circus (5.12a), and

Grip Clip (5.12a).

Roger Hurtado, "Rain Dance"

Reimers (north band): **Hand Beyond Wall**

Sun conditions: Morning sun is nice in the winter. All day tree shade on all routes except the left three.

Approach: 9 minutes via the Hand Beyond Trail described at the start of this chapter. Since this trail isn't well known, many probably considered this wall remote, but it is only 3 minutes longer than the fastest approach to Dead Cats.

GPS @ leftmost route (Camp Fire Jesus): N30°21.969' W98°07.680' (30.36615 -98.128)**GPS** @ rightmost route (Deception Pass): N30°21.979' W98°07.683' (30.366317 -98.12805)

This is a short wall full of tasty morsels, many of them plenty sustained, and the four routes on the right are as tall as most Reimers routes. Route quality is high; submissions on www.rockclimbing.com average 3-4 stars on most of the routes. The routes have a high mix of slopers and bouldery-starts over mini-roofs, forcing high feet, but without being one-move-wonders. For a 5.10 developing climber, these bouldery starts are a great thing to master. Break away from your stale Dead Cats Wall habit here and at North Shore's moderate walls.

It's hard to place three stars (meaning "out-of-towner recommended") on short routes that lack sport clips. We'll go ahead and do that, but recommend out-of-towners come here in groups to share the cleaning chores.

Access trail (Class 1). The trail comes over the cliff at the spot where it's only 3' tall. 105 paces to Hand Beyond Boulder, or 120 rugged paces to the first bolted route (Camp Fire Jesus).

Hand Beyond Boulder: a large boulder near the cliff. Its southern tip is 15 paces left of Camp Fire Jesus. Walk counterclockwise to see the TR anchors on its river side. There are two dubiously short routes. Stick-clipping is easier than top-access, by the time you scramble and protect yourself to reach low anchors.

> toprope: **Unnamed** (5.8+ TR). Only 10' of upward movement.

> toprope: **Unnamed** (5.10b TR). Reach the anchors and kiss both of them to milk the most out of the route. The climbing is pretty good, but by the time you set TR and clean...

Neil Higa, "San Antonio Drillers"

15 rugged paces from the boulder's southern tip to Camp Fire Jesus.

1. **Camp Fire Jesus**[71] (5.10d)*** 2 bolts, Curtis Mai, Todd "Notorious" McCray[72]. Starts right of a line of 5 nice little tufas.

2. **Shadowman** (5.11a)* 2 bolts, Kevin Bentz, Stephanie Bryant. 10' left of the route is a chossy little cave below a roof. 8' right of the route is a long double tufa. A nice short route, most valuable for advancing into 11a.

---

[71] The name comes from a crazy party around a camp fire, where someone decided there's a Jesus in the fire. Austin Rock listed this route as "Yet Another S.A. Route".

[72] Curtis nicknamed Todd "Notorious" because of his habit of never returning calls. Despite that habit, the two managed to bolt a whopping 30 routes (11% of the routes) at Reimers.

30' Gap Between Routes. The trail dips away from (bypasses) the next two routes.

3. **See Through Black**[73] (5.10c)* 2 bolts, Curtis Mai, Todd McCray. This route sits in mild overgrowth, 30' each way to its neighboring routes. Low pockets and "high" slopers make this look cool for a mini-route, and it feels longer than it looks. Bring your shortest partners.

4. **Tree Gnome** (5.10c)*** 2 bolts, Steve Hunt, Kevin Bentz???. Starts just right of a huge fallen-over Live Oak. Uh, Dead Oak. Zigzag bolt "line" with Bolt 2 at 11 o'clock from Bolt 1. A vertically short route with a lot of moves on a zigzag path. The tree stump is Off. Don't use the freakin' tree stump, or Gnomes will play tricks on you.

25' gap between routes. Power Squat is on gray rock with a point, left of gray-streaked tan rock.

5. **Power Squat** (5.10d)*** 2 bolts, Joe Sulak. Negative eye candy. Eye poison. Shitty looking but intense. Anchors sit almost touching those of San Antonio Drillers. Stick-clip if you're short.

6. **San Antonio Drillers** (5.10d)*** 2 bolts, Curtis Mai, Todd McCray. Start stemming a boulder and the cliff's bottom shelf. Hands have a short diagonal right-leaning crack separating gray and tan rock. The steep move is similar to that of Crankenstein. Optional sit-start, pulling the hollow choss (same grade).

7. **Harelipped Dog** (5.10b)*** 3 bolts, Mack Hargrave. Anchors sit left of the boltline. Start on a parallelogram shaped boulder, hands on big wild spongy pockets on a tan shallow bowl.

8. **Unnamed Route** (5.10a R)* 2 bolts, Curtis Mai, Todd McCray. Starts 6' right of a 5" hackberry and left of 3 post oaks. Climbs a face with pockets and points. Runout to the anchors. Solid anchor clip for tall people; "R" rating is for shorter folk.

30' gap between routes.

9. **Booger Boy** (5.10a / 5.10b)* 3 bolts, Kevin Bentz, Stephanie Bryant. Start jammed left of a big leaning live oak. The grade (which is height-dependent) assumes you keep feet off the tree. Best route name on the wall.

  variation: (5.8)*: Walk up the big live oak tree and cross onto the wall.

Big Leaning Live Oak

10. **Daddy's Girl** (5.10b)* 3 bolts, Mack Hargrave. Zigzag boltline. Starts 5' right of a big leaning live oak. The low roof is a good spot to teach pupils a hard, unnecessary, double-knee bar no-hands rest. Work your knees and feet deep.

11. **Freedom Fries**[74] (left: 5.10b / right: 5.10a)*** 3 bolts. Kudos to any bolter who gets two good distinct routes out of one boltline. One of these lines has one of our favorite types of holds, where hitting it shallow or deep makes all the difference.

  Left Fry (5.10b)***: Climbs left of the boltline over a very shallow dihedral.

  Right Fry (5.10a)***: Climbs right of the boltline over a bulge.

> A dragon can be unseen or visible, minute or huge,
> long or short.
>
> *Shuo Wen (100 C.E.)*

---

[73] This route was misnamed "Camp Fire Jesus" in Austin Rock.
[74] If you're not familiar with "freedom fries", read the Wiki page.

Reimers

8' Wide Boulder directly under Ezra's Shelf left of a 3" post oak.

12. **Ezra's Shelf** (5.10d)*** 3 bolts,
Stephanie Bryant, Kevin Bentz. Starts on the 8' wide boulder. 1st half is tan rock, 2nd half is gray rock.
Fun beta.[75]

12' Wide Boulder, 6' back from the cliff, in front of the next three routes.

13. **Monkey Boy** (5.10c)*** 2 bolts,
Kephanie. Shares a start (but not 1st bolt) with Go For the Jugular. Climbs a tan shallow bowl to pockets and an overhang.

Neil, Higa, "Go For the Jugular

14. **Go For the Jugular** (5.9+)*** 2 bolts, Kephanie. Start on a diagonally right-leaning right-facing crack to a face with a mini-bulge.

15. **Annie Up** (5.7 R)*** 2 bolts, Curtis Mai, Todd McCray. Climbs a dihedral to a right-facing flake/crack shaped like a breaking wave. Runout to Bolt 2.

variation: (5.9 R)*: Climb keeping hands right of the crack, up the white streak, using feet left of the crack towards the top.

Rounded right-leaning arête, left of a large section of tan rock and two big tan boulders against the cliff.

16. **Hidden Agenda** (5.11b)* 2 bolts, Kephanie. Human stick-clip via the stacked boulder on the left, but don't start there. Feet start on the boulder under the roof, right of Bolt 1. (Otherwise, it's the 5.8 variation.) Runout on easy climbing.

variation: **Antonian** (5.8)***. Climb Hidden Agenda, starting on the naturally stacked boulders left of Bolt 1. Runout. Nice face climb.

17. **Waste of Bolts (aka. Bluebeard[76])** (5.10d X)*** 2 bolts, Barry Wilson[77], Kevin Gallagher. Start on a large hueco with a handlebar chest-high. Deadly ground-fall runout to anchors on careful, non-crux climbing. If you don't freak out, cramp up, or pass out, you'll likely make it unless your belayer trips backwards over his backpack, in which case you'll haunt their dreams. Good mental prep for runout climbing, on a good route.

18. **Ten Foot Pole** (5.11c)*** 2 bolts, Kim Duran[78], David Black, Kevin Bentz. Starts on pretty wild-honeycomb pocketed rock. Old anchors still sit next to the new set.

---

[75] This one short route offers up three rock-on moves; we almost cried with joy.

[76] With bad weather and whatnot, Barry had nothing better to do. When Jeff asked him for the route name, he said "Waste of Bolts." Jeff didn't like the name, so he tossed out FA naming rights tradition and made up "Bluebeard."

[77] A trailmeister, Barry has had a hand in every trail project at Enchanted Rock. Vegas heavily favors Barry to win every Granite Gripper seniors category until he's 98. One day, Barry was standing on the ledge under Lip-o-suction, holding a tufa and leaning out to inspect other holds, when the tufa broke, and he fell off the ledge.

[78] Kim is one of the most impressively muscular women ever seen climbing in Texas. Kevin said she was colorful, brave, nuts at times but always awesome. Terence Smith was a partner of hers, and her example on routes basically drove him to grow a pair.

Biggest mini-roof on the wall.

19. Overlord (5.12b)* 3 bolts, Kephanie. Shares anchors with Deception Pass. Climb the right-leaning lieback crack/flake and pull the roof. Tape up your left fingers to eliminate the pain.

20. Deception Pass (5.10a PG)*** 2 bolts, Kephanie[79]. Shares anchors with Overlord. Starts on a gray slabby bulgy face, right of a chossy area. Higher up is a left-leaning chaotic ledge. Tufas are the starting footholds. Until Bolt 3 is clipped, you risk falling onto the slab.

52 rugged paces to Tit For Tom Wall. Take the ill-marked trail along the cliff and boulders near it.

> When the deal with the County was about to close, I was sitting with Milton and Joy Reimers one afternoon talking about the ranch and its future. With true emotion, they both expressed with such sincerity, "The climbers are like family." They really wanted that deal to work out for the climbers who they felt were loyal and true for so many years.
>
> *David Cardosa*

---

[79] Looks like Kevin and Stephanie's idea of a date was bolting routes! Among all the route developers in town, these two did the most work under the radar — few old timers know them. They were climbing so much, they pitched a tent (back when Reimers hosted camping) and pretty much lived there half the year. One of their favorite things to do was soloing Centipede, benefiting by its low crux and relatively easy remainder, just to freak out onlookers and count the "My God!"s.

Reimers (north band): **Tit For Tom Wall**

Sun conditions: Afternoon sun, but the six leftmost routes get tree shade.
Approach: 7 minutes
GPS @ leftmost route (Mother Buddha): N30°21.920' W98°07.643' (30.365333 -98.127383)
GPS @ trail overlooking Curious George roof: N30°21.917' W98°07.624' (30.365283 -98.127067)

While the masses hike down the Sex Canyon to Prototype Wall for excessive crimping, you can get to this wall even faster, via the Arbor Wall trail. The routes are good and contrast nicely to Prototype Wall, being generally steeper, more deadpoint-intensive, more 11+'s and more total routes. A few of the routes sport single-body-length roof pulls, and some have wild tufa formations. To identify the routes, start on the left end with Mother Buddha, because the boltlines get crazy on the right end, zigzagging near each other.

Before coming to this wall, decide where you want to warm up. Use the Arbor Wall access for each of the following options:

a.   Arbor Wall's "8 It Grand" (do a lead-downlead lap on it) and its future 5.9 (coming soon). Maybe lead Cliptomania (5.11a) bolt-to-bolt.

b.   Hike north past Arbor Wall to warm up on T-Roofic's Fearless (5.9) and Tit For Tom's two 5.10b variations listed below.

c.   Hike south to Dead Cats Wall (6 minutes from the parking lot). Warm up there and hike 5 minutes back to Tit For Tom. When not crowded, this offers the most warmup choices.

White limestone all the way up to the clifftop. The route "Tit For Tom" is at the edge of white and gray.

[space for a possible future route]

1.   **Mother Buddha** (5.11c)*** 2 bolts, Clayton Reagan. Belay from the left, though you'll still be dodging rope. (The route could use a low directional.) Rock texture is rough, just like Claytee, in a good way. Low anchors could be moved higher to add another hard move. Top out over them for 5.11d.

[space for a possible future route]

2.   **Tit For Tom**[80] (5.11d)*** 3 bolts, David Cardosa, Tom Suhler. All-air runout to the anchors.

a. variation: **Bitch Tit** (5.10b "R" or "G")* 3 or 4 bolts, Dave Phillips. One of the two warmups on the wall, it could use one bolt to make it G-rated with comfortable clipping. R rated version: start Tit For Tom, bolts 1-2. Run it out (over a leg-breaker bad landing) to The Bitch Club's Bolt 3, and up to its anchors. G-rated version: cut the runout by hunkering low to make a crowded clip of The Bitch Club's Bolt 2; use long draws on it and the previous bolt.

Gray limestone

3.   **The Bitch Club**[81] (5.11d)*** 3 bolts, Stephen Shortnacy, John Gonzales. Anchors are hidden above a ledge. Start under a shallow overhanging bowl with a white streak on gorgeous brown/black rock. Interesting all the way up. The crux shuts down a lot of people, so maybe three stars oversells it — but it's a great route if you get it. Join the Bitch Club! *Beta.*[82]

---

[80] Tom had a girlfriend whose breast size matched that of the stalactite used to pull the crux.

[81] Stephen and John kept arguing about something when they were working to get the first ascent. They often argued about stuff. During this one, John told Stephen to go join the bitch club.

[82] The start reduces to one move via big left foot far left and a "glide right" to the lumpy righthand crimp. Left-hand dyno doesn't look best but it works best. Hit the ledge in the juggy middle, even though it's higher than the right end.

4. El Presidente[83] (5.11a)*** 3 bolts, Rick Watson, Joseph Schwartz[84], John Myrick. This fine route is the Lagavulin to Blowing Smoke's Laphroiag and Wife in the Fast Lane's Bruichladdich. '00

Shallow Dihedral

5. Mikey Likes It[85] (5.11a)*** 3 bolts, Joe Sulak. Pull the chossy tufa column to the shallow dihedral. Consider stick-clipping Bolt 2.

6. Neurotica (5.11d)* 3 bolts, Joe Sulak. Joe repeated this route free-solo. Not recommended but badass. 11d's are scarce around town. Joe bolted Neurotica "out of boredom," not realizing it would become an important route for pyramiding to 5.12a in Austin. Go chase those numbers! Why not.

Big tan dihedral with wild tufas and some gray streaks, all under a tan roof and bulging gray headwall.

7. Beelzebubba (5.11b-c)*** 3 bolts, J.D. Fant. Best route name on the wall. Bolts 1 and 2 are on the border of gray (left) and tan (right) rock. Pull a bulge and then a bulging roof, to double anchors just right of a single old chain anchor (on a ginormous hanger). Bubba is smarter than he looks.

b. variation: **Beelzebubbica** (5.10b PG)* 3 bolts, John Hogge. One of the two warmups on the wall. Stick-clip Beelzebubba's Bolt 2 and start on Antiqua to its low jug horn. Traverse left under the roof and up to the clipped bolt, keep traversing up and left to Neurotica's Bolt 2, then finish Neurotica's Bolt 3 and anchors. A nice face climb, but it's difficult to second. Clean by leading and then un-stick-clipping the first bolt. Runout to the stick-clipped bolt, risking a traverse swing against an uneven surface — potential rib-buster?

The next 2 routes share anchors.

8. Antiqua (5.11b)*** 3 bolts, John Shannon. Start left of the big column full of little tufas. Bolt 1 is right of a little gray streak that's right of ribbed mini-tufas below a Geiger-esque clump of gnar pockets. Shares anchors with Underdog. It calls for moves uncommon among ATX low 5.11's. (See Antiqua in Appendix A for beta). Here's how it will likely play out: 1. You hangdog the crux 30 minutes, finally pull it, and clean Bolt 3 on the way down. 2. Your second cleans bolts 1-2, blows the crux and can't get back on, in all of 43 seconds. Ha! (Don't second the route.)

9. Underdog (5.11b)*** 3 bolts, Benji Fink. Shares anchors with Antiqua. Bolt 1 is just right of the curvy mini-tufas on the big drip formation. Bolt 2 is to the right, just over the roof. Then, a bolt on Jimmy's Rig is up and right at one o'clock, nearby, but Underdog's Bolt 3 is higher than that. '94ish.

[83] At the time, new routes were logged at Hank Caylor's climbing gym, Pseudo Rock. Rick went there to log his new route. At the time, Rick was president of Central Texas Mountaineers (CTM). Hank saw him enter the gym and yelled, "Ellllllllll Presidenteeeeeeeeeeeeeeeee!" and so the route was named.

[84] Joseph is a co-owner and technology guru of ClimbTech, the Austin company which pioneered the removable bolt and a nice all-steel permadraw (fixed draw). He says "There are only three grades: 5.easy, 5.hard, and 5.I-Can't-Climb-It."

[85] Named for a friend, Mike. Mike had cancer at the time, got on the route and loved it.

Reimers

10. **Jimmy's Rig** (5.12a)* 3 bolts, Jimmy Carse. The anchors are reaching-distance to Underdog's anchors. Bolt 1 is on an orange face above a mini-roof. Bolt 2 is on a little 30˚ overhang section. Bolt 3 cuts left on gray rock, under the anchors.

11. **Ralph's Rig** (5.12a)* 4 bolts, Ralph Vega, John Gonzales[86]. Start on Bolt 1 of Jimmy's Rig, go up and right at 2 o'clock for the next two bolts, then straight up. The route is just left of the big Curious George roof and sports cool hueco and funnel formations.

<u>variation</u> (5.??): Stick-clip Bolt 3, start under it and pull the low roof.

Huge tan roof with birds' nests over a huger featureless gray roof.

12. **Curious George**[87] (5.12b)*** 8 bolts, Mike Klein[88].
A long route, which, around here, usually means it traverses. Scramble above the ferns right of the white tufas and onto the ledge to Bolt 1 (low, right off the deck), shared with Melt Down. Pass up a stick clip and clip Bolt 2. Traverse over a 50' wide roof and up at its left end. Somewhat run out to Bolt 4 over the boulder on the ledge. 35-meter rope is fine. A classic adventure story.

13. **Melt Down**[89] (5.12b)* 4 bolts, Patrick O'Donnell.
Scramble up the ledge to Bolt 1 (low, right off the deck), shared with Curious George. Climb the arête just right of Curious George's roof.

14. **Nobody's Hero** (5.10d)*** 3 bolts, Benji Fink. 6' right of Melt Down's arête. Belay up on the boulder stack right of the leaning tree, under the boltline. Bolt 1's shaft sticks out too much, as of this writing. Stay off until it's fixed (soon).

55 rugged paces to T-Roofic Wall.

Mike Klein repeating his route, "Curious George"

---

[86] Ralph and John used the route to teach themselves how to bolt on lead (aid), to prepare for the high walls of Mex. One of Ralph's hooks blew off of the rock, and he fell and clubbed John hard. Ralph was fine, and John was annoyed. Bolting ethics originally called for working from the ground up (no rappelling). Consider the terror of fully weighting yourself and all your gear onto a little metal hook balancing on a fragile limestone pocket, the lip of which is ready to blow apart and propel that hook into your right eye, and then pressing the drill hard into the rock to drill a hole. Think about taking a lead fall with heavy drill, hammer, hardware, and other tools strapped to you. It's ugly. (Bolters use slings and trad equipment when possible, but often it's the hooks.) Nowadays, rap bolting is common, but ground-up ascents at short cliffs such as Reimers are still done, either for practice or pride, and ground-up is still necessary at tall cliffs wherever the top can't easily be accessed. Ground up is also an effective way of feeling out the best bolt placements. Mistakes are often made on a fast rap bolting job.

[87] aka. Lucky's Longy

[88] Mike likes traverses. Early in his climbing career, David Cardosa found him clunky and not very good. David advanced fast, but, well, Tom Suhler put it this way. David was the best climber Tom knew who was also the most weenie. One day, David was gripped shitless on Ripple, near but out of reach of the next clip. Mike was traversing a route near him, and David stammered, "Dude, could you please clip my rope for me?!?!" Mike did so. Climbing is a team sport, after all.

[89] Bolting can be such fun. In Patrick's words, "I had just supercharged the drill, and while I was drilling bolts, some wires got crossed and melted together. Meanwhile I was in 100 degrees Texas sun with branches stabbing me in the back and drill not working and so i nearly had a 'Meltdown'."

Reimers (north band): **T-Roofic Wall**

Sun conditions: All day shade
Approach: 6 minutes.
GPS @ T-Roofic Detour: N30°21.896' W98°07.604' (30.364933 -98.126733)

This wall is home to the beloved route T-Roofic Detour. Fearless (5.9) is an excellent warmup for this wall[90] and all walls north of here. Most people come here for T-Roofic Detour/Direct before proceeding to Arbor Wall and Tit For Tom Wall, or they come here after a day at Dead Cats Wall.

T-Roofic Detour and Fearless are the easiest routes to identify. Incredible Journey and T-Roofic's Big Brother crisscross each other, forming a sort of "X" bolt pattern.

See also The World's Great Boulder (page 131) for sport routes and bouldering down-hill from this wall.

1. **Rust Never Seeps** (5.12c)*** 4 bolts, Jeff Jackson. Climb the overhanging orange streak. Sweet looking stone. Benji Fink and Mike Klein love this route, and someone else spoke fondly of it.

Large high roof under a rounded gray headwall, cut in the middle with a large slanting tan wedge, forming a slab on the left, a rounded arête in the middle, and an overhanging face on the right. Much of the rock is chossy looking.

2. **Incredible Journey** (5.12a)*** 7 bolts, Greg Brooks. This route starts on a ledge well left of the arête described above, traverses right under the big "left side" roof, crosses the arête, traverses under some of the "right side" roof, and up to anchors left of T-Roofic Detour and right of T-Roofic's Big Brother.

3. **T-Roofic's Big Brother** (5.12c)*** 6 bolts (2 are permadraws), Jason Syesta, Tommy Blackwell, et al. Starts under the big roof left of T-Roofic. '08

4. **T-Roofic Detour** (5.10d)*** 5 bolts, Jean Hudson[91], Scott Hudson[92], Greg Brooks. Scramble up to the top of the weird ramp/slab under the right half of the big upper roof. Traverse the orange face up and right to big holds leading straight up. The locals call this T-Roofic.

   a. variation: **T-Roofic Direct** (5.11a)*** Tommy Blackwell. Begin directly under the second bolt of T-Roofic Detour. This variation looks poor and squeezed from the ground, its start being just right of the main route's start, but the start has a lot of moves, and we like it better than the main route. Do the main route only if you prefer the lower grade or lack a stick clip.

Low Roof, 15' up, right of the big upper roof.

5. **Flea Circus** (5.12a)* 4 bolts, Rick Watson. Walk up the right side of the weird ramp. "PG" rated unless you stick-clip Bolt 2. An exciting roof-pull.

20' gap between routes.
Right-leaning dihedral with two routes.

---

[90] Austin Rock hated the route, and graded it 10a. We like it. Considering the lack of warmups north of Dead Cats Wall, it's worth your giving it a chance or three.

[91] A friend described Jean as tenacious. She had trouble developing climbing skills, but stuck with it and came on strong. She won second place at the first National Women's Speed Climbing comp at Snowbird in 1988, behind a gal who became Electra on American Gladiators. The contest was tilted Electra's way, however, when Jean had to run the route an extra time due to a no-show by another contestant.

[92] When Scott Hudson went to Reimers to hike with a pal (Bill Clap), they climbed the boulders, and Scott continued bouldering there for several years before installing the very first bolts. Scott was largely self-taught, using Royal Robbin's book, and so Scott was insecure about his own skills. He'd venture out to Erock, very shy about being seen climbing by the experienced climbers there. Scott was a gymnast before climbing, and on a 5.8 Bill saw his potential and told him he was already capable of much tougher terrain. Armed with that thought, Scott jumped two number grades within a day. At Reimers, Scott bolted a dozen routes before others joined in. With relatively little climbing experience and no bolting experience, he identified and bolted stellar routes, some of the best in the park. Soon he began mentoring new climbers. At a time when developers were territorial and guarded about strangers bolting their turf at Reimers and Greenbelt, and some Austinites viewed Dallasites as outsiders, Scott was a mellow, welcoming guy to newcomers. Now in Colorado, Scott is 52 and pulling as hard as ever (5.12a-b).

Reimers

Andrew Temple, "T-Roofic Indirect"

6. **Grip Clip** (5.12a)* 3 bolts, Jeff Fenaros. Scramble up the big mossy pyramid to the dihedral. Climb a tall bulge on the dihedral's left face. Bolt 2 is left of Bolts 1 and 3. End on Fearless' anchors.

7. **Fearless** (5.9 PG)*** 3 bolts, Jeff Fenaros. Scramble up as described under Grip Clip. Runout to Bolt 2, Bolt 3, and the anchors, which are out of sight until you top out. But the runouts are well-designed. Belay up at the start to keep the leader from falling onto the rope. Unfortunately, Bolt 1 is sunk deep in the dihedral, forcing a committing freaky lead. It should be moved right, out of the dihedral, to avoid wrecking ball falls. For warmup purposes, just stick-clip Bolt 2. Maybe, the first time up, enjoy a spooky pure redpoint. *Beta*.[93]

Fifteen paces south reaches Arbor Wall's leftmost route.

> Rock climbing grades are largely subjective. It is your right as an American to disagree with the rating of a particular climb or boulder problem. All complaints should be addressed to: The President of the United States, District of Colombia, U.S.A.
>
> *from Texas Limestone II, by Jeff Jackson*

---

[93] The easiest start doesn't pull up the dihedral. Instead, hands traverse the bulge right; right hand to the sidepull.

Reimers (north band): **Arbor Wall**

Sun conditions: Afternoon sun.
Approach: 5 minutes via the Arbor Wall trail described at the start of this chapter.
GPS @ Mrs. Johnson: N30°21.875' W98°07.581' (30.364583 -98.12635)
GPS @ access trail south of 8 It Grand: N30°21.866' W98°07.571' (30.364433 -98.126183)

This wall used to have a huge live oak shade tree. The tree broke apart about 8' off the ground. The stump is coming back with new growth all over its top. The Arbor Wall up-top trail gives this wall the shortest approach (5 minutes) other than Sex Cave. It boasts a nice warmup (8 It Grand), stellar routes, and proximity to T-Roofic Wall's classic route. An alternative warmup plan is to take the Arbor Wall Trail to Dead Cats Wall (6 minutes), then make the short hike back here.

18" Hackberry, 6' from cliff.

1. **The Finest and the Flyest**[94] (5.11b PG)*** 3 bolts, Dave Teykl, Rupesh Chhagan. Runout to Bolt 3. Easy runout to the anchors.

The next 3 routes share anchors, not visible from the ground.

2. **Ferntasm Twice Removed** (5.11b)* 3 bolts, Curtis Mai, Todd McCray. Starts 6' left of the center of the dihedral climbed by the next two routes. Cuts right to share anchors with them. A stick clip isn't crucial, but the route's more fun pre-clipped. The grade has been carefully calibrated. See beta[95] to avoid pain and get the fun move.

3. **Left of Ferntasm** (5.10a)* 3 bolts, Curtis Mai, Todd McCray. Start in Ferntasm's dihedral and cross left and up after clipping Bolt 2. Cut right to shared anchors. Short runout to Bolt 3 over an ankle-tweaker shelf.

4. **Ferntasm** (5.10b R)*** 3 bolts, Scott Hudson, Jean Hudson. Climb the dihedral in front of the large broken leaning live oak. Runout to Bolt 2. Consider stick-clipping Bolt 1 or 2.

Large broken right-leaning live oak at cliff base. (This oak was the namesake of Arbor Wall; then it broke in half.)

5. **George of the Jungle** (5.10b R)* 3 bolts, Joey Phillips[96]. Start just right of the tree's roots. Careful getting to Bolt 2; runout with the tree in the fall zone. A stick clip isn't necessary if you're tall enough. *Beta*.[97] The climbing is wild and would garner 3 stars if it were safer. Feet come, and feet go.

15' Gap.

The Remains of Joey's Greenbelt Treehouse

---

[94] Austin Rock had it as "The Finest *of* the Flyest". That blew the veiled hint to the back story. There were two Amys who hung out with Dave at the time. One was the finest, and one was the flyest.

[95] After mounting the roof, you're likely going to poke around at all those painful sharp gnars and try a static ascent. You'll just shred your tips doing that. Find a left hand sidepull crimp and the best right hand crimp, both part of all the gnar. Crouch low under roof and deadpoint right hand to a juggy pinch on the right side of the big gash.

[96] After years of climbing at Rogers Park and running a dojo nearby, Joey moved to Austin and opted not to pay anyone rent by building a tree house in the Greenbelt, downstream from Beehive Wall, high above the canopy where he would not be discovered. (Fortunately, such alleged and actual crimes reported in this book are all past the statute of limitations.) He lived there close to a year. Access up the tree was a spooky bit of soloing.

[97] The runout gets you to a solid stance to high clip, so it's not as nasty as it looks from the ground. But it's still nasty. An old timer suggested a new lower bolt; it wouldn't change how high you get over Bolt 1, but it would offer a reachable Bolt 2 stick-clip.

Reimers

6. **Deferred Adjudication** (5.11b)*** 3 bolts, David Phillips. Mild runout to the anchors.

9' wide flat boulder in front of next 2 routes.

7. **Arborcidal Tendencies** (5.11b)*** 3 bolts, David Phillips. Start in front of (not on) the flat boulder. The route goes with no holds shared with Cliptomania. Some folks cut right after Bolt 2, for 5.11a. We're glad a route is here instead of yet another tree. Best route name on the wall.

8. **Cliptomania** (5.11a)*** 2 bolts+, Scott Hudson, Jean Hudson. In case you lack a stick clip and don't lack guts, Bolt 1 is 15' up over a bad landing, on fairly safe climbing. When the low-grade warmups in the area become monotonous, try bolt-to-bolting this.

a. variation: **Cleptomania** (5.11b)***
2 bolts, John Hogge. Stick clip Bolt 1. Keep
hands right of the boltline.

9. **Mrs. Johnson** (5.10b)*** 3 bolts,
Suzanne Johnson[98]. Mild runout to Bolt 2. Lowest
1st bolt ever. The route doesn't look like much, but
you might spend a lot of quality time figuring it out.

---

[98] Suzanne and Paul Johnson made climbing history by publishing Austin's first (and only?) climbing zine, Toprope Magazine, along with Team Toprope t-shirts, which now sell on Ebay for four digits. (Youngsters: Zines were blogs before the days of computers.) Regarding the route name...Suzanne was only engaged to Paul at the time of the FA.

17 Paces to Arbortrary.

The Smoking Lounge: a cool body-sized cave.

<u>bouldering:</u> **Butt Traverse** (V0): Start at the smoking lounge, end near "8 It Grand". Scrunchy warmup material.

APPLICATION: Arbortrary (5.9+) to be 3 bolts. 30' left of "8 It Grand." Start and climb the face just left of the cave.
  <u>variation:</u> (5.11a)*. Pull the upper bulge.

APPLICATION: Tree Talk (5.10d-5.11a) to be 3 bolts. 20' left of "8 It Grand." Start on the upper right jug of the cave and climb the face just right of the cave.

APPLICATION: Juniper (5.11a) to be 3 bolts. 10' left of "8 It Grand." Climb the face left of the ribbed water streak.
  <u>variation:</u> Arborcidal Dependencies (5.11b-c)***. Climb the ribbed water streak until it thins out; then cut left to merge with Juniper.

10. **8 It Grand** (5.8)*** 3 bolts, Brenton Buxton. Climb a short face with a deep dark hueco. It's probably a great 1st lead for a 5.9-5.10 gym type person who wants air falls. It's a nice warmup route; consider saving anchor-cleaning time by downleading.

  <u>toprope:</u> **Ate It Bland** (5.10c TR)* John Hogge. Set TR on "8 it Grand" anchors. Start 2' right of where the rope hangs, on the left end of the mini-roof. It's useful as a stiff warmup after the lead route. *Beta.*[99]

To exit the park via the Arbor Wall Trail (described on 66), walk 7 paces right to the low roof. Slouch under it and grovel to a minor creek's waterfall spot and climb it.

The main trail is downhill from the Arbor Wall routes. From the point overlooking "8 It Grand", hike right 60 rugged paces, across a steep creek valley, to the start of the Millennium Traverse.

Ten Commandments

I. Thou shall have no other sports before climbing.
II. Thou shall not make for thyself an idol and climb it.
III. Thou shall not speak thy commands in vain.
IV. Remember thy climbing plans and keep them holy.
V. Honor thy belayer and gear purveyor.
VI. Thou shall not murder thy canine nor feline that pee-eth on thy rope.
VII. Thou shall not commit poor belay technique.
VIII. Thou shall not steal thy partner's gear.
IX. Thou shall not bear false witness against thy partner's redpoints.
X. Thou shall not covet thy partner's rack nor thy partner's girlfriend.

Allen Corneau

---

[99] Fight for a high right foot after hitting the two thin handholds.

Reimers

Reimers (north band): **Millennium Wall**

Sun conditions: Afternoon sun.
Approach: 6 minutes via the Arbor Wall trail described at the start of this chapter.
GPS @ rightmost route: N30°21.853' W98°07.559' (30.364217 -98.125983)

This wall starts left of Rhetorick Wall's raised landing. The landing and the big arête separate the two. This wall has a 4'-7' deep roof over ferns and chossy tufa-fronted ledges. Keep walking the trail and you'll see the wall is quite wide. The headwall above the roof is home to a traverse that is Reimers' longest route. The right end has two uproutes.

1. **Millennium Traverse** (5.10b)*** 11 bolts, Mario Cantu. Use a minimum 50-meter rope. Climb to the chossy ledge on a few fun huecos (5.7, using the tree on the ledge). Clip in and traverse right until you see Mexico. The route has a couple mild runouts over all-air falls. After Bolt 10, climb up and right to Bolt 11, then to the right of two sets of anchors. (The left set serves Food Rage. The right set serves this and Rags to Riches.) Kudos to Mario for not calling this Y2K, which is a little tinny for our liking. "Millennium" is nice and woody[100], and rolls off the tongue like an orgasmic puff of a fine cigar. This route is long, so its description also should be. Sip this route like a fine cabernet, enjoying delicious big bites of chocolate for the first two thirds of the bottle, and then avoid choking on the last big glassful.

> variation: (5.10a-b) 10 bolts. Exit early, straight up, to Food Rage's anchors. This is handy if you have trouble finishing the main route. Bring a long draw for the right-angle detour on Bolt 10.

2. **Food Rage** (5.13a)* 4 bolts, Rupesh Chhagan, bb Scott Isgitt. A very bouldery start to quality face climbing.

> variation: (5.11 A0), Scott Isgitt. Hang start from Bolt 1.

Left end of a Raised Landing, where Rags to Riches and the Rhetorick Wall routes all start.

3. **Rags to Riches** (5.11b R), 4 bolts, Scott Hudson, Greg Brooks. Beware of loose rock. Start on the left edge of Rhetorick Wall (up on the landing) and traverse left around a huge arête. Easy runout at the top. Named for the chossy start (rags) and the high quality flake at the top (riches). With the choss, you'll feel better stick-clipping Bolts 1 and 2.

Reimers (north band): **Rhetorick Wall**

Sun conditions: Morning shade; afternoon tree shade
Approach: 6 minutes via the Arbor Wall trail described at the start of this chapter.
GPS @ rightmost route: N30°21.839' W98°07.550' (30.363983 -98.125833)

This wall has a lot of orange rock. Routes span it and Dead Cats Wall (to its right) seamlessly; the two walls are arbitrarily separated by a huge live oak 6' behind Lessa the Puramatic 6000 Kitty and its gnarly starting-footholds on a left-leaning flake. Rhetorick Wall's routes belay from a big ledge that drops off.

Two starting bolts of the left-and-up traverse on Rags to Riches, 25' left of Talk It Up.

1. **Talk It Up** (5.8)*** 5 bolts, Tygress Distenfeld[101]. Climb the choss to a ledge on the left, then on or right of the huge Texas-shaped right-facing flake. Bonk it for a nice bass drum sound.

> a. toprope: **Choss it Up** (5.10c TR)*** Anthony Stevens. Set TR on Talk It Up. Belay well left, wedged between the tree and cliff to prevent the climber swinging into the belayer-side rope. Start on Schizophrenic Calisthenics. Climb up the mini-dihedral left of SC's Bolt 1, over the mini-roof, then arc gradually to the left towards the last bolt of Talk It Up. A fun route on suspect-looking holds risking a big, safe swing.

---

[100] Search www.youtube.com for "woody tinny".
[101] Tygress (Rona) Distenfeld started climbing just short of age 50 and generally hasn't stopped. The hammer drills for bolting routes are bigger than she is.

/ b. traverse: **R.O.S.**[102] (5.10b G/PG)*** 6 bolts, Mountain Madness. Best route in the whole Rhetoric/Dead Cats area. Start on Lessa (see Dead Cats Wall) and traverse left on all the big holds across the entire Rhetorick Wall. The "PG" rating is for the second: cleaning Bolt 5 risks a down-and-left swing fall onto Talk It Up's ledge. Reduce the risk greatly by continuing past the bolt (pulling a little rope) before cleaning it. The belayer then quickly takes up the slack, leaving you exposed to a much smaller swing fall. The route traverses as follows: Bolt 1 of Lessa, Bolt 2 of Punctuation Mark, long draw on Bolt 2 of Rhetorick, mild runout to Bolt 4 of The Quest for Zest (which is at 10 o'clock from the previous clip), Bolt 2 of Schizophrenic Calisthenics, then finish on Talk It Up's last bolt and anchors.

2. **Schizophrenic Calisthenics** (5.12d R)* 2 bolts, Joe Sulak, bb Josh Pierce. Runout to Bolt 2 on easy terrain. Joe says it's a horrible route. Someone else said "3 star movement on 2 star rock." Past guidebooks reported that you climb left of the anchors. This is not the case; Joe says it calls for some cool beta.[103]

3. **The Quest for Zest** (5.12c)* 4 bolts, Matt Twyman, Joe Sulak. Originally named Twyman's Folly[104]. Start in a small dihedral at a diagonal down-facing thin crack. Bolt 1 is really low (6' up), for rope management.

c. variation: **Summon** (5.13a R)*** 4 bolts, Clayton Reagan. Start on Twyman's Folly, bypass the drilled pocket, and cut left at the steep section onto Schizophrenic Calisthenics.

4. **Rhetorick** (5.12a)*** 3 bolts, Rick Watson[105].

5. **Punctuation Mark** (5.12a)* 3 bolts, Rick Watson. Climb the blank water streak, staying off of all the big holds on the right. Some will say that's contrived...we quote an old timer: "All climbing is contrived, because you can always walk around to the top."

6' space between Punctuation Mark and the leftmost route on Dead Cats Wall.

---

[102] Run-on sentence.

[103] Texas Limestone II called this route Bad Language (5.12-) for reasons unknown. Austin Rock then listed Schizophrenic Calisthenics correctly, but also listed Bad Language (5.12a) between The Quest for Zest (Twyman's Folly) and Rhetorick, where there are no bolts.

[104] Red tags on a route are a sign to stay off it until the bolter can accomplish the first ascent. Many have objected to the practice, perhaps because no time limit was ever adopted. Joe had a red tag on this route for a while, but Matt was told Joe's red tag had been up for two years, so he and his friend worked the route, and Matt made the FA. Joe learned of this and said, fine, name the route. Matt said "no mang, it's your route. You name it." Joe said "No, FA's get to name routes." Matt said "come ow, dawg, don't make me name it." And Joe said, "fine, I'll name it." So Joe named it Twyman's Folly. Later he lamented and changed the name.

Why do some bolters want red tags and first ascents? Most FA's are historically irrelevant, and most routes can be sent by a lot of climbers in town, that afternoon. But, go through the entire process of obtaining drill and tools, buying hardware, investigating and cleaning a line, applying to a committee, bolting it, and working it, and you'll see how some bolters feel. You want to climb it before any vicegrippers break holds. You want naming rights to complete the creative experience, and so you don't have to remember the route by some name you don't like. You want the visceral experience of solving a problem before anyone else. For your hard work, you deserve it all...even money!

But red tags fail. They are like the wrapper on a Christmas present. A beacon saying "SEND ME FOR A CHEAP FA!" A smart bolter never trusts them. Bolters have to resort to silly tactics. Bolt it on a Monday, rest, and try to send it that day. Come back each day to try it; pull the hangers Friday evening so it doesn't get stolen over the weekend. Heck, Joe borrowed an idea from others and locked pots and pans on the bolts to keep others from stealing the FA. Some bolters just wire their routes on TR before bolting, kind of spoiling the adventure. Others just use the easier, time-proven tactic of "oh, I sent it already."

[105] Rick was working on a PhD in American Studies, when climbing and bolting took over. He and Kirk Holladay started a guiding service, Rock-About, in 2001.

Reimers

b.

c.

① ② ③ ④ ⑤

Reimers

82

Reimers (north band): **Dead Cats Wall**

Sun conditions: Sun hits it hard around 1pm, though 5-6 routes get tree shade.
Approach: 6 minutes via the Arbor Wall trail described at the start of this chapter.
GPS @ low trail way below leftmost routes: N30°21.832' W98°07.545' (30.363867 -98.12575)
GPS @ rightmost route (Centipede): N30°21.818' W98°07.541' (30.363633 -98.125683)

The busiest wall at Reimers. Great for warmups and projecting quality routes from 5.9 to 5.10+. Beginners have four routes under 5.9 plus a few more on the neighboring walls. There was a law in the 90's dictating that Dead Cats routes shall have no more than 3 bolts. This wall sees an injury every year or two and many near-misses due to leader errors, poor lead-belaying[106], and some runouts. The wall was named after a nearby tombstone that read, "Here lies Emma Peel. She was a good cat." Steven Shortnacy called the left section he bolted Live Cats Wall.

See also Digitron Boulder (page 130) for sport routes and bouldering down-hill from this wall.

Steven Shortnacy   Steven & Calvin, 2011

1. **Lessa the Puramatic 6000 Kitty** (5.5)*** 2 bolts, Stephen Shortnacy[107]. A lot of people's first lead, this route gets great remarks in www.rockclimbing.com. A small tree grows on the cliff on a ledge just right of the start. The route's starting foot holds include a gnarly left-facing flake.

2. **Rolly Poly Cocoa Kitty** (5.7)*** 3 bolts, Stephen Shortnacy. Another popular first lead.

Low Triangular Mini-Roof, 8' over a mini-ledge and over a 100° angle dihedral.

3. **Hissing Cloe** (5.7 PG)*** 3 bolts, Stephen Shortnacy. Starts where gray rock on the left meets burnt orange (Go UT!) on the right and the triangular mini-roof. Runout.

White Streak (the left of two big white streaks the wall) running down a high dihedral and down the entire cliff.

4. **Clawing Zoë** (5.6/5.7 PG)* 3 bolts, Stephen Shortnacy. Climb 6' left of a small tree on a ledge half way up the cliff. Runout on a slab fall to the anchors; reachy anchor clip creates the slash grade.

The next two routes share bolts 1 & 2:

5. **Smelly Cat Calvin** (5.8)*** 3 bolts, Stephen Shortnacy. Bolts 1 and 2 are just right of the white streak. Use a stick clip the first time up.

6. **Great Unknown** (5.11a)* 4 bolts, John Gonzales. Bolt 4 is hidden. After two bolts, climb right and up onto the left side of the bulge described below. The anchors are below the cactus. Leading is better than TRing so your hand doesn't compete with the rope for the crux hold.

---

[106] Lead belayers should always stand, stay near the area under the first bolt, and maintain only a mild arc in the rope when not feeding for a clip. Belayers should never move their break hand off the rope – not even when using a Gri-Gri. (Find Gri-Gri instructions for this at www.petzl.com.) Lead belaying is tricky. Seek instruction/mentoring beyond your first lead-belay class.

[107] Stephen bolted routes here to give his wife something to climb. His wife named them after their five cats. Four of them are still alive! Lessa, the loud purring one, is freaking 20 years old. She and Cocoa were found at a truck stop. Cocoa was huge, but still lived to age 14. Calvin was neglected by a neighbor, so the Shortnacy's adopted him. Back then, he had anorexia/bulimia and really smelly turds. He got better. Cloe is a calico, which go from seemingly normal to crazy in an instant. She hisses at all other cats except daughter Zoe. They found Cloe in a neighbor's trash can with the lid shut tight. They found Zoe in a rabbit cage with no food nor water. She's fine but won't be held. Stephen wrecked his body via hard climbing. The Shortnacys now teach tango classes.

Big 20' wide bulge at clifftop, over a large tan bowl that the next two routes climb.

7. **Mario's Route** (5.12a)*** 4 bolts, Mario Cantu. Centered over the big choss section under the 20' wide bulge.

8. **Ralph's Route** (5.11c)* 3 bolts, Ralph Vega. The rightmost route on the big overhanging chossy spot. Nice one-and-a-half-move wonder.

9. **Hello Kitty** (5.10a)*** 3 bolts, Ralph Vega. Starts on the big double-pocket handle bar.

10. **Scott's Pelotas**[108] (5.8)*** 3 bolts, Scott Hinton. Nice warmup.

11. **Water Ballet** (5.10b)*** 3 bolts, Scott Hudson, Jean Hudson. Climb left of the water streak and over a small cave above Bolt 2. *Beta.*[109]

   toprope: **Emma Peel** (5.11b TR)*. Climb the water streak under the strict "belly rule" composed by Karl Vochatzer: thine belly shall always stay overlapping the white water streak, whilst hands and feet go anywhere. A surprisingly fun contrivance.

---

[108] Pelotas is a part of the male anatomy. Scott's friends named the route after he moved away, based on certain shorts he was wearing during a climbing session.

[109] The cave topout can be done elegantly (directly over the water streak). Miss the beta and you'll go left and away from Bolt 3, up, traverse the ledge with the tree in your face, and curse our three stars.

White Streak (the right of two big white streaks on the wall) runs off a ledge near anchors and down the entire cliff.

FIXED/4 BOLTS

12. Backflip (5.9 R)*** 3 bolts, Curtis Mai, Todd McCray. Climb the line right of the small cave. Backflip sees inverted (head-first) fall injuries: blankness forces leaders above and right of Bolt 3; then they let the rope get behind their leg and fall while traversing left towards the anchors. If you're tall enough, traverse on low hand holds so your feet stay below Bolt 3. We clip Bolt 3 with a quickdraw, then hang a single biner upside down on Bolt 3 and clip it to reduce fall distance a bit and to keep the rope's position more stationary. The quickdraw backs up the single biner, which might get cross loaded in a fall.[110]

Low-cut tree stump, shaped like a turtle, 1' from the cliff base.

13. Madrone (5.9)* 3 bolts, Curtis Mai, Todd McCray. Starts at the left edge of the low stump, reaching a big early sidepull or gaston jug. The route has two paths at about the same difficulty: traverse right under the roof, or go up and traverse over the roof, to the anchors. The low traverse seemed more fun. Todd says the bush at the anchors is a Madrone.

Skinny post oak 5' from the cliff.

14. Dead Cats Don't Meow (5.10c)*** 4 bolts, David Cardosa & Tom Suhler. Start right of the skinny post oak. Fairly safe climbing to the high first bolt. *Beta[111]*.

15. My Name is Mud (5.9 PG)*** 3 bolts, Curtis Mai[112], Todd McCray. Climbs left of the cave. This route sees occasional injury and near-deckings; read this *beta*.[113] Curtis liked night hours, and so this route was FA'd by headlamp. In the poor light, Todd kept attempting the crux and then retreating to the muddy cave to rest.

---

[110] The public was split in '08 on whether to retrobolt the route. One prolific bolter recently said, "This entire bolt scheme is pathetic. Every bolt should be moved down, and a new bolt added." The scheme looks fine from the ground, but the sketchiness becomes apparent after you're committed above Bolt 3, looking at falls onto ledges below you, without an easy downclimb for bailing. Another old timer said the leader must always make as many moves as it takes to keep the rope from going behind their legs. Perhaps this route is practice for that. All that aside, the moves make it a great route.

[111] Kneebar school is in session. It's hard to spot and set.

[112] Curtis was known as "the Borg". An insomniac, he'd work incredible hours during the week and then climb half asleep on the weekends. He was a machine that worked, climbed, bolted, and partied. For a while, he was obsessed with putting up routes. Two of his (and Todd McCray's) best known routes in Mexico are Space Boyz and Snot Girlz, which pioneered their vision of moderate multi-pitch sport routes, at a time when there was only one 5.9 in the canyon. Curtis left climbing and moved on to extreme catch-and-release shark hunting, competing successfully in tournaments involving hooking sharks from kayaks, enjoying a little towing action, and removing the bait out of the shark's mouth. www.sharkathon.com describes Curtis as a "grassfire....quickly spreading and difficult to contain," in his successful organization and promotion of this tournament.

[113] Bolt 3 is commonly clipped high, from a hidden left-hand jug. Sometimes the leader pumps out while pulling rope to clip. With a sloppy belay and pulled slack, you might deck. The high clip is so far up the cliff that this doesn't even look possible, but we simulated this fall and were shocked at the result. New leaders must learn to sense when they don't have enough gas to clip. High clips take extra time, and new leaders sometimes pull more rope than necessary. Become adept at downclimbing to rests or shorter falls.

Reimers

Large live oak growing from the ledge at the cliff base.

16. **Almost Nothing To It** (5.9 PG)* 3 bolts, Sharon O'Keefe, John Parsons. Starts in front of a large live oak growing out of the cliff. Runout to Bolt 2, with the tree in the fall zone. A blown high clip of Bolt 3 could also result in a short visit to this tree. However, accidents aren't heard of (yet) and it's stellar climbing.

17. **Reimerama** (5.10a)*** 4 bolts, Scott Hudson, Jean Hudson. The boltline has a severe zigzag (bolts 2 and 4 well right of bolts 1 and 3). This route has a tasty slice-of-bread pinch on it. *Beta[114]*

  a. variation: **Last Meows** (5.10a)* David Phillips. Climb the 1st two bolts of Reimerama and run it out on easy turf up and right to finish on the last two bolts of Dude, Where's My Cat? Nice project route for those not ready for Dude's 10c-d low section.

18. **Dude, Where's My Cat?** (5.10c)*** 4 bolts, David Phillips[115], bb Jan Salinas. Starts centered over the right end of the long low ledge. It takes a long time to climb this. '10

19. **Power Snatch** (5.10d PG)* 3 bolts, Jay Stein. High Bolt 1. High Bolt 2. Hell, high Bolt 3 (runout over a slab, like at Erock). Starts on a tufa; left foot on the end of a long low ledge. Remove the "PG" by cutting the slab runout to Bolt 3 via a runner on the upper bolt of Centipede. You climb close enough to it to clip comfortably.

White Tufa low on cliff.

20. **Centipede[116]** (5.11a)* 3 bolts, David Cardosa, Duane Cardosa, Tom Suhler. Steepest route start on the wall. Bolts 1-3 slant slightly left, but the anchors cut right.

11' gap to Bolted Like Mex (at Dead Cats Annex)

> I saw my fat cat make this very move early this morning. He mistimed his morning leap to the bathroom sink. He panicked for a moment and then he reached into his bag of cat tricks and pulled out the mantel. He made it. As with most mantels it looked awkward and hard!
>
> *David Cardosa*

---

[114] Right hand on the low shelf, right-foot semi-match to the curved jug just under the shelf, to release the hand to reach high. You can pull this route without the match, but not at 10a.

[115] Dave managed to find a good new line right in the middle of an old, busy wall. Dave recently had a tooth ache, got sick of it and pulled the molar out with his fingers. The only person to ever KO Dave is his tough-fisted grandmother. Dave and his brothers Joey and Donald pioneered Rogers Park bouldering. They sent and named most of the lower grade problems and did not get all guidebooky. Later, others sent what they thought were FA's and got their invalid problem names published. (Dave should publish "The Real Rogers Park.") The Phillips brothers built trails and kept the place under wraps for a few years. When word finally got out and unauthorized cars began alerting the Army Corp of Engineers to trespassers, David Phillips and Paul Johnson contacted the corp and won permission for climber access.

[116] After bolting and the first ascent, a 10" long centipede crawled out of a pocket they had been using all day.

Reimers

Sun conditions: mostly tree shaded routes.
Approach: 6.5 minutes via either the Arbor Wall trail or Canyon Trail described at the start of this chapter.
GPS @ the leftmost route: N30'21.818' W98'07.541' (30.363633 -98.125683)

This wall is the right end of Dead Cats Wall's cliff. The two are separated by only an 11' gap between routes and two post oaks behind Bolted Like Mex.

These routes get less traffic than they deserve. Warm up at Serpent's Wall or on the juggy 5.9's here to prep for the bouldery 5.10's. There's a bee hive between two of the routes, but don't bee a wussy. They're bees, not wasps. Active but not aggressive. I once stuck my hand on the edge of the bee hive cave...in the winter, when they are less excitable. The bees may come out and say "hi' to you or your belayer. From the ground, just spot the cave, watch it a while, and you can tell whether bees are flying in and out fast and furiously, or slow and sluggishly. Someone posted online that they got stung. Joel Schopp posts that the bees look cool coming out their little cave, reminding him of ships coming out of the Death Star. He says DO NOT FEAR — they smell it.

2 Post Oaks at cliff base.

1. **Bolted Like Mex** (5.10b R)*** 2 bolts, Kevin Bentz, Stephanie Bryant. Start in front of two post oaks in the fall zones, making the runouts "R" rated. But a toprope is easy to set from Hilti Highway's anchors. Runout to Bolt 2 on fairly easy climbing. Runout to the anchors on easy balancy climbing, risking a slab fall that crashes into the trees. Kephanie had just returned from Mexico, inspired to place the bolts boldly, as is common down there. Kevin recently said, climbing is about decisions, and he didn't want to see a retro take that out of the equation. *Beta.*[117]

Manly Hilti Power Drill for Bolting Routes

2. **Hilti Highway** (5.10c)*** 3 bolts, Kevin Bentz, Stephanie Bryant. Bolt 1 is way right of Bolt 2. Find this route via a cool telephone shaped hueco under Bolt 2. This route has one of Reimers' best "Oh GOD YEEEESSSSS!" hand holds, somewhat hidden though.

> extension: **Drill Bit** (5.10d). Sit start on the low-profile tufa. Pull straight up to Hilti Highway's right hand starting triangular jug pocket.

3. **Unnamed** (5.10b)* 3 bolts, Joey Phillips?[118] The anchors are right of the big cactus grove at the top of the cliff. Feel free, but not obligated, to start 3' right of Bolt 1.

10" hackberry against the cliff.

4. **The Sting**[119] (5.9)*** 4 bolts, Jim McCray & David Phillips. Start 9' right of a tree growing against the cliff. Bolt 2 is up and left of Bolt 1. There's an active bee hive cave 6' right of Bolt 2. Once climate change kills off all the bees, hit this route allot before all hell breaks loose. See the wall description for more about the bees here.

5. **Mammazz Boyzz** (5.9)*** 3 bolts, David Phillips. Startzz in a mild dihedral split with two popcorny vertical slotzz forming a pseudo-crack. Bolt 1 is left of the mild dihedral. Slight fun runout to the anchorzz, which are low on the upper slab. Lotzz of movezz in a short space. See the wall description for more about the nearby beezz.

6. **Quality Ivy** (5.10a PG)* 3 bolts, Joey Phillips. Runout to anchors on an easy slab. High Bolt 1 is stick-clip-optional. Bolt 2 is left of bolts 1 and 3. If poison ivy is present, please adopt the route and keep it pulled.

26 paces to Serpent's Wall.

---

[117] The crux can be solved multiple ways. One time we hit a fun sequence of fist jam, foot lock, and finger jam, FTW!
[118] Two brothers fought over the bolting of this route. Dave Phillips wanted it to start from the right, to capitalize on easier holds and make it less of a one-move-wonder. Joey Phillips wanted to start direct, to bag a bitchin' 5.10 FA. They left. Dave came back later to bolt it and found it had already been bolted. Joey's the prime suspect. Maybe he invoked Older Brother rights. We almost took the liberty to name this route Sibling Rivalry.
[119] Dave Phillips was cleaning this route and chose to cut the branch he was standing on. It swiped the cave on the way down and pissed off the bees. He hid his face, but they stung him twice. Paul Johnson took a sick photo of a bee lodged in Dave's neck. Once bolted, Dave was in no mood to go back up for the FA. This guy Jim McCray from Dallas came by and piped up, "I'll Do IT!"

Sun conditions: Tree shade on the leftmost routes. The rightmost routes get all-day sun. They're great for cold days.
Approach: 6 minutes via the Canyon Trail, or 7 minutes via Arbor Wall Trail, both described at the start of this chapter.
GPS @ the leftmost route: N30˚21.818' W98˚07.533' (30.363633 -98.12555)
GPS @ the rightmost route: N30˚21.792' W98˚07.513' (30.3632 -98.125217)

With new routes added in 2010-11, this wall is now one of the best warmup and advanced-beginner walls at Reimers, just off the trail to Dead Cats. It faces the Pedernales River, at the north corner of the big creek canyon that's the home of Sex Canyon and other walls. Routes span two prominent arêtes towards the top of the cliff, and they're near a wild pair of 5.9-5.10 roof pull routes on Sunshine Roof. A gray segmented snake was spotted here during guidebook work. We reached for our camera but the battery was shot. Therefore, it didn't happen. Routes went up one-at-a-time and grades might need adjusting. El Primero gets accused of 9+/10a. IRS gets accused of 5.9, or maybe it's 5.8+ or 5.8/5.9. Antivenin is hot off the press!

1. **Slither** (5.7)*** 3 bolts, Jan Salinas, Dave Phillips. Easy runouts to Bolts 2 and 3. The grade on TR is probably 5.6, without having to clip. '11

2. **El Primero** (5.9)*** 4 bolts, Mario Cantu[120]. The anchors are just left of the overhanging arête. Bolt 1 is high, but it's safe climbing to it. Wire this for a great warmup sequence starting with God Bless the IRS and/or Antivenin. The kids ate too much candy Christmas morning. Now they're bloated.

Overhanging Rounded Arête at clifftop. 12" hackberry flattened against cliff.

3. **God Bless the IRS**[121] (5.8)*** 5 bolts, John Hogge. Nice warmup. Start between the two hackberry trees and climb the right side of the overhanging arête. Bolts are placed tightly because the trees are close. Bolt 1 was meant to be a little lower, for all to ground-clip. Whoops. '10

---

[120] Mario first suggested installing sport anchors across Dead Cats Wall, due to the numerous accidents (enough accidents to concern the Reimers family) as gym climbers ventured outside and tried to clean anchors. The demographic was young male leaders, getting their newbie girlfriends to second and clean their routes.

[121] The route was planned out the day of the single-plane attack on the IRS offices in Austin.

4. **Flakey Tygress** (5.8)* 4 bolts, Tygress Distenfeld. Climb to a large left-pointing flake near and at the anchors. '10

5. **Antivenin** (5.8)*** 5 bolts, Karl Vochatzer. Great warmup. Start at the left edge of the low roof. The bolts slant slightly right. Do not climb this and route #6 at the same time. They share no holds but they do share fall zones. '12

Arête at clifftop, slabby on the left side, overhanging on the right side. The next routes start on a ledge formed by flat stacked boulders.

6. **Moroccan Snake Charmer**
(5.8)*** 5 bolts, Jan Salinas & David Phillips.
Start on a boulder to the right of a low (chest-high) roof. Climb the slabby left face of the arête. Do not climb this and route #5 at the same time. This route is like eating a bowl of M&M's while walking a balance beam. '10

   a. underline: variation: (5.11b)*, John Hogge. Stick-clip Bolt 2 and sit-start under the roof, hands starting on the right side of the long horizontal crack.

   b. underline: toporope: (5.9 TR)*, Eric Patrick. Start under the arête, then (risking swing) climb the arête. Looks harder, doesn't it? EP might apply to bolt this.

7. **Sidewinder** (5.10c)*** 3 bolts, Kevin Bentz. Just right of the arête. Tension builds, like your first ever home-alone horror film. There are a lot of moves in a short space.

8. **KB-5** (5.9)*** 2 bolts, Kevin Bentz. High first bolt, and you're committed to make it, if you don't stick-clip it.

9. **Blank Page** (5.11a)* 2 bolts, Kevin Bentz. High first bolt. The blank section is flanked with good holds on the right that aren't far enough to feel off–route. Those probably drop grade to 10d.

Jan Salinas & David Phillips, "Moroccan Snake Charmer"

Around the corner to the right, you can reach Sunshine Roof via a scramble over boulders. Or, go down the main trail's steep part and cut left up a small trail.

Reimers (canyon, north side): **Sunshine Roof**

Sun conditions: sunny early and often. The routes are great for cold days.
Approach: 5 minutes via the Canyon Trail described at the start of this chapter.
GPS @ intersection of the main trail and the spur trail to the roof: N30°21.775' W98°07.508' (30.362917 -98.125133)

This big orange-colored roof is at the north corner of the big canyon and the river valley. It's very visible from the main trail leading out of the canyon on the way to Serpent's Wall, Dead Cats Wall and all other north-band walls. It is home to two wild roof-pull routes.

To find this roof, take the main trail from Sex Cave past Sex Canyon and the King Bee Memorial Buttress. Look for a sign saying "Fragile Area Please Stay on Trail" and a creek overlook. The nearby spur trail on the right is the rough/ slow trail up to Zoey's Wall. Hike 25 paces further to a pair of spur trails only 5 paces apart. The second spur trail goes to Sunshine Roof. (The first is the best trail to Zoey's Wall.)

1. **Deviance (aka. 5.10 Roof)** (5.10a)*** 5 bolts, Kevin Bentz & Mario Cantu. Belay just right of the 9' tall boulder. Super high Bolt 1. Bring a big brush to clean the top of the starting ledge, as your topout holds may be buried in choss. If you lack a stick clip, dig around for a key crimp. Use long draws on Bolts 3 and 4 to minimize rope drag. Bolts 1-3 are on the chossy slabby face, Bolt 4 is on the short right dihedral face, and Bolt 5 is above the roof over the short dihedral. Roof-pull photo-ops.

2. **Double Take (aka. 5.9 Roof)** (5.9 PG)*** 3 Bolts, Curtis Mai, Todd McCray. Climbs over the right end of the same starting ledge as "5.10 Roof". The starting ledge is overgrown and dirty. Bring snips and a big brush, or access by traversing from a long draw on Deviance's Bolt 1. A wild route with unusual moves and a little actual crack jamming. Consider taping to protect knuckles from millions of tiny teeth.

Reimers (canyon, north side): **Zoey's Wall**[122]

Sun conditions: Tree shade.
Approach: 5 minutes via the Canyon Trail described at the start of this chapter.
GPS @ intersection of the main trial and the first spur trail : N30°21.771' W98°07.503' (30.36285 -98.12505)
GPS @ rightmost route: N30°21.785' W98°07.492' (30.363083 -98.124867)

This wall is left of the King Bee Memorial Buttress. It offers short routes for beginners and good first-time leads. TR's are fairly convenient to set from the crushed granite trail out of the south end of the parking lot. Progress conveniently from here to Serpent's Wall.

To find this wall, take the main trail from Sex Cave past Sex Canyon and the King Bee Memorial Buttress. Look for a sign saying "Fragile Area Please Stay on Trail" and a creek overlook. The nearby spur trail on the right is the rough/slow trail up to Zoey's Wall. Hike 25 paces further to a pair of spur trails only 5 paces apart. The first goes to Zoey's Wall. (The second spur trail goes to Sunshine Roof.)

1. **Light Buzzyear** (5.8)* 3 bolts, Brenton Buxton. Use the tree to reach right and clip Bolt 1. Then climb from there, or for a longer 5.8, go back to the ground to start. This feels like a safer first 5.8 lead than Zoey's First Step. Best route name on the wall. '06

---

[122] Named after Greg Brook's daughter. Zoey climbed Zoey's First Step on Father's Day, 2005.

2. **Zoey's First Step** (5.8)* 2 bolts, Tom Suhler and Rick Tamplin. See *beta*[123] for inexperienced leaders.

3. **Maggie's Farm** (5.6)* 2 bolts, Tom Suhler and Rick Tamplin. A great place to teach kneebars. Save time cleaning anchors via a comfortable down-lead.

4. **I Never Called You a Beast**[124] (5.6)*** 2 bolts, Tom Suhler & Rick Tamplin[125]. Save time cleaning anchors via a comfortable down-lead.

5. **Clambering Kimberly** (5.7)*** 3 bolts, Brenton Buxton. Save time cleaning anchors via a comfortable down-lead. '06

Committed Knee-Bar. No pain, no gain.

Pass through a bit of overgrowth.

6. **Sunny Fun** (5.7)*** 3 bolts. Snake your way up this shitty looking route that isn't. For extra 5.8-5.9 fun, down-lead instead of cleaning.

   variation: **Western Exposure** (5.9)*** 3 bolts. Keep hands strictly left of the boltine, working the arête and holds just right of it.

On the other side of a small tree are the two leftmost routes on The King Bee Memorial Buttress.

Rona Distenfeld & Jesse, Zoey's Wall. Parallax in this shot makes Jesse look like a bear.

---

[123] Difficult anchor clip. Tough clips are dangerous situations for new leaders, where you are pulling up rope, fall before clipping, and fall far due to the extra pulled slack. You must master clipping far better than your mastery of climbing. Your mind is overloaded, concentrating 110% on two tasks: 1. Keeping hand, feet, and body rigid under tremendous muscle strain and fear, 2. Like a wizard in the most epic magic battle ever, down to 1 hit point, confidently performing a complicated one-handed spell. In this case, the dexterous, fast, yet relaxed feat of clipping the rope in all situations, be they gate facing left or right, swinging draw, rotating draw, draw crowded against the rock, and rope drag. Lead climbing is, well, as Pete put it…most people shouldn't climb!

[124] Rick had a girlfriend who, one day, leveled a foul, venomous tirade at him. After they had broken up, they ran into each other, got to talking about the argument, and Rick was able to list verbatim everything she had screamed at him. She thought about it and calmly said, "Well Rick, I never called you a beast."

[125] Rick had the rare skill of being able to pick up strippers in a New York minute.

Reimers (canyon, north side): **King Bee Memorial Buttress**

Sun conditions: Morning shade; afternoon tree shade. The canyon's temperatures are cooler than other areas.
Approach: 4 minutes via the Canyon Trail described at the start of this chapter.
GPS @ main trail below Alvin's (5.12): N30°21.786' W98°07.473' (30.3631 -98.12455)

This wall is an arbitrary western division of the Sex Canyon. The right boundary of the wall is defined by Rock Mound #2 and the rounded arête described under Sex Canyon. The wall name comes from a Limestoner route list and derives from a pre-County-ownership destruction of a bee hive, probably to make some route go. Most of the public has been in the dark on route information, due to errors in Austin Rock and new routes done after it was published. Using info from Rupesh and Matt, the following route list is rock solid.

We asked several people if any of the routes above 5.11 deserve the three-star recommendation for road-trippers. Slick Willie got the nod, and the others are considered worth doing, but not before doing taller routes elsewhere. Alvin's sure looks pretty. We want to deal with the poison ivy soon and get on it.

The next two routes are not visible from the main trail, due to vegetation. These two routes are squeezed-together. Left of them, past a small tree, is the rightmost route on Zoey's Wall.

1. **Friends and Lovers** (5.11a)* 3 bolts, Mike Klein[126]. This route and the next route are good, but because this route's bolts are jammed 2.5' away from Snuff the Rooster, and because this route's anchors are higher and invisible, read the following "path" beta to keep from climbing too much of Snuff. This route uses (right-handed) three holds on Snuff. Left hand holds are all left of the boltline and work increasingly away from it, onto the arête, so that you reach far right to clip Bolt 3. If this isn't enough beta, check the footnote.[127]

2. **Snuff the Rooster**[128] (5.11b-c)* 3 bolts, Steve Hunt, Mack Hargrave. Bolt 3 is invisible from the ground. Path finding is obscured by the boltline, so read the following beta. After Bolt 2 you are tempted to skip Bolt 3, since it jigs right and the anchors are so close by. Don't skip it. Move right to Bolt 3 and then far up to the mini-roof with the hole in it, at clifftop. Then reach left to clip the anchors. This dogleg path milks some fun, technical moves. Someone move the anchors up and right, and this line will lose its weirdness and become a cult classic.

20' gap between routes, with a tall 12" hackberry pressed against the roof. 10' wide section of white rock all the way up to a gray mini-roof at the clifftop. The roof has the anchors for the next two routes.

3. **Repulsive Attila** (5.12a)* 4 bolts, Alex Catlin. Anchors are over the left part of the high mini-roof. Bolt 2 is right of the other bolts.

4. **Donne Moi Tête**[129] (5.12c)* 2 bolts, Thu Doan, Josh Gary. Anchors are over the right part of the high mini-roof.

---

[126] James Harrison and Rupesh Chhagan bolted the route for Mike to FA for his birthday.

[127] Yep, grab the juggy undercling block far left.

[128] All the early climbers at Reimers had to tolerate the Reimers family's freakishly loud rooster, cockadoodledoing every 23 seconds.

[129] On a road trip, some crazy gal in her early 20's tried to push an underage friend of Thu's into a tent to perform an illegal act on him. Thu and pals prevented the lawlessness, for which the lad was no doubt thankful. Somewhere in all the confusion, the crazy gal taught them "donnie moi tête" is the (likely broken) French-Canadian expression for "Give me…"

Big gray bulge over small white spot. Above the bulge are the anchors for the next two routes.

5. **The Tonic Clonic Episode**[130] (5.13c)* 2 bolts, Rupesh "Shep" Chhagan. Anchors are over the left third of the big bulge. Uses the left of the two dark pockets on the big bulge.

6. **Bros Before Hoes** (5.12d)* 3 bolts, Tom Scales. Bolts are close to Alvin's. Bolt 1 is on gray rock just left of the mini-dihedral described under Alvin's. Bolts 2 and 3 are on the steep bulge. Anchors are over the right third of the big bulge, slightly left of Bolt 2.

7. **Alvin's** (5.12)* 2 bolts, Alvino Pon, Mark Pell. Start on a pseudo-mini-dihedral formed by facing edges; the left edge is gray, the right is a white streak. Bolt 1 is just right of the white streak. (Note that Bros Before Hoes' Bolt 1 is just left of the left gray edge.) Bolt 2 is at the start of a real dihedral over the mini-dihedral. Bolted on lead as sort of a statement to rap bolters of the time.

Flattened bulge above a short 25' wide section of white rock above a low roof.

Rock Mound #1: large, fractured, flakey, and rounded, mostly gray, at ground level. (See another Rock Mound landmark under Sex Canyon.)

8. **Slick Willie**[131] (5.13a)*** 3 bolts, Tom Scales. Scramble up Rock Mound #1. The route is centered over the mound. Goes up and slightly right. Bolt 1 is a ring-shaped hanger above the roof/bulge. Bolt 2 is above a little 45° section. The high bolt runs just right of the high triangular mini-roof. (Under that roof's right edge is a downward pointing flake).

25' gap between routes.

9. **Unfinished Route,** 2 bolts. Bolt 1 is 6' left of Rock Mound #2, in the roof right of a hairline crack running the roof from a low tufa, blobby on the bottom and knife-thin on the top. Bolt 2 is 2' up, left of the crack.

10. **Out of the Shadow** (5.13b)* 2 bolts, bb Rupesh Chhagan. Shares start with The Tipping Point, pulling a round double tufa on the roof. Project.

11. **The Tipping Point** (5.13a)* 2 bolts and No Anchors, bb Rupesh Chhagan. Cut left to Out of the Shadow's anchors. Project.

---

[130] After sending this route, Rupesh was eating at Rosie's Tamale House, when he cried out and fell down, from a sudden crushingly painful abdominal hernia. He lay on the floor in agony for a while. When he recovered enough to lift his shirt, a bulge shaped like some hideous alien head protruded out next to his abs.

[131] It refers to either our 42nd president (Bill Clinton) or to Ace-Jack in Texas Hold em.

Reimers (canyon, north side): **Sex Canyon**

Sun conditions: mostly shaded on route; belay areas catch some afternoon sun. Other than topouts, routes are sheltered from rain. The canyon's temperatures are cooler than other areas.
Approach: 3 minutes via the Canyon Trail described at the start of this chapter.
GPS @ Blood of the Dead: N30'21.795' W98'07.442' (30.36325 -98.124033)
GPS @ rightmost route: N30'21.785' W98'07.437' (30.363083 -98.12395)

Sex Canyon (which park staff refers to as Climber's Canyon) is a long, overhanging wave-shaped wall running much of the canyon just downhill from Sex Cave. Tufas are plentiful, and the canyon is slightly cooler and breezier than the rest of the park.

Jaime Cavazos, "Super Cruiser"

Rock Mound #2: 10' tall, blobby chossy tufa-fronted, tan with gray streak in the middle. (See another Rock Mound landmark under King Bee Memorial Buttress.)

1. **Snaggletufad**[132] (5.13b)* 2 bolts and No Anchors, bb Rupesh Chhagan. Runs just right of a dong-shaped tufa. Bolt 1 is high at 2 o'clock from the dong. Project.   ⌜?

---
[132] Rupesh bolted this the same day Dave Teykl yanked a tufa off of another route, smashing apart his two front teeth.

Rounded Arête/Bend in the cliff.

2. **O.R.A.L. (aka. ORB)**[133] (5.12b)* 4 bolts, Matt Twyman. On a white rock section and a rounded arête bend in the cliff. Goes up a right-leaning vaginal slot.

3. **No Recess** (5.12c)*** 5 bolts, Wayne "Dr. Thrill" Crill[134]. To ID this route, look for the wall's biggest starting tufa and a higher smaller tufa that sticks out at 45°, perpendicular from a 45° section of the wave formation. The belay is at the base of a tall leaning hackberry with shallow roots. Intimidating due to the tree, cracked/hollow tufas, and (at this time) drippy rusty bolts. This route was considered for an upgrade; see Appendix A.

4. **Learning to Crawl** (5.12c)*** 5 wire permadraws, Greg Brooks. Starts on an overhanging section of stalactites. Tops out over a small cave. Climbers well under 5.12c can enjoy working the first portion. Bolt 3 is optional, useful for working the next moves. It's near Bolt 2 enough to make for slow clipping on a redpoint attempt.

   variation: **Yearning to Brawl** (5.12d)*, Adam Strong. Climb Learning to Crawl without using the manufactured pocket. (Note that two of the three original manufactured pockets have been filled in.)

5. **Super Cruiser** (5.13b)*** 4 wire permadraws, Tom Scales[135].

6. **Learning to Fly** (5.12b)* 3 bolts, Jimmy Menendez.

   a. bolted variation: **Hyper Salivation** (5.13b)*** 6 bolts, Mike Klein. Climb the first two bolts of Learning to Fly, then traverse right to this route's own bolt, then to Bolus' third bolt, then finish on Bolus. Don't traverse too high, or else you're on Pavlovian Response. This variation provides (*beta spoiler*) a sustained alternative to Bolus, using the hard moves on Learning to Fly and the hard traverse to Bolus.

   variation on a bolted variation: **Pavlovian Response** (5.12b-c)* Jordan DeLong[136], Thu Doan. Go high on the Hyper Salivation traverse section.

7. **Bolus**[137] (5.12d)*** 5 bolts, Mike Klein. Starts 6' left of the 6' tall black streak. Bolt 5 is invisible from the ground.

6' Tall Black Streak spanning the bottom of the wave section.

8. **Love is a Fist** (5.12c)*** 6 bolts, Josh Pierce. Starts right of the 6' tall black streak.

9. **Let Them Eat Flake** (5.11d)*** 5 bolts, Jeff Jackson.

   extension: (5.12a)*** 5 bolts, Jeff Jackson. Top out. Most routes in the canyon were originally designed to top out.

---

[133] ORB (Over-Rated Bullshit was its original name, then Matt settled on O.R.A.L., which stands for Over-Rated Asshole League. It's said Matt was in his over rated period, somewhat like Picasso's blue period.)

[134] The route is named after the chorus of a Nirvana tune. Wayne once BASE-jumped 200' across from the RLM building on the U.T. campus, grabbed his chute and jumped into a waiting pickup truck. Later he jumped alone at Mt. Evans, Colorado, but winds accelerated him into a boulder at the landing. He lay for three days and cold nights in shorts and a light jacket, with a compound-fractured femur, broken feet, ruined elbows, extensive face and skull fractures and frontal lobe damage. Finding him in a huge field of talus was pretty much a miracle. After surgeries and massive facial reconstruction, a doctor said this type of brain injury dampens impulse control and the ability to stay socially acceptable. Friends commented that these parts of his brain weren't working well anyway! Six months later, he looked just fine. His sense of smell is gone. The jump occurred the day before his first job, at the CDC in Fort Collins, where he works to this day on the dengue virus.

[135] Tom developed McKinney Falls bouldering. He had a strong reverence for the band Fu Manchu. The names of a lot of the classics at McKinney are Fu Manchu references.

[136] A few years ago, Jordan was known for being one of the skinniest 5.13 climbers, with an incongruous inability to pull V4 boulder problems. He was proof of the power of technique and connective tissues over muscle. He eventually bulked up for bouldering at Hueco. Way back, Jordan was a lively online presence and garnered at least two threats of assault.

[137] (from Latin b*olus*, ball), a wad of chewed food ready for swallowing.

A scramble-up ledge has a narrow break between these two routes. Clifftop cactus is between Flake's and Blood's anchors.

10. **Blood of the Dead**[138] (5.11c)*** 3 bolts, Joe Sulak. Start on a suspect-looking (but long-surviving) flake. Go up, then traverse left a little on a horizontal band of holds till underneath Bolt 3.

11. **Telegraph Road** (5.11c)* 5 bolts, Greg Brooks. Start on the right end of Blood's starting boulder. The anchors got moved down, so the last bolt is optional. The last couple bolts slant right a little towards anchors on the right end of the upper roof.

25' gap between routes
Graffiti (a weird face) below a low mini-roof.

12. **Dark Energy** (5.12b)*** 5 bolts, Matt Twyman. Belay from the ledge to avoid rope drag. Bolt 1 is left of the main boltline, which is 6' left

[138] This route's holds were sharp for a while and made Joe bleed every time he got on it. After watching a B-horror flick, Joe named this "Sangre del Muerte," the Spanish version of the name. We would restore the original Spanish, but "Blood of the Dead" is just too fucking cool.

Reimers

of the big weird tufa on Mistaken Identity. Traverse right on a mild runout to Bolt 2, then up and right on Bolts 3-4. Bolt 5 is just above the roof. Matt says the progression of moves and the crux represent the universe and its death in a Big Rip, in which first galaxies lose sufficient gravitational pull to hold them together, then stars and planets are similarly torn apart, and finally all atoms explode to smithereens. Except, fortunately, after the crux, an unforeseen force sucks everything back in. '12

13. **Mistaken Identity** (5.11c)*** 4 bolts, Greg Brooks. The route's boltline is 10' right of the weird silver graffiti face below the starting roof. It starts pulling a low roof forming the bottom of the rest of the route's wave formation. Bolt 1 is just above the low roof. Huge gnar choss and gray blobs flank the middle of the route on the right side. The route works up and left.

Skinny, sickly downward-pointing tree growing out of a tall slot above the roof above the ledge.

14. **High Anxiety** (5.10b / 5.10c)*** 4 bolts, Mario Cantu, Chris Sandoval. The trail narrows between the route's choss scramble-up and a 6' tall pointy boulder. The route climbs through a tall slot with a skinny downward-pointing tree growing from it. It climbs cool formations with fun footwork. It's a great project route for low 5.10 climbers, or hit it on your way out for a decent well-bolted burn. Or, it's a convenient warmup for the hard canyon routes.

15. **Pulmonary Choss** (5.11c)*** 3 bolts, Mike Klein. Bolt 1 is under a diagonal-running inverted ramp. Bolt 2 is up and right. Come face-to-face with a wild array of broken-graham-cracker rock, then climb to wild moves, a flat tufa, and bizarre shaped holds. The repulsive name may keep people off this route as much as the suspicious (but hard) rock. Butt ugly from the ground — get your butt on this route.

Sun conditions: Shaded climbing and belaying.
Approach: 2 minutes via the Canyon Trail described at the start of this chapter.
GPS @ rightmost route: N30°21.789' W98°07.407' (30.36315 -98.12345)

Sex Cave (which park staff call Climber's Cave) is a picturesque stalactite filled cave full a fun, sheltered from sun and rain. Most routes have some bad falls, due to the raised landings underneath them. Spider Grind is all-air, and Lip-o-suction is usually all air. Mud Lip is safe. 5.10 climbers ought to ignore the grade and work the roof section of Lip-o-suction, which runs about 5.10c when wired. Also work Spider Grind, whose grade is largely on endurance. The cave's bouldering is good, and there's a head-lamp V5 traverse deep in the cave.

Roger Hurtado, "GLAMorous Pink Elephant"

Big Cave Roof. Bolts of routes 2-3 are the only ones visible on the left end of the roof. Laputa's bolts traverse the entire headwall above the roof. Routes 1 and 3-10 all start on the raised landing at the roof's right end.

1. **Laputa**[139] **(5.12b)* 10-11 bolts & belay station, 2 pitches,** Matt Twyman. This route was under development, as of this writing. Climb Lip-o-suction to the body-sized slots on the headwall left of the boltline. Traverse left on a Laputa bolt, Donkey Lady's Bolt 5, Elephant Man's Bolt 6, and continue on more Laputa bolts to a belay station on the massive stalactite that resembles a floating castle. As of this writing, a 2nd pitch is expected to traverse the wave shaped wall and top out at a bulge to anchors over a platform just below the clifftop. Lipo always sees traffic; as a courtesy, consider reaching back to strip Lipo draws as you climb. '12

2. **Hungry Horny Ghost (5.unknown**[140]**) 5 bolts,** bb Rupesh Chhagan. Starts near the left end of the roof, low over the floor of the cave. Pulls small tufas to the face, clipping the two roof bolts, the first bolt of 38 Special on the face just past the roof, and finishes on 38 Special. The roof bolts are a little hard to spot; get deep under there and look around.

3. **Project (5.13d-5.14) 11 bolts.** Climb the following two pitches without rest. A single rope would go through three 90° turns, so use the two-rope belay technique described under Donkey Lady.

---

[139] aka. Castle in the Sky. Laputa is a Jonathan Swift novel and a floating island in the novel. It's also a floating city in the animated film Castle in the Sky.
[140] Was 5.13c-d prior to holds breaking. Now the route might be stillborn.

a. Pitch 1: **Roman Orgy** (5.13b)*** 8 bolts & 38 Special's 1st bolt, Mike Klein. This spectacle starts Elephant Man and arcs under the curving roof edge to end at 38 Special's Bolt 1. The bolt sequence runs: Bolts 1-3 of Elephant Man, then 5 independent bolts, the 1st of which is just beyond and left of Elephant Man's Bolt 4. Currently some of those 5 bolts' hangers are missing. End on 38 Special's Bolt 1. Assuming this route gets restored, the thick mosses on the stalactites are Off Route, you don't need them, and the better footholds are off the moss anyway.   '05

b. Pitch 2: **38 Special**[141] (5.13c)* 3 bolts, Mike Klein. To do this pitch without Roman Orgy, hang a sling on Bolt 1 and pull up. Bolt 1 is just over the roof, 6' from the last bolt of Roman Orgy and 6' feet from the last roof bolt of Hungry Horny Ghost. Climb the wave-shaped headwall.

4. **Elephant Man** (5.13a)*** 7 bolts (4 are permadraws), Duane Raleigh[142], Jack Mileski. Starts in the cave left of Lip-o-suction's bolts. Climb the roof stalactites on 4 bolts and finish on the face and high roof. '89

www.toprope.com · Jack Mileski

variation: **GLAMorous Pink Elephant** (5.12b-c)* 5 bolts, Roger Hurtado. Start Lip-o-suction, move under roof at the large hanging tufa, merge onto Elephant Man, and finish on EM's first face bolt after the roof. For less intimidation while working it, stick-clip Lipo's Bolt 2, clip its Bolt 3, then clip Bolts 1-5 of EM. For less rope drag, instead stick-clip EM's Bolt 1 and risk a big swing off Lipo.

5. **Donkey Lady** (5.12c)* 9 bolts (No Anchors).[143] Runout to the last bolt. Climb Elephant Man's Bolts 1-2, turn 45˚ towards Lip-o-suction, and head towards Bolt 3 under the roof edge and the headwall above it. Bolt 4 is about 10' left of the big tufa and barely over the roof, on orange rock. Due to horrible rope drag, consider a two-rope belay[144].

The next three routes share various bolts.

6. **Lip-o-suction**[145](5.12a)*** 7 bolts, Greg Brooks[146]. Start standing just under the roof, on the landing below the line of stalactite blobs bordering the big roof and the headwall. Most people stick-clip Bolt 2. A few do pure redpoints from Bolt 1, climbing head-first for better fall protection. The first two bolts protecting the roof section are on the headwall just above the blobs, with Bolt 2 near the big half-person-sized stalactite. Climb the line of roof blobs, go up at the big stalactite and up that section of headwall. Clip the anchors right-to-left to avoid rope drag when seconding. If no one wants to second it, you can clean every bolt via stick clip. '90

variation: **Lipo Variation** (5.12)* 6 bolts, Russell Rand, Karen Rand. Start Laputa, use long draws before and on Donkey Lady's bolt, and finish Elephant Man. This route preceded (by many years) Laputa, which provided it a runout-cutting bolt before Donkey Lady.

7. **Discharge** (5.12c-d R)* 6 bolts, Rupesh Chhagan. Borrows Lip-o-suction's (real) 1st bolt, last bolt, and anchors. Start Lipo, pull to the face on an independent bolt under the slanting mini-roof that is 3' above Lipo's grand roof jug line. Bolt 3 is up and left and runout. Bolts 3-5 are lined up, close together, and continue up and left. Finish on Lip-o-suction's last bolt and anchors.

variation (13c): Lip-o-suction's low (roof) holds are off.

---

[141] Sent on Mike's 38th birthday.

[142] Duane and Jack took turns leading out to install each next bolt, hanging onto a tufa, girth-hitching and tying themselves onto it, to sink the next bolt, then lowering for the next guy to take over. The bolts were glue-ins which would take days to set, in the cold. Once done, they couldn't wait for that and both redpointed the route. If they had fallen, they would have ripped bolts out and decked. Duane is a partner in the publishing company that produces *Rock & Ice* and *Trail Runner* magazines. He was the first editor and publisher of *Climbing* magazine. Goomba says Duane would run high (e.g. 70') before placing the first bolt on a new route, regularly enough that people started calling him "Death Duane".

[143] No FA info on this bad boy? Really?? Kind of a high profile spot for a route to go in under stealth. Come on--you know who bolted this. Give 'em up.

[144] Tie rope#1 to a locking biner on your harness. Tie rope#2 to your harness. Lead with rope#1, then clip rope#2 into the last roof bolt and remove rope#1's biner off your harness. Do not miss-sequence these steps!! Nervous about a cross-loaded lead fall? Use a DDM steel locking biner and duct tape, or a Black Diamond Gridlock Screwgate.

[145] Early route lists altered this original spelling to Liposuction. Greg pronounced it "lip o suction", a play on words with the well known surgical procedure vs. your body being sucked to the lip of the cave. This route is greatness. One of Austin's most loved climbers, Pete Bishop, sent this nearly every weekend through age 65. Pete likes how this route rejuvenates him at the end of the day, with its painless holds and its load on muscles not usually worked at Reimers. You can often repeat Lipo no matter what you've climbed that day.

[146] Greg did a mixed first-ascent before bolting it, using slings wrapped on the various tufas, a couple of pieces and a piton. Greg was the first guy to really take advantage of hard routes around town to push himself and progress fast, while wearing a huge 'fro. It is said that he never sweats; one time he climbed a route in his slow, controlled style, lowered and said, "I was terrified!"

The next two routes share Bolt 1.

8. **Head** (5.12d R)*** 4 bolts (No Anchors), Greg Brooks. Shares Bolt 1 with Lucky Strikes, just above the slanting mini-roof that is 3' above Lip-o-Suction's grand roof jug line. Head and Lucky Strikes start standing just outside the roof, off right of Lip-o-suction's (real)1st bolt. Both routes have committed sections where you have to make it to the next clip or else deck. Spotters and pads are useful on these routes and Body Wax.

9. **Lucky Strikes**[147] (5.13b R)*** 5 bolts (No Anchors), Mike Klein. See comments on Head. The last bolt is just above the roof near the clifftop.

    c. variation: **I'm Bringing Hairy Back** (5.13b R)*** 5 bolts, Rupesh Chhagan. Climb Bolts 1-3 to dueling slots. Reach right and clip Bolt 3 of Body Wax. Traverse right into Body Wax, up to its Bolt 4, then right to finish on Spider Grind's anchors. '12

10. **Body Wax** (5.12b R)*** 4 bolts (No Anchors), Jeff Jackson. Rightmost boltline on the lower landing near the flat creekbed on a wall full of tufa ridges. Pick up your feet if you fall. Use a sharp belayer and a crash-pad on the ledge underneath the route's top section.

    toprope: **Viper** (5.12 TR)***. Use Spider Grind's anchors and climb the long tufa right of Body Wax.

Queanh Gip

John Hogge not ever sending "Body Wax"

At this spot, the creek widens out downstream (left, when facing the routes).

11. **Spider Grind**[148] (5.11b)*** 4 bolts, David Cardosa[149], Tom Suhler, Chris Suhler, Duane Cardosa. Climb a short span to the roof and traverse left. Bolt 1 is the left of only two boltlines in the creek's short wall before the creek widens and drops down to the lower starts of Body Wax/ Lucky Strikes/Head/Discharge/Lip-o-suction. This is one of the shortest longest routes you'll ever do. One crazy day, Matt Twyman, Thu Doan, and two others simul-soloed it. For even more fun, lead past the anchors, tagging the top, and down-lead it (5.11d).

    d. variation: **Mud Lip** (5.11c)*** 2 bolts, Russell Rand. To prevent swinging into the belayer, stick-clip Spider Grind's Bolt 2. Stick-clip and start under its Bolt 3. Climb to it, then to Lip Service's bolt that sits on the left side of the roof's point. Fun climbing and a creepy, safe swing-potential before reaching Bolt 1. Plus you have to work it ground up.

    variation: **Sex Grind** (5.12)*. A long, traversing route. Climb Spider Grind and keep going on bolts on other routes to the last bolt of Lip-o-suction and finish on Lipo's anchors.

---

[147] The route name has nothing to do with the cigarette brand. Mike Klein was so skilled and successful on routes that his buds Jeff Jackson and James Harrison began saying, "Oh, YOU'RE just lucky!" Jack Mileski loved to give everyone nicknames and invented "Lucky" Mike Klein. Lucky Strikes was freed by Mike, saving it from someone who was planning to manufacture holds on it. Jack himself loved masterful manufacturing, and he'd chip high footholds just for Mike (who was the shortest hard climber around).

[148] A huge spider sat under one of the ledges, staring at the developers all day, thinking its little spider thoughts of violence, torture and slow death. Productive member of nature, or heinous monster?

[149] A long-time partner of Dave's said "No one can find limestone routes like Dave." Many developers walked past Spider Grind until Dave noticed the potential. David was known as "New Wave Dave", in his bright green lycra tights.

Reimers

12. Lip Service[150] (5.12a)* 7 bolts, Jimmy Carse. Bolt 1 is over the left end of a large bed of ferns and near choss at mid level on the bulging roof overlooking the flat creek bed. This is the first bolt in the creek, but probably not the first bolt you'll spot. Traverse left on the high line of bolts above Spider Grind's bolts, finishing on Spider Grind's anchors. 🪨🍺💧👤🤸🤸🤸🤸?

extension: **More Lip Service** (5.12a or 5.12b-c)*, Thu Doan. Climb Lip Service, then keep traversing left on the last bolts of Body Wax and Lucky Strikes, hands dancing on the horizontal ledge system just under the roof, then top out on Lip-o-suction's anchors. If you take a rest in the big cave after Spider Grind, then it's 5.12a. If you don't take any no-hands rests then it's 12b-c. 🪨🍺💧👤🤸🤸🤸🤸🤸?

Entrance into the Sex Cave / Sex Canyon (aka Climber's Cave, Climber's Canyon) is up the creek right of the first bolted routes (Lip Service and Spider Grind, both of them traversing the left end of the creek's short cliffside).

Jini Perkins, "Spider Grind"

---

[150] Stephen Shortnacy and others were badgering Jimmy on what the name of the route should be. He named it Lip Service because of that, and because of the holds that are used on the lip of the cliff.

Reimers (canyon, south side): **Landfill Wall (aka. The Dark Side)**

Sun conditions: All day shade and canyon breezes under cool looking walls and comfy patio boulders.
Approach: 8 minutes via the Canyon Trail described at the start of this chapter.
GPS @ rightmost route: N30°21.741' W98°07.501' (30.36235 -98.125017)

Despite the shade, canyon breezes, cool looking walls, comfy lounge boulders, and stellar routes, this wall has not been popular, probably due to spotty route information. Now you hold in your hands the key to The Dark Side. This wall rocks! It also has the best views of the creek's pond and cypress trees. For lower grade climbers, it's convenient to visit along with Shortcake Wall. For higher grade climbers, it's close to the trail, has good warmups, and a few routes over 5.10 to do before harder south band routes.

Landfill Wall is the wide wall on the other side of the creek from Sex Canyon. The Reimers family used to dump trash here. Hike the trail past Sex Cave, Sex Canyon, and the King Bee Memorial Buttress. Turn left to cross the creek (over a tiny water channel and up two slabby boulders). Count 50 paces from the little water channel, along the trail towards Prototype Wall, looking for a huge rounded steep arête under the right side of a roof, and turn left on a steeper, somewhat overgrown trail. It soon goes up a steep balancy slab boulder near the routes.

The trail comes out at the rightmost routes, near an easy-to-identify route, Jugfest, which starts on a big blobby tufa. Warm up on Jugfest or Hidden Pockets. The routes have elbow room! They're spread out enough that the topo photos only show a few of them.

Annette Pelletier, "Monkey Pajamas"

Cool looking Arête across from Sex Canyon, viewable from the trail below the route "O.R.A.L." Two routes are over there, past a lot of jungle. We're scared. We're not going to go over there and check them out. Bushwhack to reach them, or let them rust in peace.

1. **Pika Peak** (5.10), 3 bolts, Kevin Bentz, David Black.

2. **Dos Vatos**[151] (5.10d), Kevin Bentz.

A Huge span of Jungle separates the above two lone routes from Slopeamine.

3. **Slopeamine** (5.11d)***4 bolts, David Phillips.
Easy runout to anchors. Bolt 1 is 6' left of Heathers, just under the roof. Bolt 2 is just above it. Bolt 3 is at the start of the slab. The route has a cool basketball sized hueco. The stick clip is unnecessary if you're tall enough (~6'). Once anchors are clipped, push the tall tree with your leg. Woooo!

Big wide open-book dihedral with 3 stacked mini-roofs at top and center. Mild wave formation spans the left face of the dihedral.

4. **Heathers**[152] (5.11c)*** 3 bolts, Curtis Mai, Todd McCray. This route is 25' left of Monkey Pajamas. Bolts 1 and 2 are on the short wave formation on the dihedral's left face, under a diagonal left-sloping slab. Bolt 3 is on the slab. One Heather is short, another is skinny, and the other one is really tall.

---

[151] Two Dudes.
[152] Named after the movie about vicious, popular high school girls and the actual girls Curtis and Todd hung out with.

5. **Monkey Pajamas** (5.10a PG)*** 2 bolts, Curtis Mai, Todd McCray. Climbs the dihedral center. Bolt 1 is on a mild bulge on the right face of the big dihedral. Bolt 2 is up and slightly right, above the bulge. Anchors are over the stack of 3 mini-roofs, under a wedge-shaped prow sticking far over the cliff. Belay from the ledge under Bolt 1. Cruxy 1st clip; consider a stick clip. Soft belay any falls above Bolt 2 to avoid wrecking-ball impact. This route has the best view of the canyon. Fun sit start, at the same grade.

40' gap between routes, with 2 pointy mid-cliff roofs.

Oddly shaped flowstone. The bottom of it is flat and curving like a tape worm, terminating 3' above the ground, forming a great "ramp" starting foothold.

6. **Tapeworm** (5.9+)*** 3 bolts, Curtis Mai, Todd McCray. Starts on the flowstone described above. Bolt 1 is super high (20') above the right end of a 9' wide mini-roof. You don't need a stick clip if you dominate 5.9 and do the best *beta*[153]. Bolt 2 is above a tiny tufa. Bolt 3 is in a scoop. Anchors up and right. A comfy lounge boulder is in front of Tapeworm, sporting seven cool knobs here and there. The tapeworm offers a fun sit-start, with left hand underclinging behind the formation. You know you want to.

toprope: **Garbage** (5.11b / V2)*. Start centered under the tapeworm, left-hand behind it on an undercling. Climb up and right on the tapeworm to the left-facing block below and right of the tapeworm's rounded top. Traverse right on the face of the rounded ledge, using slopers and the prominent diagonal edge. Top out over the middle of the ledge, on a hidden right hand jug and nearby crimp.

Triangular Roof connected to the Huge Amphitheater Formation mentioned below. This roof is over a wide bulge over a ledge over a roof low to the ground. The bulge's top is splattered with a long span of sprague[154] and popcorn. The Bulge has two routes.

7. **Little White Trash Boy** (5.10c)*** 4 bolts, Curtis Mai, Todd McCray. Bolt 1 is 9' left of Hanging Garden's Bolt 1, on a bulge below the sprague layer. Bolt 2 is on choss between spragues. Bolt 3 is on a white lichen triangle area. Bolt 4 is up and slightly right, above the roof. Poison ivy sometimes obscures the anchors, but you can finish via the variation.

variation: **Trash the Garden** (5.10d)*: Cut right to finish on Hanging Garden's anchors.

8. **Hanging Gardens** (5.12)* 5 bolts. The ledge is too dirty to mount; stick-clip and yard up to Bolt 1. Bolt 1 is 10' left of Sometimes I'm Dreamin's Bolt 1, on a bulge below the popcorn. It's over the low ledge's wet mossy spot. Bolt 2 is at 11 o'clock. Bolt 3 is straight up, 2' under the first upper roof. Bolt 4 is just over this roof's left side. Bolt 5 is at 10 o'clock on the point of the neighboring roof to the left. Anchors are left of that.

Huge 35' wide amphitheater roof formation over a mini-roof on its right side. On the left end, you'll see refuse from the Reimers family dump.

9. **Sometimes I'm Dreamin'** (5.11d)*** 5 bolts. This route climbs on chaotic terrain, including a high, left-facing "blade" formation over left and right facing bulges. (The lower bulge is chossy and right facing.) Scramble up the starting ledge's easiest spot, on its right end, under a small pointy bulge. Bolt 1 is on the right side of a mini-dihedral, just above the left end of the big low roof under the wide amphitheater. Bolt 2 is 3' away, at 10 o'clock. Bolt 3 is on the left side of the bulge topped with white lichen. Bolt 4 is on the bottom right of the blade formation. Bolt 5 is above the left side of an arcing mini-roof. Anchors are just over the roof. Use a long draw on Bolt 2.

10. **Get Yer Fill** (5.12c)* 6 bolts, Rupesh Chhagan, Mike Klein. Bolts are left of the arête on the right end of the huge amphitheater formation. Bolts 1-4 slant slightly left. Bolt 5 is a double bolt on the roof. The right one is older, and it recently pulled out. Rupesh hammered it back in and tightened it. With suspect rock quality up there, best clip both bolts. Bolt 6 slants slightly left, and anchors are to its right. '05

---

[153] The start is about 5.8; cut left to mount the ledge over the tufa formation.

[154] Sprague isn't the most common term, but it comes in handy. A sprague hold is a collection of monos onto which you can chaotically arrange fingers. Spragging your fingers means separating them to pull on sprague. Popcorn monos jut out more, offering pinches. It's a fine line between sprague and popcorn. Climbing Dictionary credits early use of the term at McKinney Falls on Evil Eye, and credits Jack Mileski for inventing the term.

11. J.P. Court (5.12a)* 3 bolts. Bolt 1 is high over a handhold ledge over a roof. The route continues on white rock for 2 more bolts, then it's runout to the roof. Anchors are over the roof.

12. Jugfest (aka. No More Tears) (5.8)*** 3 bolts, Curtis Mai, Todd McCray. Start on the cool blobby tufa over a natural cheat stone. Bolt 1 is up and left of the tufa. Bolt 2 is above and right of a double-triangles hueco, below a jutting arête. Bolt 3 is above a blocky outcrop. Anchors are below and between two gnarly mini-roofs. It's one of the best 5.8's at Reimers. We prefer it without a stick clip, prompting you to do more solid, more interesting beta. This route is like a short first marriage to someone hot and crazy, followed by years of marriage to someone hot and sweet.

variation: **Tufafest** (5.11c)*. Sit-start centered under the sweet tufa.

13. Hidden Pockets (5.8 R)*** 3 bolts, Tommy Blackwell, Luke Bowman[155], Evan Jackson. Bolt 1 is above and right of the blobby tufa. Runout to Bolt 3 over a slab, making for the "R" rating, on easy (5.6) but balancy climbing. This route would be "G" rated at Erock. '05

One can scramble south (right) along and near the cliff to reach Shortcake Wall, but the trail isn't well developed, as of this writing.

[155] Luke has been known for colorful and plentiful hair. Vinny once wrote, "I respect that guy and his amazing facial hair is not to be taken lightly. I've seen his beard swallow gerbils whole and fend off the gnarliest of javalina."

Sun conditions: Morning shade; mostly afternoon shade
Approach: 10 minutes via the Canyon Trail described at the start of this chapter.
GPS @ rightmost route: N30˚21.743' W98˚07.508' (30.362383 -98.125133)

This short wall gets good reviews on www.rockclimbing.com, with all routes averaging 3 stars. It gets regular traffic, but it's rarely crowded. The short routes really beg for sport anchors. In the mean time, consider leading and (carefully) downleading to spare the cleaning time.

The main trail along the south creek bank has a steep spur trail going directly to this wall, near Teva slab. (You can see the top of this slab boulder below and to the right of the main trail.) Or, take the mellower path to Prototype Wall and then hike left and uphill, past Dr. Seuss Wall. Shortcake Wall is separated from Dr. Seuss Wall by a pile of boulders you hike over, against the cliff.

Sarah Moore, "Karen Carpenter"

bouldering: **Calories** (V2-3)***. Traverse the cool features just below all the routes' first bolts, left or right. No need for a pad, being careful over the one boulder on pretty good holds.

1. **Got a Dollar?** (5.7)* 2 bolts, Curtis Mai & Todd McCray.

2. **Crack Ate The Pipe** (5.8)* 3 bolts, Curtis Mai & Todd McCray.

3. **Karen Carpenter** (5.10d/5.11a)* 3 bolts, Brenton Buxton[156], Joel Schopp, Frank Curry. Height-dependent grade. This route and Gut Punch have a similar feel to Yertle towards the top, with the pump hitting as you reach slopers.

---

[156] Brenton is a 25 time (and counting) Pike's Peak Marathon runner. We hiked Pike's Peak in two days. Running it is unthinkable. Brenton is known for never not smiling.

4. **Gut Punch the Buddha** (5.9)* 3 bolts, Curtis Mai & Todd McCray.

   a. toprope: **Pinch the Buddha** (5.10c TR)*. Start 3' right, right-hand pinching a mini-tufa. Climb up, into the tall grass under the tree, then move left.

9" Post Oak 3' from cliff, 6' right of Gut Punch the Buddha.

5. **Fat Chicks Tryin' To Be Sexy** (5.10a)* 3 bolts, Curtis Mai & Todd McCray.[157]

6. **Hat Dance** (5.9 PG)* 3 bolts, Curtis Mai & Todd McCray. Runout on easy terrain. For more fun, and more jugs, tie in and sit start.

   free solo: (5.6). Climb the natural slab/stairs right of Hat Dance. It's a nice fast access to route anchors along the south band; however, the downclimb is harder than 5.6. You can also use this route while someone's taking their time leading Hat Dance to solo, beat them to their anchors, and so demonstrate that all climbing is contrived.

Pile of boulders; hike 27 rugged paces south (right) over the boulder pile to Dr. Seuss Wall.

Reimers (south band): **Dr. Seuss Wall**

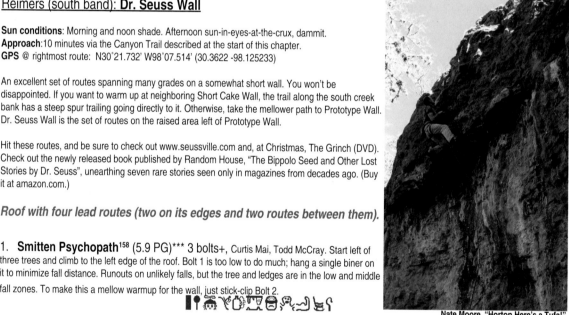

Nate Moore, "Horton Here's a Tufa!"

Sun conditions: Morning and noon shade. Afternoon sun-in-eyes-at-the-crux, dammit.
Approach:10 minutes via the Canyon Trail described at the start of this chapter.
GPS @ rightmost route: N30°21.732' W98°07.514' (30.3622 -98.125233)

An excellent set of routes spanning many grades on a somewhat short wall. You won't be disappointed. If you want to warm up at neighboring Short Cake Wall, the trail along the south creek bank has a steep spur trailing going directly to it. Otherwise, take the mellower path to Prototype Wall. Dr. Seuss Wall is the set of routes on the raised area left of Prototype Wall.

Hit these routes, and be sure to check out www.seussville.com and, at Christmas, The Grinch (DVD). Check out the newly released book published by Random House, "The Bippolo Seed and Other Lost Stories by Dr. Seuss", unearthing seven rare stories seen only in magazines from decades ago. (Buy it at amazon.com.)

Roof with four lead routes (two on its edges and two routes between them).

1. **Smitten Psychopath**[158] (5.9 PG)*** 3 bolts+, Curtis Mai, Todd McCray. Start left of three trees and climb to the left edge of the roof. Bolt 1 is too low to do much; hang a single biner on it to minimize fall distance. Runouts on unlikely falls, but the tree and ledges are in the low and middle fall zones. To make this a mellow warmup for the wall, just stick-clip Bolt 2.

2. **Buttered Side Up** (5.11c PG)* 3 bolts+, Josh Pierce. Pull the roof's left half. This route is bolted boldly (runout to Bolt 2) and badly (at the roof).[159] The high Bolt 2 isn't pleasant to head towards, but the climbing is fairly safe. *Beta.*[160]

---

[157] First Snake Ascent, Karl Vochatzer. While reaching to clip Bolt 3, a snake flipped out at Karl and landed on his bicep. He held on and lowered his shoulder to shake it off. It fell to the ground. It was a nasty, vicious water moccasin!! Actually no, just a garter snake. Karl proceeded to get his first send and FSA.

[158] aka. Ragin' Angel. Named for an ex-girlfriend.

[159] A retrobolting is likely, using the conventional scheme of a roof bolt near the lip, and perhaps moving down Bolt 2 so leading is more attractive on this seldom-climbed route.

[160] We clipped Bolt 3 high via a slippery (dangerous) left knee bar; shorter folks probably can't set it.

3. **Horton Here's a Tufa!** (5.11c)*** 3 bolts, John Hogge. Bolts 1 and 2 are left of a large low-profile tufa formation with vertical slots. Climb left of this formation to the roof. Runout to anchors on the left face of the upper dihedral. '11 🏃🎒🚡🦅🏔️⛺ 🏕️

    a. variation: **Thing 1 Thing 2** (5.11a)* 3 or 4 bolts. Start Horton Here's a Tufa!, clipping Bolts 1-2 and optionally a long draw on its Bolt 3 to cut the next mild runout. Traverse right under the roof to the jug just over the roof and high clip the last bolt of Star Belly Sneech. Merge onto S.B.S. by going up and right of the bolt, then come back left to its anchors. Lots of moves on a short wall. 🏃🎒🚡🦅🏔️🏃

    b. variation: **Star Belly Sneech Direct** (5.11b)* 3 or 4 bolts. This variation is full of sneech-snatches. Stick-clip Bolt 1 and use the 3 or 4 bolts described under Thing 1 and Thing 2, but start and climb the low profile tufa formation right of the boltline, traverse right to the right-hand jug over the roof's right end, and pull the roof up and left to the anchors of Star Belly Sneech. Starting right of the boltline, in this manner, is how the original toprope route went, before Horton was bolted. Non-purists can just start left (on Horton) for an easy Bolt 1 clip, then work right and up the tufa formation. 🏃🎒🚡🦅🏔️🏃

4. **Star Belly Sneech** (5.10c)*** 3 bolts, Joe Sulak. Anchors are over the right end of the roof, left of the boltline. Climb up to the right end of the roof, then Bolt 3 sends everyone wrong. Just cut right and up, then come back left to the anchors. 🎒🚡🦅☕🏃

    Free Solo: **Toilet Solo** (5.9 X), Josh Pierce. Start Star Belly Sneech; climb straight up. But soloing is evil, disrespecting all who love you. Don't do It. Thanks.

Overhung face.

JAN 2016

5. **Socks On Chicks** (5.10d)*** 3 bolts, Todd McCray[161], Curtis Mai. Start left of the 6" hackberry growing almost against the cliff. Reimers routes tend to be squeezed, but this one has actual unbolted space to the right, behind the tree. If you feel the best hold selection is out there, tap it. The route name is out of the Dr. Seuss book Fox in Socks. 🦅☕

5" Hackberry 6" from cliff.

FEB 2016

5.11a/b

6. **Blowing Smoke at the Monkey**[162] (5.11a)*** 3 bolts, Curtis Mai, Todd McCray. Starts right of the tree. Mild runout. Like working out on a treadmill, when suddenly a loud crash is heard outside. Running to see what happens, you smash your nose on the closed glass door to the patio. 🦅🏃

---

[161] Back in the day, Todd was an outlaw's lawyer by day and a party animal by night. We imagine he often took the opportunity to say, "As your lawyer, I advise you to run it out!" In remote Mexico, friends Curtis and Trip once had to tackle him, as the tequila had turned him into a crazy dick. (Todd disputes this account, saying he was having fun kicking rocks, some of which hit hit the fire, and his pals didn't like it. They got all Police on him, saying someone might get hurt. They became the man, suppressing Todd's freedom of expression. Todd felt, if there's anywhere you should be allowed to kick rocks, it's in remote Mexico.) Todd teamed with Curtis Mai on many Reimers routes and famous routes in Mexico such as Space Boyz and Snot Girlz. SB took them a year of road trips to bolt. At some point they decided they should bivy on this big project, and so they rigged two cheap Walmart lounge chairs with some extra suspension and spent a couple nights on the route on their portalounges.

[162] Named for smoking cannabis through a rock pipe in the vicinity of the route. (Can you find the pipe?). Rock pipes are a common practice at crags, using a 1/2" drill bit for the loaded part and 3/8" bit for the mouth side. One old timer has drilled pipes at all Austin area walls he climbs at.

7. **Yertle the Turtle** (5.12a)*** 4 bolts, Joe Sulak, Shawn Treadaway[163]. Yertle is a great route with complexity and a lot of moves in a short space. *Beta.*[164] Yertle was "retro-chipped" by parties unknown. After the FA, a left hand half-pad mono was expanded into a much bigger hold.

8. **Flinch** (5.12c)*** 4 bolts, Matt Twyman, Thu Doan. The bolts are over a left-facing flake. Harder than Grinch.

9. **Grinch** (5.12c)*** 3 bolts, James Harrison, Josh Pierce. Easier than Flinch.

6" Hackberry rooted against the cliff

10. **Rolling Out the Red Carpet**[165] (5.12b R)* 3 bolts, Rupesh Chhagan, Shawn Treadaway, Joe Sulak. Start to the right of the tree rooted against the cliff. Runout.

11. **Buttered Side Down** (5.11b R)* 3 bolts+, Josh Pierce. Both this route and Wreckin' Ball climb over a downward-pointing thin crack. Runout to Bolt 3 with a bad-fall cruxy waist clip or 5.12ish high clip. Great climbing as a TR. At least 3 people want to retrobolt this to make it a great route, and there's committee support for it.

12. **Wreckin' Ball** (5.12a PG)* 3 bolts, Tony "Jungleman" Faucett. Both this route and Buttered Side Down climb over a downward-pointing thin crack. Shares a start with 8 Flake (Prototype Wall). Runout.

Brian Mihealsick, "Yertle the Turtle"

Right of here on the same big ledge are the routes on Prototype Wall. The arbitrary wall separation is defined by belayers on this wall staying up at the start of the routes, while belayers for "8 Flake" and the rest of Prototype Wall belay from below the ledge.

My mother had warned me:
"Stay out of the dirt."
But there, there I was
With a spot on my shirt!

Dr. Seuss

I hurried upstairs, and from over the tub
I grabbed a big towel and I started to rub.
I rubbed at that spot and I rubbed it real keen.
I rubbed it till, finally, I rubbed the shirt clean.
But then...*then* I looked, and I let out a howl.
That spot from the shirt! It was now on the towel!

Dr. Seuss

[163] Aka Shawn of the Tread. Aka Tiny Dancer for his perfect footwork.

[164] Many stick clip Bolt 2; otherwise, locking off on the ledge to high-clip it and to make the next move gets excruciating. But that reduces a 4 bolt route to a 2-clip half-led route. Plus, leading unclipped to Bolt 1 is pretty fun when wired. It seems a shame to get rid of that portion of the lead. Well, it turns out that one can skip the high-clip and instead climb past Bolt 2 and crotch-clip it, so low that you must pre-clip that draw onto the rope. Footing is tricky and balancy, and you must work out which hand will clip and which way to rack the draw so that you don't backclip. Rehearse all of it on TR.

[165] Shawn left a red tag so long that Rupesh sent it and named the route accordingly.

Reimers

Reimers (south band): **Prototype Wall**

Sun conditions: sun hits it hard around 1pm.
Approach: 10 minutes via the Canyon Trail described at the start of this chapter.
GPS @ Bolt Talk: N30°21.702' W98°07.522' (30.3617 -98.125367)

Thank goodness Prototype Wall gets afternoon sun, else these routes would get no rest! Many locals start their routine at this wall and move to other stuff. The wall has stellar face routes with juggy low starts. It has a couple of warmups, and it's near walls with alternative warmup material. The routes have more exposure than much of Reimers, due to the high starting ledge.

An aggressive squirrel used to pop out of the big slot/cave right of Bolt Talk's Bolt 4 and harass (and even bite!) climbers. We wish that squirrel were still around for YouTube postings.

Take the Canyon Trail and its south band fork described at the start of this chapter. The south band fork goes along the creek's south bank for a while and dips downhill. It branches; take the left branch going uphill around a nice tall V0-filled boulder. Soon you'll reach Prototype Wall.

The best landmark for identifying routes is the boulder column at the bottom of a thin curving crack, on the right side of the big open area. The smallest boulder, on top of the stack, has the 1st bolt shared by Bolt Talk and Unnatural Selection. 12' left of that bolt is Prototype's Bolt 1.

Immediately left of 8 Flake's start is the rightmost route on Dr. Seuss Wall.

The next three routes share a last bolt and anchors.

James Fierbaugh, "Bongo Fury"

1. **8 Flake** (5.8)*** 5 bolts[166]. Mount the wall 8' left of Bolt 1 unless it's stick-clipped. Climb the long upward-pointing flake running diagonally up and right. A great, exposed TR for beginners. The route is close to PG rated, with rare ankle injuries on lead falls. Shares anchors and top bolt with Bisector and Clone Call.

    variation: **Let Them Not Eat Flake** (5.11a)*. Keep off the entire flake system, staying below and to the right of it. At times you use holds just under horizontal sections of the flake system and just right of vertical/diagonal parts, especially when clipping bolts and the anchors. The lower of two ledges below and right of Bolt 3 is *on*. This and Some Flake are fun when you have to put up 8 Flake for other people for the 1,000th time.

    variation: **Some Flake** (5.10b PG)*. Start Let Them Not Eat Flake, but after clipping Bolt 5, merge onto the flake/crack.

2. **Bisector** (5.10a)* 4 bolts, Curtis Mai, Todd McCray. Start left of Bolt 1. Climb two bolts on the face under 8 Flake's anchors to Clone Call's upper two bolts and 8 Flake's anchors. Nice warmup.

3. **Clone Call**[167] (5.9)*** 4 bolts, Scott Hudson, Jean Hudson. Climb the left-slanting dihedral to 8 Flake's last bolt and anchors. This route seems more valuable than 8 Flake in a warmup sequence. Bolt 1 is just right of the deep part of the dihedral.

4. **Demasiadas Cervezas** (5.12a)* 3 bolts, Scott Steiner. Bolt 1 is just right of Clone Call's Bolt 1. Hands stay right of the starting crack.

The next two routes share Bolt 1.

5. **Mas Cervezas** (5.11c)*** 5 bolts, Rick Watson, Tony Faucett. After Bolt 1, traverse left a little on allegedly painful jugs. The accusations are false if you're careful. Bolt 4 cuts up and right. Folks often set TR via Prototype's anchors.

---

[166] We tried hard to track down the FA of this centerpiece route. But none of the old timers we reached knew. The bolts just grew out of the rock one day.

[167] Clone Call was the second route on the wall and was bolted before 8 Flake. Clone Call and Unnatural Selection were named after Star Trek TNG episodes. We regret that they weren't called The Trouble With Tribbles and Kobayashi Maru.

Jen Knowles, "Bolt Talk"

6. **Prototype** (5.10c / 5.10d)*** **5 bolts,** Jean and Scott Hudson. Bolt 2 is up and right, above a big left-facing flake. Bolts 4-5 and anchors angle right, and the anchors hang over Sugar's start. A classic route you want to project, but there's a group of 5.11+ climbers using it like a cheap whore to warm up. Wait till they're gone...

7. **Sugar** (5.11b PG)* **5 bolts,** Rebecca Gonzales. Bolts 1-3 are left of the dihedral. Bolts 4-5 slant slightly right. Runout to Bolt 5; watch leg position to avoid an inverted fall. A much maligned route due to the squeeze job, this reporter found it as good as anything on the wall, with wild low moves and unpolished holds. "Sugar" uses Prototype's big jug. Variation "Spice" skips it. Skip the scary lead and set TR from Prototype, or lead Sweet and Low.

   a. variation: **Sweet 'n Low™** (5.11a)* **6 bolts.** Climb Sugar through Bolts 1-4, putting a long draw on Bolt 4. Traverse left (to avoid Sugar's runout) and clip a long draw on Prototype's Bolt 4 and finish Prototype. Various newcomers have sent this variation accidentally while misidentifying the start of Prototype.

Boulder column at the bottom of a thin curving dihedral crack.
The next two routes share Bolt 1. Dig that bolt! Sunk in a boulder atop the column.

8. **Bolt Talk** (5.11a)*** **6 bolts,** Jean Hudson, Scott Hudson[168]. Austin's king of face climbs. Bolt 2 is right of the curving dihedral crack. Both this and Unnatural Selection have cool pebbles.

---

[168] Bolt Talk was the first route on the main cliffs of Reimers, circa 1987. Scott used to get several people to TR his lines and smack chalk where they liked bolt placements. They'd talk about it and work to prevent long reaches.

Reimers

9. **Unnatural Selection** (5.11a)*** 5 bolts, Jean Hudson, Scott Hudson. Bolts 2-3 slant slightly right. Easy runout to Bolt 4. Austin's queen of face climbs. The king and queen have the same grade, but most people find one harder than the other, and they are divided in which is harder. Some will have trouble starting this route, while others will have trouble finishing Bolt Talk.

    b. variation: **Half-a-Hoof** (5.11b)*** 8 bolts, John Hogge. Climb half of Hoof, exiting early on Unnatural Selection. Aside from traverse cleaning chores, it's a better route than Unnatural Selection, lacking Unnatural Selection's irritating start and its easy walk in the middle. And the traverse holds are cool. Accidentally sent this while trying for Hoof and exiting too early.

The next two routes share Bolts 1-2.

10. **Bongo Fury** (5.11c)*** 3 bolts, Rick Watson, Tony Faucett. Boulder up the right side of the big boulder stack for variety, or the left side for safety. Traverse right and up over all-air falls till you're onto the upper face. Easy runout to Bolt 3.

    c. variation: **Bongo Direct** (5.13a)*, 3 bolts. Start from the ground under Bolt 1.

    d. variation: **Unicorn Hooves** (5.10d PG)* 12? bolts, Sean O'Grady[169]. Start "8 Flake" and follow the mild horizontal features, clipping bolts on other routes, including a high bolt on Bolt Talk, and finish on Bongo Fury. Bad fall runout after Clone Call's bolt. Consider climbing Hoof or Half-a-Hoof instead.

    e. variation: **Hoof** (5.11b)* 8 bolts, John Hogge. Climb bolts 1-3 of Prototype. Traverse the obvious line of jugs right and slightly up, clipping Sugar's Bolts 3 and 4, Bolt Talk's Bolt 4, Unnatural Selection's Bolt 4 (long draw), Bongo Fury's last bolt (long draw), and finish up on Bongo Fury. Mild runouts.

11. **Her Majesty's Secret Traverse** (5.12a)* 7 bolts, Andrew Gale[170], Eric Patrick, Karl Guthrie. Start on Bongo Fury, doing its opening right traverse and its moves up its first two bolts. Then traverse right on one bolt of its own, one bolt of ReKleiner, two more bolts of its own, then up one bolt and up to its anchors.

12. **The ReKleiner** (5.13b)* 5 bolts, Rupesh Chhagan, Mike Klein. Stick-clip the really high Bolt 2, and also Bolt 1 to manage the rope. Climb left of the cactus. Runout past Bolt 3; cut this by threading a sling through a cave.

    variation: **Lazyboy** (5.13b)* 6 bolts, Rupesh Chhagan, Mike Klein. Start ReKleiner and traverse right on Her Majesty's Secret Traverse.

Hike south (right) till you cross a low bridge. Hike 10 more paces till you have a view of Herbivore Connoisseur (on Mai Tai Wall).

It is a little known but well established fact that Texas cowboys were adept at toeing pockets and dangling from heel hooks. Rope work, honed on the rock, translated easily to the ranch in the form of the lasso.

from Texas Limestone II, by Jeff Jackson

---

[169] Sean wrote the much-needed guidebook Austin Rock, after Jeff Jackson's guidebook became out of date from a lot of new route development. Sean had planned a second edition, and we had a chance to see him as he started at Hand Beyond Wall, on the left, climbing every freaking route one-by-one, to consider 2nd edition updates. His hands-on work ethic had a big effect on this guidebook. Sean also started www.ErockOnline.com and ran it for a decade.

[170] For which the route is also called The Limey. Andrew has freakish 5.13 ability "off the couch."

Reimers (south band): **Mai Tai Wall**

Sun conditions: Morning shade. All day belay-shade from trees (except during winter when the leaves are gone). Best climb in the morning, late afternoon, or all day on cold days.
Approach: 10.5 minutes via the Canyon Trail described at the start of this chapter.
GPS @ trail to Crack Smack: N30°21.679' W98°07.528' (30.361317 -98.125467)

www.about.com reports that "mai tai" is Tahitian for "out of this world." The drink is 1 oz dark rum, 1 oz light rum, ½ oz lime juice, ½ oz orange curacao, ½ oz orgeat syrup, maraschino cherry garnish. But this wall was also named after Curtis Mai. It spans a raised landing right of Prototype Wall, with a great view of the "S" curve in the Pedernales River. Hike past Prototype Wall's Bongo Fury and look for a side trail on the left, which leads up to Crack Smack. To get to Mai Type and Tree, move left along the wall until you're at Mai Type's low roof. Nearby vegetation prevents good topo-photos, so find Crack Smack or Mai Type and use the below land marks to locate the other routes. The route "Tree" used to have a tree, then it got cut, but there were other trees, and eventually few people knew which route was which.

The wall is deceptively steep — the routes with slabby-looking tops are mostly vertical faces. The routes mostly have nice finishes with some tricky, secondary cruxes up there. If Prototype Wall's "8 Flake" is busy, come do Mega Lounge (5.8) which we like even better.

1. **Mai Type** (5.11d-5.12b R)* 4 bolts. Bolt 1 is over the rightmost end of the roof that's under Prototype Wall routes (Bongo Fury and The ReKleiner). Start by dynoing from the ground (ledge) to a block 3' left of Bolt 1. Bolts 2 and 3 slant slightly left. Easy runout to Bolt 3. Runout to the anchors over a bad slab fall. However, it's wild looking up there. Go see! We backed off via careful download to Bolt 1 and un-stick-clipped the remaining bolt. We're a wuss.

2. **Tree** (5.9)*** 5 bolts. Bolt 1 is 6' left of a 9" hackberry almost against the cliff. Stand on the big stump (the route's namesake) to clip Bolt 1. The route was bolted before the tree was cut, so go back down and start on the stump's roots, or start 4' left of the stump (using a right-facing polar-bear shaped blob on the shelf). Both starts are fun. Pull the outcrop to a winding thin crack. Very cool pebbles are a sight at the top. *Mild beta spoiler.*[171]

Big tree stump inches from the cliff, under a mini-roof. Don't sit on the stump — you'll bonk your head on the roof and fall to your death.

9" Hackberry almost against the cliff.
30' Gap between routes.

3. **Mega Lounge** (5.8+)*** 3 bolts, Curtis Mai, Todd McCray[172]. Bolt 1 is 12' up. The thin holds make it wiser to warm up on Let the Wallies Loose. Cool pebbles at the top.

Two horizontally growing Spanish oaks.

4. **Let the Wallies Loose** (5.9)*** 4 bolts, Curtis Mai, Todd McCray. Start over the right of the two horizontally growing trees. A great warmup for the wall. You don't need to step on the tree to start it.

Right-sloping dirt and tree-root landing.

5. **I Speak For the Trees** (5.10a PG)*** 3 bolts, Curtis Mai, Todd McCray. Start over the right sloping landing, on a left-hand pocket and right-hand ledge. Best route on the wall and one of the best 5.10's at Reimers. Mild runouts. Runout to anchors on a short traverse swing fall across the slab. *Mild beta spoiler*[173].

---

[171] Three full rests usually make a route suck; in this case, you're busy looking at what's next, and here the three rests form four nice boulder problems.

[172] M&M were sort of the "Warren Harding" to Jeff Jackson and Alex Catlin's "Royal Robbins." Most bolters back then were climbing hard shit, but M&M were just solid 5.10 and viewed the other bolters as Gods. M&M went into the Potrero for their first time, looked up at the right peak where Space Boyz now runs, and thought, "Wow, wouldn't it be sweet to bag that peak?" And they did. They also looked left where Snot Girlz now runs and thought, "Wow, *that* peak looks pretty cool *too*." Largely self-taught at climbing and bolting, they caught their share of chuckles developing SB over a year's time. But they persevered, bagged both peaks' FAs, and, in the process, sold Mex developers on their vision of moderate sport multi-pitches for the common man. Along the way, Curtis developed his own rope walkers and battery systems. Curtis ended up supercharging lots of developer's drills to perform much better than the primitive systems they were rigging.

[173] Cool contortions and cross moves. You're a snake, slithering gracefully between tree branches.

6. **Crack Smack** (5.10b R)*** 4 bolts, Curtis Mai & Todd McCray. Climbs a lieback "crack" formed by a boulder stack. High first bolt. Climbing to it is easy (power-wise) but tricky. The route has lots of moves. Runout above the upper ledge, which could break ankles on a fall. Theorized safety beta: it might be safer to not clip Bolt 4 high; keep climbing till you're stood up and on jugs. A fall during the standup might fly you cleanly past the ledge.

7. **Herbivore Connoisseur** (5.11a)* 3 bolts, Rupesh Chhagan. On this route is a fang shaped tan/orange scar between two reddish streaks and over a squirrel cave. Bolt 1 is 15' up on the banded slab. Beware of a disguised loose block on the last ledge. Severe slab-fall but mild climbing runout to Bolt 2. Nice face moves. Clean fall to the anchors.

From Mai Tai Wall's spur trail, hike 30 paces south (right) along the main trail to the 6' tall head-bashing boulder and access to Check Your Head Wall.

> Trouble was, we'd been experiencing a spell of bad weather: It would rain for a couple of days, look like clearing, then rain some more. We lived in fear of the dreaded Royal Robbins appearing to take over the climb. Worse, we were in danger of becoming "overtrained." All summer we'd trained hard—eating, drinking, loafing. Now, as we waited out the bad weather, the excitement of the impending climb precipitated almost constant partying.
>
> *Warren Harding, in Downward*

Reimers (south band): **Check Your Head Wall**

Sun conditions: Morning shade; afternoon mostly shaded.
Approach: 11 minutes via the Canyon Trail described at the start of this chapter.
GPS @ trail leading under the head-whacking boulder to the climbs: N30°21.664' W98°07.530' (30.361067 -98.1255)

Hike carefully under the 6' tall head-bashing boulder next to the main trail. This boulder is cut forming a choss mini roof with a point on the right saying "That way to Jade and Crankenstein." The day Rupesh Chhagan showed us this wall, he said the name was from him constantly ducking under the 6' boulder. We hiked with him to Insect Wall to become enlightened on the history of Wild Spider and the Reimers Renaissance. Then, on our way back, we found a group approaching Check Your Head Wall, when suddenly we heard, (Whap!!!!!) "Ouch!!!!!!!!!!!!!!!!!!!!!!!!!!"

1. **Chop Suey Style** (5.11d R), 3 bolts. 5.3 climbing to the high Bolt 1. Bolt 2 is at 11 o'clock. Bolt 2 doesn't protect falls back onto the ramp, and Bolt 3 has no good clip stance. FAIL. On top of that, the Limestoner rating of 11+ is probably sandbagged. Mid 5.12? Someone pass up the stick clip for Bolt 3. Maybe a retrobolting would make this a better route.

2. **Check Your Head** (5.12c)*** 3 bolts, Rupesh Chhagan. Runout over a clean fall. Bolt 1 is above a diagonal left-leaning "crack". Bolt 3 is up and far left.

3. **Swingers** (5.12d)* 3 bolts, Rupesh Chhagan, bb Kirk Jones and Marisa Hinton. Bolt 1 is at the bottom right of a large guitar-pick shaped flake. The flake edge is along the bottom, left, and top. The guitar pick points up and right. The bottom of the pick is a diagonal formation completing the pick. The anchors are up and left from the last bolt.

4. **Pocket Change** (5.10d)* 4 bolts, Scott Hudson. Tall route. At the last bolt, use the arête to clip and climb up the arête to the anchors.

original version: (5.12a)*, Scott Hudson. The arête is on to clip the last bolt, but then move left and finish straight up above the bolt. This was Scott's original style for the route.

Hike 16 rugged paces south (right) to Crack Attack (on Insect Wall North).

Sun conditions: Late afternoon sun, but belayers and starts mostly get all day shade.
Approach: 11 minutes via the Canyon Trail described at the start of this chapter.
GPS @ Crack Attack: N30°21.663' W98°07.563' (30.36105 -98.12605)

This wall has great views of two bends in the river. Crack Attack is pretty easy to identify. Vegetation makes it hard to shoot topo-photos. Fortunately the boltlines are simple, straight-up.

Insect Wall (North, Central, South) was the sight of a renaissance of hard-route development around 1998. Before that, it had just a few routes. Rupesh did many of the lines, but he reported that James Harrison was the driving force behind the development. James is a hardcore adventurer, driving and kayaking everywhere in search of new stuff and bolting routes in the middle of nowhere.

1. **Crack Attack** (5.11a)*** 4 bolts, Jean Hudson, Scott Hudson. Squeeze through a narrow 8' tall fissure just off trail. Scramble to a downward facing diagonal crack with a hackberry growing at the bottom of the crack and leaning against the cliff. A lonely gifted child at an adult party. An excellent warmup for tough nearby routes. For the rest of us, hit this occasionally on your way to War on Rugs Wall or Crankenstein. Fantastic surface shapes and great climbing.

Low Roof.

2. **Three Slackateers**[174] (5.11d)*** 3 bolts, Rupesh Chhagan, Bonner Armbruster, Marisa Hinton. Two starting options, both equally hard. The FAs likely stood on the boulder under the boltline and leaned over the pit to reach starting holds. (They don't remember…freaking slackers!) But you can start to the left on the ledge under the right end of Crack Attack's crack, go up and traverse right. That start is longer and probably more fun, but risks a swing onto the boulder. Runout to the anchors. Bolt 1 is 7' above the roof. Three stars may be a stretch, but the upper section is the type of face people like around here, the route has three distinct styles (as does Crack Attack), and these two seem like good warmups into the rest of Insect Wall.

3. **Power Pig** (5.12b)* 5 bolts, Christina Jackson. Start on the ground and pull the same roof as Three Slackateers. Bolt 1 is 3' above the roof. Bolt 2 is up and right. Bolt 4 is up and right.

4. **Deflower Power** (5.12a-b)*** 6 bolts, Rupesh Chhagan. Pull a white-lichen bulge. Stick-clip Bolt 2 to avoid decking and to keep the rope out of a bad position. Bolt 2 is a double. Bolt 3 is up and right. The world has one less tree and one safer route.[175]

The Low Roof rises up 4' higher.

5. **Dragonfly** (5.12d)*** 3 bolts, Wayne Crill. Bolt 1 is on the edge of the roof at the right of a pair of rimmed black water streaks 3' apart. A big bush of American Beauty Berries (purple in season) grows on the starting ledge. On bolt placements, the Doctor says, "I got a lot of shit from punters of the day for Dragonfly because the crux was a good little bit above a bolt, it's steep so perfectly safe and not a long fall, but you couldn't hangdog and work the crux w/o taking the fall repeatedly."

6. **Malaria** (5.13a)*** 6 bolts, Mike Klein. The bolts are on a white area just left of several big black streaks. Bolt 1 is just below the roof, left of the upper boltline.

7. **Mantis** (5.13b)*** 7 bolts, Rupesh Chhagan, James Harrison[176]. Bolt 3 is above the roof, and it's a double bolt.

---

[174] All three developers cut class, called in sick to work, etc. the day they bolted it. Speaking of slacking…be sure to watch the old movie Slacker, shot in Austin, which expressed the local vibe, back in the day.
[175] The tree was cut after the FA. Rupesh named the route from the tree's potential to pop cherries on a lead fall.
[176] The route required so much expensive glue to reinforce holds that James considered naming it Money Pit.

Short 15' Wide Flat Tabletop Boulder on Mai Tai Wall Ledge, typically with a cheat stack on it.

8. **Scorpion Child** (5.12c)*** 7 bolts, Joe Sulak[177]. Bolts 3-4 are left of the big 8' tall black tufa on the headwall. Scramble onto the left end of the 15' wide boulder on the ledge.

9. **Project** (5.13d/5.14a), 8 bolts, bb Clayton Reagan. Height dependent grade. Scramble onto the right third of the tabletop boulder on the ledge. Bolts 1-3 are below the roof. Bolt 1 is low, on the starting bulge. Bolts 1-2 slant right, and Bolt 3 cuts hard left near the headwall. Bolt 8 is up and left.

10. **Wild Spider**[178] (5.13c)*** 5 bolts, Mike Klein. 2 bolts in the roof. Bolt 1 is left of a half-cantaloupe sloper (often chalked completely white). Bolt 3 is left of a tall hueco. Fun runout to the anchors.

11. **Alip** (5.13b)* 6 bolts, Matt Twyman. 6' right of Wild Spider. Left of a hackberry on the trail. Bolt 1 is on the roof 18" down from the little baseball tufa. Bolt 2 is 18" up from the baseball tufa.

12. **Rotten Oasis** (5.13c-d PG)* 4 bolts, Rupesh Chhagan. Right of the hackberry, centered on three stacked bands of low-profile bulges angled steeply. There's a tiny tufa just below the top of the bulge. Runout to Bolt 4 on easy climbing.

Jordan "Ryan Jordan" Ryan, "Scorpion Child"

13. **Texas Hold'em** (5.13b-c)* 6 bolts, Rupesh Chhagan, Scott Isgitt[179]. Bolt 1 is on the right side of a middle band of three stacked low-profile bulges.

12' gap and big American Beauty Berry bush between Texas Hold'em and Backslider Direct.

Reimers (south band): Insect Wall Central

Sun conditions: Afternoon sun, but belayers and starts mostly get all day shade.
Approach: 11.5 minutes via the Canyon Trail described at the start of this chapter.
GPS @ Backslider Direct: N30°21.652' W98°07.534' (30.360867 -98.125567)

> Never Say TAKE.
>
> *Jack Mileski*

A slanting mini-ramp, under a roof, high on the left, low on the right, identifies the first four routes in this section. Their lines are complicated, but the ramp is a great landmark. Under this ramp is a big American Beauty Berry bush growing out of the ledge.

---

177 Josh Pierce did early work on the route; Joe rebolted and FA'd. This and other classics at Reimers have one or two manufactured holds. Some have proven climbable without them, at grades not terribly higher. Climbers hold their opinions about hold-creation, enhancement (e.g. making a pocket a little deeper), and comfortization (knocking off sharp bits), often ignoring that all sport routes are a manufacturing process of breaking loose holds, removing dirt and plants, and installing hardware. With Scorpion Child, Joe turned an abandoned, already-chipped project into a great route, one that was absolutely not climbable without chipping. Someone else chipped this famous route in Colorado, called The Nose. Chipping can be abused, but it also can be used. May we have the wisdom to recognize the difference. Check out the *Rock & Ice* issue 191 (Jan 2011), both the Jeff Jackson editorial and the article on this topic.

178 For years, Insect Wall had just a few routes, including Wild Spider. At that time, Wild Spider was probably the hardest route in Central Texas. It became considered untouchable for a time and did not see a second ascent for at least a decade. The Reimers Renaissance of the late '90's filled in the wall.

179 Scott is a former owner of both Austin Rock gyms. Before the County purchased Reimers and North Shore, Scott helped them become more comfortable with rock climbing. He pointed out the similarities to other user groups (hiking and biking), describing sport routes as "vertical trails." Park management still uses that terminology on occasion, and it was likely important in putting climbing on equal terms with the other user groups.

14. **Backslider Direct** (5.broken[180]), 4 bolts, Rupesh Chhagan. Bolt 1 is below and left of the left end of the slanting ramp formation. Bolt 2 (shared with Backslider) is on a bulge at 2 o'clock from Bolt 1. Climb straight up to merge onto Backslider, clipping its last three bolts and anchors.

15. **Morcheeba** (5.13d)*** 5 bolts, Rupesh Chhagan, Josh Gary, Matt Twyman. Bolt 1 is below the slanting ramp formation and centered between (higher) Bolts 2 and 3 of Backslider. Climb to the ramp and traverse left, clipping Backslider's Bolt 3 (our Bolt 2). Pull the roof up and slightly right to Bolt 3. Cut hard right to Bolt 4, then up to Bolt 5 and anchors. Cryptic moves.

16. **Backslider**[181] (5.12c)* 6 bolts, Wayne Crill, Benji Fink, Jimmy Menendez. Traverse up and left along the slanting ramp formation on four bolts, then continue up and slightly left on two more bolts to anchors. The bottom of the route is often wet; pull up to skip the start.

17. **Singularity** (5.13a)* 6 bolts, Matt Twyman. Shares Backslider's 1st bolt. A 12" hackberry tree stands about 6' back from the route's headwall. While projecting, Matt bailed clipping the 3rd or 4th bolt, surfed the tree, and got a heinous arm gash. Bolt 2 is up and right, in the roof at a spot left of the cool flowstone below.

18. **Stickbug** (5.13c)*** 5 bolts, Rupesh Chhagan & Mike Klein. Start on low flowstone. Bolt 1 is far right of the thin flake. Bolts 1-3 go up and right to just left of the tree that presses against the roof. Bolt 3 is a double.

8" Hackberry in middle of trail, pressing against the roof.

19. **Cinching Up the Rootlock** (5.13d)*** 6 bolts, Rupesh Chhagan. A tree's canopy is growing left of Bolt 2 and overgrowing over Bolt 3 on the lip. Bolt 2 is at 11 o'clock from Bolt 1. Bolt 4 is a double.

20. **Dreamkeeper**[182] (5.13b)*** 6 bolts, Mike Klein, Jeff Jackson. Bolt 1 is a little higher than that of Cinching. Bolt 3 is just above the funny left-pointing giant ear flake. Jeff drilled a pocket, but Mike was able to FA without it. Get ready for the really cool exit.

21. **Brainstem** (5.14a)*** 7 bolts, Rupesh Chhagan & Clayton Reagan. The route has a namesake formation resembling a spinal cord and brainstem (the thin tufa). Bolt 3 is a double; use the lower one. Bolts 1-4 lead up, then cut left to Bolts 5-7 and finish on Dreamkeeper's anchors, thus avoiding the beehive.

variation: **Evolution of Choss** (5.14a)* 5 bolts, Clayton Reagan[183]. Start on Brainstem and clip its first 5 bolts, then go up and slightly right, past an active bee hive on the right, to finish on Too Many Donuts. Kudos to Clayton for dodging bees.

Hike 7 paces south (right) to the 2 annoying boulders left of the scramble up to Too Many Donuts.

---

[180] It was 5.12d before holds broke.

[181] A Toadies song.

[182] The route was named in tribute to the late Jack Mileski, a much missed mentor to climbers and the school kids he taught in Dallas and Colorado Springs. Jack invented the climbing term "beta". A legend in the Gunks, he moved to Dallas to teach inner city kids. He and Duane Raleigh were the first to explore routes up to 13b in Texas, back when that approached the top of the sport. He developed a lot of routes at Miller Springs and The Burn, and was known for naming not only routes, but the holds on them as well. (Wrath Wall had the Orange Gland, Steel Wheels, Drangonfly, South America Pocket, and the Vampire House.) He'd name every hold on any route of significance. The term "beta" came from studying climbing moves, video-taped on Beta-max format (which lost out to VCR tapes, which gave way to DVD discs, which are getting elbowed back by Blueray… Jack loved to ask climbers, "You want the beta, Max?"). He mentored many climbers, including Jeff Jackson. His motto was "Never Say Take", and he lived it, pushing every pump to the anchors or a fall.

[183] Clayton is known to actually surf in Texas. He has been active in the growing boat flotilla and hard DWS sending around Lake Travis. Clayton evolved in the gyms of Dallas and outlaw climbing at The Burn, a hard bouldery wall with some manufactured holds. One day Jack Mileski was found at The Burn, filing down one of them. Asked why, he cracked an impish smile and said, "I gotta make it a little harder for Clayton." Terry Andrews reports that Jack had magic skills at chipping. Jack might say, "this foothold just doesn't belong. We need a fine smear here." And with a tap of hammer and screwdriver, that hold was gone. Other times he might say, we need a little something here. In the blink of an eye, "Whap!" and the most perfect hold emerged.

Reimers

Reimers (south band): **Insect Wall South/Roof**

Sun conditions: Afternoon sun, but belayers and starts mostly get all day shade.
Approach: 12 minutes via the Canyon Trail described at the start of this chapter.
GPS @ Block Party: N30°21.625' W98°07.548' (30.360417 -98.1258)

The Limestoner route list calls this area the Great Roof. The trail dips down right at Block Party, which is easy to spot with its left-traversing permadraws under the roof.

Two annoying boulders jam up the trail into a narrow zigzag. From the trail, see the cave referenced below in the route description for Too Many Donuts.

Wide high roof over an 8' Tall Ledge with big belay area for routes right of Ship of Fools.
The next two routes share bolts 1-3.

22. **Too Many Donuts** (5.11b/5.10d PG)* 5 bolts, Mike Klein. Boulder carefully up the dirty ledge. No, that juggy-looking edge is not good — slick as glass! Traverse diagonally up and left three bolts on solid but micro-fractured rock. Then cut hard left to Bolt 4 under the cave. Runout to Bolt 3 (on solid climbing) and to Bolt 4 (risking road rash across the arête). A great route for short pupils adept at thin faces to finally pwn their tall masters. Seek your revenge. If you have to bail at the crux, cleaning via downlead isn't too sketchy.

23. **Ship of Fools** (5.12a)*** 5 bolts, Russell Rand. Boulder carefully up the chossy ledge. The boltline goes up and left on a slab for three bolts, then up.

The next two routes share 3 bolts:

24. **The Hard Sutra** (5.14a)* 6 bolts, bb Rupesh Chhagan. Shares a start and 3 bolts with Om Shanti, then goes left for 3 bolts, then goes right to finish on Om Shanti's anchors. Project.

25. **Om Shanti** (5.14b)* 7 bolts, bb Rupesh Chhagan. Start on the curvy crack and pull the roof. Bolt 4 is a widely placed double bolt. Project.

26. **Ill Ninja Skills** (5.13d)* 7 bolts, Rupesh Chhagan. Located at the center of the big ledge, this route is basically "Block Party Direct". Climb 5 of its own bolts, then straight up to Block Party's Bolt 5 and finish on Block Party's Bolt 6 and anchors.

27. **Block Party**[184] (5.13a)*** 7 bolts (6 are permadraws), Mike Klein. Located at the right end of the big ledge. Climb to the roof and traverse left. The first bolt (with no permadraw) isn't used.

Hike south (right) 70 rugged paces to the House of Pain.

> If you fall, I'll be there for you.
> *The Ground*

---

[184] During development, Mike found a huge block with a crack line running all around it. He tried and tried to pry it, but it wouldn't come out. Later, on an FA attempt, he grabbed it with both hands, the rope running under the block. He reached up to clip the next bolt, which moved the rope out from under the block, in time for the block to pop off and send him falling. If it had popped before then, it would have dragged the rope and whipped Mike down under it, a scenario that has killed other climbers.

Reimers (south band): **House of Pain**

Sun conditions: All day belay shade. Afternoon shade until late afternoon sun hits the top of routes. Bastard in the Brothel has all day shade.
Approach: 13 minutes via the Canyon Trail described at the start of this chapter.
GPS @ Jade: N30°21.604' W98°07.568' (30.360067 -98.126133)

This is a hard wall with tall, stellar, sustained routes.

1. **Ivy League** (5.11b-d)*** 5 bolts, Russell Rand. Poison ivy takes over this route — then people earn huge karma points by clearing it. Take up some gloves and it's no big deal. Adopt a route! This route starts 15' left of Bastard's anchors. Scramble up the ramp-shaped part of the short ledge. Rap from the anchors to avoid rope drag. Toproping is doable but you fight the drag. Small rusty bolts as of this writing, but interested parties will rebolt it.

[A future route right of Ivy League seems likely. DP calls dibs. It might additionally branch, cutting left on the obvious traverse and cross Ivy League.]

[A future route for leading Bastard Direct seems likely. Dibs. It would branch right to B.D.'s anchors but also might cut left to separate anchors.]

Sweet Tufas under tall dihedral across from the trail head. Routes 2-5 branch off of shared bolts.

2. **Bastard in the Brothel** (5.11a)*** 5 bolts, Rupesh Chhagan[185]. Use Bolts 1-2 of Jade. Climb the tall dihedral, traverse the face left under the mini-roof, and left and up to anchors left of the roof. Runout to Bolt 4 on an easy section and runout to the anchors. After Bolt 5, you'll see Catharsis Roof anchors (to the right) before you'll see Bastard's anchors. Keep going straight up. A great, long climb on mostly big holds.

toprope: **Bastard Direct** (5.10d-11a TR)*. Set TR on Bastard in the Brothel. Start just right of the mini-roof and climb straight up, merging onto Bastard at the big horn. Bastard Direct may teach you the best way to do Bastard in the Brothel.[186]

3. **Catharsis Roof** (5.12c)* 6 bolts, Rupesh Chhagan. Climb Jade's Bolts 1-5. Break slightly left to a roof bolt on an air-fall runout, to separate anchors. Soft belay the wrecking-ball-fall section: let out two armloads of slack as soon as Bolt 5 is clipped.

Cavason Sutton, "Rain Dance"

4. **Jade** (5.12a-b)*** 6 bolts, Mike Klein[187]. Starts on the sweet tufas. Soft belay as described under Catharsis Roof. Bolt 1 is just above 2 little white puffs right of bigger icicle tufas. Bolt 4 is just above the lowest roof. Bolt 5 is up and right. Bolt 6 is high, above the hueco right of the highest roof

---

[185] Voted most likely to dwarf his own legs with the rest of his body. Rupesh hit a high mark recently, sending a 5.14c at Flat Creek (private land).

[186] Use a right-hand scar sidepull at the last crux, instead of that thin edge usually used on Bastards in the Brothel. B.Brothel can be pulled the same way, crossing into that sidepull.

[187] Mike named this around the time of his parents' "Jade" wedding anniversary. For 10 years, Jade had only one experimental bolt on it (probably set as a directional for TR's), before Mike tackled the project. Mike is one of the shorter hard climbers in town, and he can heel hook, effectively, 5'3" over his left ear. Despite being a baker, he's not fat. In the mid 90's, Mike was arguably Austin's top climber.

Brittany Ryan, "Jade"

section. The all-air runout to Bolt 6 is much loved and often taken! [188] You'll never forget this route and two of its memorable holds. This route's grade is largely on endurance, having no harder than 5.11+ cruxes. A great 5.11+ project is just hangdogging every bolt.

5. **Angular Momentum** (5.11d)*** 7 bolts, Karl Guthrie[189]. One of the longest 5.11's in the park. Like Jade, this route is long and has a lot of character and variety. Climb Bolts 1-3 of Jade, then cut right on a 2 o'clock path clipping four bolts. Bolt 5 is just left of the arête, Bolt 6 is Bolt 3 of Spanish Fly, and Bolt 7 is above and right of a cave. Climb over the cave and right to anchors shared with Irreverent Youth, or left to Spanish Fly's anchors (which have sport clips).

---

[188] Some of us fondly remember the day of local John Dwyer's confirmation-send attempt on Jade. He cruised it all the way past the runout to Bolt 6, grabbed for a draw, and had none left. <CENSORED DIALOGUE>. Then he struggled to take his ATC's locking biner off the back of his harness, and pumped out. John has the loudest voice ever. The canyon shook violently as he bellowed "NOOOOOOOOOOOOOOOOOOOOOOOOOOO OO!!!!!!!!" and took the long fall.

[189] Karl and his partner Joseph Schwartz invented and marketed the world's first "RB" (Removable Bolt), a handy tool for many industrial applications, including the manufacture of sport routes. On steep routes, when the bolter can't aid on anything to reach the next hole to drill, s/he drills a small intermediary hole to temporarily hold an RB and move onto that RB to reach the bolt hole s/he wants to drill. One night at Guero's, I asked Karl for his most outlandish climbing incident. He began an animated storytelling and I realized, yet again, my impaired hearing was sorting out only a word here and there, amongst the restaurant's crowd noise. But Karl was on a roll and I didn't stop him. Here and there I heard words like "big wall… rope…up…crashing…blood…big…blood everywhere…OH GOD…back…rescue..HA HA HA…" and so forth. Finally he stopped and I apologized that I didn't hear the story, but I was glad our other companion (Jaime Cavazos) enjoyed it. Jaime chuckled and replied, "Short story…KARL'S A BADASS!"

6. **Spanish Fly**[190] (5.12c)*** 4 bolts, James Harrison. Bolt 1 is as high as Bolt 2 on Irreverent Youth, on medium gray rock between a white lichen arête and Irreverent Youth's dark streak. We've never seen anyone on this, but two groups recently got on and loved it.

7. **Irreverent Youth**[191] (5.13d)*** 6 bolts, Clayton Reagan[192]. Bolt 1 is centered on a 12' wide, mostly dark streak. Borrows a jug rest hold from House of Pain.

variation: **Irreverent Spoof** (5.14a)*, Rupesh Chhagan. Climb Irreverent Youth but skip House of Pain's jug rest hold on the ledge immediately below its Bolt 4, and the right-hand crimp above it.

8. **House of Pain** (5.13a)*** 5 bolts, Jeff Jackson. Bolt 1 is on light gray rock above the right-lower-end of a diagonal mini-roof. Bolt 2 is a double. Bolts 1-4 angle slightly left.

variation: **Symbiosis** (5.13c)***, Josh Gary. Skip the two drilled pockets (one is the normal starting hold; the other is a 3-finger jug pocket just above Bolt 2). Rupesh considers the moves way better than those of House of Pain.

variation: **House of Youth** (5.13b)*. Climb House of Pain to its rest jug. Follow the natural line from there, crossing onto Irreverent Youth.

9. **Lord of the Dance** (5.13a)*** 4 bolts, Matt Twyman. Start where House of Pain starts. Move right onto Lord of the Dance's line of 4 bolts. Bolt 1 is just right of a really white blocky blob, down and left from mini-tufas. Use of the manufactured pocket is optional, and there is debate about whether it's easier and a lower grade to use it.

6' Tall Pointy Boulder — the base of the next three routes.

10. **Rain Dance** (5.12b)*** 4 bolts, Russell Rand. Runout to Bolts 1 and 2. Stand on the tip of the pointy boulder and traverse left. Bolt 1 is above the steep part and lined up at the pointy boulder's left tip. Bolt 3 is a piton. All bolts slant slightly left.

11. **Strangle Hold** (5.12b)*** 5 bolts, Greg Brooks. Stand on the tip of the pointy boulder. Bolt 2 is runout — don't fail the clip. Bolt 5 cuts up and left.

12. **Velcro Rodeo** (5.12a)* 4 bolts, Jeff Jackson. Stand on the pointy boulder. Super high Bolt 1, 3' above a hueco, over the right third of the pointy boulder. This route was bolted on lead with a deathfall runout on the easy section that has since been retrobolted.

8' gap to Pearl (on War on Rugs Wall).

Lucas Johnson, "Jade"

---

[190] Named after a Beavis and Butthead episode and also a particular move on the route.

[191] This route was a long standing project known as Black Shadows.

[192] Jefe says Clayton's idea of fun isn't sending in front of a lot of people. It's loading the boat with 15 pads and cruising across the lake to crush some obscure V6.

Reimers

Reimers (south band): **War on Rugs Wall**

Sun conditions: Morning shade; afternoon sun. All day shade on Die Hard.
Approach: 13.5 minutes via the Canyon Trail described at the start of this chapter.
GPS @ Natural: N30˚21.585' W98˚07.571' (30.35975 -98.126183)

The left end of this wall extends seamlessly from House of Pain, delimited by a separate boulder (and piled cheat stack) under Pearl. Also the landing area becomes a little wider with more Persimmons. The right end transitions into Crankenstein Wall after the cool arête/dihedral pair and roof of You Bet Arête.

This wall and Crankenstein Wall include a set of mild-overhang face routes rivaling Prototype Wall, with a wider range of grades and usually less crowding. A mini-renaissance of bolting started in 2011 when Karl V scoped out a couple routes on a lousy looking (but good-climbing) face. Now the far-south band has a good warmup (How to Counter Your Apprehension) and a nice set of new routes. The next best warmup is probably bolt-to-bolting Ant Encounters, or any of the other easier 5.10's. Back Off Crack (on Crankenstein Wall) is creepy but physically the best warmup.

1. **Pearl** (5.11b/5.11c)*** 4 bolts, Mike Klein. Start standing on the left end of a low boulder, usually made taller with a cheat stack. The slash grade is for tall-and-flexible/not. Some of the holds are a tactile pleasure; feel around on the edges for sweet-spot pockets. Others are a little sharp.

   a. bolted variation: **Nudity** (5.10c)*** 6 bolts, John Hogge. Long! Start Sunday Mass. Traverse up and left, angling at 10-11 o'clock along the diagonal shelf and across the face, and end on Pearl. Bolts used: Sunday Mass Bolt 1, All Hail Broke Loose's Bolt 2, Grass Attack's Bolts 2 and 3, a lone bolt only for Nudity, Pearl's last bolt, then straight up to Pearl's anchors. '11

   b. variation extension: **No Guns** (5.10d PG)*** 9 bolts, John Hogge. One of the longest 5.10's at Reimers. Start Ant Encounters. Be careful seconding; go past Bolts 2 and 3 to unclip for less swing near ground and boulder stacks. Traverse up and left on Ant Encounter's Bolt 1, Apprehension's Bolt 1, About Face's Bolt 2(long draw), down and left to Sunday Mass's Bolt 1 under the ramp (long draw), then continue and finish on Nudity.

2. **Grass Attack** (5.11b)*** 4 bolts, David Phillips. Start on the right end of Pearl's low landing boulder, just left of the chossy low profile tufa. Bolt 1 is up and left of the choss area. Bolt 3 is at 11 o'clock from Bolt 2. Beta[193]. '11

3. **All Hail Broke Loose**[194] (5.11d-5.12a)*** 4 bolts, Karl Vochatzer. No Dave-kwon-do on *this* route. All Karl-kwon-do. '11.

4. **Sunday Mass**[195] (5.10c/d)*** 3 bolts, Mike Klein. Bolt 1 is below a diagonal right-leaning ledge. Start 2' right of the spot under Bolt 1 on thin crimps. There's usually a cheat stack under the route. Beta[196].

5. **About Face** (5.11b)*** 4 bolts, Karl Vochatzer. Right hand starts 3' right of the boltline. Often there's a cheat stack under the start. Two nice boulder problems separated by the ledge. This route and the next one may have been passed over for decades because they appear like one-hard-move to a full ledge rest and then easy climbing to the top. Nope. Wild, unintuitive moves on this one. '11

   variation: (5.10d-5.11a)*. Start Sunday Mass and immediately merge right onto About Face.

---

[193] A topout hold is often covered by the tall grass.

[194] The weather was great most of the day — then angry clouds began collecting fast. I advised bailing ASAP to the beer-stocked van parked near the topout, but Karl was hell bent to bolt his anchors. Dave ascended the fixed line first and got hit with small hail and rain. Then I jugged up the wrong line, cursed my way past a knot, and got soaked and muddy on my way to the van, as the rain got heavier. Dave and I drank and waited until the rain lessened. Then I went back, expecting that Karl had hiked out or found shelter just below the fixed line. Shockingly, he was on the line, finishing the anchors, totally soaked.

[195] Erroneously renamed Natural. Mike bolted Pearl and Sunday Mass on the same day, solo leading, in an escape from crazy weekend crowds at Prototype Wall. On Saturday morning, approaching Prototype can be creepy, like walking into a party where everyone's sober, the lights are on, and the music's off. On Sunday after late night parties, it's a zombie apocalypse. One friend proposed putting zero stars on the routes there, due to the crowds.

[196] Right foot on the big flake. Dyno (5.10c) or power (5.10d) up to the hueco.

Britta Kakacek, "Apprehension"

Reimers

6. **Apprehension** (5.10a)* 5 bolts Karl Vochatzer. The start is just right of the boltline on a 3-finger horizontal right-hand slot just left of the chossy drip. A harder (5.10c) start is just left of the boltline on a sharp right hand pocket above the mini-roof and a crowded left-hand 2-finger pocket. Climb to a smooth face under a rounded ledge below the anchors. At mid route, you can go onto the ledge or stay off it for harder climbing (10d). '11

     c. variation: **How to Counter Your Apprehension** (5.10a)*** 4 or 5 bolts, Karl Vochatzer. Best warmup at the wall. Start on Ant Encounters, then immediately traverse left to Apprehension. To lead it, stick-clip Apprehension's Bolt 1, or without a stick, lead on Ant Encounter's Bolt 1 and then all bolts of Apprehension. (The first method avoids rope drag; the second method gets acceptable drag if you have long draws on Bolts 1-2.)

7. **Ant Encounters** (5.10d)*** 5 bolts, Tom Suhler, Chris Suhler. Start 7' left of a 6" hackberry.

8. **Mona Peligrosa** (5.11d)*** 3 bolts+, Jimmy Carse. The arête at the top is on-route. Avoid it for a harder variation. Classic sea-of-holds to solve. Scary bolt scheme unless a retro moves Bolt 3 higher.

     d. bolted variation: **Peligrosa Right** (5.12b? X)* 3 bolts. Uses Bolt 1 and anchors of Mono Peligrosa. Way up and right you'll find Peligrosa Right's own two bolts. Ground-fall runout to Bolt 2 on easy jugs (if you find them all).

Dihedral up high; Mini-Roof 3'-4' off the ground under the next 3 routes.

9. **Die Hard** (5.10a)*** 4 bolts, Luke Bowman, Tommy Blackwell, Evan Jackson[197]. Starts pulling a mini-roof left of an 8" hackberry (while it's alive) growing 2" from cliff. The rest of the route goes up the prominent dihedral. Bolt 3 is up and left, Bolt 4 up and right.

Evan Jackson

Rona Distenfeld   John Hogge, "Mona Peligrosa"

[197] Three very tight friends, known for many days of volunteer work rebolting aging routes at Reimers and other Austin climbing areas. Tommy is a retired SWAT team commander and currently works on public safety software. This year, he published "Tales of Travis County" on all his wild stories of law enforcement (available at www.rockhoundbooks.com). Evan once ate 12 chili dogs in one hour. Luke used to color and cut his hair like one of those toy trolls.

Because they spent far too much time together, slapstick mishaps were inevitable. Tommy wrote up the following examples. One day Tommy and Evan fell off a boulder together, and Evan rode him down like a sled to a soft and safe landing, whereas Tommy got jacked up. Another day they were hunting for new routes, and Evan pulled a huge block off into his own forehead, causing a gushing bleeder between his eyes. Tommy exclaimed, "Damn! I wish I had brought my camera!" While replacing Lip-o-suction's Bolt 2, somehow Luke fell and landed on Tommy's head, driving him to the ground.

Pranks were also inevitable. They used to sandbag each other into using handholds infested with "fire weed", a small nettle that burns like fire. On one occasion, they had seen a snake nearby. After just the right amount of time, Evan saw opportunity to tickle Tommy's ankle with a crow bar, and Tommy's nervous system screamed "Snake tongue!" He pounced three feet off the ground and ran like Wile E Coyote just leaving the cliff's edge.

10. **Dude, Where's My Hammer**[198] (5.11b)*** 4 bolts, Luke Bowman, Tommy Blackwell, Evan Jackson.

11. **Unknown Route at Hollow Flake** (5.???), 4 bolts. Centered on a prow below a rounded tower. Start on a big hollow flake. Climb to the face and cut right to Teenage Parties' Bolt 3, 4, and anchors.

12. **Teenage Parties** (5.11b)* 4 bolts, Rick Watson, Tony Faucett.

13. **War On Rugs** (5.10d)*** 4 bolts, Scott Hudson, Jean Hudson. This route is ounces away from 5.11a.

Acute-Angle Dihedral/Arête Pair

14. **You Bet Arête** (5.11c)*** 4 bolts, Kevin Gallagher[199]. Bolt 4's hanger is missing, as of this writing. Start in the dihedral left of the arête. Bolt 1 and 2 are just right of the arête. "R" rated unless you stick-clip Bolt 2.

15. **More Wasabi** (5.12a-b)* 4 bolts, John Myrick, Karl Guthrie. Bolt 1 is just above the curved edge of the roof. Bolt 2 is at 2 o'clock atop the bulge. Bolt 3 is on the roof. Bolt 4 is a double.

Hike south (right) 7 paces to the start of Santeria/Gang Bang.

I must not fear. Fear is the mind-killer. Fear is the little death that brings total obliteration. I will face my fear. I will permit it to pass over me and through me. And when it has gone past, I will turn the inner eye to see its path. Where the fear has gone there will be nothing. Only I will remain.

The Bene Gesserit Litany of Fear,
from Frank Herbert's Dune

---

[198] A girl first proposed the name Teenage Hard-Ons, rifting on the neighboring route names. Before bolting, the name and route were discussed online, drawing accusations of obscenity, objections that kids climb at Reimers, and intensions of shunning the route. (We assume none of those folks ever climbed Gang Bang.)

Bolting a route can go smoothly, or things go wrong and it's a frustrating time sink. Batteries run out before the last bolt. Hardware is dropped. Everything's set to sink the first bolt, and the drill bit is not there in the bag. On this occasion, the developers began cleaning and planning the route, then could not find the hammer Evan had used earlier in the day. They searched and re-searched all their gear and the route's landing area, and finally concluded one or two parties of friends nearby were playing a trick on them. They asked and got denials; they re-searched everything including those friends' packs, for two hours. Tempers were flaring. Finally, Evan spotted the hammer, hung on a tree 25' up and blending in with the canopy. The tree had snagged it off his harness, somehow opening a carabiner in the process, as he was lowered through the tree branches.

[199] Kevin was second author on the late great Texas Limestone II guidebook. He was first owner of a charming VW Westfalia Camper, which he sold to Jeff Jackson, who eventually sold it to Dave Phillips, who built a shanty around it to live in at Monster Rock.

Sun conditions: Morning and early afternoon shade. Late afternoon sun with big tree shade over Crank.
Approach: 14 minutes via the Canyon Trail described at the start of this chapter.
GPS @ Crankenstein: N30˚21.575' W98˚07.580' (30.359583 -98.126333)

The routes start under a series of big-flat-boulder landings. This wall and nearby War on Rugs Wall (to the left) include a set of mild-overhang face routes (most with steep starts) rivaling Prototype Wall, with a wider range of grades and a less crowded setting. There's way too much attention paid to Crankenstein here. Crank's start is polished slick! Wife gets its traffic, but notice triple stars now on other routes, and the Scary Munchies (5.10d) variation. See War on Rugs Wall for warmup suggestions.

Flat, Sloping Boulder Landings under the next bunch of routes.

1. **Santeria** (5.13.choss[200]) 3 bolts, Jeb Vetters. Start on Gang Bang and move left to a bolt left of Gang Bang's choss. Climb over a small struggling oak tree.

2. **Gang Bang** (5.13.choss[201]) 3 bolts, Jeff Jackson FA. Bolt 1 is right of a funky slot above the choss.

   variation: **Wang Dang** (5.10b-c A0)* 3 bolts. Don't undertake this lightly. Stick-clip Bolt 1. When the belayer steps off the ledge, jump and you'll soar close to Bolt 1. Jug the rope up to it. Climb to the anchors. While Bolt 1 is acceptable, the remaining bolts and anchors are sketchy (at this time). We clipped the anchors, traversed right to Bride's anchors, then back left to clean Gang Bang's anchors. Lower to clean the 3 bolts. With new hardware, this would be pretty fun.

Low Left-Leaning Pseudo-Parallelogram Formation on the cliff.

3. **Bride of Crankenstein** (5.11c)*** 4 bolts, Karl Guthrie. Bolt 1 is high, atop the parallelogram formation. Bolt 2 is on a tufa. Bolt 3 (invisible from ground) and 4 angle left. Mild runout to anchors. Stick-clip Bolt 1, and also clip a short draw on Crankenstein's piton for the belayer. Start on a left-hand 3-finger-pocket above the left edge of the big low block. Climb the blobby stuff up and right (away from Bolt 1), then work left to Bolt 1, then up to Bolt 2. Shares some space (but no handholds) with Crankenstein, but it sure feels all its own, with wilder moves, and it's a nice alternative if you aren't feeling enough endurance for Crank. Beta.[202]

4. **Crankenstein** (5.11d)*** 1 piton and 5 bolts, Scott Hudson. This route is often stick-clipped, in violation of Travis County law. Learn the low moves, then clip a biner (sans draw) on the low piton and cruise in full redpoint glory. The piton is low on the arête edge of the pseudo-parallelogram formation. Anchors are right of a crack and the boltline.

   a. variation: **Wankenstein** (5.11b)*** 1 piton and 4 bolts. Climb Crankenstein through its piton and 1st bolt, then climb on Bride of Crankenstein's bolts 2-4. Height-dependent grade.

5. **Industrial Disease** (5.12b)* 4 bolts, Greg Brooks. Pulls the choppy bulge over Bolt 1. Bolt 2 is under a left-leaning diagonal flake. Anchors are right of the boltline.

6. **The Munchies** (5.12a)* 3 bolts, Paul Irby, Wayne Crill. High Bolt 1, 4' above the mini-roof. Bolts slant slightly left; finish on Industrial Disease's anchors. A gem of the south band, the boltline achieves a rare trifecta, with three lines (The Munchies, Cotton Mouth, and Paranoia) leadable on the same bolts. Use a spotter on the start to slow a swing fall. The bolts were arranged on the path of most-resistance, away from the juggy flake of Scary 7-11 and its former poison ivy. With the PI gone, the route's a good eliminate. Take the direct line between the bolts, staying off the lumpy long sidepull and the entire juggy flake system. You can get very close to the flake system, using a jug below its horizontal ledge between Bolts 2 and 3. Near the anchors you can use the cool half-moon sidepull on Industrial Disease and solve the thin section straight up to the anchors. Nice safe runouts, by the way. Many climbers will need a cheat stack to reach the downward facing flake undercling. This route is difficult to second (cleaning Bolt 1).

---

[200] Reported 5.11c in Austin Rock, this is now much harder since Gang Bang's low jug broke.

[201] Formerly 5.11a, its low jug flake loosened on a Last Ascent by Merrick Ales, and it fell apart during a stabilization attempt. Rupesh Chhagan then got the First Choss Ascent on loose choss, too unstable to be worth grading.

[202] LH 2pocket, RH ledge jug. RF far right ledge; dropknee. RH sloper horn; bump to higher sidepull. RF jam, LH sloper sidepull, bump to flat sloper atop blobby formation. RH "A frame" shaped 2pocket sidepull, for reach. LH far left edge past obvious sloper pocket. RF "match" RH, above it, on flat sloper. A few more snatch moves to easier climbing. Lots of moves in a little space!

b. <u>variation:</u> **Cotton Mouth** (5.11c)***. A fantastic eliminate, easy on the hands (once you know it). At Bolt 1, use a tall lumpy sidepull formation far off right to get to the horizontal crack under the mini-roof. Use that crack, pull the roof and stay off the big flake system that's right of the boltline. The jug pocket under the horizontal ledge of the flake system is on route.

c. <u>variation:</u> **Paranoia** (5.11b)***. Climb Cotton Mouth, but exit it early onto the juggy flake system when it's time to clip Bolt 3. Ride the flake to the anchors.

d. <u>variation:</u> **Toxic Munchies** (5.12a-b)*, Pete Bishop, Jeff Olson. Start Cotton Mouth, climb for 2 bolts, then cross left onto Industrial Disease. Pete and Jeff climbed this back when The Munchies had poison ivy in the flake system.

Queanh Gip, on her 1st send of "Crankenstein"

Huge right-facing flake system starting 15' up, slanting slightly left, running to the clifftop.

7. **Scary 7-11**[203] (5.12a?)* 3 bolts, Todd McCray, Curtis Mai. The start goes up to the flake system that's been cleaned of poison ivy. If you see regrowth, the flake is so wide you will be able to avoid touching it. Or Pull it! Pull it, for us ALL!! Bolt 1 is high, on a light gray flat outcrop, lower than The Munchies Bolt 1. Runout on a juggy flake section to Bolt 2 right of the flake. Bolt 3 is straight up and left, then anchors are straight up.

Queanh Gip, "Wife in the Fast Lane"

---

[203] Originally called Squirrel Cage, during its hayday as a TR-only route. According to international law, since leading is more badass than TRing, those who lead a TR route get to rename it. But, the law is inconsistent, since, if someone free solos a route, which is supremely more badass, they don't get to rename it. But themz the rules. The name "Scary 7-11" reflects the former (broken and now harder) 5.11 crux, 5.7 aftermath, and the runout. The 12a grade was suggested by a 5.13 climber; we imagine it might be harder.

variation: Scary Munchies (5.10d/5.11a)***. This fun variation "salvages" Scary 7-11's broken start and coincidentally gives the south band another 5.10 (if you or your cheat stack is tall enough). Stick-clip Scary 7-11's Bolt 1 and start to the left, on The Munchies. Use a spotter to slow your swing in the event of a low fall. Traverse the horizontal jug/sloper line right to merge onto Scary 7-11.

Big 4' Tall Slanted Flat-top boulder, roughly 3' from cliff.

The next two routes share Bolt 1:

8. **Short Term Memory Loss** (5.11c PG)*** 4 bolts+, Rick Watson. From the boulder, clip Bolt 1 of Wife, then go down to start on the ground. Bolts and anchors slant slightly left. Runout to Bolt 3 over a ledge hazard. Rick and several committee members support a retro.

9. **Wife in the Fast Lane** (5.10d or 5.11a)*** 5 bolts, Jean Hudson. Start on top of the big 4' tall slanted flat-top boulder (5.10d) or down on the ground (5.11a). Both starts are plenty interesting.

10. **Bolt Happy**[204] (5.11d)*** 6 bolts, David Phillips. Stick-clip Bolt 2 (and clip Bolt 1 for the belayer). Start off the right end of the big 4' tall slanted flat-top boulder. Bolts 1-3 slant up and right under the prominent diagonal ramp. When seconding, unclip Bolt 1 from the ground. Climb this route wrong and you'll curse the grade. *Beta.*[205] This route is the ugly person you kept resisting dating who ended up totally great in bed. '00

topropes: (5.12a & 5.11c-d TR)*. Use Bolt Happy's anchors and start right of its start. 12a on the left side, 11c-d on the right side.

The next two routes share anchors.

11. **Bolted Like Reimers** (5.10c)*** 5 bolts, Stephen Shortnacy. Climb the face left of Back Off Crack to BOC's anchors, staying out of the crack (Britta!). Zigzag boltline. Nice view of the lake from the anchors. Kwai Chang Kane glides silently over the rice paper. '00

variation: (5.11b)*. Stay off the ledge left of Bolt 4, including hand holds over it. The block over Bolt 4 is on for hands and feet. After that, climb the face, the arête being on, but not necessarily providing the best holds. Runout to Bolt 5, enough that a TR may be preferable.

12. **Back Off Crack** (5.9, X without gear)* 1 bolt and gear placement, or use of 1-2 neighboring bolts. Injinio Jones, Scott Hudson. This is a left-facing flakey crack. There is some committee interest in adding bolts. Until then…

Leading this with trad gear: some limestone cracks are sturdy enough for pro; some aren't. Please use good, conservative judgment. New tradsters sometimes experiment with gear at Reimers and blow apart the stone. You would get much more practice moving along the bottom of Enchanted Rock's granite routes, setting pro and test weighting it to learn what's effective. You should apprentice with someone to see how they set pro as you second their ascents. That said…on this route you can use a small/medium cam before the bolt.

Leading this without trad gear: this route is reasonable (but X protection) to lead if you dominate 5.9, and as such it's a useful mellow warmup for the south end of the park. Stick-clip Bolt 2 of Bolted Like Reimers and start climbing. The fall from that bolt to the first (way high) bolt of this route is a grounder, but it's easy climbing and falls are unlikely. (Alternatively, you can cut this fall distance by a solid, reachy, clip of Bolted Like Reimers' Bolt 3. Get on the full-rest ledge, then there are various clip stances for the high bolt, even for short folks. Take time and work it out from the ledge.) We would not go to lengths figuring all this out, if a 5.9 warmup weren't so useful on this end of the park.

[County-Suspended Application. Paul Brady applied to bolt a route near the fence line. The committee approved it, but the County was uncomfortable with activity that close to the neighbor's property. Now the County owns that property, Paul might get his route!]

---

[204] Dave is somewhat addicted to sinking bolts. Been there. He bolted this on lead. As he approached the top, he was pleasantly surprised to find anchors already bolted for him.

[205] Don't pull up onto the easy-looking ramp; you'll have problems climbing and clipping the next bolts. Stay low under it.

Reimers

Reimers (riverfront): **Digitron Boulder (aka. T-Rex Boulder)**

Sun conditions: All day sun facing the river; all day shade on Digitron and Unknown.
Approach: Reach this boulder by bashing trail downhill from Dead Cats Wall.
GPS @ T-Rex: N30˚21.793' W98˚07.560' (30.363217 -98.126)

Early developers at Reimers also called this big boulder the World's Second Greatest Boulder. The left two routes are about 40' tall, and T-Rex is a long traversing route. There are several boulder problems that are toprope-protectable via bolts on T-Rex (bring a stick-clip), and nearby World's Greatest Boulder offers more routes and problems. Both boulders are next to the river. Both catch a lot of sun, so the most fun plan is early or late route climbing, bouldering, and swimming.

The bolted slab side faces away from the river. You'll likely reach T-Rex first. Get to the other two routes by scrambling clockwise around the boulder. Digitron and Unknown had poison ivy as of this writing, but T-Rex was clear.

1. **Digitron** (5.10c)* 3 or more bolts. Bolts are just right of the acute arête. ⌘⚓?

2. **Unknown** (5.11d-5.12a X Mixed)* 1 bolt. Place a cam in the hole before the bolt. ⌘🐾?

3. **T-Rex** (5.12a)***, 5 bolts, Ralph Vega, John Gonzales. On the overhung river-facing side of the boulder, the route starts up the right end of the boulder (at the spot closest to the river) and traverses its top edge left to the other end. Soft belay to Bolt 4. The below topropes are listed left-to-right as usual, though the traverse's bolts are numbered right-to-left.

🎣🔥🎣🔥🎣🍖🐚🎯🐾🏃

a. toprope: **Diplodocus** (5.8). Set TR on the anchors and climb just left of the arête. Too short to go out of your way to climb, but the rope will end up there after doing T-Rex.

b. toprope: **Digitalia** (V6)***. Aka Digitalis. Set TR on Bolts 2 and 3 and tie into the end below Bolt 3. Use a spotter to slow the swing on a low fall. Climb straight up under Bolt 3.

c. toprope: **Triceratops** (V?)***. Set TR on Bolts 2 and 3 and tie into the end below Bolt 2. Start on Digitalia, then slant right to Bolt 2.

d. toprope: **Stegosaurus** (V?)***. Set TR on Bolts 2 and 3 and tie into the end below Bolt 2. Climb straight up to Bolt 2.

e. toprope: **Ankylosaurus** (V0)*. Boulder the start of T-Rex to Bolt 1 and continue straight up to topout.

Reimers (riverfront): **World's Greatest Boulder**

Sun conditions: All day sun
Approach: Bash trail downhill from T-Roofic Wall, or hike Sex Canyon to the rope swing, cut right, pass Digitron Boulder, and keep hiking.
GPS @ Pocket Rocket: N30˚21.854' W98˚07.602' (30.364233 -98.1267)

A big boulder at the river's edge, downhill from T-Roofic Wall. A sketch pad is recommended for the bouldering and extra protection leading these routes. The bolts looked rusty as of this writing, though Pocket Rocket's most important (high) bolt looks good. Climb some Reimers history!

TR's can be set scrambling the back side of the boulder. Bring slings to extend over the edge. Pocket Rocket was the first bolted route at Reimers. Scott Hudson wrote on www.mountainproject.com the following Reimers history. In 1986, he, Bill Gooch, and Jeff Johnson (not to be confused with Jeff Jackson) TR'd Pocket Rocket and decided the first to boulder it would sit and watch the other two sink one bolt each (tediously via hand drill) and would get first crack at the lead FA. Scott won. Scott was the first to muster up the highball send, watched as the other two labored at the bolting, and then Scott sent it on lead.

bouldering: Left of Screaming Yellow Zonker's are many boulder problems and variations.

bouldering: **Screaming Yellow Zonker's** (V1)

1. **Pocket Rocket** (5.10d)* 2 bolts, Scott Hudson.

2. **Size Ain't Shit** (5.11c)* 2 bolts, No Anchors, Charlie Chapman. Uses Pocket Rocket's anchors.

3. **Love Shack** (5.12)* 2 bolts, Paul Clark[206], Jeff Jackson.

Reimers (south band): **Huge Leaning Live Oak**

Sun conditions: all day tree shade (duh!)
GPS: N30°21.687' W98°07.535' (30.36145 -98.125583)

This huge live oak leans onto a huge cypress tree, downhill from Mai Tai Wall.

Back in the day, old timers such as Scott Hudson loved to scale this huge live oak, chill in the canopy of the huge Cypress tree it leans against, and smoke some herb. It was the thing to do. Matt Twyman considers this tree route the best route at Reimers.

Solo the leaning oak (or lead on slings), but bring equipment to rappel down. The solo upclimb is easy, but the solo downclimb is tricky. Many will have trouble making the solo just because of the height. Do not do this route often; the tree bark needs time to recover. Climb it barefoot, to minimize impact, and because you'll have a better grip.

---

[206] Paul has big wide lats that look like wings. On route, he looked like a flying squirrel. Check out his photo of a figure-4 on The Gauntlet, in Texas Limestone II.

Reimers: **Buildering**

Back in the day, there were no masonry buildings on the ranch. Now the County has built the bathroom and pavilion for climbers, not realizing some won't be able to resist climbing them. Will they allow it? The pavilion has all sorts of problems, and traversing the corners isn't easy with those cement beams creating reaches.

buildering: **Once Around the Crapper (V1)*,** A.S. on the FA.

buildering: numerous problems on the Pavilion.

Reimers: **History**

Like many Texans west of Austin, the routes generally look butt-ugly and ornery. In 1984, Bill Gooch and Hank Caylor looked it over for an hour and figured it had limited potential. Scott Hudson showed up for some hiking and spent several years bouldering here. He, Bill, and another guy installed the first bolts in 1986 as part of an early mini-competition. (See notes under The World's Greatest Boulder). While Bill was injured, Scott borrowed his drill and began putting up the first routes. By '89, Jeff Jackson, Kevin Gallagher, Duane Raleigh, Jack Mileski, Scott and Jean Hudson, and Greg Brooks got busy bolting. Jack Lawrence printed a one-page list of 52 routes in early '92.

Scott Hudson

Long before all that, starting around 1977, John "Goomba" Sanders would go into Reimers, cross the river and climb the boulders and cliffs. Over there, he found all sorts of route grades, up to and beyond 5.12.

All of the early bolting was "outlaw," without permission of the land-owners, Milton and Joy Reimers. Milton raised livestock and opened his ranch for hiking, swimming, fishing, and camping, years before climbers showed up. Through the early '90's, the Reimers family had no idea this tough climbing bunch of vandals were sinking bolts in their cliffs. Drills were snuck in, inside backpacks. Greg Brooks FA'd Lip-o-suction on slings, out of concern for sinking its present highly visible bolts. Scott and Jean Hudson brought in the other bolters, but fostered a concern for keeping a low profile, since bolts hadn't been discussed with the family. Knowing the family would eventually find out, the bolters adopted mankind's time-tested strategy of *keeping it on the down low* and seeking forgiveness, not permission.

Back then, the family took a $2 admission fee (or $3 if you camped) and provided you a receipt that said:

> No Guns
> No Teenage Parties
> No Repelling[207] (sic.)
> No Nudity

David Black Collection   BITD shot of 3 Reimers developers
Steve Hunt (3rd), David Black (4th), Kevin Bentz (last)

The Reimers didn't want any trouble. Well, climbing *is* trouble. Eventually, a climbing accident occurred, and the Reimers were sued. The climbing community rallied and showed their support for the family, who seemed much appreciative. It's also said that climbers from Oklahoma built a friendship with the Reimers and perhaps helped them become more comfortable with this unusual activity on their ranch. As more climbers devoted time from the Greenbelt and Erock to Reimers, climbers became their biggest group of customers. Milton and Joy Reimers became very, very close with the climbing community over the years.

---

[207] The Reimers' response to a complaint from non-climbers that someone was bolting in the Sex Cave.

In 2000, the 1st Annual Limestoner climbing competition at Reimers was conceived and organized by Rebecca Gonzales. Each year, this friendly comp raises money for CTM to fund the replacement of rusty bolts and worn anchors. Contestants score their hardest clean ascents, and judges use score clumps to place each contestant into Beginner, Intermediate, and Advanced categories. One year, this skinny guy Jordan Delong scored so high, the judges created a new category: God.

At one point, there was an annual *climbing in drag* day.

Reimers saw a gazillion ascents over the years. Milton maintained the huge ranch, served on the City Counsel of Drippings Springs, and played poker with friends. Four days a week, for freaking decades, Milton greeted visitors outside his house, often smoking a nice cheap cigar, and collected fees and waivers. Joy shared the duty, and she was sunshine to Milton's partial cloudy. It takes a rare personality who can be cheery through decades of retail customers. For roughly 120,000 times over the years, Milton got his day interrupted to come out to yet another car of scruffs and say, "Y'all got yer passes?"[208]

Nick Brown Scott Isgitt, on his first send of "Hyper Salivation"

And, customers sometimes caused big problems. Around 2000, a climber let their dog run loose, and it chased a horse over the cliff at Shortcake Wall. That was the Reimers' granddaughter's favorite horse. The smell of the decaying horse shut down climbing in that area for a whole season. But the Reimers also must have had a lot of positive experiences with climbers, including this one written by Scott Isgitt:

"It took me a number of years to break the ice with Milton, but I finally got him to start laughing at some of my jokes. Either that or he was just laughing at me. He started letting me use his Kawasaki Mule to pull my portable rock wall in and out of the mall each summer and Christmas. I was bringing it back to the ranch one time on a trailer and had an interesting run in with Milton's herd of cows.

A few of them were blocking the road from the parking lot back to the house where I had to turn around so I could unload the mule. I decided to honk the horn to try and scare the cows away and without paying attention, I got out of the van to check the trailer. When I looked up after checking the trailer, the 3 cows that were blocking the road had miraculously multiplied into about 30 cows. I squeezed between a couple of them to get back to the van so I could honk the horn again. When I did, the cows started ramming and bucking into me. They were going a little crazy and seemed to be getting more and more agitated. So, not being the smartest kid in the class, I decided to honk the horn again (I obviously didn't put 2 and 2 together). By this time, I was all but pinned up against the van with a cow's ass in my face and I got kicked and stepped on a few times. I made my way back inside the van and decided to just sit there and wait. By this time, Joy had heard all of the noise and came out to see what was going on and then realized what had happened. She just started laughing at me and told me that a honking horn was what they used as the dinner bell for the cows. They thought I was there to feed them.

The next time I pulled up to the house to go climbing, Milton came out with a big ol' grin on his face — the first time I ever saw him start off with a smile — and said, "I heard you learned how to ring the dinner bell" and then just started laughing out loud. He said that when Joy told him what had happened, it was the funniest thing he had heard in a long time. I just laughed with him and said "just don't make me sound too dumb when you repeat the story."

Milton didn't just sit back collecting the cash. He and Joy had 1,267 acres to ranch, and, in Texas, that means daily chores and a lot of cedar clearing, to keep grasslands clear for grazing and spring waters running. A wise rancher cuts the cedar with loppers, before they grow big enough to require a chainsaw or bulldozer. The workload on Milton averaged probably one or two acres, *per day*, year in year out. One year, he hired a couple of South American women to lop, and he was astounded how fast they worked. They literally ran from cedar to cedar, across the entire ranch. The next year he drove out of state trying to find them.

Ranching and hosting visitors was in Milton's blood; his great grandfather homesteaded the three Reimers ranches in 1887, and the first visitors came in wagons to camp in the early 1900's. In 2005, Milton and Joy sold the ranch to Travis County, simultaneous with the County purchase of North Shore. (See the chapter on North Shore for some history on that.) They bought another ranch in Dripping Springs and retired from the business of serving rock climbers, bikers, hikers, and fisher folk.

Todd McCray
Todd McCray collection

Curtis Mai & Todd McCray
Todd McCray collection

[208] Estimating 80 cars per week, 50 weeks per year, for 30 years.

Those first sport climbers in the early 90's were a mix of folks including dirtbags, crazies, students, and yuppies. Today's lot has shifted heavily towards weekend warriors, soccer moms, and even Republicans. The number of homeless climbers in Austin can now be counted on one hand. The amount of herb burning in the air is way down, though we're told the quality is way up. Some Reimers routes were a little crazier than they are today, with big runouts and some use of trad equipment. And the mindset was mostly very different. Peek into the mind of one old timer (Tony Faucett):

"I'll tell you a couple or three stories...

One day we were on Crankenstein at Reimers. There were five of us. The sky got black. I said "it looks like rain, we better head for cover". Rick (Watson) replied, "ahhh, it's not going to rain". Right then, BOOM! A lightning bolt hit right above us, and a turd floater it was. The five of us huddled in a pile, soaking wet.

Another time, Rick, Rene Payne and I were on a road trip. We were at Penitente Canyon. We hooked up with Hank and Calvin. Hank flashed a 13a and everyone was a partying. Right left of it was "Los Hermanos de los Wienie Way"...a damn good 5.11, and we were burning runs on it. The sky got black. I said, "It looks like rain, we better head for cover". Rick replied, "Ahhh, it's not going to rain". So he took off on the Wienie Way. Right then, BOOM! A lightning bolt hit right above us, and a

Dmitrii Makarov 📷   **Rick Watson & Alvino Pon**

turd floater it was. Rick's glasses were fogged over, and his chalk a milky paste. He yelled "I'm outta here", took a backwards flight, and I dropped his ass fast. We all huddled under a boulder for a smoke.

Did you know, I spent four days in the back of a pick-up truck with Rick waiting for a blizzard to pass at Hueco Tanks. FYI, Rick snores Like a muthafucker!

Ask Scott Harris about the time I knocked the contact out of his eye shadowboxing at the base of "Pags to Pork". Were fucked man, were fucked!!!

Rick and I just finished bolting Mas Cerveza, and I think also Bongo Fury. It was a sultry day, as Texas summers can be. Everyone was sweating like a pig. Jason Spear gave Mas Cerveza a run. It was a little sporty at the top, and Jason soon found himself in No Man's Land. With the chains right in his face, he yells "I'm gassed, I can't make the clip". Rick replies "just grab the chains dude". Oops, wrong answer! The chains weren't looped, and the sweat was a pouring. Jason went for the chains alright, slipped off them, and the air mail was delivered.

Somehow Rick was wired to the first bolt, and Jason about two feet off the ground.
— T"

Erik Moore 📷

A motley crew of bolters, boulderers and badasses
Cody Ramsey, Cody Cox, Chris "Vinny" Vinson
Rick Rivera, John Gonzales, Greg Brooks, Merrick Ales

Reimers

North Shore Trail Map

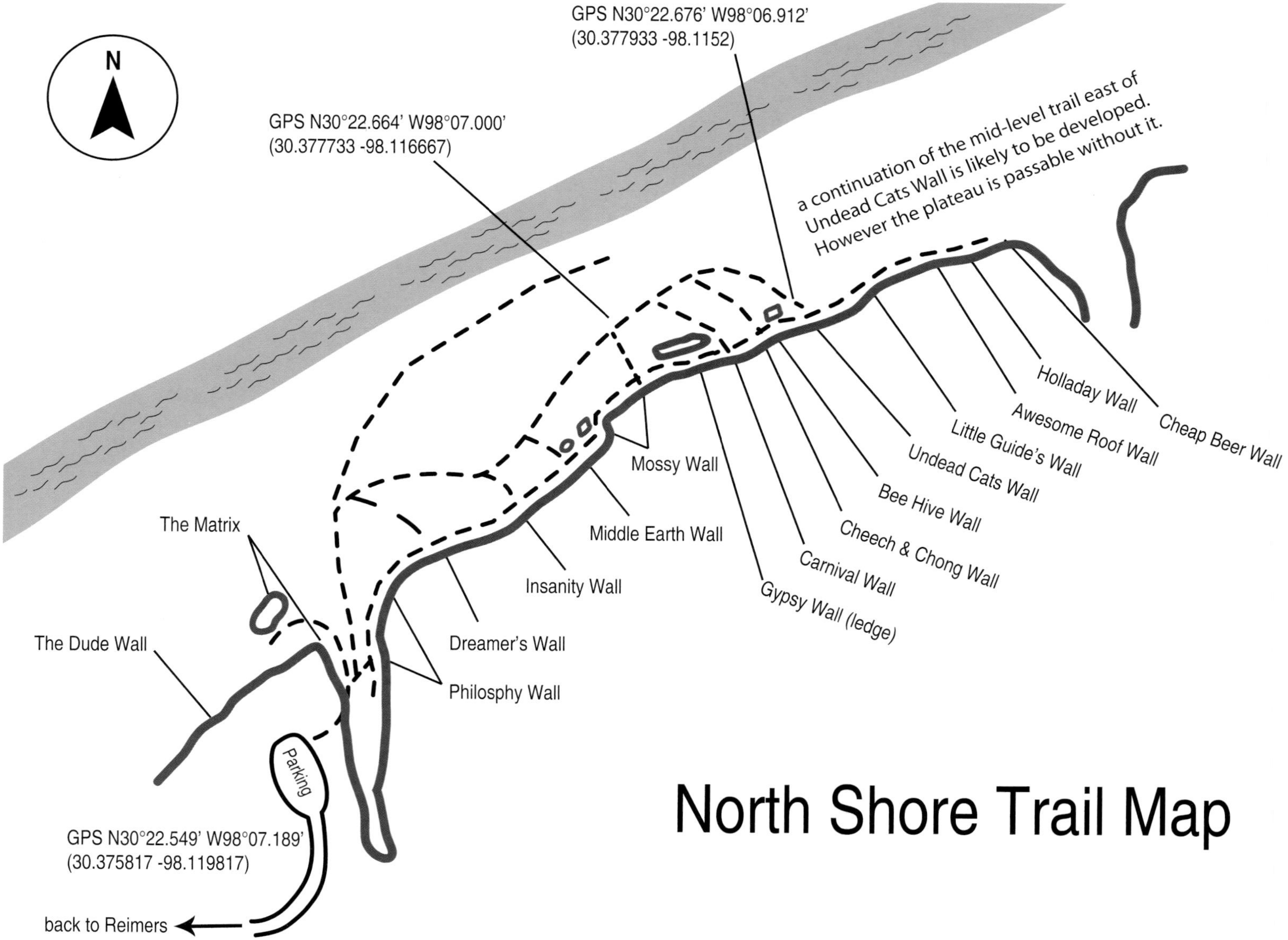

N

back to Reimers →

GPS N30°22.549' W98°07.189'
(30.375817 -98.119817)

Parking

The Dude Wall

The Matrix

Philosphy Wall

Dreamer's Wall

Insanity Wall

Middle Earth Wall

Mossy Wall

Gypsy Wall (ledge)

Carnival Wall

Cheech & Chong Wall

Bee Hive Wall

Undead Cats Wall

Little Guide's Wall

Awesome Roof Wall

Holladay Wall

Cheap Beer Wall

GPS N30°22.664' W98°07.000'
(30.377733 -98.116667)

GPS N30°22.676' W98°06.912'
(30.377933 -98.1152)

a continuation of the mid-level trail east of
Undead Cats Wall is likely to be developed.
However the plateau is passable without it.

Grant Isaac

Ralph Vega
"Astro Zon

Climbing Area: North Shore

North Shore is a new climbing area within the Milton Reimers Ranch Park of Travis County. The climbing area is a 2,000-foot wide cliff that runs along the Pedernales between two wide creek valleys, plus cliffs and boulders just west of the western creek. It seems likely to open to the public this year (2012). Ask for access status and directions when the ranger greets you at the park entrance. As of this writing, road signs point to "North Bank" rather than "North Shore." Until it is open, work access for test climbing, bolting, and trail building is available to folks approved by Central Texas Mountaineers. Contact CTM at www.ctmrocks.com for more information.

North Shore's two-minute approach to its popular west walls, and its short drive-time from Reimers parking, makes it practical to hit projects at both areas in the same day. Since noon sun hits Reimers' popular Dead Cats and Prototype Walls, a great strategy is Reimers in the morning and North Shore after lunch. See the Battle Plan for Out-of-Towners chapter for other comparisons of the two areas.

Since it's a new area with relatively little traffic, expect a high chance of hold breaks. Consider wearing helmets, especially for the belayer. Consider stick-clipping high bolts. One climber broke his foot, clipping high off a bomber-looking starting jug that had survived a dozen ascents. Lots of traffic has solidified grades from 5.11a down. Less traffic has occurred above that, and so the grades above 11a are suspect. Please send us your grade opinions when you've done enough redpoints to find your best possible beta.

All walls, landmarks, and routes are listed east-to-west, left-to-right facing toward the cliff. The trail enters from the right (west) end. Along with existing routes, this chapter points to spots where new routes are likely to be developed. We estimate the number of future routes and list the existing committee-approved route applications. As new routes go in, look for downloadable updates to this book at www.AustinClimbingBook.com.

David Phillips, "Hexed"

Evacuation:

A possibility for Starflight (helicopter) evac is in a meadow next to the river at GPS coordinates N30° 22.669' W098° 07.019' (Digital Degrees: 30.377817 -98.116983), downhill from Mossy Wall. We don't know whether they can land there, but they can probably drop a line there.

Trails:

The North Shore parking lot is at N30°22.549' W98°07.189' (30.375817 -98.119817). The trail map guides you from the parking lot into a big creek valley. The trail branches at a creek crossing; staying straight goes to The Matrix and The Dude Wall. Turning right at GPS N30°22.591' W98°07.138' (30.376517 -98.118967) and crossing the creek gets you to the long mid-level trail that runs parallel to all the other climbing walls and the river. This mid-level trail is fairly flat and fast compared to the trail along the cliff. People often drop down to it to move between walls.

Various short spur trails lead from the mid-level trail to the walls. As of this writing, trails are not developed beyond Undead Cats Wall. The following describes how to get to each wall.

The Matrix & The Dude Wall:

The Matrix Wall (left end): almost at the bottom of the rock stairway into the creek valley, cut left and hug the short cliff band for 40 paces.

The Matrix Boulders & The Dude Wall: continue all the way down the stairway and along the trail on the left bank. Don't take the creek

Jan Salinas, "A Mortal Life"

crossing; stay straight for 95 paces. A spur trail is likely to go uphill from there to the tall Oracle Boulder. To reach The Dude Wall, hike counter-clockwise around the Oracle Boulder.

For the rest of the walls, take the rock stairway all the way down and then walk left to the creek crossing to start on the mid-level trail. The following describes where each wall's spur trail is along the mid-level trail. For example, to get to Middle Earth Wall, read from Philosophy Wall through Middle Earth Wall, but don't take any of the spur trails to Philosophy Wall, Dreamer's Wall, and Insanity Wall. (It's been proposed that the Park add signs at each spur trail.)

Philosophy Wall: after crossing the creek, hike the trail 40 paces, then cut diagonally up hill on slabby boulders. This spur trail is marked after the slabby boulder section.

Dreamer's Wall: the mid-level trail bends around the point of the creek and river. The spur trail on the right goes somewhat steeply uphill. It starts at N30°22.630' W98°07.105' (30.377167 -98.118417).

Insanity Wall: continue on the mid-level trail 50 paces to cross a 6' tall gully and 25 more paces to a spur trail at N30°22.641' W98°07.056' (30.37735 -98.1176). It angles left and then cuts straight to the route Fangoria.

Middle Earth Wall: 80 paces further is a fork in the trail at N30°22.651' W98°07.026' (30.377517 -98.1171). The right branch is a spur trail that snakes sharply right and leads to Middle Earth Cave (a tall, deep tube). The left branch is the rest of the mid-level trail.

Mossy Wall: after another 38 paces, a spur trail at N30°22.650' W98°07.010' (30.3775 -98.116833) cuts right to the route Man's Best Friend.

Carnival/Gypsy Walls: after 130 paces, a spur trail at N30°22.673' W98°06.951' (30.377883 -98.11585) is marked by a 15' long burnt cedar trunk. As of this writing, the spur trail is rough over messy rock.

Bee Wall/Cheech & Chong Wall: the mid-level trail goes over a hill and starts angling uphill after 50 paces. 20 more paces, a spur trail at N30°22.658' W98°06.918' (30.377633 -98.1153) cuts sharply right and comes out at the leftmost Cheech & Chong Wall route.

Undead Cats Wall: after 90 paces, the trail will have worked up hill to a big roof (a County-designated clifftop overlook) in the middle of Undead Cats Wall. Right of that is the route Pie in the Sky at N30°22.676' W98°06.912' (30.377933 -98.1152).

Eastern Walls: no spur trails were established, as of this writing. Take the mid-level trail to the Carnival/Gypsy Walls spur trail. Then work left and downhill to a plateau near the river but still high above it. Hike to a big boulder on the left side of this plateau. Straight uphill from it is Holladay Wall. A little further is Cheap Beer Wall, obvious from its huge three arêtes divided by two open book dihedrals.

Rona Distenfeld   **John Hogge, "Global Warming" FA**

North Shore: **Bouldering**

Most of North Shore's bouldering is at The Matrix (page 173). The rest is scattered around. Working right-to-left (West to East) there is:

- A pointy boulder in the creek downhill from the Matrix Boulders.

- Philosophy Wall (page 168) offers relatively easy highballs on the described TR lines and a few unanchored lines.

- Waste of Time Boulder, below the little canyon of Carnival Wall & Gypsy Wall, between the cliff and the mid-level trail. An overhanging face is on the east side. A nice guy with dreads improved the landings, to the point where he could safely check out the problems. He was disappointed and said, "It was a waste of time."

- Next to that is a boulder with an easy slabby face on the west side and an arête and other problems clockwise from the face.

- A boulder with hard problems underneath Little Guide's Wall.

- A balanced (stacked) boulder 40' downhill from the route Opticalrectuminitus on Holladay Wall. Working clockwise:
    Roughly 4 roof pull problems on the uphill side.
    Bad-landing sit-start problem right of the acute arête.
    Acute arête problem on the downhill side.
    Bad-landing crowded up-and-left face traverse left of the arête.

- Downhill from the stacked boulder, on the river side next to the mid-level "trail" is a big boulder:
    Roughly 7 easy slab and face problems near the trail on the west side
    Roughly 5 overhanging problems and a crack traverse on the downhill side.

- A high-ball boulder at Cheap Beer Wall at the corner of the Pedernales River valley and the big feeder creek.

- A little low cliff bouldering in the creek valley just around the corner.

- The big creek valley east of Cheap Beer Wall is OFF-LIMITS to climbers and hikers. For years, the County has been concerned about trespassing, and they delayed route development at North Shore to decide how to prevent it. Please stay out of that creek so that climbers' reputations and access to North Shore are protected. The bouldering in various spots of the creek is off-limits and not good enough to violate the park's trust. Prior to the County purchase, the main spot was called Wizard's Wall, and the general area was called Wizard's Water.

- A little untried highball bouldering deep into North Shore in the Lick Creek valley. We recall some choss and some cool looking stuff. Access status is unknown, and it's far unless you're on a mountain bike on the old jeep trails. The park design specified that off-trail hiking is acceptable. What's unknown is how much of the Pogue Hollow ranch will be open for hiking. If you see a fence and No Trespassing signs before you get to Lick Creek, that's your answer. Part of the reason we mention this is to guide people away from hiking the entire ranch in hopes of finding more bouldering. We hiked the entire ranch over the years before the County purchase, but only found this and the off-limits creek areas.

As you develop any new problems here, please send us detailed descriptions, grades, and names at AustinClimbing@pobox.com[209]. If you send something on an unnamed boulder, please send us a boulder name too. Landing work is encouraged.

> Creating a new theory is not like destroying an old barn and erecting a skyscraper in its place. It is rather like climbing a mountain, gaining new and wider views, discovering unexpected connections between our starting points and its rich environment. But the point from which we started out still exists and can be seen, although it appears smaller and forms a tiny part of our broad view gained by the mastery of the obstacles on our adventurous way up.
>
> *Albert Einstein*

---

[209]Get your name here for 2nd edition. But wait -- unlike route developers, boulderers get to name problems but don't list themselves as FA's. Never understood that, really. Well, how about this. FA it and name it "(your name)'s Bitchin' Boulder Problem "

North Shore: **Cheap Beer Wall**

Sun conditions: All day shade.
Approach: 13 minutes via the mid-level and some bushwhacking. See the section on trails at the beginning of this chapter.
GPS @ leftmost route (Milwaukee's Beast): N30°22.725' W98°06.720' (30.37875 -98.112)
GPS @ rightmost route (Schlitz My Liquor): N30°22.711' W98°06.730' (30.378517 -98.112167)

Named for the top choice of beverage fueling North Shore development, beating out water by huge margins. But there's a coincidental historical tie-in. In the 60's, former North Shore land owner Johnny Reimers built what is now La Cabana Grill at H71 and Reimers Rd, a few miles west of Hamilton Pool Rd. He ran it as a beer joint called The Horseshoe Lounge, serving up Lone Star and Pearl, back in the sad days before Shiner Bock was widely distributed. His place was one of the few around. His special was catfish, caught from North Shore's riverfront.

Highball Boulder at the cliff's corner.

Short cliff area with two cracks.
   [potential easy routes, about the height of Zoey's Wall.]

Arête #1 (of 3 — together they look like enormous monster teeth, projecting out from open-book dihedrals.)
   [1 likely future route]

1. **Milwaukee's Beast** (5.7)*** 4 Bolts, Louie Graham, Chris Keistler. Climbs the face right of arête #1. Great beginner slab climb with a knee-bar instruction opportunity, and a great warmup. Bolts 1-3 slant left; Bolt 4 is at 1 o'clock. '05

2. toprope: **Mickey's Big Mouth** (5.7 TR)*** TR anchors only, Dave Phillips. [Bolt this for lead.] Climbs the crack in the 1ˢᵗ dihedral. '05

Arête #2

[An undeveloped 5.9 on arête #2 that was TR'd in 2005.]

3. **Lonestar Tallboy** (5.10d)* 5 Bolts, Kirk Holladay. Climb the meandering crack on the dihedral right of arête #2, left of the boltline. Beware of wrecking ball falls left into the dihedral's left face. '05

4. **Icehouses** (5.11c)* 4 bolts, Dave Phillips. Climb the vertical face, then pull the roof. *Beta[210]*. '05

Arête #3

5. **Red Dog** (5.11c R)* 4 Bolts, Dave Phillips. Climb straight up arête #3; exit right through the dihedral. Bolt 1 is just left of the arête's slanting edge. The next bolts slant slightly right, crossing over to the other side of the arête, which is chaotically shaped higher up. The anchors are hard to see; they're on a slabby face at clifftop. Consider stick-clipping Bolt 2 due to the sharp boulder in the fall zone. The tree is also in the fall zone on non-crux moves. '05

    a. variation: **Steel Reserve** (5.11c)*** Dave Phillips. Climb Bolts 1-2 of Red Dog. Break left and finish on Icehouses. Some folks will like the variation better than Red Dog because of the fun roof pull.

Low Roof under a 30' wide 12' tall blob

6. **Schlitz My Liquor** (5.11b)*** 4 bolts, Kirk Holladay[211]. Climb the chossy left-pointing flake system. Mild runout to the anchors. '05.

[1 likely future route]

North Shore Bolting Fuel

---

[210] We failed to start this and wondered if a hold broke. DP says start with a right-hand gaston.

[211] Kirk loved beer, bolting routes, and climbing, all with portable tunes blaring. He was creative, and one day he opted to keep the beer super-cold via dry ice in the cooler. But by the time it was Beer Thirty, the beer had fused into a rock solid block of ice. Chipping efforts ensued.

North Shore: **Holladay Wall**

Sun conditions: All day shade.
Approach: 13 minutes via the mid-level trail and some bushwhacking. See the section on trails at the beginning of this chapter.
GPS @ Optical Rectuminitus: N30˚22.724' W98˚06.771' (30.378733 -98.11285)

This wall is named in honor of Kirk Holladay, a major contributor to routes at North Shore, a pioneer of DWS and bolted routes at Pace Bend, FAs in and out of Texas, and guiding through his company, Rock-About.

Shortly after his death, a client wrote about how effectively he had shared his passion for rock climbing. He was also talented at rolling doubles. He'd set up a chill spot above the water soloing at Pace Bend and beat all comers at backgammon.

At El Potrero Chico, he established many routes, and he and his friends began the wild New Year's Eve tradition of shooting off fireworks, around midnight, at parties rappelling off of multi-pitch Space Boyz. Friends shot his ashes into the sky over Space Boyz.

He was a delightful friend to many. Kirk Holladay (1969-2009).

Kirk Holladay, R.I.P.   (Kaci Myrick 📷)

Triangular boulder- fractured cliff section (still against the rest of the cliff).
>   Access free solo on right side of this fractured section.

Chaotic shaped face.
>   [3 likely future routes]

Roof (30' wide, over a face with three cracks)
>   [3 likely future routes]

Mild Angle Face

1. **The Quatch**[212] (5.9)* 3 bolts, Kirk Holladay. '05

>   [5 likely future routes]

Low Roof under Face (on the left side) and big bulge (on the right side)

2. **Opticalrectuminitus** (5.10c)*** 3 bolts, Dave Phillips. 50' right of The Quatch. Start under a low dihedral roof; pull a long left-pointing edge. Runout to Bolt 2; we recommend stick-clipping it. Primo face moves. '05

>   [1-2 future routes on the face; 2-4 routes on the big bulge]

Prow.
>   [0-2 future routes]

Mild angle right-slanting dihedral.
>   [3 likely future routes]

---

[212] "Quatch" is some local Mexican slang (possibly *really* local, as in just one crazy guy) for "sh*t."

Holladay Wall's 30 foot wide roof

North Shore: **Awesome Roof Wall**[213]

GPS @ left end: N30°22.723' W98°06.793' (30.378717 -98.113217)
Approach: 12 minutes via the mid-level trail and some bushwhacking. See the section on trails at the beginning of this chapter.
Sun conditions: All day shade.

Slabby Face with 3 Trees and a Little Starting Roof.
    [4 likely future routes]

Bulge (30' wide).
    [1 likely future route]

Awesome Roof over 15' Tall Face having 3 Horizontal Crack Lines and a Dihedral on the left third.
    [7 likely future routes]

Bulge (80' wide with big choss area towards the right and a short bulge with ledges at the right end).
    [12 likely future routes]

---

[213] A working name until someone bolts a route here (after obtaining permission from CTM). According to tradition, once that happens, that person gets to name the wall.

Sun conditions: All day shade.
Approach: 11 minutes via the mid-level trail and some bushwhacking. See the section on trails at the beginning of this chapter.
GPS @ 70' Wide Slabby Wall: N30°22.704' W98°06.810' (30.3784 -98.1135)

This wall has no bolts yet, but many 5.low free solos by Dave Phillips and Birddog. Both were at the wall during a period of FA fever in '05, when Birddog started soloing lines starting in the middle and working right. Dave said, "Fine! You go that way, and I'll go this way," and he started soloing lines working left. Here are the main wall features:

70' Wide Slabby Wall. [5 likely future routes]
Fractured Rock Stack on Ledge.
Pointy-Triangular Roof with Big Hackberry Tree on the Right [2-3 likely future routes]

Slabby Sloper Face
Hike-Under-Boulder with V.Hards on it.

So, with that little said, we're stuck with a lot of boring white space on this page. Let's fill it up. This wall, like all sport route walls, will undergo roughly the following process of development:

1. Climber topropes a line to get a feel for its quality and grade. Sometimes the exact line is not obvious, and different paths are explored. Sometimes multiple lines are planned together, such as branching or joining lines, or traverses across uproutes. Occasionally, one bolt line serves two paths. During this toproping, some or all of the loose-hold and vegetation cleaning is done.

2. Climber figures out where bolts could be clipped and sometimes marks positions with chalk or tape. Tall climbers try to remember to reach each position and then bring the hand back some, to simulate the clipping situations for shorter climbers. Climber hammers lightly on each position to assess rock quality. On limestone, a high "ping" indicates good rock. Lower "whack" means bad hollowness.

3. If existing routes are right next to it, climber assesses the extent of shared holds and whether the squeeze job is worth while.

4. Climber photographs or draws the line and obtains permission from a committee.

5. Climber completes cleaning the route of loose holds and interfering vegetation. The level of cleaning varies a lot. Some clean lightly, giving holds a chance to survive, but risking hold breaks. Some clean more aggressively, with small pry bars. Some clean very aggressively with smashing hammers. In wet conditions, mud can be a big task to dig out of the holds. When you find a dirty new route, it may be because mud could not be completely cleaned out earlier. But usually it's because the developer was lazy.

6. Sometimes holds are reenforced with glue or Sika AnchorSet™. Sometimes choss surfaces are reenforced via different texture strategies.

7. Now it's time to bolt. Climber rigs all tools and hardware and (ignoring past ground-up ethics) generally rappels to install all hardware. Climber must be able to reach each placement well enough to dill holes and hammer in the expansion bolts. On overhangs, this may mean holding onto climbing holds, heel-hooking in climbing shoes, drilling one handed, and precariously doing likewise to place and hammer a bolt one-handed on a long reach. Climber can often avoid all that by clipping single biners into previously installed bolt hangers, or Aiding off of rock features via hooks or trad gear. For limestone, we like slings and fabric knots instead, because metal gear blows apart good holds too often. Alternatively, Climber can also drill small intermediary holes and Aid into them via ClimbTech's removable bolts.

8. On each hole, the hammer drill is kept as straight as possible. The bit has to be the exact size specified for the bolt. Climber sets the bit to drill about 1/2" deeper than the bolt shaft. While drilling, if the drill encounters a pocket, the drill will jump in or move sideways a little, and generally the hole has to be abandoned. Climber also watches the color of the dust coming out of the hole. Light brown is good; medium-to-dark brown is bad (for limestone). Graininess (dirt!) is bad.

9. Climber uses a tube to blow out the hole to be extremely clean, to avoid a spinning (useless) bolt placement. A small brush can help also. Climber adds a hanger onto the bolt and taps the bolt slightly into the hole, then hammers it fairly hard all the way in. Once in, Climber must ignore all distractions so as to remember to tighten the bolt. Climber tightens till it's not easy to continue tightening, and avoids overtightening and damaging the bolt. If Climber has used Fixe™ bolts, some advise use of Locktight™ to prevent the nut from traveling off the bolt. (Fixe bolts are interesting but are advised against, by many in ATX, for use in limestone.) If the bolt does not tighten, climber swears profusely, being tired of sitting in the harness that long, removes the hanger and bolt head, and drills a new hole. Or perhaps Climber used a glue-in and will never have this happen.

10. Exhausted, climber sends the route for the FA, or else risks someone stealing that. In a fit of inspiration, a route name comes to mind.

North Shore: **Undead Cats Wall**

Sun conditions: All day shade.
Approach: 9 minutes via the mid-level trail. See the section on trails at the beginning of this chapter.
GPS @ leftmost route (Live in the Cat's Lane): N30°22.691' W98°06.850' (30.378183 -98.114167)
GPS @ left of viewpoint, route Rushin Brunette: N30°22.694' W98°06.870' (30.378233 -98.1145)

This wall bears no resemblance whatsoever to Dead Cats Wall, but it was designated by a two person committee as the place to poke fun at Reimers Proper route names. It's full of lively, pumpy routes and it-ain't-over topouts. Warmups are nearby at Beehive Wall and Cheech & Chong Wall.

A big cedar tree grows out of the cliff, 4' below the top. Huge fractured rock chunks comprise the cliff underneath this tree.

Access free-solo (class IV or 5.7)***. Climb a suspect-looking stack of boulders, on the face and left corner just left of the tree described above. To free solo (class IV), start under roof and work diagonally right up the stack. For a long time, a fixed rope hung for convenient Gri-Gri/Cinch toprope solos (5.7), starting on the "face" formed by the pile of boulders, going diagonally right and up. We grew fond of the little route. More solid than New Wall? Maybe it's worth bolting for lead.

Long Bulge.
Tree 8' up on a ledge under the next routes.

1. **Life in the Cat's Lane** (5.10d)* 3 bolts, John
Hogge. Climb to an undercling-looking block mid-cliff. '09

The next two routes share Bolt 1:

2. **A Thousand Meows From Beyond the Grave**
(5.11a PG)* 4 bolts, John Hogge. Climb the dihedral left of
the column. Runout to Bolt 2. '09

3. **Dead Cats DO Meow** (5.11b PG)*** 4 bolts[214],
John Hogge. Start on A Thousand Meows and cross right
onto the column. Runout to Bolt 2. There is a dangerous high
clip stance you may be tempted to do from having climbed A
Thousand Meows From Beyond the Grave. Instead, stay low and
reach high for a safer clip. '09

Lots of space between routes.

4. **Catflip** (5.11c)*** 4 bolts, John Hogge. Bitchin' choss route[215]. Climb near the big white downward-pointing flake and smaller flakes, and pull a small (3' deep x 20' wide) roof at the top. A cat runs through a slaughterhouse, out a window and onto a steep roof. '09

Wave

5. **Sleeper Cell** (5.11b / 5.12a)*** 4 bolts[216], Dave Phillips. Climb pockets to a big left pointing sidepull flake. 5.11b requires reach and
secret beta, otherwise it's 5.12a. '09

---

[214] Two bolts without hangers show the original start, hosed when holds broke.
[215] The bolter sincerely apologizes for globs of cement on the low left jug horn. His cement-containment measures failed; he intended all the cement to be hidden behind the horn.
[216] "Never put a bolt where they can use it to work the crux." –Jeff Jackson

North Shore

6. **Werecats** (5.12b)*** 4 bolts, Dave Phillips. The boltline is right of a wild blobby tufa just above the landing. '09

7. **Rhino Ballet** (5.12c)* 5 bolts, Rupesh Chhagan FA, bb Dave Phillips. Bolt 1 is above and right of a white right-facing flake. '09

8. **Rushin Brunette** (5.12a)* 5 bolts, Dave Phillips. Bolt 1 is framed by a right-angle flake. Shares its Bolt 5 and anchors with Nac Nac. '05

9. **Nac Nac** (5.11c)*** 4 bolts, Ben Gayler, David Cardosa. The rightmost route under the left end of the huge roof. Start on the face right of Rushin Brunette's starting flake system. Go up on Bolts 1-3, then up and left to finish on Rushin Brunette's last bolt and anchors. At one point, things look like they're going well, then they keep getting worse and worse. *Incredible Beta.*[217] '11

County-suspended application:[218] Guinness Stout (5.12), to be 10-15 bolts. It would start on Nac Nac and traverse along the obvious lip under the roof for 100', under the designated viewpoint, and then top out.

Trailhead.
Huge Upper Roof (its right edge is over Nac Nac)

[217] The crux beta is wearing laced shoes! From the two-handed undercling, change left-hand to gaston that same feature. Reach high and right to a flat semi-jug. Feet bicycle the feature and turn right shoulder up. At this point I snatched the little tufa to bump up, but Ben goes for a higher intermediary, and, each time, his left shoelaces snag that tufa! (Dab? Aid? IDK.)
[218] We've opted to leave such information to provide you a heads-up on possible future lines. You can mark through these descriptions to record final bolt counts, grade, etc. Suspended applications are less likely for bolting, but the County might some day accept them.

Viewpoint (30' wide, at the center of the roof). [9 likely routes east of viewpoint; 5 west of it]

Long Bulging Cliff with a series of 6 slightly-separated rock island belay areas running from Bee Wall. These islands may be easiest to identify hiking right-to-left. Get up on top of them.

Rock island 6: 30' long, connected to the cliff, full of loose big & small rock. Belay these routes from the ground.

10. **Pie in the Sky** (5.11a)*** 3 bolts, Kirk Holladay. This was Kirk's last route. High Bolt 1 is left of the mini arête-dihedral pair. Bolt 3 is left of the wide "V" crack at the top of the cliff. Rope drag on lowering can get you stuck. To prevent that, clip anchors left-to-right, then separate the rope ends before lowering. '09

Rock island 5: 25' long, against the cliff but barely detached from it underneath. Belay these routes from atop the island.

    <u>expired application:</u> Pontufacator (5.10+), to be 5 bolts, Start on a Jimmy Durante nose shaped tufa.

11. **Electric Hellfire** (5.11d-5.12a)*** 3 bolts, Ralph Vega. '09

12. **Unfinished Monkey Business**[219] (5.11c)*** 4 bolts, Karl Vochatzer, Annette Pelletier. Bolts 1-2 slant right along a thin diagonal left-pointing flake system. Bolt 3 stretches right, just left of a pocket. Climb from there up to Bolt 4 and anchors. The route is hard to second; maybe stick-unclip Bolt 1. That monkey looked all cute and cuddly, right before it bit your nose off. This route has three traversing variations across 1-3 permadraws. They were unplanned, and bolt placements protect them via shear dumb luck.

    a. <u>variation:</u> **Monkey Grind** (5.11c)* 3 bolts & 1 permadraw, John Hogge. After Bolts 1-3, head up and right to the ledge and traverse it right, clipping a permadraw (Lessamir's last bolt). Finish straight up to Lessamir's anchors.

    b. <u>variation:</u> **Monkey Grinder** (5.11d)* 3 bolts & 2 permadraws, Karl Vochatzer. Climb Monkey Grind but continue traversing to the 2nd permadraw (Hello Netherkitty's last bolt), then finish straight up to Hello Netherkitty's anchors.

    c. <u>variation:</u> **Monkey Grindest** (5.12a)* 3 & 3 permadraws bolts. Climb Monkey Grinder but continue traversing to the 3rd permadraw (Power Scratch's last bolt), then finish straight up to Power Scratch's anchors. Project, but not for long. Three guys are gunning for this while we go to print. Variation: finish on route #16's anchors (likely easier and less rope drag).

Rock island 4: 10' long, fully detached from the cliff. Belay these routes from the ground. The next four routes pair up, forming two sets of "Y" boltlines.

Sharing 1 bolt and the starting move:

13. **Lessamir the Slashamatic 1431 Hellkitty** (5.11c)* 3 bolts and 1 permadraw, John Hogge. Start left of Bolt 1, then slash diagonally left for two bolts, then slash right a little to Bolt 4 and anchors, leaving a heinous blood trail. *Beta*.[220] '09

14. **Hello Netherkitty!** (5.11c)*** 3 bolts and 1 permadraw, John Hogge. Start left of Bolt 1. Branch right. *Beta*[221]. '09

---

[219] Karl and Annette took 11 months to develop the route, with 4-5 months between bolting the anchors and the rest of the route. They described the moves of the first half of the route as "monkeying" with long reaches and quick movement. The route name evolved thusly.

[220] Lessamir and Hello Netherkitty share an improbable-looking starting dyno on solid holds to a solid target. Then, Lessamir's beta is to move a hand down to a lower hold to the easiest (lower) diagonal traverse to Bolt 2.

[221] See the beta footnote for Lessamir, plus, well, this route is like that time the cat leapt to a chair top, then jumped to an all-legs clawing onto the nice drapery, then sprung onto the ledge where your fine pottery collection sat precariously. Packed with three big deadpoints, though the third one might just as easily be replaced with static moves.

North Shore

Rock island 3: 12' long, fully detached from the cliff. Belay these routes from the rock island.

Sharing 2 bolts and the starting move:

15. **Power Scratch** (5.11d)* 4 bolts and 1 permadraw, John Hogge. Step off Rock Island#3 onto the mild bowl-dihedral to the jug flake. After two bolts, branch left. Enjoy the chossy right handlebar sidepull while it lasts; do not clip high from it. Sort of like that weird sport where two guys box and play chess at the same time, boxing for one round and then each playing one more move in the chess game. '09

16. **My Name Was Muffin** (5.11c)*** 4 bolts, John Hogge. After two bolts, branch slightly right. The route is too long for three bolts, and too short for four. *Beta.*[222] '09

17. **Almost Nothing Screw It** (5.11b)*** 3 bolts, John Hogge. Start on the right end of Rock island #3. Levitation is within your grasp. Believe!

[222] Clipping strategy is an interesting part of the route and your beta.

North Shore: **Bee Wall**

Sun conditions: All day shade. This wall has some potential hard lines.
Approach: 8 minutes via the mid-level trail. See the section on trails at the beginning of this chapter.
GPS @ leftmost route (Bee-Roofic): N30°22.695' W98°06.894' (30.37825 -98.1149)

Low Roof hovering over Rock island #2, which is long and separated from Rock island #1 by a crack and big 12"
wide hackberry tree. Belay these routes from the island.

[1 likely future route]

1. **Bee-Roofic** (5.10bee)*** 4 bolts, John Hogge. Start just right of an 8" hackberry on the big cheat stone at the edge of Rock Island #2. If the cheat stone isn't tall enough for you, stack a backpack until left hand is on the crack's jug. Climb between the tree and the cliff. A nice, tricky warmup with a lot of moves for its length.

2. **Peace Breaker** (5.9 PG)*** 3 bolts, Taylor Reilly, Bird Dog, Alvino. Start 12' right of Bee-Roofic in the mild dihedral. A great warmup for the area. Easy runout to Bolt 2.

[possible 3 more future routes along this rock island]

expired application: Happy Days (5.9), to be 3-4 bolts. Lean out off the rock island to an obvious block; after getting on, traverse right 4' and top out.

Face (30' wide) with low 8' dish on left end, in front of Rock Island #1.

3. **Bee-otch** (5.12b)*** 5 bolts, Ralph Vega. Start on a tufa-featured dish above the ledge. Break just right of the dish. Human stick-clip Bolt 1 from the ledge to the right of it.

[likely 2 future routes]

Bulge-shaped cliff with upper bulgy roof (60' wide)

[likely 2-3 future routes along this bulge]

Large Beehive left of Stinger.

4. **Stinger** (5.12a)*** 3 bolts, David Cardosa[223]. Starts at the "V". Runout to Bolt 3. Exit left of the cactus. From the ground, you'd think the holds are thin. Consider using a two-rope belay to execute the clips better protected. The route could use a low directional bolt to manage the rope. '09

---

[223] Of the old timers we've met, David looks least likely to crush like he can. Not overweight, but just not that tall or tiny or broad-shouldered look of the rock gods. On routes near his limit, he lets out all these high pitched pain-yelps that sort of lampoon Sharma. He came back to the sport in recent years, bolted some North Shore routes, then broke the sad news that his shoulder was destroyed. Asked how, he said "Cat Flinch." He was staring down a cat for fun, the cat swiped claws at his arm, and he flinched it away, ripping the shoulder.

North Shore

North Shore: <u>**Cheech & Chong Wall**</u>[224]

Sun conditions: All day shade.
Approach: 7.5 minutes via the mid-level trail. See the section on trails at the beginning of this chapter.
GPS: N30˚22.675' W98˚06.919' (30.377917 -98.115317) @ Mickey's Crack

This wall is a little ugly, but it has high route quality and healthy warmups for harder stuff. Still Smokin', and Up in Smoke are good warmups once wired.

Right-leaning Dihedral

1. **Mickey's Crack** (5.11a)* 4 bolts, Taylor Reilly. Bolts are right of a right-leaning dihedral. '09

2. **Pluto's Hole** (5.10b PG)*** 3 bolts, Birddog. Start on a rounded arête. Climb to a big wedge below the roof and right of Bolt 3. Runout to Bolt 3 but with a solid clip stance. Cool topout over the anchors. '09

[potential route]

Slabby Face below a roof on the cliff's right side. Mini-roof at mid-level.

3. **Glass Slipper** (5.12a)*** 4 bolts, Alvino Pon. Climb past a curvy zigzaggy horizontal crack at mid-wall. Constipation followed by great relief. '09

Gnarly flattened cedar stump

expired application: Walt Loves Children (5.9-5.10), to be 3 bolts. Located over a cedar stump. Climb through a white tear and small sharp plates-tufas.

4. **Corsicane Brothers** (5.10a)*** 5 bolts, Birddog. Bolt 1 protects the climb onto the starting ledge. Climb up and right to two huge huecos that look like big monster eyes. The monster is staring at you. You sneak by, and then as darkness falls, you hear its footsteps… '09

15' Wide bulge-arête.

expired application: Brain Like a Sieve (5.hard), to be 4 bolts. Start 5' left of Mostly Labrador. Climb the right side of the bulge-arête.

5. **Mostly Labrador** (5.8+)*** 4 bolts, Chris (Birddog) Keistler. Bolt 2 is just right of a bowling ball sized hueco. Pull the cedar stump to get onto the starting ledge. '05

6. **Still Smokin'** (5.9)*** 3 bolts, Chris (Birddog) Keistler. Bolts are right of two big stacked huecos. '05

7. **Hey Mr. Lizard Man** (5.8 PG)*** 4 bolts, Kirk Holladay. Bolt 1 protects the climb onto the starting ledge. Anchors are left of a point on the mini-roof. Runout to Bolt 3 over a short fall onto the ledge. '09

David Phillips,
"Dave's Not Here"

---

[224] The left side is also known as Disney Wall.

8. **Up in Smoke** (5.10b)*** 4 bolts, Chris (Birddog) Keistler. Bolt 1 protects the climb onto the starting ledge. Mild runouts to Bolts 3 and 4. Anchors are right of a point on the mini-roof. Cheech gut-punches you for fun, then Chong passes you a big fatty. '05

Unbolted space[225]

Dihedral & Arête on Left Side of Steep Overhang (of Carnival Wall)

9. **Dave's Not Here** (5.11b)*** 5 bolts, Kirk (Kirkdog) Holladay. Bolt 1 protects the climb onto the starting ledge, but not very well, as you have to climb left of it. Climb a slight arête. Like climbing Blowing Smoke at the Monkey, but your arms explode. '05

North Shore: **Carnival Wall**

Sun conditions: All day shade.
Approach: 7.5 minutes via the mid-level trail. See the section on trails at the beginning of this chapter.
GPS @ trail head: N30˚22.664' W98˚06.946' (30.377733 -98.115767)

This tall, dramatic, steep wall has some hard-route potential, though some of it is off limits due to a proposed County overlook.

Big Low Roof under a Steep Overhang
[2 likely future routes]

[Viewpoint — for now, keep route applications 15' away from the caution tape at top of the cliff.]

expired application: Retro Cowboy (5.hard), to be 5 bolts. There's a directional bolt. The line runs up the middle of the wall.

abandoned application: "The Carny". Ends 15' left of Carnival's anchors. Dave advises this line not be bolted; too many pretty formations are choss that will break and yield no route.

Nose / Bend in Roof

expired application:, Crazy Mtu (5.12-13), to be 5 bolts. Starts under the big roof below Carnival, goes straight up and left to the arête, and finishes on Carnival's anchors. One school of thought: instead of (or in addition to) this line, do a low traverse under Carnival. '09

[1 likely future route]

1. **Carnival** (5.10d PG)*** 6 bolts, Dave Phillips. Start on the Gypsy Wall ledge; traverse up and left over the nose. Shares a belay station with two Gypsy Wall routes at the edge of the ledge. Bad right-swinging wrecking ball fall on a runout mild section. The family vacation road trip starts out fine. The kids start asking "Are we there yet?" a third of the way there. The wife forgot to pack lunch in the cooler. Bickering occurs over poor navigation skills, a missed exit, and a 20 mile run to the toll road's next U-turn. Tempers flare from that and the unfinished business of 20 years of marriage, and then it starts to hail. On the new car. '05

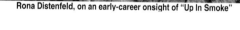
Rona Distenfeld, on an early-career onsight of "Up In Smoke"

---

[225] There is room for another line on cool upper features, but the start is way harder than the 5.8 mid and finish. Could come from the start of Up in Smoke, but that move is still much harder than the rest of this line. IMO, leave it unbolted.

Sun conditions: All day shade.
Approach: 7 ½ minutes via the mid-level trail. See the section on trails at the beginning of this chapter.
GPS @ western approach from Mossy Wall: N30˚22.667' W98˚06.940' (30.377783 -98.115667)
GPS @ eastern approach from Carnival Wall: N30˚22.666' W98˚06.906' (30.377767 -98.1151)

This wall is a sweet little climbing sanctuary, over a landing 10' above the floor of a little mini-canyon formed by a rock island. From the East (Carnival Wall), hike into the canyon and scramble up using a tree at the edge. From the west (Mossy Wall), hike that mossy canyon to the ledge's westernmost tip. Most of the routes are on the left end of the landing, with one lone route right of them.

Wildly featured face, the left half of the Open-Book dihedral listed below.

Carnival (on Carnival Wall), Living on the Edge, and Love Potion No. 9 share low bolts and a belay station. When seconding (TRing), clip the belayer-side-of-the-rope to Bolt 1 to prevent the belayer from crashing left into the rock.

2. **Living on the Edge** (5.10b)*** 5 bolts, Jan Salinas, the Black-clad Backstepper. Start on the crack between the two belay stations. Traverse left on Carnival's Bolts 1-3 and go up the arête. See belay station notes above. '09

   a. variation: (5.10b). This variation traverses onto the arête higher than Living on the Edge does. Traverse left on Carnival's Bolts 1-2, up on a bolt of Love Potion No. 9, traverse left onto the arête and up on Living on the Edge's Bolts 4-5 and anchors.

3. **Love Potion No. 9** (5.9)*** 5 bolts, Louie Graham, Jan Salinas. Start as with Living on the Edge. Traverse left on Carnival's Bolts 1-2 and go up the face on drips. See belay station notes above. Magic's in the air. '09

4. **Rock Gypsy** (5.7)*** 4 bolts, Jan Salinas. Chris (Birddog) Keistler Free Solo '05. Use the belay station near the tree. The boltline runs left of an hourglass shaped hueco. Great beginner's lead. '09.

   access solo: (5.5) Climb the dihedral book formation, exiting left at the cedar tree.

Open-Book dihedral with a short crack part way up.

5. **Hexed** (5.9/5.10a PG)* 3 bolts, Louie Graham. Climb the dihedral. Unclean fall on the way to the anchors, due to the ledge. The grade is height-dependent. '09.

   b. variation: **Freakshow** (5.8 PG)***, John Hogge. Start on paper thin jugs directly below the anchors. Go straight up. At Bolt 3, traverse the ledge right, go up to the clifftop 3' right of the anchors, and hand-traverse the clifftop to make the anchor clip.

   c. toprope: **Vagabond** (5.8)***. Set TR on Hexed' anchors. Start 5' right of where the rope hangs on an undercling crack. Follow the crack diagonally up and left to gain the ledge. Finish on Freakshow. A backwards "S" path and a big helping of underclings.

Face with an upper mini-roof under an arête. [Viewpoint — for now, keep route applications 15' away from the caution tape on the cliff.]

   solo: **Dream Weaver** (5.9), David Phillips. Start on Vagabond's undercling crack but go straight up, over the slightly overhanging ledge, and topout the face up and slightly right. '05

   Application on hold (in viewpoint area) Dream Weaver, to be 3 bolts. '09.
   Application on hold (in viewpoint area) Tramps and Thieves (5.11-), to be 3 bolts. 5' left of Crystal Balls.'09.
   Application on hold (in viewpoint area) Crystal Balls (5.10+), to be 3 bolts. 10' left of Gypsy's Magic. '09.

Mild Dihedral with a full-cliff right-facing crack

6. **Gypsy's Magic** (5.7 PG)*** 3 bolts, Louie Graham[226], Roger Werner. This was North Shore's first bolted route. Climb the right-facing crack in the mild dihedral. PG rated because of the dead tree, but it will eventually leave on its own. '05 ▮𝄆❊⛯☝𝍠⛏⟁⚞⚟⛐⚓ ⚐

Middle-of-Ledge access point from the narrow mossy little canyon, approaching from Carnival Wall.
Arête and Smooth dihedral
    [3 likely bolted routes].

Ledge's western-tip access point, approaching from Mossy Wall.

┌──┐

Gypsy Proverbs:
Burn your enemy's caravan and you burn your future.
Bury me on my feet—I have spent my entire life on my knees.
Credit is better than money.
A witch-wife and an evil is three-halfpence worse than the devil.
After bad luck comes good fortune.
In the hour of your greatest success are sown the seeds of your own destruction.
He who is late may gnaw the bones.
It is better to be the head of a mouse, than the tail of a lion.
The winter will ask what we did all summer.

└──┘

---
[226] Some developers are all about the FA; Louie is all about the picnic, bringing the best crag food to work on routes.

Sun conditions: All day shade.
Approach: 6 minutes via the mid-level trail. See the section on trails at the beginning of this chapter.
GPS @ Man's Best Friend: N30˚22.648' W98˚07.005'

Mossy Wall has a stellar set of tall (for Texas) routes that remind people of Prototype Wall, but they are prettier, more sustained, slightly taller, slightly steeper, and slightly tougher. Route character varies; some have thin crimps/pockets/footholds, one has juggy crimps on good footholds, and there's even a jug haul. The wall is steeper than it looks. It dries faster than other walls at North Shore, as it juts out and catches more air flow.

The right end of this wall is at the crack in the big open-book dihedral bordering Middle Earth Wall. The leftmost route is at a little canyon; hike that and scramble up the ledge to reach Gypsy Wall, a good place to warm up for this wall when Middle Earth Wall is occupied.

Mossy Canyon
Tree near the cliff

1. **Moss Cerveza** (5.11b)*** 5 bolts, John Hogge. Start between the tree and cliff. Ernst and Young have verified that this route has absolutely no resemblance to Mas Cerveza, and the two routes have negative market correlation. '10

2. **Deceptive Warmup** (5.11a)*** 6 bolts, Karl Vochatzer. A stiff 11a; 40% of sampled climbers think it's 11b. The last bolt goes out of sight by the time you're looking for it under the mini-roof. Go up and right to find it. '09

3. **Fancy Feast** (5.11b)*** 5 bolts, Kareem Al Bassam and David Cardosa. Climb left of Bolts 4 and 5; they might get moved leftward at some point. '09

variation: **Fancy Feast Indirect** (5.11b)*. Climb Deceptive Warmup's Bolts 1-3; cross right onto Fancy Feast. This variation was climbed before the direct route, and the developers prefer it. '09

4. **The Stain** (5.11c)*** 6 bolts, David Cardosa. Climb the white streak with black edges. '09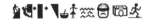

5. **Katrina** (5.12a)*** 5 bolts, John Myrick[227]. Bolt 1 is on top of the ledge. Bolt 4 is over the big tufas. At this point in the guide, we'd like to mention

---

[227] John "Power Merchant" Myrick started climbing at age 7. In high school he juggled climbing with wrestling, track, and power lifting. Weighing only 125, he could bench press 310 and squat 450. He's a Nationals Sport Climbing and Bouldering competitor, beloved coach of Team ARG (Austin Rock Gym), and a 5-time USA Nationals coach. John envisioned, organized, and currently directs the Collegiate Climbing Series tournament, initiating climbing as a college sport. Stocky doesn't even begin to describe John's physique. He's a Mack truck fueled by cheeseburgers. Back before John became such a productive member of society, he burned the candle at both ends. His pals Todd McCray and Curtis Mai had a rule: everyone had to take responsibility for their selves and not pass out. One night at the Potrero, John violated this rule, and out came the blue magic marker to decorate his sleeping face. The next morning, no one told him about his face, and they started climbing multi-pitch Snot Girlz. Somewhere up there, he noticed blue sweat dripping all over himself.

that Climbing is Inherently Dangerous. **For instance...**it was the summer of '05 and Kirk Holladay was TRing this line prior to its bolting. Several folks were milling about, below. Kirk fell; Dave Phillips took, but Kirk kept falling and almost decked. "WTF!?!" After *one of those* brief exchanges, they both looked up and saw the anchors had dropped 10' below the clifftop. Evidently, Birddog had anchored to a truck above the cliff, but the truck was not in Park and had rolled. However, on that summer day of '05, the truck did not kill Dave, Kirk, Birddog, the Watsons, Greg Brooks…

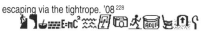

6. **Mossatopia** (5.11c)*** 5 bolts, Dave Phillips and Greg Brooks. Climb to the diamond-shaped cave. Slight runout to the anchors. '05

John Garcia, "Mossatopia"

7. **The Ghost of Johnny Reimers**

(5.12a)*** 6 bolts (1 permadraw), John Hogge. AKA "the blank route." From the ground it looks like there aren't any holds, but that's not the case. Big all-air runout to the anchors. The climbing is like wrestling the circus strongman, dodging the knife thrower, then escaping via the tightrope. '08 [228]

[1 bolt is approved for a linkup from route #7 to route #8's midsection. It's not well investigated yet, so it may not happen.]

8. **Beyond All Likelihood** (5.11d)* 6 bolts,

John Hogge. Climb to the big ledge. Bolts 3-5 slant steeply left towards cool little tufas. Hollow rock forced bolt placements that make onsighting ridonculous. Avoid frustration, read the footnoted beta and go for the flash.[229] At the top, pull a small roof below the anchors. The route is hard to second. The crux is truly mad at the world. '09

Trail Head

9. **Man's Best Friend** (5.12d)* 4 bolts, Eric

Patrick. Start up on the right side of the big pointy ledge. Bolts 2-4 slant left slightly. '05

---

[228] While all of the early crew began by picking eye-candy lines, I planned to just bolt a couple lines and go back to projecting at Reimers. I walked the clifftop the first day of development and threw two ropes semi-randomly over the cliff on walls I liked. One landed over the route, Dreamland; the other landed over this route.

[229] The boltline suggests traversing higher than the easiest path, but it's on super thin holds exceeding the route's grade. Bolt 3 is way high and right of the easiest path of the climb, because hollow rock left of it prohibited a bolt placement. Beta: left hand on the dark pocket, righthand clip Bolt 3, downclimb back to the ledge. Now move right hand to the dark pocket and traverse left on cruxy left hand and right hand fractured crimp sidepulls… while they last. If those should break, the higher more natural path probably becomes the route.

Prow-Arête

10. Astro Zombie (5.12c)*** 5 bolts, Ralph Vega. Climb just left of the left-leaning prowl-arête. Tasty big-air runouts. ⌂☝🗻☝☝ ⸮🐍⸮

11. The Beast Maker (5.12c-d)*** 4 bolts, Long Ta, Ralph Vega. Climb the left-leaning prow-arête. Bolt 1 is below the ledge. ⌂☝🗻 ☝⌂☝⸮

Left face of a big open-book dihedral.

12. ctrl alt delete (5.11c-5.12a)*** 4 bolts, Ralph Vega. Climb the white streak right of the prow-arête. ⌂☝☝⌂🗠🏃🥁

Lori Bergeron, making the wall look tall

13. 28 Year Engagement[230] (5.11d)*** 4 bolts. Climb the face to the choss hand holds over Bolt 3. Traverse right, under the roof, to the anchors. (You can also cut the corner to the roof, through tufas, probably at a higher grade.) Use long draws on the Bolts 1 and 4 to reduce rope drag clipping the anchors. ⌂☝☝🏃 $E=mc^2$ 🏃

extension: **Project** (5.hard). Clip 28 Year Engagement's left anchor. Pull the mini arête left of the anchors and top out left of the arête. Jump or walk off far west to the scramble-down mentioned under Philosophy Wall.

[potential route right of 28 Year Engagement, possibly sharing its anchors]

Right of the routes is the middle of the big open-book dihedral. It has 2 mini-roofs forming inverted stairs.

Downhill from Mossy Wall is a reasonable-looking Starflight (helicopter) evacuation spot in a meadow next to the river at GPS coordinates N30˚ 22.669' W098˚ 07.019' (Digital Degrees 30.377817 -98.116983). We don't know whether they can land there, but can probably drop a line from there.

> Joy comes in a rush as the muscles work swinging upward in balance past an occasional runner. The easy going is interspersed with bits of questioning calling for quirky answers. A hand jammed and the opposite foot set high in a hole and move up in one fluid motion pivoting and changing the jam to a lieback and reaching for the next spike above.
>
> *Royal Robbins*

---

[230] Johnny and Lenora owned North Shore and its 2,500+ acres for decades. Johnny was a momma's boy. Mama really was his best friend. But momma didn't like Lenora. Thus, they lived together for 28 years, until momma died. Then they got married.

Sun conditions: Morning shade; afternoon sun is from the side.
Approach: 5 minutes via the mid-level trail. See the section on trails at the beginning of this chapter.
GPS @ Hello World: N30°22.621' W98°07.040' (30.377017 -98.117333)

One Wall to rule them all…One Wall to find them, fleeing the noon sun at Dead Cats Wall for shadier climbing. This stellar wall has slightly more easy-to-moderate routes than Dead Cats, with bolts generally closer together. Five routes, however, climb over boulders near the cliff. Blown clips and bad (excessive slack) belays seen at other walls might result in severe injuries or deaths on these boulders. If you've never seen a bad belay, chances are you are badly belaying! Please seek more instruction.

This wall is wide, with two tall chimney caves dividing the routes into three sections, and two big boulders further subdividing the routes. Routes vary from juggy to crimpy, so the lower grade routes aren't necessarily the most recommended warmups. We like warming up on Tookish, Blood of the Dwarves, A Mortal Life, Orcs Drool, Elvin Beauty, My Precious, and Halfling's Leaf.

David Phillips, "Blood of the Dwarves"

Pocketed right face of a big open-book dihedral.
(Several Mossy Wall routes are on the left face.)

1. **Troll Teeth** (5.10b)*** 4 bolts, John Hogge. Start just right of the crack. '08.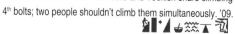

2. **The Fellowship** (5.9+)*** 4 bolts, Alvino Pon[231], Kirk Holladay. '05

Big Boulder (7'-8' tall) with rounded top, in front of the next two routes

3. **Bilbo's Bag** (5.9)*** 4 bolts, Kirk Holladay. High Bolt 1; we recommend the stick but also like this particular high bolt for an extra fun, careful, intimidating redpoint. '05

4. **Elvin Beauty** (5.10c)*** 4 bolts, John Hogge. Climb to the left side of the high rock outcrop, then traverse right to anchors. Shares a hold with Bilbo's Bag. '09

5. **Tookish** (5.8)*** 4 bolts, Kirk Holladay, Alvino Pon, Chris Keistler. WARNING: this route and Blood of the Dwarves share space at their 4th bolts; two people shouldn't climb them simultaneously. High Bolt 1 on easy climbing. This route breaks right after Bolt 3. '05

6. **Blood of the Dwarves**[232] (5.8)*** 4 bolts, John Hogge. The starting ledge under this climb is a shallow dish with wild little drip formations. WARNING: this route and Tookish share climbing space at their 4th bolts; two people shouldn't climb them simultaneously. '09.

---

[231] Alvino did a lot of ground-up style route development in Colorado, and developed a couple hundred routes around the U.S. He went the opposite direction of many climbers mentioned in this guidebook, actually moving *from* Colorado *to* Texas. Smart guy; short winters! "Alvino Pon" is an alias he uses on all of his routes. He first became known locally for handling hot coals at an Erock campfire, where he grabbed them out of the fire and held them in his palm, using some shamanesque hand-vibration magic. He'd also take the coal between two fingers and maintain it there, repeatedly blowing the Breath of the Yeti on it. Years ago, he solved a bolting closure in the Greenbelt; see the Greenbelt history.

[232] Long after the route was named, stone drip formations at the base of the route proved to be dwarven blood.

Between the next two routes, the ledge has a cool almost half-round tube indention.

7. **Hobbit Hole** (5.7)*** 4 bolts, Luke Bowman & Tommy Blackwell '05

8. **Fallohide** (5.7 PG)*** 4 bolts, Chris Keistler & Kirk Holladay. This route goes just left of a roughly 12" diameter tube divided by a handlebar. Runout to Bolt 2; stick-clip it if you don't dominate the grade. '05

Slanting Landing (downhill towards the right) under the next two routes

9. **One Ring to Rule Them All** (5.8+ R)*** 3 bolts, John Hogge[233]. All bolts and anchors are runout; unclean falls above Bolt 3 to the anchors. It's tempting to add a bolt up there, but we like the slow careful moves that would become hurried and trivial with a bolt. Some routes are just better run out. '09

10. **Amazing Legacy of J.R.R.Tolkein** (5.10a)*** 4 bolts, John Hogge. Start with foot on a blocky outcrop with a left-pointing flake. Pull to a hueco. '08

11. **A Mortal Life** (5.10a)*** 4 bolts, Jan Salinas & Dave Phillips. Pull the hard face to the runnel left of Moria Cave.

Moria Cave (a large vertical cave)

12. **Hello World** (5.8)* 3 bolts, Neil Higa. Pull the left edge of Moria Cave, clipping bolts on the left, to the anchors below the roof. '09

<u>extension:</u> (5.10d)*** 1 more bolt, Neil Higa. Bring two extra draws to do the extension. Above the low anchors and roof are one bolt and high anchors. To reduce rope drag, clip a draw on the left of the low anchors before pulling the extension. '09

[233] FA via a slow, tedious lead rope solo using a Cinch and quickdraw chains, because noone was around to belay and it seemed easy. Never again.

13. The Mines of Moria (5.11a)*** 4 bolts, John Hogge. Climb the runnels right of Moria Cave and left of the boltline; pull the roof. Runout cartwheel fall potential while trying to clip the anchors.'09

    a. variation: **Duran's Bane** (5.11a)*** Climb with hands right of Bolts 1-3, on the sweet tufas. (Are there any other kind?)

    b. variation: **Dwarven Greed** (5.10b)*** 5 bolts. At Bolt 3, traverse right clipping the 5th bolts of Ringbearer and Dwarves Rule and finish on Dwarves Rule.

Big Boulder (20' wide, 5'-6' tall) in front of the next 3 routes. WARNINGS: Use directionals on TR!! Belayers must be extra sharp for the next three routes to keep climbers from colliding with the big boulder.

14. Ringbearer (5.11a R)*** 4 bolts + 2 permadraws, Dave Phillips[234]. Climb through two black tufas left of the boltline and out the roof. Bad potential falls until Bolt 3 is clipped; consider just stick-clipping it on your first runs. Clip the anchors right-to-left, then place the belayer's end of the rope onto the right side of Bolt 6, to keep it out of the mini-crack. When seconding, belay from the big boulder top to reduce rope stretch, but also spot the seconder to avoid collision with the big boulder. The permadraws help seconds stay on the wall and help clean without seconding. '08

15. Dwarves Rule (5.10d)*** 5 bolts, John Hogge. Runout. Climbs the left side of a water streak. Use directionals when seconding to prevent collisions with the big boulder. '08

16. Orcs Drool (5.10a)*** 4 bolts, John Hogge. Climbs the right side of a water streak. Runout to the anchors. Use directionals when seconding to prevent collisions with the big boulder. '08

    [Potential tough face route.]

Slanting landing (downhill towards the right) under the next set of routes through Smeagol

17. My Precious (5.9)*** 5 bolts, Brian Wann & Kirk Holladay. WARNING: keep off the poorly supported thick ledge-outcrop left of the anchors. '05

Middle Earth Cave (a large chimney-tube formation)

18. toprope: Middle Earth Cave (5.6 TR)*** TR anchors, Dave Phillips. Anchors bb Kirk Holladay. '05

    a. toprope: **Mystic Wonder** (5.7 TR)*. Shares TR anchors with Halfling's Leaf. Start just inside the cave, facing outwards, pull its right arête, then break onto the right face.[235]

19. Halfling's Leaf (5.8)*** 5 bolts, Dave Phillips. Climb the thin crack. Excellent warmup. '05

20. Smeagol (5.9+ R)* 3 bolts+, Kirk Holladay, Alvino Pon. Bolt 3 is runout on hard moves[236]. '08

21. Worm Tongue (5.9 PG)*** 3 bolts, Kirk Holladay, Alvino Pon. Bolt 3 is somewhat runout but on easy moves. Be sure to hit the piston-grip-pinch-gaston-with-an-elbow-lock. '08

---

[234] Dave honed his crag wit from years of banter with his older brother and identical-twin brother. (Unbelievably, there are *two* carriers of Dave DNA.) A day climbing with Dave is almost guaranteed fun. Dave is most apt to say, "You're climbing it wrong," "This ain't no God Damn 5.10c," and, "Oh, you only get one more try, then I'm lowering ya." Over the years, Dave and bud Terence Smith came to define two types of climbers. Type 1 are those who climb only for themselves, not for the sake of relationships with partners and peers. Climbing is truly part of their soul. Type 2 are there to socialize and stoke their egos. We later added a postulate reminiscent of "I lost *The Game*". Identifying a climber as Type 2 automatically makes you Type 2. Also, Type 3 is weak climbing with "the fam" or a romantic interest. But all this is child's play compared to what Warren Harding published in 1975 — a scale of 10 climber "zones", ranging from elite-skill evangelical climbing-ethics-purists such as Royal Robbins (Zone 1) down to depraved, lowly-regarded shallow characters such as Harding himself (Zone 10). Harding had big balls — he published teasing discussions of 61 of his peer climbers, assigning each of them to a zone.

[235] Jan Salinas has dibs on a lead route that the committee twice denied. The application was for four bolts and anchors right of the cave. A handful of people like unique aspects of this climb and its convenience leading to set Middle Earth Cave TR.

[236] Several of us recommend lowering #3 and adding a 4th bolt.

Lori Baggins Bergeron, "Halfling's Leaf"

> Fantasy is escapist, and that is its glory. If a soldier is imprisoned by the enemy, don't we consider it his duty to escape?. . .If we value the freedom of mind and soul, if we're partisans of liberty, then it's our plain duty to escape, and to take as many people with us as we can!
>
> *J.R.R. Tolkein*

Little Dihedral Roof.

22. Earth's End (5.10a R)* 4 bolts, Kirk Holladay, Christopher "Fozzy" Reaves. This fun roof pull is not well protected[237]; you are committed to not fall. Runout to Bolt 4 on easy climbing. '09

Sick bulge (which transitions on the right to Insanity Wall's reverse stair step roof)

23. Beyond the Sea (5.11b / 5.11c)*** 6 bolts + 1 permadraw, Tommy Blackwell & Luke Bowman. Climb the weirdness to the big ledge. Pull the bulge and clip the super-long-chain permadraw. Height-dependent grade. Lacks sport anchors as of this writing. '05

    [POTENTIAL 5.12 up the middle of the bulge.]

---

[237] Not much can be done besides moving Bolt 3 up a little.

North Shore: <u>**Insanity Wall**</u>

Sun conditions: All day shade.
Approach: 4 ½ minutes via the mid-level trail. See the section on trails at the beginning of this chapter.
GPS @ Fangoria: N30˚22.613' W98˚07.092' (30.376883 -98.1182)

This wall was once covered in poison ivy stemming from a trunk the size of a tree. In a fit of literary genius, Chris Keistler penned the perfect name for this crazy mix of cliff shapes. The high roof area houses a great 5.9 warmup (Illusionary Mentor) and a set of low 10's on creepy terrain (micro-fractured rock that's holding up well) with some steep moves. The high roof-pulls look sketchy over a slab, but they are well bolted. The insanity continues across the low roofed overhanging headwall with uproutes and traverses across low huecos and a high horizontal band of mini-caves. The features keep coming with another high roof, a big offwidth crack (Insane Tree Hugger and branching routes), a wave-shaped cliff, a roof crack route (More Fun Than Bubblewrap)…crazy!

Reverse Stair Step Roof.

1. **Big Huking Chicken** (5.11a R)*** 5 bolts (1 is a permadraw), Luke Bowman, Sean O'Grady, Tommy Blackwell. Climb the left end of the low roof. Hang a long draw on the bolt above the roof to decrease rope drag. Consider stick-clipping the reachy roof permadraw. The roof can be solved at least two ways. '09

2. **Lithium** (5.11d R)* 4 bolts, Evan Jackson, Dave Street, Russell Gaskamp. Runs above the tall hackberry on similar formations as Big Huking Chicken. Scramble high on the ledge to Bolt 1 just before the top of the ledge. Consider stick-clipping Bolt 3, by climbing the tree.

High roof (near clifftop) over crazy formations, insane shapes, choss, and fractured holds spanning the following five routes. 3 of the routes are marked intimidating due to runouts and clips on suspect looking holds, but they've had extensive cleaning and have held up well.

3. **Illusionary Mentor** (5.9)*** 5 bolts, Chris Keistler. Climb the offwidth crack and cross the arête higher up. Reachy Bolt 3. Reasonable runout to Bolt 4. A great climb and healthy warmup. '08

4. **Dr. Jekyll** (5.10b PG)* 5 bolts, Alvino Pon & Chris Keistler. Bolts 1 and 2 are on the middle of the ledgy protruding boulder stack. Climb to a large detached-looking outcropping and a small tufa. Two runouts. '08

Routes 5 & 6 share Bolt 1. Routes 6 & 7 share Bolts 1-3.

5. **Mr. Hyde** (5.10b)* 4 bolts, Alvino Pon & Chris Keistler. Bolt 2 is at 11 o'clock, near the top of the ledge. '09

6. **Psycho Killer** (5.10b)*** 5 bolts, Chris Keistler. Bolts 1 and 2 are on the right end of the ledgy protruding boulder stack. At the upper roof, climb just right of the unusual horizontal horn. Beware: a big choss section right of that has a hairline crack all around it. Use it lightly or use other holds. '08

7. **Huevos Locos** (5.10a PG)*** 5 bolts, Christopher "Fozzy" Reaves, Chris Keistler, Alvino Pon. Runout on easy climbing. Clip Psycho Killer's Bolts 1-3. Cross an arête right and go up towards a small cave. (Option: use PK's Bolt 4 to temporarily protect reaching to clip around the arête.) Runout to Bolt 5 on easy climbing; the PG rating applies to Bolt 4.

   a. extension: **Lenora's Wrath Kept 'em Lawful**[238] (5.10c)*** 4 bolts + 6 permadraws, John Hogge. <u>35-meter rope minimum</u>. Bring a 5th draw for the optional pro described under Huevos Locos. Climb Huevos Locos' Bolts 1-4, then traverse right on permadraws across the wild little caves, finishing on Fangoria's anchors. Soft belay the final moves. To clean most safely, pull the rope and lead Huevos Locos. Or second this route, avoiding a bad cartwheel pendulum fall by climbing past Bolt 4 to get a solid stance in the bowl, before unclipping it. This route is like a long, stormy vacation in a tropical paradise. *Beta.*[239] '09

---

[238] Years ago, young friends of Johnny were trying to talk him into letting them grow *stuff* on the ranch. But, fearing Lenora, they opted not to.
[239] The 10c path is hard to read across the caves. Going too low or too high at the wrong points will trap you.

Rona "Tygress" Distenfeld, "Psycho Killer"

Big Overhanging Headwall over an outward-arcing roof that's over a high starting ledge.

8. Global Warming (5.11c)* 4 bolts + 1 permadraw, John Hogge. At Bolt 1, climb the ledges to mid-roof (if you're a purist, else skip this hard ledge topout and just scramble to the right on Pave the World). Maybe pass up the stick to clip Bolt 2. The clip is solid spooky fun for a 6' tall type. The roof looks imposing, so few pull this sweet route. Come on. *Bring it.*[240]

9. Pave the World (5.12a)* 2 bolts + 3 permadraws, John Hogge. Scramble up near Fangoria's Bolt 1 and walk left on the ledge. Start on a high hold, right of Bolt 2, which is shared with Pollution and Erosion. All-air runout to the last permadraw. A hold got smaller after the FA; it might be harder than 5.12a now. The cement dab is actually a reinforcement layer, on a different hold.

> **b. variation: All Part of my Evil Plan** (5.11c)* 3 bolts + 3 permadraws, John Hogge. Offers an interesting longer alternative start to Global Warming. Climb Pave the World's Bolts 1-3; traverse the line of huecos left and finish on Global Warming. This variation is easy to clean, whereas the next one requires seconding.

> **c. variation: Game Over, Man. Game Over!** (5.11d)*** 3 bolts + 6 permadraws, John Hogge. Climb All Part of my Evil Plan to its highest permadraw, then traverse the caves right on Lenora's Wrath Kept 'em Lawful, which finishes on Fangoria's anchors. This wacky, long line goes up, traverses left, goes up, and traverses right, for the weirdest boltline in Austin. It hits every cool hold on the headwall, and it's the longest route at North Shore.[241] ESTIMATED MINIMUM ROPE LENGTH: 35 meters.

10. Pollution / Erosion (5.12c)*** 5 bolts & 1 permadraw, Long Ta[242], bb John Hogge. Climb Fangoria's easy start and clip its Bolt 1. Scramble up and left on the ledge. Borrows a starting hold from Pave the World, using it left-handed. Rupesh says the moves are great, and it's a good route despite the choss. '09

11. Fangoria (5.12a)*** 5 bolts, Ralph Vega. Starts to a big white tufa under a bulge. R.A. says it's as good as Tunnel Vision. '09

---

[240] I took 40 minutes of solo hangdogging and quiet contemplation to solve the crux; Rupesh took 10 seconds.
[241] I bolted Pave the World primarily to serve this variation, and didn't count on ever sending Pave the World.
[242] This route had some obvious suspect holds left after bolting and cleaning, but *five* broke during Long's attempts, including one during the FA.

Steep Face with high roof and offwidth crack (left), transitioning into a prow (middle) and then a wave formation (right).

The next four routes share bolts. (#12 and "d" share finishes. "d", "e" and #13 share starts.) If you like onsights, go for #12 and either route "e" or #13 so you can get in two start-to-finish onsights.

12. Anger (5.11b)*** 4 bolts & 3 permadraws, John Hogge. Climb the two-boulder-stack column, clipping Bolts 1-2, to the large landing. Go up the face, clipping Bolts 3, 4 and 5 (the permadraw) just under the steep part. Work up and slightly right to a hidden permadraw above the 1st roof. From there you finish on Festivus, working left and up clipping one more permadraw and pulling the ledge. Expect rock fall at the choss band.[243]

d. bolted variation: **Festivus, for the Rest of Us**
(5.11a)* 3 bolts & 4 permadraws, John Hogge. Climb Insane Tree Hugger's Bolts 1-3. On four permadraws, cut up and left across the Rachel Harris Picnic Cave, continue up and left and end on Anger's anchors. Can be cleaned quickly by seconding the low part of Insane Tree Hugger. Festivus or Grievances was originally proposed by David Cardosa. There are feats of strength, and it doesn't end until someone gets pinned!

e. bolted variation: **The Airing of Grievances**[244]
(5.10d)*** 3 bolts & 3 permadraws, John Hogge. Climb Insane Tree Hugger's Bolts 1-3. Cut up and left to the Rachel Harris Picnic Cave, and continue straight up from there on permadraws to separate anchors. Can be cleaned quickly by seconding the low part of Insane Tree Hugger. Semi-beta: this route can't feel like 10d without perfect strategy.

13. Insane Tree Hugger[245] (5.11a)*** 6 bolts, Chris Keistler. Climb the big overhanging offwidth crack. Bolt 2 seems too low. Mild runout to Bolt 3. Very popular; watch how many people climb the crack wrong. '08

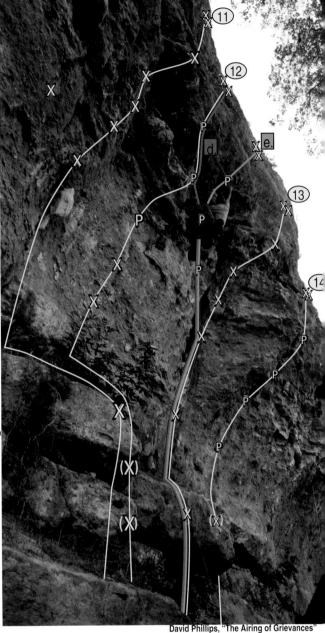

David Phillips, "The Airing of Grievances"

14. Bulimia[246] (5.12c)*** 1 bolt and 4 wire permadraws, Cody Ramsey, bb Karl Guthrie and Vinny Vinson. Climb the big prow. '09

expired application: Hill Country Hobo (5.12-5.13), to be 4 bolts. Climb to the huge orange and black cave. '09

---

[243] I took a long blind lead fall, when a hold broke and sent choss into my eyes.

[244] References a Seinfeld episode and commiserates six separate airings of grievances that occurred during the development of North Shore.

[245] Originally a TR named Texas Toprope (Dave Phillips '05), falls caught a manly-sized swath of Texas sky. Some still have fun TRing this without any directionals; however a low fall results in a collision with the tree. Chris bolted this route on lead. His aiding hook failed and he hit the tree hard, gashing his forehead, and preventing him from decking as he bear-hugged the tree and slid down it. Then he went back up to see what failed. The hook (borrowed from Kirky) hadn't popped off the rock — rather, the sketchy shoe-lace Kirk used to cord the hook had finally broken.

[246] The core intensive mid section almost caused Cody to puke.

15. **The Heart is Deceitful Above All Things** (5.11d)* 4 bolts, Ralph Vega. Climb right of the orange and black cave. '09

16. **Identity Crisis** (5.12a)* Dave Phillips, partially bolted. Start 8' left of Imaginary Friend on small dihedral stair steps. Large suspect block. The route was still under development, as of this writing.

    [-1 hard future route]

17. **Imaginary Friend** (5.11c)*** 2 bolts + 3 permadraws, Jeff Jackson, Dave Phillips. Scramble up the messy boulder stack left of the route and onto the ledge. Climb a seam through the wave and out a steep roof formation. All-air runout to the anchors. This route requires a lot of Dave Kwon Do, and it has the most Bling of any route at North Shore, with Tree Hugger a close second. '08

18. **HE Ain't My Brother...** (5.11c PG)* 4 permadraws, John Hogge. Scramble up as described under Imaginary Friend and walk right. Falls are typical getting hands above Bolt 3 to clip; even with a sharp belay, leaders will lightly deck onto the ledge at the bottom of wave. After Bolt 3, traverse left one bolt and then pull onto the ledge to out-of-sight anchors that are up and right. Like when a magic trick goes horribly wrong, then is salvaged before the audience notices.

    f. bolted variation: **...Never WAS, and never will BE!**[247] (5.11d PG)*** 5 permadraws, John Hogge. Climb HE Aint' My Brother...'s Bolts 1-4, then traverse left to the Neil Higa Mini-Cave, clipping this route's only independent bolt, then up and left to Imaginary Friend's anchors. At Bolt 4 you could go up to get hands onto the ledge, then shuffle them to the anchors, but it's boring. The low cave traverse is exciting, so do that.

Roof architected straight out of the original Flintstones cartoon. The roof is over a landing about the same size.

19. **More Fun Than Bubblewrap** (5.10a)*** 3 bolts, Tommy Blackwell, Evan Jackson, Sean O'Grady. '08. Trad FA Mike Klein, nearly pissing himself, while trespassing the property circa 1998. Chimney your way up under the anchors to the ledge. Traverse Bolts 1-2 left along the crack at the left edge of the roof. Mild runout to Bolt 3. This route is fun, pumpy, and longer on moves than it looks like from the ground.

    g. extension: **Pop!** (5.10b R)***. A long low creepy fun boulder-problem traverse tacked onto the start of Bubblewrap. Clip Bolt 1 and walk the ledge 21' right to the right-facing flake. Boulder the horizontal crack left to Bolt 1 and lead Bubblewrap. The lead line doesn't protect the traverse; use a spotter to help stay on the ledge after a fall. The spotter can crouch low behind the climber and use the low undercling crack to stay on the ledge. The dirt landing is sloped, but it could be flattened out more to help stop falls. The flake has some crumbly spots that are the main risk of falling. This hybrid route came about because Tommy wasn't enthused with how Bubblewrap came out, with rock conditions forcing low anchors. The idea for Pop *bubbled up* three years later.

[potential sick routes on the roof, though the two flakes under the headwall are loose and will need to be trundled]

bouldering: The ledge under Bubblewrap and the big roof is fronted with an excellent face with juggy bouldering for warmups convenient to west Insanity Wall and Dreamer's Wall.

---

[247] The names of the main route and variation are Milton Reimers' reply to a realtor who mistakenly called Johnny Reimers his brother. (They were cousins.) Some of my friends took to randomly blurting out this cute quote. Milton and Johnny were probably cool together, though, as they played poker together. Maybe the realtor caught Milton on a bad day. Lenora Reimers also did the poker thing, late in life, enjoying internet Omaha Hold'em, which is one brainy complicated messed up game, if you ask me.

North Shore: **Dreamer's Wall**

Sun conditions: All day shade.
Approach: 3 ½ minutes via the mid-level trail. See the section on trails at the beginning of this chapter.
GPS @ the head of the spur trail leading to Lenora Reimers' Turkey Call: N30˚22.613' W98˚07.100' (30.376881 -98.118333)

The routes on this wall and the rightmost routes of Insanity Wall appear pretty short for sport routes, but they have a lot of moves or other exciting reasons to exist. The wave on the right is the little prettiest formation at North Shore. The two cracks and the diagonal traverse between them offer a nice warmup sequence. Another good warmup area is the bouldering described under Insanity Wall.

Bulge/Arête right of Flintstones cartoon architecture roof

1. **Huck of a Deal** (5.10d)* 2 bolts, John Hogge. Scramble up the little dihedral under the landing, underneath I Double Dog Adair Ya. Bolt 1 is up and left on the bulge. Bolt 2 is at 11 o'clock on the face. Anchors are out of sight. '09

Raised landing under a big "open book" dihedral

2. **I Double-Dog-Adair Ya** (5.7)* 2 bolts, FA free solo Jodi Adair[248] '05. bb John Hogge '09. Climb the left-leaning hand crack. One of the worst looking little routes, yet it offers some teaching moments.

   a. bolted variation: **Charles Bergh Fan Club** (5.9)* 3 bolts, John Hogge. Clip Eternal Love's Bolt 1. Climb diagonally left and traverse under the roof to I Double-Dog-Adair Ya's anchors. A wild little traverse through a cool space, with cryptic optional beta. '09

3. **Eternal Love** (5.8+)* 2 bolts, FA free solo Dave Phillips '05. bb John Hogge, '09. Climb the right-leaning flake-crack.

   [Center of the thin-shelf roof has multiple cracks; a safe route is doubtful.]

The next two routes are a right-traverse and an uproute crossing it. They share the traverse's 2ⁿᵈ permadraw.

4. **Open Spaces** (5.11b)*** 5 permadraws, John Hogge. Climb the blob under the dihedral. Lean out right to clip Bolt 1. Traverse right across the entire face, around (or over) the arête, and up to The Arête Twin's anchors. Not unlike the complicated Iraqi War, culminating in a surge.

5. **Water Quality** (5.10d)*** 3 bolts (1 is a permadraw), John Hogge. Climb just right of the blob under the dihedral; pull the right side of the roof. Borrows Open Space's Bolt 2. Runout from there to Bolt 3. Don't play on the roof's left side; it has fractures.

   [Right of that is a mediocre-looking uproute. A very hard painful one-move-wonder start to easier climbing, though the top might have a secondary crux. It's worth checking out.]

Two arêtes separated by a short, 4' tall crack.

6. **L'arête Des Jumeaux (The Arête Twins)** (5.11c)*** 3 bolts, Karl Vochatzer & Annette Pelletier.[249] '08. The boltline is on the left arête, left of the dihedral. Pick from the two general paths shown on the topo. Will you pick wisely?

   [POTENTIAL 5.hard route up the runnels on the right face of the dihedral, squeezed between Duex Arêtes and Lenora Reimers' Turkey Call. TR route off DA anchors?]

---

[248] Jodi, a rookie climber, soloed to the area where the anchors are now. Afraid to lean back and pull on the juggy but suspect-looking boulder stack, as advised, she instead traversed left on dirt, pulling off loose rocks, putting herself over a death fall. No longer able to spot, Dave Phillips then ran up the access crack at Philosophy Wall to get on top to pull her up by the hair, in the event she needed that. She didn't.

[249] They bolted the route on their first date. Developing this route led to developing their daughter Lillyana, 18 months later.

Small beautiful wave; Trail Head

7. **Lenora Reimers' Turkey Call** (5.11b PG)* 4 bolts (3 are permadraws), John Hogge. Unclean fall potential (wrecking ball onto pointy part of arête or ledge). Bolts run just right of the rightmost of the double arêtes, on the left end of the small wave formation. After mantling the ledge, start straight up the arête. '08

    b. underline:variation: **GO TO HELL**[250] (5.11b PG)*. Pull right of the arête onto the wave for a chill. Then work left back onto the main route on higher holds than you used to get onto the wave.

    c. extension: **Goats and Cattle**[251] (5.11c PG)*** 4 permadraws, John Hogge. Climb Lenora Reimers' Turkey Call, skipping her anchors and traversing right in an arc across the top of the wave formation to Dreamland's anchors.

    d. extension: **Cattle and Goats** (5.11a)*, John Hogge. Climb Dreamland or Years in the Making, rest thoroughly, then climb Goats and Cattle right-to-left; exit on Lenora Reimers' Turkey Call anchors. '09

    [potential hard line or two, middle of wave]

8. **Dreamland**[252] (5.11a PG)* 3 bolts, John Hogge. Start on a divot in the roof, under a wide black streak on the wave. Pull the roof left of Bolt 1 and chill before attacking the wave. Unclean wrecking-ball fall potential on a runout to the anchors. A short pretty gal gets furious at you, for a moment, till you give her an ice cream. '08

Rounded Arête

9. **Years in the Making** (5.11a)* 4 bolts, John Hogge. Starts on the little roof; traverses diagonally left across the rounded arête to anchors above a ledge. Belay on the ledge at the start. '09

---

[250] Lenora once countered a low offer on her land by scrawling GO TO HELL on the contract and faxing it back.
[251] Goats were ranched here for decades, followed by Cattle. '09
[252] My original name for North Shore, inspired by the awesome beauty of the ranch, the potential climbing, and the dream of somehow creating a permanent climbing park at the far end of 1,159 acres that I couldn't afford to keep. Its difficult journey into the public hands was a dream-come-true.

North Shore

North Shore: **Philosophy Wall**

Sun conditions: Morning shade; afternoon tree shade.
Approach: 2 ½ minutes via the mid-level trail. See the section on trails at the beginning of this chapter.
GPS @ the corner of the river-facing and creek-facing problems (at The Golden Rule): N30°22.609' W98°07.110' (30.376817 -98.1185)

This wall has over thirty TR-protected boulder problems ranging V0- to V3 (5.7 to 5.11d). They are generally tricky and harder than they look. All grades are tentative, on very little traffic. Several routes have chossy tops; watch for rock fall.

The 2010 Routes Committee and some advisors considered how to utilize this wall. The routes are too short for quality lead routes, too easy to appeal to most boulderers, and too high with marginal landings for beginning boulderers. Consensus was to install TR anchors. Development work was done by Dave Phillips, Birddog, Jodie Adair, Louie Graham, Jan Salinas, John Hogge, Chris Barton, Rona Distenfeld, Adam Mitchell, and Carlos Garza. Dave and John installed the anchors in 2010. FA credits on this wall are for first ropeless ascents. Since "V" grades aren't real expressive in this grade range, we give both "V" and YDS number grades.

Location: This wall is the closest from the trail leading east from the creek east of the parking lot. As you cross the wide creek, you'll see the right end of these routes. Most of the routes are on the cliff along the creek valley, but on the left end they continue on the cliff as it bends to face the Pedernales River. The cliff connects into the first bolted lead routes on Dreamer's Wall.

Rona Distenfeld, "The Early Bird Gets the Worm"

Equipment: For setting the topropes, bring 24" slings, locking biners, and some 50' minimum ropes. If you like the wall enough for repeat visits, retire some lead lines and cut them into 50' ropes to handle all routes here. We keep a kit of slings and 50' ropes that cover a third of the wall at a time.

Setup: The toprope anchors are mostly above the cliff for easy TR setting, and most are not visible from the ground. Go up top with your gear and find the leftmost or rightmost anchor, then read the **underlined anchor descriptions**, which explain each anchor location and the problems it protects. Hang your ropes, then on the ground the descriptions of rock features (*in bold italics*) and problems should sync up with the ropes you've hung.

Top Access: (left to right) Unnamed Dihedral (a 5.7 lead route), Access Crack (5.7 solo, but it's hard when toting gear), The Jodi Adair Show (a 5.6 lead route, aid-able with long draws in case you have no lead belayer), and a rock stairway access (uncool when wet).

The following descriptions start on the left with the river-facing rock features and routes, and transition to creek-facing rock features and routes.

--- River-Facing Routes ---

Slab to the right of the lead route "Years in the Making" on Dreamer's Wall.

1. **The Far Left** (V0, 5.9) No Anchors, Dave Phillips free solo FA. Climb the slab at a dish right of the bolted route.

15' foot wide Column. Climbable cracks flank its left and right end.

Lead Route Anchors (right of the dihedral, when facing over the cliff. These anchors serve the next lead route.)
2. **Unnamed Dihedral** (V0-, 5.7) 1 bolt, Chris Keistler. Bolted for convenient access to the top. Climbs the crack line in the wide dihedral with a pocketed right face.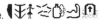

TR Anchors (overlooking a huge hackberry and the river.)
3. **Social Anxiety** (V2, 5.11b)*. Stand on the right side of the ground-level patio boulder. Climb the rounded arête.

TR Anchors (bolted either side of a mini-crack, in front of small boulders. They serve the next two routes.)
4. **Buddhism** (V0, 5.9)*. Pull crimps left of the thin flake onto the little slab and to the big plate.

5. **Bud-ism** (V0, 5.10b)*. Start at the thin flake. This featured problem looks easier than blank Buddhism, but no.

6. **Access Crack** (V0-, 5.7)* No Anchors. Climb the body-jamming wide crack. Often soloed for access, it's awkward, technical, and ill-advised with a backpack. Hiking access is described below.

16' foot wide Face left of the rounded-arête.

<u>TR Anchors</u> (sitting on a low ledge next to the wide Access Crack. They serve the next three routes.)
7. **Living on the Edge** (V0-, 5.7)***. Pull the access crack's arête.

8. **The Early Worm Gets the Bird** (V0, 5.10a)***. Optional sit start. Climb just right of the arête, staying off of it, including its diagonal upper section.

9. **Fairness Can Not Be Measured** (V2, 5.11b)***. Sit-start in front of the weird clumpy tree with many little trunks. Pull the ladder of pockets on the face right of the wide crack.

<u>TR Anchors</u> (on a 20' wide rock island's right side as you're facing over the cliff. They serve the next three routes.)

10. **ProcrastiNation** (V1, 5.10d)*** Dave Phillips. Start 5' right of weird clumpy tree, where hold density (pockets & runnels) is highest, just left of where the cliff rounds the corner. Optional sit start.

James Showery, "The Golden Rule"

--- Creek-Facing Routes ---

Rounded Arête corner separating river-facing and creek-facing routes. 18' foot wide Face just right of the rounded-arête, with a low bulge transitioning to a steep slab.

11. **The Golden Rule. aka. Do Unto Others** (V0, 5.10b)*** Dave Phillips. Climb the arête.

12. **Elitism** (V3, 5.11c)*. Start just right of The Golden Rule, on a left-hand sidepull, feet on a big ledge at the ground. Stay off the obvious juggy holds of The Golden Rule.

<u>TR Anchors</u> (sitting on a rock island's left side as you're facing over the cliff. They serve the next two routes.)
13. **The Path of the Weekend Warrior** (V1, 5.10c)***. Start on crimps above and left of two slots 5' up.

14. **Staunch Liberal** (V0, 5.10a)*** John Hogge. Sit start and pull to a right-hand crescent moon shaped pocket; climb to and over the big flake at the top.

<u>TR Anchors</u> (sitting a little low on a rock coffee table. They serve the next two routes.)
Crack slanting slightly left

15. **Unnamed Crack** (V0-, 5.7)*. Chris Keistler.

24' wide Slab over a starting bulge.

16. **Fascist Reality** (V0, 5.9)*** Adam Mitchell[253]. Climb the slab right of the V0 crack.

---
[253] Adam now owns the guiding service company Rockabout, Inc.

17. Honesty is the Best Policy (V0, 5.8)* Dave Phillips. Start left of the dish/bulge formation described below, left-hand in a 3 finger pocket with a visible thumb catch. Exit right to the anchors. This and the next three routes were squeezed mercilessly together, but they have distinct starts. Their easy slabs were thrilling solos, but boring topropes. We *honestly* advise just staying on rope to pull all four starts to the slabs and immediately lowering. Or bring pads and use these slabs for head gaming. Expect some dirt up there.

18. Bleeding Heart Conservative (V0, 5.8)* Dave Phillips. Start on the left side of the dish/bulge formation.

Dish/Bulge formation (a low dish under a pronounced bulge).

19. Pinko Commie (V0, 5.9)* Dave Phillips. Start left hand on three vertical slot-pockets on the right side of the dish/bulge formation.

TR Anchors (under a big balanced boulder protruding far over the slab section. Access the anchors via a safety line or quick-draw chain on the anchors for route #23. These anchors serve the next three routes.)

20. Nanny Culture (V0, 5.10b)* John Hogge. Squeezed just right of Pinko Commie. Start below a 5' wide shelf that's 8' off the ground. Stay off the left blocky pinch.

21. Pragmatism (V0, 5.10a)* Chris Barton. Start below the right-pointing flake.

Shallow Dish under a High Rounded Arête.

22. Anarchists of the World Unite (V0, 5.10b)*** John Hogge. Start under the high rounded arête, pulling to and past the low shallow dish and up the arête. Since the toprope hangs well to the left, you can cut the swing by flicking the climber's side of the rope right to a slot 2' right of the high arête's top.

TR Anchors (sitting low under a Persimmon grove, next to the fractured-top roof.)

23. Put Your Best Foot Forward (V0, 5.8)* Dave Phillips. Start right of the arête in a mild dihedral.

TR Anchors & Rappel Station (over the wide offwidth crack, accessed via the ledge under the overhanging cliff near route #23's anchors. These chain anchors serve the next two routes.)

24. Elijah Rock (V0, 5.8+)* Jodi Adair. Pull the low sprague pockets, staying off the jug ledge on the right. Short, but it will take a while to get up it.

Wide offwidth crack.

25. John the Baptist's Belt (V0-, 5.7)*** Jodi Adair. Climb the wide offwidth crack to a little landing. Short but tricky and very instructional, with viable finger, fist, arm and body jams.

variation: (old school 5.7)***. Climb using nothing but crack jamming until the crack runs out.

12' Wide Column Boulder.

TR Anchors (at the right side — when facing over the cliff — of a grove of three oaks)
26. An Eye for an Eye (V0-, 5.7)*** Dave Phillips. Climb the slight dish and exit through the left-leaning dihedral.

TR Anchors (at the middle of a grove of three oaks)
27. A Tooth for a Tooth (V0, 5.9)* Dave Phillips. Climb the cave's left edge and top out at any of the three or so topout points. The steepest move on the wall.

Cave.

Lead Route Anchors (at the left side — when facing over the cliff — of a grove of three oaks. The anchors are centered over the dihedral. They serve the next two routes.)
28. The Jodi Adair Show (V0-, 5.6)* 3 bolts, Jodi Adair, bb David Phillips. Climb the cave, exiting right. The bolts are close and could have been reduced to one bolt, but they do come in handy for quick access via solo aiding. We don't trust the upper holds enough to solo this.

Face with low roof (2' off the ground on the left, higher on the right) and lots of ground-cover.

29. Path of Zen (V0, 5.10a)***. Start matched on Women Whiskey and Weed. Traverse left to the next hueco, then up, keeping hands right of the boltline of The Jodi Adair Show.

TR Anchors (left — when facing over the cliff — of a coffee table boulder resting at cliff edge. These anchors serve the next two routes.)

30. Women Whiskey and Weed (V3, 5.11d)***. Start matched on the shallow triangle hueco just left of the rounded arête. Climb up the arête (or the face left of it) to the chossy roof. Touch the roof and take. The roof can't be trusted to pull on. Extension: start on the low deep double-hueco pinch directly behind the toprope. The topo shows the extension. The route uses Zenister's anchors, but the topo doesn't show that, since the route stops well short of them.

North Shore

Mild Dihedral

31. Zenister (V3, 5.11c)***. Start slightly right of the toprope.

TR Anchors (low, below a mini-roof, out-of-sight from above. To set them, climb Zenister and traverse right to them. They serve Prison Planet.)

32. Prison Planet (V2, 5.11b)***. Just left of the big tree.

Big tree growing 6" from the cliff.

TR Anchors (opposite the left branch of the big oak tree. These anchors serve the next two routes.)

33. Shit Happens (V1, 5.10c)*** Dave Phillips. Climb the thin crack just right of the big tree, leading to an outcrop left of the choss bowl.

34. Pwnership (V0, 5.10a)* John Hogge. Start on a left-hand crimp under the 2' wide mini-roof. Pull up the mini-roof and then right to the ledge and up. Or, start with a big dyno straight to that ledge.

TR Anchors (7' left of the anchors for routes 33-34, on a caprock whose edge is diagonal to the cliff. They serve the next two routes.)

35. Hedonism (V0, 5.7/5.8)*** Dave Phillips. Climb at the huge triangular hueco with a mouth shape in its center. Several big dynamic moves rarely found on routes at this grade. The grade is height-dependent.

36. Do What Thou Wilt (V0, 5.9)*. Lay-back start the right-facing edge. Pull straight up, staying right of the huge triangular hueco on Hedonism. Exit left to the anchors.

37. Consumerism (V1?)*, No Anchors. Start on big slots. Bad landing. Exit left of the suspect band at the top.

38. The Far Right (V1?)*, No Anchors. Pull the chossy roof's non-chossy left side. Exit left of the suspect band at the top.

bouldering: V?, A traverse that starts on the big slots on The Far Right. Traverse left to the thin crack before the tree; continue on the thin crack on frog-legs to the cave.

Short hike between routes and the access.

Access up the obvious rock stairs: The stairs go up and right to a ledge. Traverse carefully left, posing rose moves. Avoid hitting your backpack against the overhanging rocks. This access is impassibly slick from seeps after rain; go a ways further right.

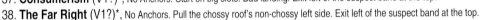

> If more of us valued food and cheer and song above hoarded gold, it would be a merrier world.
>
> *J.R.R. Tolkein*

North Shore: **The Matrix**

Sun conditions: All day shade.
Approach: 1 ½ - 2 minutes. See the section on trails at the beginning of this chapter.
GPS @ The Matrix Wall left end: N30˚22.576' W98˚07.147' (30.376267 -98.119117)
GPS @ Oracle Boulder: N30˚22.592' W98˚07.165' (30.376533 -98.119417)

The Matrix is a short wall (roughly 18' tall) and several boulders with a few routes and bouldering, across the creek from Philosophy Wall, on the west side of the creek. Some landings still need improvement. Problems will be published in the next edition.

See the overhead map at the start of the North Shore chapter. From the North Shore parking lot, hike the trail into the creek valley, stay on that side of the creek, and work uphill near the Oracle Boulder. The Matrix Wall faces the creek and then bends west into a canyon. The canyon portion is the short cliff line behind the tall Oracle Boulder, in the ravine between the wall and the boulder, guarded by two tall trees. On the other end of this ravine, you can climb up and out to The Dude Wall's left end.

Boulder with left-leaning crack and gnarly cedar on top.

The Matrix Wall, Creek Side, left end

The Matrix Wall, creek-side. *This wall starts just right of the boulder. It's roughly 18' tall cliff, with a rounded overhung dihedral with a thin crack and a bowl in the center.*

Roughly 10 problems.

The Matrix Wall, canyon-side.

1. **Trinity** (5.7), 2 bolts, Louie Graham. Climb the short fracture double crack near the creek-side entrance into the ravine, 40' left of The Blue Pill's anchors. '08 ?

solo: (5.???): access crack ?

toprope: Welcome to the Real World (5.10b TR)*, Dave Phillips. Use The Blue Pill's TR anchors. Climb 4' left of The Blue Pill. '08 ?

2. toprope**: The Blue Pill** (5.11b TR)*. TR anchors, John Hogge, David Phillips. Start in a dihedral left of a bulgy arête, near the ravine's narrow exit to The Dude Wall. 40' right of Trinity. '08 ?

Tilted flat boulder downhill.

Oracle Boulder. Its creek-facing end has a ledge stack forming a highball problem. The boulder and The Matrix Wall form a canyon. Topropes can probably be set via slings on vegetation atop the boulder.

Rabbit Hole Boulder. A rectangular boulder downhill. The boulder has a crawl space under it.

Short Boulder
360 degree traversing for little people

Oracle Boulder (right), The Matrix Wall riverside (left)

Sun conditions: All day shade.
Approach: 2 ½ minutes. See the section on trails at the beginning of this chapter.
GPS @ rightmost route (The Dude Abides): N30˚22.587' W98˚07.191' (30.37645 -98.11985)

See the trail map and Trail section at the start of the North Shore chapter. Hike counter-clockwise around the Oracle Boulder and scramble up and over a hill till you find the nearby lead routes.

1. **Project** (5.hard)* 2 bolts, bb Dave Phillips. Start on the boulder under the roof and pull the short lieback crack. Possible unclean fall at the anchors. The route is in front of a tall 2' wide post oak. A hold broke, sending this way up from the projected 5.11d. '09

2. **Don't Mess With the Jesus** (5.9+ PG)*** 3 bolts, Kirk Holladay. Climb the thin crack left of a leaning cedar tree on the ledge, then work left to anchors. Runout to Bolt 2 and the anchors. '08

   toprope: **Shut the Fuck Up, Donny** (5.12a TR)*** John Hogge. Start up the choss divot on the ledge. Climb fairly straight to the anchors.

3. **Just Checked In** (5.9 R)* 2 bolts, Rick Watson. High Bolt 1, above the roof. Runout to Bolts 1 and 2; do not fall. We usually dislike runouts but kind of like these. '08

4. **Nothing** (5.8)*** 4 bolts, Christopher "Fozzy" Reaves, Alvino Pon. Good warmup. '08

5. **The Nihlists** (5.8+)*** 4 bolts, Christopher "Fozzy" Reaves, Alvino Pon. Steeper than it looks. The jar is full of candy, but you can't open it. '08

6. **The Dude Abides** (5.7)*** 4 bolts, Kirk Holladay FA, Birddog trad FA, Dave Phillips FBA[255]. Climb the ledge to the large right-facing crack. '08

   toprope: **The Dude** (5.10a TR)*** Kirk Holladay, Rick Watson. Climb the face under the anchors. '08

   [abandoned application: (5.9). Abandoned due to poor route quality.]

> If my memory serves me right the girls that would date you back in the day didn't mind the fleas a bit!
> *Kirk Holladay*

---

[254] Route names are references to the movie The Big Lebowski. If you have no time to see the movie, you'll get a lot of laughs reading www.wikiquote.org/wiki/The_Big_Lebowski. This thing is growing…check out ww.lebowskifest.com.
[255] FBA = first beer ascent; a redpoint done holding a beer at all times. Dave executed a beer-jam during the ascent.

North Shore: <u>**History**</u>

A Sketch of Johnny and Lenora

Not many marriage engagements last *twenty eight years.* Hold that thought, while the story starts slowly and ramps up to crazy. Johnny ("J.R.") Reimers and Milton Reimers were cousins, each with a lot of land. They ranched goats and cattle, and somehow kept cedar suppressed on several thousand acres, leaving us beautiful open views and gushing springs.

Johnny's wife Lenora was very pleasant and quiet around me, but the neighbors knew not to mess with her. Even then, I imagine she had her hands full with Johnny. In these here parts of Texas, ranchers did have their fun. Johnny used to say people in Spicewood only ever get half drunk. (Ergo, they can always keep drinking.) Land rich and money poor, ranchers sometimes play poker for acres. The cash doesn't simply roll in from raising livestock, so ranchers did what they could to make ends meet. Lenora worked for the phone company, and Johnny built a beer joint on Highway 71, called The Horse Shoe Lounge (unrelated to the one in Austin). He'd catch catfish out of the Ped and prepare it as a special every week.

And he'd chop cedar and sell it for firewood. One day this didn't go well; his eye got slashed and blinded by his chainsaw. With rattlesnakes to eradicate around the ranch and meat to put on the table, hunting was a way of life. Lenora had a killer turkey call and hunted wild turkey on the property. One day Johnny spotted a rattlesnake in the house. He grabbed his shotgun and blasted a hole right through the floor. We do not know what Lenora said about that.

Nor what she said, if she knew, about the following shenanigans. Johnny and a friend were drinking a lot and driving, when a cop pulled them over. Probably long ago, without video cameras and decent radio connection to police backup. We don't know what words were said and what was personally at stake for them facing a DWI, but their solution to this problem, allegedly, was to take the cop's gun, rough him up, and flee. They got away with it.

Despite this one alleged lawless ethical breakdown, Johnny is described as a really kind, family man. Big, gentle, and always smiling. Family was first. And he was a momma's boy. Momma was his best friend, and she didn't like Lenora. Johnny's solution to this dilemma was to get engaged to Lenora. For *28 years.* After momma died, they got married, and stayed married decades longer than most of us. They had no biological children, but they raised Lenora's two nieces as their own. Some day when you're hiking deep into the ranch and come along some spring water…sip a little toast to J.R. and Lenora.

The Park Beyond All Likelihood

After Johnny died, Lenora settled the estate by putting up half her ranch (North Shore) for sale. She accepted an offer from me and my former wife, and then arose the first (of many) roadblocks to North Shore becoming parkland. Lenora felt she was selling too cheap, and she wanted out of the contract. Under contract terms, if the survey showed the ranch was a few acres above or below that of a decades-old survey, she had the right to cancel the sale. Well, that old survey had been done *old school*, prior to lasers and GPS, *by rolling a freaking wagon wheel along the borders and doing math on paper.* Fortunately, in this case, this old method was pretty accurate, and we were able to buy the property.

We hoped to somehow develop the North Shore riverfront as a climbing area while recouping the investment via an environmentally friendly housing development on the rest of the land. I became too busy to climb here, or anywhere else, but occasionally scoped the walls and bouldered.

Soon we learned that Travis County was looking for parkland, and I spent the next four years crossing my fingers and talking with Charles Bergh at Travis County. But we became ready to sell before they could buy. I lost patience, gave up my dream of preserving the climbing, and accepted a contract from a 1-acre-per-lot type land developer. With various properties to sell off to settle my divorce, it was a bitter-sweet opportunity. However, after a couple months, the developer changed plans and cancelled the contract. Fortunately, the County was still interested.

For most of 2005, many people worked to assemble the park deal, but it was tough going. While it thrashed through various obstacles, I opened up the ranch to some experienced developers to bolt routes, hoping to "knock it out" that year, maximize route safety and quality, and save the County the process of development oversight.

Chris "Birddog" Keistler on the cold, FA of "Psycho Killer"

The crew put up 28 routes until I casually mentioned it to the County, whereupon they firmly asked we stop developing routes. The County needed to follow their process of hearing all public interest groups, including other user groups and environmentalists. Objecting to that process did not seem worth risking the park acquisition, so we stopped development and just climbed on the existing routes. And always eager for FAs, several of the crew free soloed about 10 more routes, done in wild style, without pads, over unimproved landings, unpreviewed, untrundled, and dirty.[256]

Meanwhile, the park deal was under threat at every turn, with price re-negotiations among five different parties involved, a difficult third-party road deal, a bond election to win, and a seller's tax deadline to make. (Thus, the route called "Beyond All Likelihood.") Fortunately, on the platform of providing recreational opportunities, open spaces, and water quality, the bond election passed by a wide margin. Final negotiations and the closing happened a few hours before the tax deadline was up. Thanks to many hard working people and the voters' blessing, Travis County bought Milton Reimers Ranch and Pogue Hollow (North Shore) in late 2005.

Visitors have always been amazed at Pogue Hollow's immense beauty. I feel fortunate to have enjoyed its many sweet spots and to have played a part in its permanent preservation. Driving to sign the final papers to sell the ranch, I realized everyone in the surrounding traffic jam was about to buy themselves some amazing land. The cost to the public: under $20 each, in property taxes, spread out over several years.

Best Thing Since Sliced Bread

The Bolter's Gold Rush of 2008

The County graciously kept Reimers open immediately after their purchase, but they spent several years planning future park facilities, during which they kept North Shore closed. Climbers crave new rock and tire of old rock, and several of us were stirring and talking about how to get it open. During this time, Tommy Blackwell suggested the name North Shore. By 2008, a few of us were talking about filing formal complaints, when *out of nowhere* a parks official said "let's get you guys in there to develop routes". Soon they generously ordered thousands of dollars of hardware for the bolted routes. After some trail work, the gates opened for development and The Gold Rush of 2008 was on, with the original 2005 era bolting crew hungry for more routes. Kirk, Birddog, and Alvino led a fast pace. Others jumped in, fearing all the good lines might disappear. I'd intended to do a just few lines and then go back to projecting other areas, but I caught the fever. By the end of summer '09, we had 115 routes.

It would be fun if the bolting crew had pulled a lot of hilarious pranks on each other to report... but no. Just the one. One morning, several of us arrived at different times in three cars: Birddog's truck, Kirk's truck, and, lastly, my Suburban. We worked on different routes that day. A spool of fat yellow caution tape was out there for various uses. Dave and I were the last to leave that afternoon. When we hiked back to my Suburban, it was *completely* wrapped in this goofy caution tape. We knew Birddog or Kirk had done it. Days went by and Dave finally

talked to Kirk. Yes, Kirk had done it, but he asked Dave if *we* had first wrapped *his* truck that morning, on our way in. Dave said no, and Kirk started laughing, realizing Birddog had hiked out first that afternoon and had wrapped Kirk's truck before driving off. Then Kirk hiked out, found his wrapped truck in the parking lot and my unwrapped burb next to it, and assumed Dave and I had wrapped his truck that morning. So he unwrapped his truck and wrapped mine! Moral of the story: *what goes around, doesn't always comes around.*

**Gypsy Wall Development by
Louie Graham, Jan Salinas and David Phillips.**

During development, the crew and rangers found two cases of carcass-dragging that could only have been done by a big cat (cougar/mountain lion). The name Undead Cats Wall had been proposed earlier than that, but it then seemed even more apropos.

The Fires of 2011

Drought, 100-degree weather, and high winds fueled a devastating wildfire in Bastrop and a smaller fire in Spicewood. The Spicewood fire torched roughly 70 homes, and it jumped Highway 71 and

---

[256] The way God intended FA's to be. Anything else is CONTRIVED.

ran up the dry left bank of the Pedernales River, torching a lot of overgrowth below the North Shore cliffs, opening up river views, creating better camera angles, and generally improving the environment below the cliffs. However, it also crossed land up top and killed most trees above the cliffs, all of which we use for anchoring while developing routes. And it destroyed huge hundred-year old oaks along the hiker's riverside trail from Reimers to North Shore. A week later, lightening strikes set a fire at Reimers and the neighboring tract, torching six buildings of the set built for the movie, "The Alamo". These fires came at the end of almost 100 straight days of 100 degree weather, while most Republican candidates for President (including Texas Governor Rick Perry) remained un-conservative with the environment, saying "chill out," Global Warming is not proven to be man-made.

Special Thanks

The preservation of Reimers and North Shore came about by many people from diverse groups interested in open spaces, water quality, and recreational spaces:

Dave Phillips and Scott Steiner for assessing the cliffs back in 1999 and recommending that they were awesomely worth buying for climbing.

Pete Gutierrez, Brett Schuchert, Jan Capps, and Dallas-area climbing gyms Exposure and Stoneworks for giving me this incredible sport, ultimately resulting in North Shore climbing.

Milton and Joy Reimers for their decades-long work keeping their ranch open to climbers and for preserving their ranch via the park acquisition. Their ranch was the lead deal, and North Shore might not have been preserved without them.

Michael Luigs (Land Water Sky), a real estate broker on a mission to preserve Texas ranchlands. He was prepared to buy these ranches and preserve them, in some way, if the bond election had failed.

David Phillips, "Ringbearer" FA

Charles Bergh, Joe Gieselman and their County staff. They dreamed big and worked hard for it.

Travis County Commissioners Gerald Daugherty, Karen Sonleitner, Ron Davis, Margaret Gomez, and Judge Sam Biscoe for valuing this park, testing the public's interest and protecting the public's financial interests. They drove a hard bargain on your behalf.

The Commissioners' appointed citizen's advisory committee for recommending the budget be expanded to buy both ranches.

Travis County voters. Few people vote even in the presidential elections. This set of voters was savvy enough to understand that local and state elections have a big impact on their lives, and they voted for a legacy we and future generations will immensely enjoy.

Tom Mercer, a gifted real estate developer, for helping me understand North Shore's complicated issues and making personal sacrifices to make this deal happen.

David Braun (Plateau Land & Wildlife; Braun and Associates) for his advice in accomplishing this type of conservation deal.

Stephanie Renea for supporting the park deal instead of alternatives that would likely lead to roads, rooftops, and no climbing.

Significant support for the park acquisition and the bond election efforts by various groups including the park bond's PAC, The Nature Conservancy, Hill Country Conservancy, Hill Country Alliance, Central Texas Mountaineers, and Austin Rock Gym. Some of the many individuals were Valerie Bristol, George Cofer, Mike and Pam Reese, Christy Muse, Scott Isgitt, Kirk Holladay and John Myrick.

Members of the press for valuing the park story, including the Austin American Statesman, Austin Chronicle, and KEYE.

David Phillips, "Ringbearer" FA

John Hogge, "Cattle and Goats" FA

North Shore

Scott Chapman, "Hastur's Semi-Liquid Fishy Things"

David Phillips, "Demonic Hordes and the Evil Eye of Orms-by-Gore"

Donna Kwok, "Nyarlathotep Arises from the Blackness of 27 Centuries"

Blaine Burris, "Insane Whisperings from a Yuggothian Braincase" traverse

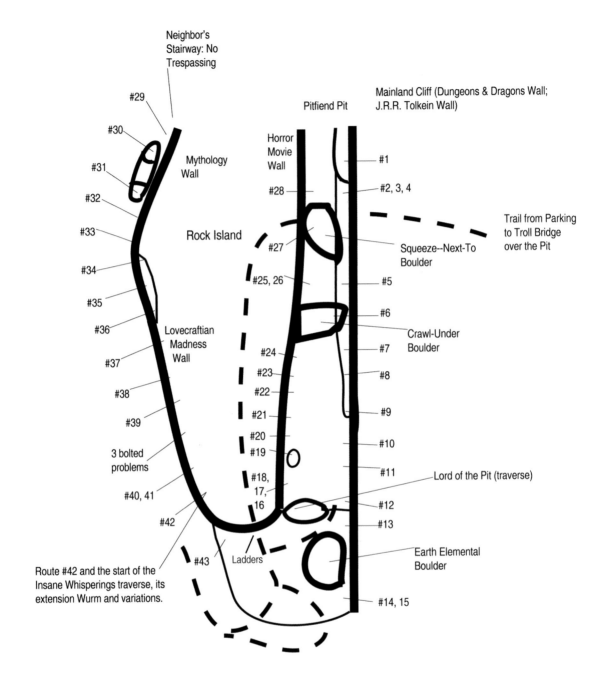

Neighbor's Stairway: No Trespassing

#29

#30

#31

Mythology Wall

#32

#33

Rock Island

#34

#35

#36

Lovecraftian Madness Wall

#37

#38

#39

3 bolted problems

#40, 41

#42

Route #42 and the start of the Insane Whisperings traverse, its extension Wurm and variations.

#43

Ladders

Pitfiend Pit

Mainland Cliff (Dungeons & Dragons Wall; J.R.R. Tolkein Wall)

Horror Movie Wall

#28

#27

#25, 26

#24

#23

#22

#21

#20

#19

#18, 17, 16

#1

#2, 3, 4

Trail from Parking to Troll Bridge over the Pit

Squeeze--Next-To Boulder

#5

#6

Crawl-Under Boulder

#7

#8

#9

#10

#11

Lord of the Pit (traverse)

#12

#13

Earth Elemental Boulder

#14, 15

Monster Rock
Trail Map & Route Starts

Climbing Area: Monster Rock

Monster Rock (Mrock) is my rock climbing park about 35 minutes west of Austin. It has 52 lead and TR routes stuffed miraculously onto a mere 1 acre, 75' wide home site. Grades range 5.6 through 5.13a, concentrated at 5.9-5.12. Since it has fewer routes than the other areas, it's less suited for regular climbing habits. It's a change of pace, and it serves niches: cool-air climbing in a canyon, closely bolted routes for new leaders, excellent long traverses and variations for endurance training, a stellar set of 5.11's, and core-intensive 5.12-5.13. The 5.10's are good enough, and most repeat customers are 5.10 climbers.

All the routes have super-shut anchors similar to sport anchors. One difference is you cannot safely climb over them to top out, since their upward direction makes them essentially "back clipped". Bring 8 draws (and a couple long draws for variations). Each route has a (now weathered) sign that has guided visitors before this book was written.

David Cardosa, rage-sending "Revenge of the Shoggoths" after a 10 year break from climbing.

Days of operation and fees have changed over time. The latest info on access is kept at www.MonsterRock.info. As of this writing, the latest is:

- Inform me before you come at 512-658-2275 or hogge@pobox.com. Last minute plans are fine.

- Leave $5 in the box near the port-a-potty, along with your signed release form (available on the website). Leave the signed release form only on your first visit.

- Open every day, daytime hours.

Directions from Austin/Dallas: set your GPS to 2208 Pace Bend Road South, Spicewood, Texas, 78669. Old school directions:

1. From I-35, take 290 west and exit Southwest Parkway. (Or from Loop 1 aka. Mopac, take the Southwest Parkway exit.) Southwest Parkway starts at Mopac, goes west and dead-ends into H71.

2. Go right (west) on 71. Go past the Village of Bee Cave, past Hamilton Pool Rd (on the left, which goes to Reimers), and assorted hill-funk businesses and restaurants.

3. Look for a big Chevron on the right and a sign that says "Lake Travis / Pace Bend Park". The Chevron is at the corner of 71 and RR2322 (aka. Pace Bend Rd). Turn right.

4. Go roughly a mile, passing under minor power lines and then slow down at the major lines suspended on steel towers. Mrock is the 2nd lot on the left after the major lines. Look for the mail box with "2208". GPS N30°23.560' W98°04.164' (30.392667 -98.0694).

The property is narrow and long with parking spots nestled in trees on both sides of the dirt drive, from the gate to the shed & shack. Walk down hill between two houses to the **Troll Bridge** stairway spanning across a dark chasm. Thou standeth over **Dungeons and Dragons Wall**. The bridge bringeth ye to **Sauron's Tower**, a rock island with **Horror Movie Wall** in the pit facing D&D Wall and **Lovecraftian Madness Wall** and **Mythology Wall** facing towards the river. Walk ye left to the Ladders" marked on the trail map and go down. ***These ladders are impassible to dogs and young children.***

The ladders terminate at a big ledge with scramble-downs to access Lovecraftian Madness Wall, Mythology Wall, and various boulder problems. Or you turn back to the main cliff to access J.R.R. Tolkein Wall, which has two pairs of routes separated by Earth Elemental Boulder. Turn left and scramble down into the Pit Fiend Pit to access Dungeons & Dragons Wall and Horror Movie Wall.

Directions from San Antonio:

Take the loop to 281 and go north for 65 miles. Go east on 71 for 16 miles. Go over the Pedernales Bridge and immediately take a left on 2322 (aka Pace Bend Rd.). Then see #4 above.

Weather Conditions:

Monster Rock's pit contains 24 of the 52 main routes. Rain, fog, and high humidity can shut most of these down, and the pit dries slower than other crags. But the six routes deep in the pit stay drier and dry as fast as other crags. If you find the routes you want to do are wet, get back your $5 admission and try Reimers (or Pace Bend DWS). While Reimers is 40 minutes away, your wasted side trip to Monster Rock only cost 20 minutes round-trip.

Monster Rock

Sun/Shade Conditions:

The walls in the pit are shaded in the morning and late afternoon (around 3pm). They get sun from the side for a few hours around noon-3pm (times varying throughout the year), which affects your vision but does not bake the rock, climber, or belayer. Most people show up early morning to beat the heat, but if you start late, the pit may boost your energy since it's much cooler than the outside air (e.g. 85° vs. 98°).

The four routes on J.R.R.Tolkein Wall, just outside the pit, get all-day shade from trees. The riverside walls (Lovecraftian Madness Wall and Mythology Wall) get morning shade and some afternoon tree-shade.

Warnings:

- In the pit between the two cliffs, climbers might contact the cliff behind them on a fall, on both lead and toprope. Consider wearing a helmet.
- Mrock's fallzone hazards (boulders, opposing cliffs) leave no room for sloppy belays. Belayers must be sharp, on their feet, and ready to take up fast. Keep only a mild arc of slack in the rope; do not let the rope droop.
- Before climbing the pit's traverse, coordinate with everyone in the pit so that your lead falls don't strike belayers and other climbers.
- Do not climb above the (super shut) anchors, since falls can easily "back clip" you out of both anchors.
- Z-clipping is common on some of the pit routes where bolts are placed closely to minimize fall distances toward the opposite cliff.
- If a rope is hanging on a top-rope route, assume it's a static line (unsafe for lead climbing).

Policies:

- See www.MonsterRock.info for the release form and any changes to the access information in this book.
- No climbers under the age of 18 unless supervised by a parent experienced in lead climbing.
- No children visiting who would not be safe on the tall, steep ladders.
- No dogs are allowed due to ladder access and limited space.
- No glass containers.
- Pack in/pack out, especially cigarette butts. Since the City recently banned smoking in all parks, and the County is considering following suit, Mrock and (ironically) Georgetown Hospital are positioned as the last bastions of climbers' tobacco rights.

Contacts:

- Local Emergency Services: 512-264-1476
- John Hogge (owner): 512-658-2275 or hogge@pobox.com.

Karl Vochatzer, onsighting "Green Slime vs. Bag of Dev

Monster Rock (mainland cliff): **Dungeons & Dragons Wall and J.R.R. Tolkein Wall**

The routes here range 30-50'. These two connected walls are on the main cliff overlooking a rock island. Cross the bridge, walk left on the rock island, and climb down two fixed ladders (*impassible by young children and dogs*) to a rocky landing. The cliff over this landing is J.R.R. Tolkein Wall, with four routes divided by a pointy boulder. The left two are good, popular 5.9 warmups, while the right two are tricky 5.10's, good as warmups only when wired. Healthier (juggier) warmups are in the pit: Swordmaiden of Rohan (5.7), Kraken's Deadly Dance at Sea (5.8), Creeping Doom (5.8), and Demonic Hordes (5.10b).

From the leftmost route (Herman Munster), scramble down into the chasm between Dungeons & Dragons Wall on the right and Horror Movie Wall on the left, arriving at D&D Wall's "Seven Gorgons Breathing." Deeper into the pit, two big boulders jam against the cliffs and divide the routes and provide landmarks. Warning: expect occasional pebble-fall from the tallest routes on Dungeons & Dragons Wall.

Routes 1 and 2 share anchors:

1. Gelatinous Cube's Deadly Solvent

(5.11c)*** 5 bolts, John Hogge. This route is at the far end of the pit, past both big boulders. Clip the safety rope to reach the start on the wedge-shaped boulder; sometimes it's slippery even when the rest of the wall is dry. The belayer can go up that boulder and sling Bolt 1, or else belay down below the boulder. After Bolt 2, use the jug off right, then climb the crimps straight up the boltline to the cool area at the top. '99 🔨⚡️🔧🎷🐁🐸😊⤴🦅⛰

a. variation: **Tim, the Goatheaded Wizard** (5.10d PG)*, Roni Beer. Keep hands left of the boltline until they're over the last bolt. The fall looks bad — consider leading Ray of Disintegration and just TRing this route. 🔨⚡️🔧🐸👁⛰🦅🏃

Routes 2-4 share Bolts 1 and 2:

2. **Specter's Touch** (5.10c)*** 6 bolts,
Roni Beer, John Hogge. Start right of the wedge shaped boulder, feet off the various surrounding boulders. The belayer can clip into the nearby fixed rope to keep out of the fall zone. After Bolt 2, branch left. Cut left again after Bolt 5 to merge with Gelatinous Cube's Deadly Solvent. '99
⚡️🔨⚡️🐒🔧⚡️🎷🐸⚓🏃🚂 $E=mc^2$ ☕⛰

3. **22-Eyed Beholder Hovering Near**

By[257] (5.9)*** 5 bolts, John Hogge. After Bolt 2, branch right on Bolts 3-5 that slant right to anchors right of the bridge. '99 ⚡️🔨⚡️🐁👁🐸😊⛰🔫

b. bolted variation: **Ray of Disintegration** (5.9+)*** 5 bolts, John Hogge. Climb 22-Eyed Beholder Bolts 1-4, then cut left to a different Bolt 5 and continue left to shared anchors left of the Troll Bridge. This is an easy way to set TR's for Gelatinous Cube's Deadly Solvent, Tim the Goatheaded Wizard, and Specter's Touch. 🔨⚡️🔧🐁⚓🐸🦅🐁⛰🔫🏃

---

[257] A beholder is an evil floating globe-beast having a huge eyeball, sharp-toothed mouth, and typically 10 little magic-beam-shooting eyestalks.

Monster Rock

4. **Swordmaiden of Rohan** (5.6)*** 6 bolts, Jen Koschmann, John Hogge. After Bolt 2, cut a sharp right, traversing on Bolts 3-4, then climb up Bolts 5-6 to anchors on the left side above the cave. The bolt next to the anchors is for Warg Riders. '07

    c. underline: extension: **Warg Riders** (5.7/5.8)* 8 bolts, Ryan Collity, John Hogge. Climb Swordmaiden of Rohan and clip Bolt 7 just left of her anchors. *(Don't clip her anchors — never clip and lead over these super-shut anchors.).* Continue upward, traverse right over the cave on Bolt 8 and clip Sky Full of Dementor's anchors.

Squeeze-Past Boulder: squeeze between this boulder and D&D Wall to access the above four routes and two Horror Movie Wall routes (Demonic Hordes and Trollkind) at the far end of the pit. It's the biggest/highest boulder jammed between the cliffs.

5. **Sky Full of Dementors** (5.9+)*** 7 bolts, Tim Sharp, John Hogge. The belayer sits on the ledge between the two boulders jammed between the cliffs and clips into the bolt there, or climbs onto Crawl-Under Boulder and clips the bolt on the cliff. Climb the face between the boulders; pull the arête above and right of the cave. Anchors are under a prickly pear cactus. Whenever this cactus grows over the anchors, please call the me to trim it. '07

    d. variation: **Expecto Patronum!** (5.8)*** 6 bolts, Lisa Meng, John Hogge. Bring 1-2 long draws. This variation avoids the lower and upper cruxes of Sky Full of Dementors. Stem between the left boulder and cliff to ease up the low crux. At the cave, clip a long draw, then move left and clip the anchors for Swordmaiden of Rohan (above and left of the cave), which avoids the high crux. Or clip another long draw on the hanger left of the anchors and go up and right, finishing on the high anchors.

Crawl-Under Boulder: a boulder you crawl under to access D&D Wall's leftmost five routes and four Horror Movie Wall routes (Freddie vs. Jason, Thing vs. Cousin It, Demonic Hordes, and Trollkind.)

6. **Kraken's Deadly Dance at Sea** (5.8)* 5 bolts, Jini Perkins, Blaine Burris. Start on the Crawl-Under Boulder. High Bolt 1. '08

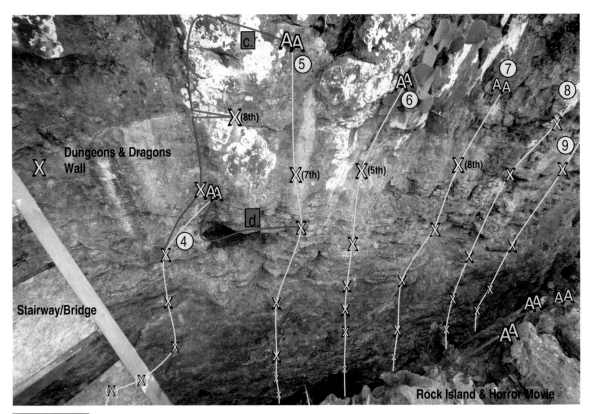

3' ledge and the floor of the pit. These routes are tall for the area (50'), not very sustained but they burn a lot of calories and are popular. Green Slime vs. Bag of Devouring is the best, with several long cruxes.

7. **Creeping Doom:** (5.8)* 8 bolts, Joel Schopp, John Hogge. On the 3' tall rock ledge just right of the first big boulder jamming between the cliffs, pull on the left-facing arête. This route is a nice warmup. '07

> variation: (5.8), Jen Koschmann. Stem between D&D Wall and Horror Movie Wall. Chimney moves!

8. **Mindflayer's Tentacles** (5.10a)*** 8 bolts, Erik Moore, John Hogge. Start near the right end of the 3' tall ledge. '07

> variation: (5.9+) Karl Vochatzer. Stem between D&D Wall and Horror Movie Wall for about 15'. Chimney moves!

9. **Dwarven Berserker/Lich** (5.10b)*** 8 bolts, Ryan Collity, John Hogge. Start on the right end of the 3' tall ledge. Rope stretch, low crux and uneven landing can make this an ankle-biter on toprope. Just lead it. '07

10. **Green Slime vs. Bag of Devouring** (5.10b)*** 7 bolts, Dave Phillips. Start in the left of two 6' tall mild dihedrals near the pit entrance. Slip through enemy lines into the open, then avoid their big cannons. '07

11. **Seven Gorgons Breathing** (5.11a PG)*** Rachel Harris, John Hogge, 5 bolts. The first route on the right from the pit's entrance. High Bolt 1. Climb the little dihedral nearest the pit entrance, to the chossy ledge. Runout to the anchors, which sit at 1 o'clock from the last bolt. The large "plate" below the ledge has multiple attachment points to the cliff, but it's hollow and might blow some day. The belayer should move to its right once the climber moves onto it. PG rated since the pit narrows behind this route; helmets are advised. '07

> variation: **The Sixth Gorgon** (5.10d)*, Dave Barre. Start to the right of the dihedral.

Bouldering:

Gray Ooze (V1). Traverse Green Slime backwards. Gray Ooze was a monster universally hated by gaming geeks.

Green Slime (V1)*. At the wall's rightmost low point (below the pit entrance), traverse low, right-to-left, down-climbing onto the 3' tall rock ledge. Another gaming-geek-hated slimy monster.

The Blob (V2). Traverse Gray Ooze, returning on Green Slime.

> As most Dungeon Masters know, the rewards are great --
> an endless challenge to the imagination and intellect,
> an enjoyable pastime to fill many hours with fantastic and often
> unpredictable happenings, and an opportunity to watch a story unfold
> and a grand idea to grow and flourish.
>
> *Mike Car, in "Advanced D&D Dungeon Masters Guide"*

Monster Rock

Chasm entrance separating Dungeons & Dragons Wall (routes 1-11) and J.R.R. Tolkein Wall (routes 12-15). The following routes are on the landing below the entrance ladder and above the floor of the chasm.

12. Herman Munster (5.9+)*** 5 bolts, John Sonzcak. Straddle boulders to clip Bolt 1, then go down to the narrow ledge to start the route. Bolts 1-4 angle slightly left. Herman had two bolts on his neck; this route has two nice cruxes.'99

13. Grendel (5.9)*** 5 bolts, Joey Phillips.[258] Bolt 2 is at 11 o'clock, near Herman Munster's boltline. Bolts 4 and 5 angle left towards Herman Munster's anchors (which Grendel used to go to), but Grendel has its own anchors at 1 o'clock from the last bolt. Lookout — here it comes again. '99

> e. variation: **Tom Bombadil** (5.6)*, 10 bolts (to Swordmaiden's anchors) or 12 bolts (to the anchors right of the bridge), Brenton Bruxton. Brenton improvised the traverse onsight, toting a lot of gear, as is his way. Here's our re-creation of the route: bring a long draw and 2 slings to reduce rope drag. Start Grendel, stemming the Earth Elemental Boulder to keep it 5.6. Go up 2 bolts, angle left with a long draw on Herman Munster's Bolt 3, then traverse horizontally across five routes (hanging long slings on two high bolts as you approach and cross the sea of wild slots). The next bolts are right of the cave and at its right end. Then dip down low across the cave, then up to clip Swordmaiden's anchors. Or continue on 2 more bolts (probably at a higher grade) to reach anchors right of the bridge. A nice walk, not ruined by golf.
>
> –Mark Twain

Britta Kakacek, "Balrog's Whip"

Earth Elemental Boulder: the tall pointy boulder to be careful with when leading nearby routes.

14. Crawling Chaos[259] (5.10a R)* 5 bolts, John Hogge. Bolt 1 is close to Balrog's Whip's bolt, but they have distinct starts. A hay bale is usually wedged behind the boulder, left of this route, to keep the climber from leading unsafely between cliff and boulder. If it's missing, stay safe and work the hard path that keeps you right of the boulder. Reach up to clip Bolt 3, then go far left of the boltline. The climb eases up but gets increasingly dangerous to Bolt 4, as you climb over the pointy boulder. Upon lowering, keep the rope out of the flake above Bolt 4. '99

> f. toprope: **Hellacious Hobbit** (5.6 TR)*. Climb the boulder left of Crawling Chaos and then transfer onto it and climb to the anchors.

15. Balrog's Whip (5.10c)*** 4 bolts, John Hogge. This route is Bolt Talk's little brother. It's at the property line. '99

Property Line.

---

[258] Dave Phillips FOSA (first old-school ascent). Dave had this wired and, one day, for reasons unknown, led this on a static (back-breaking) rope, no harness, in combat boots, leapfrogging with only two draws, with a newbie belayer. Grendel is the monster in the well-known Anglo-Saxon epic poem Beowulf. We recommend the novel Grendel by John Gardner, a retelling of Beowulf from the monster's perspective.

[259] I was stalled at the crux, when belayer Joey Phillips warned me a huge centipede was coming my way. Joey's always a joker, so I thought I was being messed with and ignored him. Until the monstrosity crawled its 9 inches of wiggly little legs between my hands. I busted the move, very very quickly. The route name was then obvious.

Chris Barton, "Balrog's Whip"

This wall is the mildly overhanging cliff forming the left side of the Chasm, opposite Dungeons and Dragons Wall. The six routes starting at Goblin Mutant are popular, similar, slightly-overhanging, and progress nicely from 5.11.easy to 5.11.hard.

WARNING: On some routes, you might contact the cliff behind you on falls (even on top-rope). Six routes are toprope-only because the opposite cliff would make leading too hazardous. The topropes kept on them are for your use on these routes only. Please do not pull the ropes.

Most of the topropes have a directional permadraw to keep you held into the cliff. Unclip it on the way up; reclip when lowering. Watch your back in a fall and consider wearing a helmet. Belayers need to avoid excess slack. There have been no injuries to date, but this setting is unusual and the risks of injury hard to determine.

Access Scramble-Down

The next three TR routes share anchors and two directionals. One dynamic rope is kept on their shared anchors.

Paul Brady, "Thing vs. Cousin It" FA, onsight

16. toprope: **Cold Damp Embrace of the Mummy** (5.11d TR)* David Cardosa[260], John Hogge. Just inside the pit's entrance, this is the leftmost of 3 routes sharing TR anchors and a single rope. This one shares a directional permadraw with the next route. Start at the access point's boulder stack on a jug flake and jug pocket. Climb left of the directional and straight up. Dodge the mummy's deadly kiss. '07

17. toprope: **Dracula's Silent Steps Approacheth** (5.12a TR)* Austin Wise, bb John Hogge. Middle of 3 routes sharing TR anchors and a single rope. Shares a directional permadraw with the previous route. Start and climb between the two directional permadraws.[261] '07

18. toprope: **Frankenstein Killed by a Mere Angry Mob** (5.12b TR)* Austin Wise, bb John Hogge. Rightmost of 3 routes sharing TR anchors and a single rope. Start standing on a small boulder and pulling a mild bulge to the rightmost directional permadraw, then up and left to a second directional permadraw. '07

19. **Goblin Mutant** (5.11a PG)*** 5 bolts, John Hogge. The left-most lead route, near the pit entrance. Wear a helmet. To minimize fall distance towards the opposite cliff: use a short draw on Bolt 3, clip the permadraw hanging from Bolt 4, move up, then clip a short draw onto Bolt 4's hanger (sharing the chain). Like reaching high for the candy jar on the shelf, hoping to not grab a live mouse-trap. '99

variation: **Jigsaw's Contraptions** (5.11a R)* 4 bolts & 1 permadraw, John Hogge. Climb Goblin Mutant's Bolts 1-3, cut right 45° to a permadraw on Lord of the Pit, then up to finish on Texas Chainsaw Massacre's last bolt and anchors. Risky fall to the permadraw in the narrow pit...the price for a nice pumpier finish to Goblin Mutant.

20. **Hellboy** (5.11c)* 5 bolts and 1 permadraw, John Hogge. A fun contrivance using only handholds between or directly on the lines defined by two permadraws. Clip Bolt 1, then climb, reaching left to clip Goblin Mutant's Bolts 2-4, then Hellboy's 2nd independent bolt and anchors. Read Goblin Mutant's description to get max protection out of its permadraw. For a true send, consider tick-marking each hold, or you're likely to grab holds off route. Hellboy's fanbase has grown, but the contrivance keeps us from giving it 3 stars. '08

21. **Texas Chainsaw Massacre (aka. Leatherface)** (5.11b)*** 4 bolts. Randy Ho, David Phillips. A stick clip isn't necessary but advised, since the footholds may be fragile. Soft belay till Bolt 2 is clipped to avoid crashing onto the roof edge. Don't miss clipping Bolt 3, which sits back in a shallow depression. The movie starts mellow, then knives start flying through the air. '07

---

[260] David dedicated this first-ascent to Scott Harris, after beating him (and me) to it!

[261] A brief hierarchy of vampires: Bram Stoker's Dracula > The Hunger > True Blood > the Bauhaus song "Bela Legosi's Dead" > Ann Rice novels > D&D vampires > Dark Shadows > Twilight

The next three TR routes each have anchors, and static topropes are kept on them:

22. toprope: **Shower Scene from Psycho** (5.11b TR)*** Paul Brady, John Hogge. Climb using the directional permadraw to keep away from the opposite wall. Unclip as you pass the permadraw and reclip upon lowering. *Beta[262]*. '07

> variation: **The Descent** (5.10a TR)***, Robyn Watts. Climb the route, stemming both walls at will. This variation and Piranha seem a lot more fun than the corresponding stemming variations on the opposite wall. '11

23. toprope: **Eye-pluck scene from The Birds** (5.11d TR)***, Mike Klein, John Hogge. Climb using the directional permadraw to keep away from opposite wall. Unclip as you pass the permadraw and reclip upon lowering. Start just left of the big matchable block. Chased by wolves across shaky ground. '07

> variation: **Piranha** (5.7/5.8 TR)*** John Hogge. Climb the route, stemming both walls at will. A tall enough climber can stem all the way to the last couple moves. Height dependent grade. '11

24. toprope: **Willard Calls Out the Rats** (5.11d / 12b[263] TR)*** Austin Wise, John Hogge. Start where the ground begins dropping into the dark hole, on the big matchable block. Power up the almost-bare section, staying off the long small arête used on Eye-Pluck. Escape the rat army across a yawning fissure. '07

> variation: **Ben's Rat Army** (5.10c TR)*** Rachel Harris. Start on Willard and go up and right (staying low, just over the boulder stack) to link into Freddie vs. Jason. Below the bare face, traverse right and up, over the sloping boulder, onto the ledge, and then up and left finishing Freddy vs. Jason. Since Freddy vs. Jason is an exciting lead, do that before getting on this toprope route.

Crawl-Under Boulder: a boulder you crawl under to access the following routes and some D&D Wall routes.

The next two routes share Bolts 1-3:

25. **Freddy vs. Jason** (5.10a)*** 5 permadraws, Trevor Brooks, John Hogge. Start between the two big boulders jammed between the cliffs. The belayer sits low with feet on stacked boulders, back against the ledge (allowing traffic to pass behind belayer). Clip into the ledge's bolt to not depend on the stacked/balanced boulder landing. Use a right-hand jug, gain the ledge, then go up and left. Shares anchors with Willard and its permanent toprope. Just clip the rope onto the anchors, letting it lay on top of the locking biners, then lower. Interesting crux[264]. '07

26. **Thing vs. Cousin It** (5.11d)*** 3 bolts and 2 permadraws, Paul Brady, John Hogge. Start the same as Freddy vs. Jason. From the ledge, climb the dihedral and then the arête, on hairs and fingernails. '07

Squeeze-Past Boulder: a boulder you squeeze next to, between it and D&D Wall, to access the next two routes and some D&D Wall routes. It's the biggest/highest boulder jammed between the cliffs.

27. **Demonic Hordes and the Evil Eye of Orms-by-Gore** (5.10b)*** 3 permadraws, Lauren Divine, John Hogge. The shortest route at Mrock, but with a lot of moves, pump, and a big long name. The belayer sits right of the highest boulder jamming between the cliffs and clips into the nearby bolt on the cliff. The climb starts on the cliff face at the top of that boulder. Traverse diagonally up and left across a rounded arête to the anchors shared with Freddy vs. Jason. Don't go up looking for a rest on the jugs with tape all over them; they are detached and suspect. '07

---

[262] Left-hand sidepull jug under the low roof. Right-hand bad crimp sidepull. Awkwardly set left kneebar right of your left hand. Static release left hand to reach high. Harder beta is still worth doing for fun: right hand sidepull; move feet right, lieback for the reach. Or, the Chere & Kareem foot-lock (similar to the kneebar beta).

[263] Height dependent grade. It's 11d if you can reach past otherwise crux holds, 12b if you can't, and 12a for nobody. We pulled (and graded) the 11d reach prior to sending any 12a's. Russell Mayes used the intermediaries, grading those 12b. Beta spoiler: 11d means doing a high right hand cross move past the thin intermediaries.

[264] It looks like 5.11, but trick beta makes it light pulling. After bolting, I came back a long time later to lead it and thought I'd gotten the grade estimate low by 6 letter grades. The ledge is like an emotional magnet. No one wants to step off and execute the crux. Stage the right foot and get a high left foot on the arête. Stretch far left to lefthand intermediaries. Slowly shift left to snatch a better left hand hold.

Monster Rock

28. Trollkind (5.9+ R)*** 5 bolts, Chris "The Wanker" Palmer, John Hogge. The belayer clips into the fixed rope around the wedge shaped boulder. Start standing on D&D Wall's little ledge, across from the route.[265] Rated "R" due to hard clips and the fall hazards from the boulder on the left and the wedge-shaped boulder opposite the climb. We advise stick-clipping the highest bolt. '07

> Heeeeeere's Johnny!!
>
> *from the movie "The Shining"*

> I want to play a *game*.
>
> *from the movie "Saw"*

"B" = Belay station

Traverses:

Lord of the Pit (5.11b)*** 10 permadraws, Greg Brooks[266]. Sit outside the Pit on the half-coffin sized boulder guarding the pit entrance. Traverse right, through most of the pit across the wall's mid section, clipping all the permadraws, over creepy, all-air falls. Bolt 10 is well above Bolt 9, to exit to Freddy vs. Jason's anchors. You'll see locking biners and a permanent toprope on these anchors; just clip your lead rope onto the anchors, sharing it with the locking biners, and lower. It's long but a 35-meter rope works fine. Never second (follow) this route — the bolts are positioned only for leading, and falls while seconding aren't clean. With the permadraws, there is no need to second it. Due to low lead falls, don't traverse over anyone in the pit. '07

Carrie (V3)*** Russell Mayes. Traverse low, left-to-right, from the start of the wall's low roof to the big matchable jug before the Pit sinks into Oblivion; exit up onto the boulder stack. Bad landings, suspect rock; spot carefully with multiple spotters.

Homonculust (V3+) Traverse Carrie to the big matchable jug and return to the start. Bad landings, bad rock; spot carefully with multiple spotters.

---

[265] Below the start, an ancient Troll free-solo battle route climbs out of the cave and up the face to the bridge.

[266] I asked Greg to bolt a long traversing line across this wall, not being sure where the best line was. Greg bolted it and came back later for the FA. I had never seen him climb. Greg crept across it with the Zen calm and pace of a pre-global-warming glacier. It looked like a 100% bet on a pump-out, on this long route, and I thought about dropping the camera and giving odds…but no. Flash FA.

Monster Rock (river cliff, left): **Mythology Wall**

This wall is connected to Lovecraftian Madness Wall at a rounded arête. Both are on the far side of the rock island, facing the river. Descend the bridge/stairs, hike left across the rock island, descend two ladders, cross the landing under J.R.R.Tolkein Wall, and bend clockwise down stone stairs. Walk past Lovecraftian Madness Wall and around the arête. You'll see the neighbor's stairway.

The wall has five routes with campus-ish starts, two long traverses (which both use the same permadraws), and variations. The variations (mostly open projects as of this writing) tack high quality endurance pumpfest traversing exits (ranging 11 to 16 bolts) onto the bouldery uproute starts. Bolt placements were coordinated for protecting both uproutes and traverses. The permadraws' biner gates all face into the cliff to protect both the rightward traverses from these uproutes and the leftward traverses coming from Lovecraftian Madness Wall.

To understand the traverse variations, first sort out Cyclops' Eye and its two (high and low traverse) variations. The rest of the traverse variations just start the other four uproutes and exit on either the high or low traverse.

29. **Cyclops' Eye** (5.12a)* 2 bolts, 1 permadraw, Tyler "T-Bone" Beattie, bb John Hogge. Stand on a boulder left of the "ruined castle wall", left hand in a huge bumpy pocket. You've stabbed the monster's eye, and he's furious. '08

> h. variation: **Siren's Song Forever** (5.12?)* 2 bolts & 16 permadraws. Climb Cyclops to good holds above the horizontal crack. Traverse Torture-iffic backwards (left-to-right); hands get anything but generally stay above the first six permadraws. After the 16 permadraws, you're done. Project.

> variation: **Deadly Breath of Dragons** (5.12+?)* 2 bolts & 16 permadraws. Climb Cyclops to the prominent horizontal crack. Traverse Wurm backwards (left-to-right); hands stay strictly below the 6 leftmost bolts. After the 16 permadraws, you're done. Project.

30. **Hydra's Hissing Heads** (5.11a PG) *** 3 bolts and 1 permadraw, Kevin Holte, John Hogge. Stick-clip Bolt 2 to avoid falling onto

Tyler "T-Bone" Beattie, "Cyclops' Eye" FA, onsight

Monster Rock

the ruins. "PG" rated without the stick; KV has taken the falls and there's some contact against the tall cheat stack. Start standing on the leftmost point of the "ruined castle wall". If you can't reach the good right handhold, stack a pack on top till you can reach it. Bolt 4 and anchors slant slightly right. The route is longer and more sustained than it looks from the ground. Slice all five heads off and you're done. '08

i. variation: **Hundred Handed Ones** (5.12a?)* 1 bolt and 14 permadraws. Stick-clip Bolt 2 to avoid the bad fall and minimize rope drag. Merge right onto Siren's Song Forever. The Hundred Handed Ones (Hecatonchires) were monster-giants so ugly that their father Uranus pushed them back into mom's womb. Project.

variation: **Gaia's Incest** (5.11b PG)*** 1 bolt and 6 permadraws, John Hogge. Start Hundred Handed Ones, but go only to the 6th permadraw, which is at the rounded arête.

variation: **Basilisk's Glance of Death** (5.12a?)* 2 bolts and 15 permadraws. Merge right onto Deadly Breath of Dragons. Project.

31. **Medusa's Snakes all Staring** (5.11c-d R)* 3 bolts and 1 permadraw, Ben Edwards, bb John Hogge. Stand on the rightmost point of the "ruined castle wall". Consider stick-clipping Bolt 2, which is up and right from Bolt 1, just under the permadraw. Medusa is the archetype of ugliness, with a hair of snakes and a stare that turned onlookers into stone. But with gnar tattoos all the rage today, perhaps Medusa deserves a second look. '08

j. variation: **Poseidon and the Sea Nymph** (5.12a?)* 2 bolts and 13 permadraws. Merge right onto Siren's Song Forever. The god and nymph *coupled* in Athena's temple; she dealt with it by turning the nymph into Medusa. Project.

variation: **Impaled by the Manticore** (5.12b?)* 2 bolts and 13 permadraws. Merge right onto Deadly Breath of Dragons. Project.

32. **Strength of Titans** (5.sick)* 3 bolts and 1 permadraw, bb John Hogge. Start on the chossy ledge. Hands go to the torn flake. Bolt 3 (the permadraw) is up and right of Bolt 2. Project. '08

k. variation: **Hercules vs. the 3-Headed Hound of Hades** (5.sick)* 2 bolts and 12 permadraws. Merge right onto Siren's Song Forever. Project.

variation: **Gored by the Minotaur** (5.sick)* 2 bolts and 12 permadraws. Merge right onto Deadly Breath of Dragons. Project.

33. **Sliced by Thor's Hammer** (5.12c)* 3 bolts and 1 permadraw, Ben Edwards, bb John Hogge. Start on the chossy ledge, just left of the arête. Hand goes to the crescent. Bolt 2 is up and right of Bolt 1; Bolt 4 is slightly left from Bolt 3. Thor had it going on, with his giant-slaying auto-returning hammer and his goat-drawn chariot that divided mountains. Thor lost a few "fixed" contests but gave them a good show. He was fooled into wrestling an old woman (who was actually Old Age) and nearly won. He lost a drinking contest since his horn of mead was magically tied to the ocean, but he managed to alter the tides in the process. '08

l. variation: **Odin's Spear** (5.12c)* 2 bolts and 11 permadraws. Merge right onto the high or low traverse (they merge here) and climb the Insane Whisperings traverse in reverse order (left-to-right). Project.

Rounded Arête: Mythology Wall transitions into Lovecraftian Madness Wall here. The low right side of the arête is the start of Starspawn of Cthulhu (see next page). That route crosses left onto Mythology Wall's rightmost section.

Monster Rock (river cliff, right): **Lovecraftian Madness Wall**

In memory of the horror writer H.P. Lovecraft. This wall is on the riverside of the rock island, nearest the scramble-down from J.R.R.Tolkein Wall. It is connected to Mythology Wall at the big rounded arête. Routes here have passable 5.9 and 5.10a contrived warmups, but most folks warm up elsewhere. Another good warmup, once wired, is the Insane Whisperings traverse, resting at various bolts. The Goths variation is extremely fun, and it's a good hangdogging warmup.

34. **Starspawn of Cthulhu** (5.13a)* 3 bolts, Tyler Beattie, bb John Myrick. Stick-clip Bolt 1. Climb to the left side of the small roof, clipping bolts left of the arête. Bolt 2 is just under a permadraw which can be skipped. '07

    m. variation: **Cthulhu Awakens** (5.13b?)* Exit early, right, on the high permadrawed Insane Whisperings traverse. Project.

35. **Sick Experiments at Miskatonic University** (5.13a) *** 5 bolts & 1 permadraw, Russell Mayes[267], bb John Myrick. Climb the face under the center of the small roof. Above the roof, look right to clip Bolt 4, then climb straight up to clip the permadraw. The university's creepy clock tower ticks off the remaining hours of mankind... '07

Snout of Shub Niggorath. This choss formation at the bottom of the cliff looks like a monster's nostrils.

36. **Fear of Evil Gods** (5.12c)*** 4 bolts & 2 permadraws, Jeff Olson[268], bb John Myrick . Start above the left nostril of the Snout. Climb the thin crack line to right side of the small roof, then work right to Bolt 4 (ignore the close bolt on your left) and right to the permadraw. Exit left to the anchors. '07

37. **Revenge of the Shoggoths** (5.11c/5.12b)* 4 bolts, Phillip Bryan, bb David Phillips. Clip Bolt 1 of the neighboring route to prevent crashes into the belayer. Start right of the boltline to the mini-roof over the right nostril of the Snout. See grade and beta discussion[269]. If you fail, do the Goths variation. Shoggoths were servants of the Elder Things until they rebelled. They were enormous masses of gelatinous flesh that they could form into appendages and organs, as needed. '07

    variation: **Goths** (5.10d)*** 4 bolts. Yard up the belayer's side of the rope to Bolt 1 and finish the climb.

38. **Hideous MI-GO Swimming Through Space** (5.12d)* 5 bolts, Dylan Jones, bb John Myrick. Start on left-hand slopers and right-hand deep 2-finger pocket. '07

    variation: **The Dunwich Horror** (5.12d) 6 bolts. After Bolt 3, head right to finish Hastur's. Project.

Russell Mayes, working "Sick Experiments" before his FA

---

[267] Russell teaches rock climbing, sings/song-writes, and models. In five minutes, Russell accelerated my pace on sending projects. Before this FA, he prepared by vocalizing every move in fine detail, including each move's "V" grade difficulty, body positioning, coring-up, sagging, and each spot where he needed to "man up". Lacking that kind of memory, I now write out detailed beta, review it a few times at home, and read it right before a send attempt.

[268] Voted most likely to make every route in Texas look short.

[269] The grade is extremely height dependent. It's been solved with a bad left kneebar to power higher and snatch, with or without use of the bad left paper-thin undercling. It's been solved as a straight-up deadpoint. All use the low left hand and high right sidepull crimp. The easiest beta works at 6'0" but likely not at 5'8": high left foot on the obvious point, lean right, then launch an arcing deadpoint left and up to bypass the awkward bulge. This arcing style deadpoint also means you don't fall backwards off the target hold (half dish or sprague atop the bulge). Arcing deadpoints are a useful move beyond this route. They execute slower than straight-up deadpoints, reducing power requirements. And as with liebacks, one arm stays straight, consuming less power. Your deadpoints might go further on less power.

Monster Rock

Tyler Beattie, "Invisible Slayer"

39. Hastur's Semi-Liquid Fishy Things (5.11d)*** 5 bolts and 1 permadraw, John Hogge, bb David Phillips. Clip Bolt 1 of the neighboring route to prevent crashes into the belayer. Start right hand in the big mail slot. Hang a long draw off to the right on Invisible Slayer's last bolt and finish on its anchors. '07

n. variation: **Fear of Infinity** (5.12a)*** 4 bolts & 1 permadraw, John Hogge. The best variation at Mrock, combining the start of Hastur's, part of the Insane Whisperings traverse, and the upper part of Fear of Evil Gods. Use Hastur's Bolts 1-2, Hideous MI-GO's Bolt 3, Revenge's Bolt 3, and Fear's last bolt and anchors. A tough little bully whaps you hard in the mouth. You get up, dust yourself off, then his big brother cracks your head open.

variation: **Fear of Being Eaten** (5.11d)* 4 draws & 1 permadraw, John Hogge. Branches left after Bolt 3 (the permadraw) to a bolt under the ledge (use a long draw), then up and left to finish on Hideous MI-GO's anchors, for a steeper finish compared to Hastur's.

variation: **Fear of Ethics** (5.11a A0)*** 5 bolts (1 long), Tommy Blackwell. Hang a fat draw on Bolt 1 and pull up on it. Climb the rest of Hastur's unaided.

Two side-by-side bolts atop a bulge protect the following three roped boulder problems:

o. bolted prob: **Reanimator** (V5-6?)* 1 bolt & 1 permadraw. Clip the bolt on the left side of the bulge. Start left hand in the big mail slot, climb the left side of the slopey bulge up and right to the permadraw, and exit right on the permadrawed traverse. Project. '07

p. <u>bolted prob:</u> **Hellraiser** (V6)* 1 bolt & 1 permadraw, Chris "Vinny" Vinson[270]. Clip the bolt on the left side of the bulge. Start left hand on the edge with three "finger prints". Go up and right to a prominent pointy thing centered on the bulge, then up to Bolt 1. Exit right on the permadrawed traverse. '07

q. <u>bolted prob:</u> **The Hidden** (V5-6?)* 1 bolt & 1 permadraw. Clip the bolt on the right side of the bulge. Start left hand on the finger jug flake. Go up right of the bolt to the roof permadraw. Exit right on the permadrawed traverse. Project. '07

The next two routes share bolts 1 and 2:

40. **Invisible Slayer of the Mad Arab Abdul Alhazred** (5.11a)*** 5 bolts and 1 permadraw, John Hogge, Dave Phillips. Bolt 3 is at 11 o'clock from Bolt 2, under the left edge of the mini-roof. Then go to the permadraw at 10 o'clock. The remaining bolts and anchors slant left. Shares anchors with Hastur's Semi-Liquid Fishy Things. '07

41. **Nyarlathotep Arises from the Blackness of 27 Centuries**[271] (5.11b)* 5 bolts and 1 permadraw, John Hogge. Go straight up the crack and up the mini-roof. The bolt count excludes Invisible Slayer's nearby Bolt 3, though some folks clip it before clipping the permadraw. '07

42. **Icy Touch of a Dimensional Shambler** (5.10c)* 3 bolts and 1 permadraw, Chris "Birddog" Keistler. Climb left of the cliff edge arête. Holds on the arête are off route to pull 5.10c. Hard to onsight. Get it wired before using as a warmup. '06

r. <u>toprope:</u> **Psychic Venom** (5.10d TR)* Lauren Divine. A fun contrivance. Set a TR on Icy Touch's anchors. Start between the cracks; both cracks are off-route. Stay left of Icy Touch's bolts.

s. <u>variation:</u> **Herbert West's Weird Instruments** (5.10a)*. Holds on the arête are on-route for this variation.

43. **Cosmic Horror** (5.7)* 3 bolts, Troy Wilson[272]. Climb the wild-featured face right of Icy Touch's crack to the landing. Climb the face left of the ladder. Clip anchors next to the ladder, or Icy Touch's anchors. '08

t. <u>variation:</u> **Cosmic Encounters** (5.9), 3 bolts and 1 permadraw, Jennifer Marine[273], John Hogge. Start Icy Touch, clipping a permadraw and bolt. Cross onto and pull straight up the arête, skipping the big rest on the ledge, clipping 2 bolts right of the arête. Clip anchors next to the ladder. This variation was devised as a warmup for the wall. Jennifer said it's the weirdest route ever. Contrived non-ledge-rest and arête pull. Named after the weirdest (but extremely fun) board game ever, Cosmic Encounters.

Lovecraftian Madness Wall Traverses

Dave Phillips and I did not have a lot of faith in the viability of routes on this wall. By early '07 it only had the 10b and 11b. None of the other route starts looked within our reach. To get one more line out of this otherwise useless wall, I kept eyeing the long ledge system across the entire wall as a potential bolted traverse, and figured some variations could exit early and up at various points, to provide a mix of routes at different grades.

So, in early '07, I asked Dave to bolt "the traverse". Dave's A.D.D. was kicking in at that moment, however, and he missed hearing exactly how to run the line, as some beetle was crawling over the nearby 5.11b, distracting him. So Dave ended up bolting the stellar Invisible Slayer of the Mad Arab Abdul Alhazred, which starts late, runs only 10' of the desired traverse, then goes up on cool moves. A 5.11a was born, and Paul Brady reported that it was one of the best 5.11's in Central Texas.

Soon we went back to the drawing board and Dave came back and bolted "the traverse" (Insane Whisperings from a Yuggothian Braincase), much of it on lead. Then uproutes were bolted which borrowed one bolt each off the traverse. And, the exit-early traverse variations worked out well, with 10c and 10d variations, and a killer 12a variation later sent by pro climber/photographer Boone Speed. The resultant 11b traverse has been so fun over the years that I decided the property was worth buying, even if it were the only route.

As far as the feared uproutes go, two of them mellowed out with cleaning and beta, but the rest are for you badasses.

---

[270] Vinny projected and sent over pads, no rope. He also redpointed it as a sport route, exiting on Hastur's.
[271] Never pronounce **Nyarlathotep** out loud.
[272] Troy purchased the Austin Rock gyms about seven years ago.
[273] Jennifer published a book on step families called No One's The Bitch, and she appeared on national TV to talk about the book on a Dr. Phil show. Climbers can't afford to have chaotic stepfamilies. See www.noonesthebitch.com.

Monster Rock

44. traverse: Insane Whisperings from a Yuggothian Braincase (5.11b)*** 9 permadraws, Greg Brooks[274]. Start Icy Touch to the little roof formation and traverse it left on 9 permadraws to the arête, then lower. Falls while attempting to clip Bolt 6 may cause some contact during the swing and require you run a few steps across the cliff. The grade is bumped up for endurance; workable by 10+ climbers. A story of ever-building suspense, this is. It never gets old. '07

extension: Torture-iffic (5.11c)*** 16 permadraws, Neil Higa[275]. Traverse Insane Whisperings. Continue around the arête and across Mythology Wall's 7 permadraws on its high traverse (hands stay mostly above the permadraws). Lower on Bolt 16. An epic fantasy trilogy, where all three books are wildly different. '08

variation: Wurm (5.12a)*** 16 permadraws. The longest sustained traverse of nicely formed horizontal features in Central Texas. Traverse Torture-iffic, but before Bolt 11, downclimb and keep hands below the line of the remaining permadraw bolts, where there's a prominent horizontal ledge formation. Lower on Bolt 16. Another epic trilogy. Project.

The "Insane Whisperings from a Yuggothian Braincase" traverse has the following eight variations, each exiting early on various up-routes, providing a variety of route grades. But first, a grim aside. The space-borne Mi-Go race (who invented Yuggothian Braincases) could transplant other beings' brains across space in the braincases, from which the brains could see, hear, and speak...but in which they could not retain their sanity...

t1. variation: Starspawn Insanity (5.11b)*** 1 bolt & 9 permadraws, John Hogge. Traverse along Insane Whisperings to Bolt 9, then go left and up to finish on Starspawn of Cthulhu.

---

[274] First Inadvertent Ascent, Onsight. Greg was trying to send Sick Insanity and went left looking for holds. Later, photos showed he had sent Insane Whisperings.

[275] With very little projecting, Neil pulled off this big endurance 16 bolt traverse, while few have managed the original 9 bolt traverse. He was pumped out of his mind. He'd probably not ever pulled a 5.11c power crux at the time. To this day, Neil downplays this accomplishment. We still get teary-eyed thinking about it.

t2. variation: **Sick Insanity** (5.11d)* 1 bolt & 8 permadraws, Carl Stewart. Traverse along Insane Whisperings to Bolt 8, then go up and left to finish on Sick Experiments at Miskatonic University.

t3. variation: **Fear Insanity** (5.12a)*** 1bolt & 7 permadraws, Boone Speed. Traverse along Insane Whisperings to Bolt 7, then go up and left to finish on Fear of Evil Gods. Walk off the top to avoid rope wear. A wild route with celebrity status.

t4. variation: **Revenge Insanity** (5.10d)* 1 bolt & 6 permadraws, Donna Kwok. Traverse along Insane Whisperings to Bolt 6; continue up and left to the small chaotic roof. Finish the last moves of Revenge of the Shoggoths.

t5. bolted variation: **Hideous Insanity** (5.10c)*** 2 bolts (use long draws) & 5 permadraws, John Hogge. Traverse along Insane Whisperings to Bolt 5, go up and left to the shelf, clip a long draw on the non-permadraw bolt under the shelf, then go up and left with a long draw on the last bolt, finishing Hideous MI-GO Swimming Through Space. The easiest traverse variation on the wall. '07

t6. variation: **Hastur's Insanity** (5.10d)* 3 bolts & 5 permadraws, Will McDonald. Traverse along Insane Whisperings to Bolt 5, then go up and finish on Hastur's Semi-Liquid Fishy Things. Bring a long draw for the last bolt (out right on Invisible Slayer).

t7. variation: **Invisible Insanity** (5.10d)* 2 bolts & 4 permadraws, John Myrick. Traverse along Insane Whisperings to Bolt 4, then go up, finishing on Invisible Slayer of the Mad Arab Abdul Alhazred.

t8. variation: **Nyarlathotep Insanity** (5.11a)* 3 bolts & 3 permadraws, Donna Kwok. Traverse along Insane Whisperings to Bolt 3, then go up, finishing on Nyarlathotep Arises from the Blackness of 27 Centuries. This is a great warmup for the harder routes.

45. traverse: **The Dreaded Colour out of Space** (5.7 R)* 5 bolts, John Hogge. Belay and start on the ledge left of the upper ladder. Lead the last two bolts of Cosmic Horror; after Bolt 2, unclip Bolt 1 to avoid rope drag. Blind belay from here on. Traverse high on the cliff, clipping the upper bolts of Icy Touch, Nyarlathotep, run out to the last bolt of Invisible Slayer, then runout to Hideous Mi-Go anchors. Don't lead this unless you dominate 5.7; bad swing falls onto slabs. Seconding is on less risky runout swing falls (PG rated). The Colour Out of Space was a creature seemingly made of never-seen-before colors, that turned flesh to dust.

The Case for Limestone Traverses

What's up with all these traverses around town? A lot of climbers don't like traversing, but traverse junkies have their reasons:

1. With our short cliffs, traverses provide long routes. Really long, because all those hand shuffles and cross moves test your endurance over a horizontal span more than does a typical vertical span of the same length. A 40' wide traverse might be the equivalent of a 60' uproute.

2. Climbers like features, and route developers like following them. On limestone, natural features often run diagonally or horizontally.

3. You don't get much of that feeling of being protected by bolts, because you constantly risk swing falls prior to clipping and on the way to the next clip. It's a good kind of creepy.

Greg Brooks, "Insane Whisperings" FA, onsight

4. We're short on exposure in Texas. Millennium Traverse, Lenora's Wrath, and others get you up "high" and you stay up there, a long, long time.

Lovecraft's literature was all about weird, outlandish, undefeatable horrors. His protagonists rarely died. Rather, they saw the *hideous actual fabric of the universe*, and it left them quite mad…

Monster Rock

Rachel Harris Bryan, "Hideous Insanity"

Monster Rock: **Bouldering**

Mrock has some decent bouldering that provides a nice set of problems for beginning boulderers and alternative warmups for the sport routes. Undead Boulder is a nice spot by the river, when there *is* a river. So far, these boulders are rarely climbed, so bring brushes.

Shub Niggorath's Pinky Boulder: Not a true boulder, it's the small slabby right end section of Lovecraftian Madness' cliff, just right of the crack on the route Nyarlathotep Arises from the Blackness of 27 Centuries.

Blind Idiot God (aka. Azathoth, the Mindless Horror Ruling Time and Space) (V1). Sit start, eyes closed en route, no peeking. Pull the roof, fumble up the featured slab, finish standing on the ledge.

Necronomicon page 666 (V1). Sit start. Right side of the boulder. Ascend to easy climbing.

Cthulhu's Knuckle Boulder: Just to the right of Shub Niggorath's Pinky Boulder, next to the trail steps. Warning: Never pronounce Cthulhu out loud! You have been warned.

Eyaaa Eyaaa Cthulhu! (V0). Sit start. Keep off the arête. Follow the otherworldly-looking crack-like formation.

Yog-Sothoth waits at The Gate (V0). Sit start. Stay off of Eyaa Eyaaa Cthulhu!'s crack-like formation.

Strength and Toughness Boulder: forms an A-Frame with Monster's Lair Boulder. This boulder is the one with the large diagonal crack on it. Both are perched on a hill between the cliffs and the river. *Please stay off the fragile topmost face of the boulder above the highest ledge full of dense shag carpet/coral type rock surface structure. This interesting rock surface breaks easily.*

Force of Nature (V0-1). Sit-start at the roof's edge at the diagonal crack. Follow the crack right and up.

Dwarven God + 7 (V0). Sit-start at the right edge of the boulder. Traverse left.

Royal Assassin/Icy Manipulator (V2). Sit-start on the curvy vertical crack. Go up to the jet-black deep pocket and then to the shelf. Don't touch anything above that shelf (it breaks). Dyno to the top edge. With a Royal Assassin and an Icy Manipulator both played, the opponent was locked down and likely hosed.

Monster's Lair Boulder: forms an A-Frame with Strength & Toughness Boulder. The face's many features will yield more problems.

Helltide (V0). Climbs the arête on the right side under the dead tree.
Shambling Mound (V0). Start on the dark scary hueco on the left side, traverse left and up, staying off of the dirty surfaces.

Magic, the Gathering Boulder:[276] lies next to S&T Boulder and Monster's Lair Boulder.

Orcish Vast-throngs (V0). Sit start at the right. Traverse left and up.

Undead Boulder: a large boulder down at the river's edge. Enjoy the view from its top. An easy ledge ("**EL**", herein) runs horizontally across the boulder's left half. Some problem grades change if EL is on or off. All problems are sit-starts and (except for the traverses) top-outs.

Necromancer (V6-7?). Start on the detached boulder next to the main face of Undead Boulder. Traverse right onto Undead Boulder and across it, staying below EL. EL is off. Project.
Zombie Nation (V2). Like Imp in a Bottle, but EL is on.
Abomination (V0 EL-on / V?? EL-off). Start on the boulder's left arête.
Army of Darkness (V0 EL-on / V?? EL-off). Start left-hand on ledge, right hand on the big pocket. Go up to the cave.
Cultes des Ghoules (V0 EL-on / V?? EL-off). Start on the big low (1' off the ground) left side-pull. Finish on the left side of the bulge.

[276] In honor of Magic, the Gathering™, a collectible card game. With its clever design by a mathematician, gaming geeks of all ages became addicted to playing it and collecting its cards. Within a few years, it had outsold a century of sales of the board game Monopoly.

Werewolfie (V0 EL-on / V?? EL-off). Start as with Cultes des Ghoules. Finish on the right side of the bulge.

Night of the Living Dead (V0 EL-on / V?? EL-off). Start in the shallow cave behind the tree. Climb out left of the tree.

Tree.

Dawn of the Dead (V1). Start like Night of the Living Dead. Exit the cave to the right of the tree.

Hand of Vecna (V4-5?) Project.

Resident Evil (V3). Climb to the slight "point" at the boulder's top.

The Hunger (V4?) Start three feet right of Resident Evil. Climb to that same point. Project.

Scratches on the Inside of a Coffin (V0). Lie-down start under the low little arête, hands left of the arête. Climb left of the two stacked arêtes.

Skeleton's Teeth (V0). Start hands on the low little arête. Climb the two stacked arêtes.

Ghost Story (V0). Start hands on the little low arête. Climb diagonally right and up.

Witch's Cackle. (V?) Start left-hand undercling, right-hand crack. Climb straight up. Not a project, but we never graded it. Moderate.

Prow 2' off the ground. **_WARNING: This piece of rock is almost 100% detached. Climbing it entails a risk of a crushing death!_**

Eye of Vecna (aka. Lich's Delight) (V?). In the game Dungeons & Dragons, a Lich was an undead wizard with a lust for power. The lich Vecna strived to become a demi-god and to kill all the other demi-gods. At some point he lost his eye and hand, and they became powerful magical artifacts, up there with Excalibur and the One Ring. If a mortal found them and agonizingly "replaced" his own eye or hand with them, the mortal would gain power. And also utter evilhood. But now, let's take it down a notch. Start on Witch's Cackle. Traverse the prow right to the short face; go up under the Hueco. Not a project, but we never graded it. Moderate.

Bloody Wooden Stake (V?) Climb the lowest point of the prow straight up over the bad landing boulder. Not a project, but we never graded it. Moderate.

Howl of the Ring Wraiths (V?) Start hands on the prow's uphill top surface. Climb straight up. Not a project, but we never graded it. Moderate.

There are more potential variations on the prow.

More excavation of the big landing boulders would open up the right side of the boulder. Anyone have a jack-hammer?

Danny <u>Paradorn, risking the crushing death on Bloddy Wooden</u> Morgan <u>Young is spotting.</u>

> Listen to them. Children of the night. What music they make.
>
> *Bela Lugosi, in the 1931 movie "Dracula"*

First there was Odin, and he saw that the rock was good, and he sent Thor to bash it up into climbable portions. Thor did his worst and clave Monster Rock in two. Likely some half-elf strolled by and free-soloed every route, dirty, without chalk.

Then in 1998 I was planning to move to Austin for its charms and its rock climbing. I was not interested in Erock and not that into the Greenbelt. I liked Reimers, but saw an aging Milton Reimers, smoking his cheap cigars[277], and figured he'd die before long, and his widow would follow the conventional wisdom of selling her ranch to developers to cover future estate taxes. So we shopped for backup climbing properties and bought Monster Rock and North Shore. (Ironically, Reimers became public, North Shore became public, and Monster Rock became a lot more routes than I ever imagined.)

In 2001, the first half-dozen routes were installed by Joey Phillips, an English grit-stoner friend of mine (John Sonzcak), and me (under their tutelage). Then I succumbed to the pressures of work and stopped climbing for about six years. During that time, I climbed Mrock maybe twice. One day I noticed a newspaper blurb about someone falling to their death on Pace Bend. There are many dozens of homes on the road, but I got a creepy feeling. I knew how short Mrock's neighboring fence was (3' at that time). A few days later, a friend felt like getting out and climbing, so we headed to Mrock for the half-dozen routes. We arrived, walked to the bridge, I looked to my right, and there was a lawn mower, pointed away from the 3' fence. Shivers ran up my back and scalp, and I *knew* the neighbor had backed the mower, tripped backwards over the fence, and died in the pit, near my deepest routes.

I shook it off and we climbed a little, when a man crossed the bridged and yelled for permission to come down and talk. He explained that his dad had died in the pit, and he wanted to recover his glasses. We helped him cross the routes and go deeper into the pit to recover them.

In 2004, Dave Phillips set up camp at Mrock, and I moved down the street. Mrock didn't progress; Lovecraftian Madness Wall appeared to have few feasible starts, and the pit was a mess of vegetation and fall zones problematic for lead routes. Dave and Terence Smith built trails, and other friends unearthed Undead Boulder. Dave had more faith in the pit routes than I did; he saw a lot more potential for good routes. By 2006, he proposed developing them and opening a small business offering Mrock access to the public.

Finally in '07, work eased up, and I turned my attention to climbing. I cleaned massive ferns and soils off of D&D Wall, bolted the rest of those routes, and hired John Myrick to bolt the hardest Lovecraftian Madness Wall routes. Dave bolted the rest of them. We opted for some toprope only routes in the pit to deal with unsafe fall zones. Mrock opened for business.

Mrock's public opening was promoted with an onsight contest, and with the opportunity for first-ascents of any route that didn't already have an FA. As part of the promotion, my free Mrock guidebook recorded First-Onsight-Ascents (FOAs) as well as regular FAs. In some cases, the FA was also an FOA. In this book, each route shows the FA and bolter(s). The FOAs are:

Annette Pelletier (Nyarlathotep Fear)
Blaine Burris (Texas Chainsaw Massacre)
Chris "The Wanker" Palmer (22-Eyed Beholder Hovering Near By)
Dan Jepson (Hastur's Semi-Liquid Fishy Things)
Daniel Culotta (Hideous Insanity)
Danny Lenz (Creeping Doom variation)
David Blankenship (Specter's Touch)
Donna Kwok (Invisible Slayer; Nyarlathotep Arises)
Jimmy James Klein (Goblin Mutant)
Jen Koschmann (Swordmaiden of Rohan)
John Hogge (Green Slime vs. Bag of Devouring; Icy Touch)

Josh Bilberry (Cold Damp Embrace of the Mummy; Psychic Venom)
Lance Waring (Torture-iffic)
Laura McWilliams
"Lucky" Mike Klein (Gelatinous Cube's Deadly Solvent)
Paul Brady (Shower Scene from Psycho; Lord of the Pit.)
Ryan Collity (Herman Munster; Grendel; Warg Riders)
Roni Beer (Crawling Chaos)
Russell Mayes (Dracula's Silent Steps Approacheth)
Sean O'Grady (Balrog's Whip)
Tim Sharp (Sky Full of Dementors)

The last piece of Monster Rock was developed a year later with the Mythology Wall routes and their extension of the classic Insane Whisperings traverse to 16 bolts. For years, the starts had looked too tough to make any decent routes out of, and we'd considered manufacturing starts. Ideas included plastic holds, huge drilled jug huecos, glued-on sandstone holds to contrast with all the area limestone, and artificial tufa drips under the roof. After some toprope study, the traverse extension was obviously good, and I felt it was time to bolt it, coordinated with the best possible set of uproutes. I opted to build a tall, ugly, permanent cheat stack for two of the routes and trusted the other three would go unaided. Now Monster Rock is completely bolted. Except for that one linkup we just spotted...

> 5.11 is way more fun than 5.12. 5.12 is basically about pain.
>
> *Jan Capps*

---

[277] We recommend Backwoods for a good cheap smoke.

N
Taylor Cove
Maugham Cove
Collier Cove
Pace Bend Park Rd.
Davis Cove
Gracy Cove
Thurman Cove
Marshall Cove
Thrasher Cove
Maxey Cove
Naumann Cove
Park Entrance
Grisham Trail
Tatum Cove
"Duende Cove" dry bouldering
Baldwin Cove
Table #400 Climbing Area
Acid Rock & Hueco Wall
Table #397 Climbing Area
Restroom 14 Climbing Area
Giles Cove
Levi Cove
Tournament Point
Mudd Cove
Map Key
Restrooms (Identified by Number)
Paved Roads (25 mph speed limit)
Unpaved Roads (10mph speed limit)
Boat Ramps & Phones
Cove is labeled but has no climbing

Pace Bend Climbing Areas

Climbing Area: A Sketchy DWS Guide to Pace mother fuckin' Bend

Pace Bend (PmfB) is a Travis County park 40 minutes west of Austin, on Lake Travis, offering excellent Deep Water Soloing (DWS) in twelve coves and the cliffs between them. The lake level varies throughout the year, and with it, the existence, safety, difficulty, quality, and highball-ity of each climb. If you were to explore PmfB at every possible lake level, you'd find roughly 800 different climbs, far exceeding the number of bolted routes around Austin. PmfB is about variety, freedom from ropes, forgetting the grades, and fun.

PmfB experiences occasional droughts that shorten or eliminate its DWS season of late spring through about mid-September. When the water is up, come out as soon as water temperatures allow and get your fix. Waiting till August may leave you high and dry.

www.bloodyflapper.com/pacebend provides a great graphic tool for picking an area that is reasonably safe and fun at the current water level. Its "More Info" link also provides the current water temperature (via wwwext.arlut.utexas.edu/omg/weather.html) in a chart entitled "LTTS Water Temperature Profile". If you're away from a computer, ask the water level and temperature at 512-264-1482 (the Pace Bend office for Travis County Parks).

Long Ta, Giles Lake Cliff

This guide provides detailed access beta for each PmfB climbing area. It breaks down the climbing areas in more detail than at www.bloodflapper.com, giving you estimated numbers of problems at various water levels. This guide also adds more coves. However, we investigated most of PmfB at 667'-672' and used rough measurements and estimates to handle all other water levels. We expect to compile corrections over time and publish them. *Every recommended water level in this chapter is untested. Do not trust our estimates; always check your landings for submerged boulders.*

Everyone's resistance to cold differs; generally people won't have fun if the water temperature is lower than 70 degrees. Beware of hypothermia, which can hit even in warm water if you're in long enough.

Directions: set your GPS for 2501 Pace Bend Road North, Spicewood, TX 78669. Old school directions: get onto Pace Bend Road using the directions for Monster Rock. Keep on Pace Bend until it dead-ends at the park.

Equipment

- Ditch your rope, rope bag, backpack, belay device, quick draws, helmet, cams, tri-cams, hexes, nuts, and belayer, for a mere swimsuit[278].

- Water & some Gatorade. Easy on the beer; dehydration happens fast with DWS.

- A float. You need a float because most areas lack resting ledges and the like. A popular float is an extra thick "noodle," or 2-3 noodles duct-taped together. (Buy these in town at Pool supply stores or maybe Walmart. The corner Chevron and other Pace Bend gas stations sell them periodically.) Maybe arrange a carrying loop for climb-out exits. We also like a thin life preserver; it's easy to carry out — but take it off for taller climbs, or it will rip you upon impact.

- A floating strap for your prescription glasses or sun glasses. The gas stations on Pace Bend often sell these.

- A secure car key holder in your swimsuit. We bring some cash and ID to leave home the wallet. We've not heard of PmfB crime, but you know it's inevitable.

- For 5.12 and up stuff, a brush for occasional lake-grime cleaning.

---

[278] And we do mean *mere*. Water weighs down those fashionably big men's trunks like a lead balloon. We hate pulling a hard move out of the water and then waiting there, pumping out, until the water pours off our trunks. So the best men's outfit is bikini Speedos™. Sorry.

Jake Archer 📷   **Thurman South Lake Cliff**

- A boat is not necessary. But, PmfB has two boat ramps if you want to add more greenhouse gasses into this doomed planet's atmosphere at $6 per gallon soze you can fish between sends or water ski.

- Climbing shoes are very optional. Bring old climbing shoes for heel-hooks, edging, better smearing capability, and extra armor on shallow landings. Synthetic shoes probably work better than leather. Or just climb in bare feet like the ancient peoples, so you can toe the hell out of pockets. Shoes probably win out on most climbs, but bare feet are more fun.

- Bring a massive BBQ picnic so the rest of us can eat. Bring us a shade tent for your picnic table. Thanks!

- The cliff divers seem active setting knotted ropes or fire escape ladders at areas that become difficult to climb out of (e.g. Acid Rock/Hueco Wall). In case the water drops further than their lines, consider stowing some static line in your car. We've seen climbers secure chalk and coolers on static line, lowering it all to hover just above the water for easy access.

Newbie Advice

Deep Water Soloing sounds about as scary as Soloing does. But we encourage all to check out PmfB, regardless of your skill level or your level of comfort bouldering or leading. It's just too fun, and the climbs are high quality. You get to pick your level of scared, by bailing early off climbs, or down-climbing, or picking shorter climbs. And, we feel PmfB is about the best place around Austin to train and enjoy easy-to-moderate steep climbing.

How to Fall

Before falling, always check for rocks lying too close to the surface. Unless the water is muddy from some major flood, submerged rock is visible from above (but not as visible while swimming). Under highballs, go under and poke around. Be careful climbing slab sections; it's hard to judge when your foot will or won't hit upon slipping. Pumping out is rarely the problem because you can push away from the cliff and clear all the rock. Slipping is the risk. Fortunately, much of PmfB is overhanging air falls to the water. Just choose your climbs wisely.

On shallow water problems…water does stop a body pretty quickly, but the distance varies with your body angle and what you do. You could put arms out and press down upon impact for quick breaking, but that's hard on the shoulders and unwise on highballs. Tucking feet (cannon ball) could protect your ankles in shallow water but could risk your tailbone and spine on submerged uneven rock. Know your submerged topography.

On a highball over deep water, close your nose with one hand, hold that elbow with the other hand, cross your legs to "cork screw" into the water, keep feet flat, and kiss your sweet ass goodbye.

The actual climbing feels different from dry-land limestone routes, as starting surfaces often have a *lake grime* whose composition is a mystery. Maybe it's a combination of dried mud cake, a trillion dead algae, and Deep Ones urine. Whatever it is, it has decent friction, it's mostly solid, and it's easy on the skin. Pulling with wet hands is interesting; they dry off quickly on the way up, and sometimes you milk rests longer to get them dry.

The submerged footholds are sometimes slimy and bad. You feel around down there, massaging that slippery mystery topography in search of a ledge or pocket. Icky at first; guilty pleasure later. There's no smearing down there; when there are no feet, our favorite DWS move comes into play: legs swim and thrash to power campus-bumps up bad handholds until you have some footing on the dry cliff. Another favorite: when there are no starting handholds, make like a dolphin and do the Ocean Dyno.

a Dolphin Dyno

Crazy Cramps, Drownings, and Drunk Boaters

A young climber from SMU mentioned he was treading water when a massive crazy-cramp hit his leg, forcing his knee to bend, and he couldn't continue treading water. He yelled for someone to throw him a noodle. Fortunately he wasn't alone. It's common to see all but one climber top out, and the lone climber continues working a problem. It's also common to see dehydration (then cramps). Be prepared to tread water with arms only, and hope they don't cramp too. Better yet, use the buddy system. Everyone differs in swimming ability, and drowning often happens silently and quickly.

If your buddy is drowning, do not touch them. They are panicked and out of their minds. They will likely grab you and pull you down with them. Do whatever is safe for you. Reach your float over to them until they grab it, if you have the energy to swim and exit the water without your float. Otherwise, arrange a 911 call ASAP.

Besides practicing a buddy system, it's good to have a lot of bodies in the water, so that boaters don't blow over an unseen lone swimmer. Boaters sometimes blow through Giles Cove's fall zones to stop at access points for cliff-diving.

Once in a while, a climber will fall funny from a roof, invert under water, and not realize it. If the water is murky, you don't know which way is up, and you risk drowning. Jordan Ryan[279] offers the following technique: 1. Force your eyes open. 2. Blow out a few bubbles. 3. Now you know which way is up.

So DWS has its risks. At least you'll never get dropped by a bad belay.

Water Level Strangeness

Perhaps a third or more of the problems' physical cruxes are simply pulling right out of the water, using slimy footholds. Grades can easily jump when the water level drops one or two feet. Repeating last week's easy problem might require a dolphin-dyno. Or, risk accusations of *Ethical Violation* and sit on your float. I like life preservers over noodles, because you can sit and ride a little higher to help start troublesome problems.

Compounding these challenges, PmfB has a time-space distortion that skews Newtonian physics by three and a half dimensions, disturbs causality, and degrades all continua into discrete elements. As a result:

> 2' *often-equals* 3'.

We shall attempt to explain this. One day we climbed an area at the 671' water level. A week later, we came back at level 669' and were shocked at the difference. See, it's like this. The guard shack could post 671' when the actual water level is 671.9'. And they could post 669' when it's really 669.000001'. Thus, a 2' (671' – 669') drop in water may actually be 3' (671.9' – 669'). Climb a great area and return at "two" feet lower, and you may find all landings compromised, or problems fewer and much-harder-to-start than before.

Usually this doesn't spoil an outing; there are plenty of nearby problems to shift to. But, steep short problems can be safe today and bad after "two" or three feet of water drop. Always check under the water.

Soap Box

1. Deep Water Solo is the worst term ever invented among all fields of activity, throughout all of eternity.

2. It's cumbersome to pronounce. No wonder the Europeans came up with another term, psicobloc. But that is impossible to spell, and it ain't English.

3. Of *course* the water is deep. Otherwise you're shallow water soloing and, incidentally, you're actually soloing.

4. There's no soloing over water, unless you're 50' up or over an angry ocean's crashing waves. On calm waters such as Lake Travis, it's Water Bouldering. Accurate, but not entirely satisfying in the way Climbing, Soloing, and Buildering are. Maybe call it Splashing, because that's mainly what happens.

Ethical Violations

Overzealous DWS projectors sometimes resort to zip lock portage of towels and chalk to stow and use *en route*, or even stepping off boats to start problems. Please consider these ethical violations and dunk them. We're not even sure we'll ever wear climbing shoes here; shoes are a *land* thing. This is *water*. It's a *slippery* slope, and we're sure we will see TR rehearsal head points of Sharma's arch problem before long.

Park Access

Directions, fees (for day use, primitive camping, improved camping, boating, etc.) are provided at www.co.travis.tx.us/tnr/parks/pace_bend.asp. Currently, day-use fees are $10 per vehicle; consider getting an annual pass ($100) that gets your vehicle into Pace Bend and Reimers/North Shore. If you use more than one vehicle, a secondary pass runs $50 per vehicle.

---

[279] Aka. Ryan Jordan. WTF?

Pace Bend

Directions within the Park

The park is over a thousand acres, with only two main roads. Simple side-roads access each cove. Ask for a map at the guard shack. Most of the coves have two roads going to them, one on the south side of the cove, one on the north. Use the next section (Picking a Cove) to decide which cove you want to visit, then read about convenient parking and access under Cove Descriptions & Access Beta.

All of our access points are designed as hikes or easy downclimbs into the water. This has the advantage of giving you a reliable, convenient way out of the water. In many cases it's faster to jump off the cliff near or at an area's problems. However, we advise scoping our recommended hikes and downclimbs, in case you can't get up any other way.

Picking a Cove

PmfB has many coves and lake cliffs to choose from. At the park entrance, you will pay your fee at one of two guard shacks. The left-most has a posting of the current water level. Use that and one of the two charts below to decide which areas to climb. Many folks do two or more areas in a day.

The general trend throughout late spring and summer is falling water levels. As the lake level drops, the climbing areas take turns becoming unsafe until you're left with several areas on the east coast of the park (the various lake cliff areas from Baldwin Cove to Giles Cove). Sometimes a big rain event will raise the water level a lot, but it takes major rains west of Austin, not a lot of rain just over Lake Travis.

If you have a favorite area you want to visit, reference it in the Alphabetic chart below to see how good it is at the current water level. After this is a second chart organizing the areas from high to low water levels. The second chart can be used throughout the season to climb the areas in the order that they will become unsafe as the water drops. Since some areas offer problems good at different water levels, they appear several times in the second chart.

PmfB: <u>Alphabetic Listing of Climbing Areas</u>

Exit Sign	Climbing Area	Total Problems at Various Water Levels	Picnic Table#	BBQ	Detail Page
Grisham to Table #399	<u>Acid Rock</u> & Hueco Wall	54@674, 44@ 672, 30@670', 28@668 (or lower)	399	yes	230
Grisham to N. Baldwin	<u>Baldwin</u> Cove North Bank and North Lake Cliff	0@676, 11@674, 40@662	406	yes	228
Collier Boat ramp	<u>Collier</u> South Lake Cliff	0@679, 11@677; all short	82		222
Middle Davis	<u>Davis</u> Cove North Bank	0@681, 5@677, 11 sketchy@676, 6@674	75	yes	222
S. Davis	<u>Davis</u> Cove South Corner and South Lake Cliff	80@680, 59@677, 20@675,	72	yes	220
N. Davis	<u>Davis</u> North Lake Cliff	43@687, 33@685, 6@681	77-78	yes	222
Grisham to S. Baldwin	"<u>Duende</u> Cove"[280]	0@677, 34@674, dry bouldering@663 and lower		yes	226
Grisham to Giles	<u>Giles</u> Lake Cliff	0@675, 10@671, 16@668 (and lower), 8@657, 14@653 (and lower)			233
N. Gracy	<u>Gracy</u> Cove North Corner	0@688, 7@685	65		219
N. Gracy	<u>Gracy</u> North Lake Cliff	0@674, 56@671, 34@669, 19@667	65		219
N. Thrasher / S. Marshall	<u>Marshall</u> Cove, Both Banks	16@685, 8@683, 6@677 and more nearby	17		217
N. Marshall	<u>Marshall</u> North Lake Cliff	14@687, 6@680	21	yes	217
N. Thrasher / S. Marshall	<u>Marshall</u> South Lake Cliff	30?@692, 7@682	16 or 17		217

---

[280] Duende Cove is what the local badasses call the southwest side of Baldwin Cove. That name does not appear on park maps.

Exit Sign	Area	Total Problems at Various Water Levels	Picnic Table#	BBQ	Detail Page
Collier Boat ramp	Maugham Cove Both Banks	18@690, 25@683, 19@678	past 89		223
N. Maugham / S. Taylor	Maugham North Lake Cliff (aka. "Mom")	16@675, 10@672	91	yes	223
Maxey / Naumann	Maxey Cove North Bank	8@692, 23@687, 12@684, 7@679			213
Maxey / Naumann	Maxey North Lake Cliff	5@685 plus those nearby at Thrasher			214
Maxey / Naumann	Maxey South Corner and South Lake Cliff	6@696, 4@682	none		214
Maxey / Naumann	Naumann Cove Both Banks	6@687, 4@683, 2@679	unmarked		214
Grisham; just past Restroom #14	Restroom #14	0@687, 5@678, 0@675, 4@670		yes	233
Grisham to Giles	Table #397	0@674, 28@670, 7@667(or lower)			232
Grisham to Table #400	Table #400	0@673, 31@670, 26@668 (or lower)	400	yes	228
N.Taylor (1st exit)	Taylor North Lake Cliff	30@684. 24@682, mostly short	105	yes	225
N. Thrasher / S. Marshal	Thrasher Cove North Bank and North Lake Cliff	23@695, 40@688, 23@686, 9@683,13-15 3@680			216
S. Thrasher	Thrasher South Lake Cliff	47@685, 8@684	9 & 10	yes	215
Thurman/Gracy	Thurman Cove North Bank and North Corner	0@693, 14@689, 17@678, 5@676	27		218
Thurman / Gracy Loop	Thurman South Lake Cliff	11@678, 22@672, 15@670, 4@668 25			218

We kindly ask the reader for feedback on the above water levels for later publication. Truly nailing down the best water levels may take years; don't hesitate to contact us through 2035. In the above table:

Exit Sign is the exit off the two main roads that gets you to the most convenient parking for accessing an area.

Detail Page is the page number where the particular area is described, with the best hiking access to the climbs and sketchy descriptions of the problems.

Total Problems at Various Water Levels gives an estimated number of safe, fun problems at different water levels. It's a summary of details provided in each area's description. Never trust these water levels — always check for submerged boulders under your climbs. As water level drops, problem counts increase as previously submerged problems see sunshine, or they decrease as submerged hazards get too close to the water surface.

Example: if an area's total problems are "6@696, 4@682", it has 6 problems reasonably safe at water level 696' and higher, and those six are iffy or unsafe at 695' and lower. Also, this area has 4 problems reasonably safe at 682'. The table doesn't summarize problem heights, so we can't tell whether the 4 are even above water at, say 694'. Those details are provided, if available, under the area description at the **Detail Page**. In this example, consider 696' and 682' the best target levels to visit this area.

Example: "0@693, 14@689". Occasionally we sneak in zeros to show when problems become too short. In this case, we have 14 short problems optimally climbed at 689', and they suck when the water rises to 693'. We didn't want you to show up at 693' and hate us.

Picnic Table# is the number painted on the Picnic table nearest to the most convenient parking.

BBQ indicates whether a BBQ pit is nearby.

The above table lists each climbing area once. You might find the next table easier to use; each area appears multiple times according to new problems that appear at the area as the water level drops.

Pace Bend

PmfB: **Climbing Areas Listed by Water Level**

Water Level	Pg.	Climbing Areas	Annual Chances	Problem Counts
696'	214	Maxey South Corner and South Lake Cliff	7%	6
695'	216	Thrasher Cove North Bank and N. Lake Cliff	7%	23
692'	213	Maxey Cove North Bank	13%	8
	217	Marshall South Lake Cliff		30
690'	223	Maugham Cove Both Banks	17%	18
689'	218	Thurman Cove North Bank and N. Corner	17%	14
688'	216	Thrasher Cove North Bank and N. Lake Cliff	17%	40
687'	213	Maxey Cove North Bank	17%	23
	214	Naumann Cove Both Banks		6
	217	Marshall North Lake Cliff		14
686'	216	Thrasher Cove North Bank & N. Lake Cliff	20%	23
685'	222	Davis North Lake Cliff	27%	33
	214	Maxey North Lake Cliff		5
	215	Thrasher South Lake Cliff		47
	219	Gracy Cove North Corner		7
	217	Marshall Cove Both Banks		16
684'	213	Maxey Cove North Bank	27%	12
	215	Thrasher South Lake Cliff		8
	225	Taylor North Lake Cliff		30
683'	216	Thrasher Cove North Bank and N. Lake Cliff	30%	9
	223	Maugham Cove Both Banks		25
	214	Naumann Cove Both Banks		4
	217	Marshall Cove Both Banks		8
682'	214	Maxey South Corner and South Lake Cliff	33%	4
	217	Marshall South Lake Cliff		7
	225	Taylor North Lake Cliff		24
681'	222	Davis North Lake Cliff	53%	6
680'	216	Thrasher Cove North Bank and N. Lake Cliff	57%	3
	217	Marshall North Lake Cliff		6
	220	Davis Cove South Corner and S. Lake Cliff		80
679'	213	Maxey Cove North Bank	70%	7
678'	223	Maugham Cove Both Banks	67%	19
	218	Thurman Cove North Bank and North Corner		17
	218	Thurman South Lake Cliff		11
	233	Restroom #14		5
677'	217	Marshall Cove Both Banks	63%	6
	220	Davis Cove South Corner and S. Lake Cliff		59
	222	Davis Cove North Bank		5
	222	Collier South Lake Cliff		11
676'	218	Thurman Cove North Bank and North Corner	60%	5
675'	220	Davis Cove South Corner and S. Lake Cliff	50%	20
	223	Maugham North Lake Cliff (aka. "Mom")		16
674'	222	Davis Cove North Bank	53%	6
	226	Duende Cove		34
	230	Acid Rock & Hueco Wall		55 (674' is best for 10 high-water problems; the rest are better at lower levels)
673'	228	Baldwin Cove North Bank and N. Lake Cliff	50%	11
672'	223	Maugham North Lake Cliff	47%	10
	218	Thurman South Lake Cliff		22
	230	Acid Rock & Hueco Wall		55 (672' is the minimum for 14 of the problems; the rest are better at lower levels)
671'	233	Giles Lake Cliff	37%	10
	219	Gracy North Lake Cliff		56
670'	218	Thurman South Lake Cliff	30%	15
	228	Table #400		31*
	230	Acid Rock & Hueco Wall		55 (30 safe problems on the left end. At 670' they get taller and more fun)

Pace Bend

	233	Restroom #14		4
669'	218	Thurman South Lake Cliff	20%	4
	219	Gracy North Lake Cliff		34
668'	230	Acid Rock & Hueco Wall	13%	55*
	233	Giles Lake Cliff		16*
667'	219	Gracy North Lake Cliff	13%	19
663'	226	Duende Cove	13%	33 (almost all appear boulderable at 663' and lower)
662'	228	Baldwin Cove North Bank and N. Lake Cliff	13%	34*
653'	233	Giles Lake Cliff	13%	14
644'			10%	
641'			7%	
632'			3%	(2011 summer level reached 637' during drought)
631'			3%	

*Acid Rock/Hueco Wall, Giles, and Baldwin especially deserve further study at lower water levels.

"Annual Chances" shows how rare it is to see the given water level during a climbing season (May through September). If it's warm and you see the current water level has a low percent chance, jump on the opportunity to check out the area or areas listed for that water level.[281]

Cove Hopping

A useful day strategy is to avoid the sun; climb one of the various west-coast coves early and move late in the day to the two east-coast coves (Giles and Baldwin), to stay in the shade. Still another strategy: *follow the beer.*

When there's nothing but cedar "trees" to look at, the drive time between coves can seem really long. PmfB mf speed limits are Twenty Five mf Miles per Hour, a crawl that makes the drive from Thurman/Gracy to Giles feel like a long rush hour commute. But *no*; that particular drive time is only 2 minutes by the optimal route (south on the main road; left on Grisham Trail).

PmfB's two roads form a big loop connecting all the areas by clockwise or counter-clockwise routes. So we were curious what time savings could be made in choosing clockwise or counterclockwise routes. The savings aren't big. The worst you can do, choosing wrong, is to waste 7 minutes. (Taking the clockwise path from Thrasher Cove to S. Baldwin (Duende Cove) wastes 7 minutes compared to the counter-clockwise path.)

Rule Of Thumb: go clockwise to Giles/Baldwin/Duende if you are at Collier, Maugham, or Taylor. Otherwise drive counter-clockwise.

Poseidon, fill our lake, so that we may Send.

Ancient Climbers' Prayer

---

[281] The chances were computed from monthly water levels collected by the University of Texas since 1945. We used only the most recent 30 years of data through 2010 but did not see much change compared to going back to 1945. Thank you, UT, you're great!

Pace Bend

PmfB: **Climbing Areas**

It's about **mf** time a guidebook gives some PmfB access beta. We hate driving to the south side of a cove when the best access is on the north. We hate hiking into a cove and swimming a long way until we see any climbs, when there's a scary looking deathfall 5.2 downclimb near the good stuff. Droughts take PmfB out of commission regularly, so we don't ever remember what we learned two years ago. This chapter nails down access, mainly through the strategic use of picnic tables.

The map you get (but don't really need) from the guard shack will show the various named coves drawn along the west and east coasts of PmfB. Climbs sometime occur on the south side of a cove, on the north side, and on the "lake cliffs" between coves. The following uses Thurman Cove to explain the terminology used in this chapter to identify climbing areas:

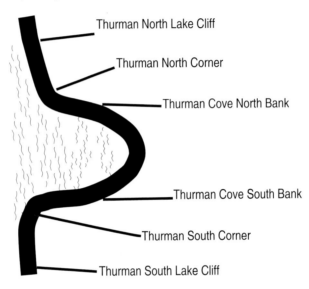

This chapter only sketches difficulty grades in a few areas. In later editions, we'd like to sketch the grades at all areas, at all useful water levels. We use YDS grades (e.g. 5.10c) instead of bouldering grades, because the low V grades span a wider range of difficulty than is useful to climbers at those levels.

For now, we've focused on good access beta and estimated problem counts at various water levels. The estimates will take a long time to refine, since Mother Nature does not always offer us the water levels we want to survey. Also, we're aged and on our slow decline towards gimptitude. Most counts were via visual inspection. Since we've seen how folks enjoy really short problems, such as Giles at high water, and, well, McKinney, we've been liberal with suggesting that a given span of cliff could offer fun pulling, even if it's 7' of pulling out of the water.

We sincerely hope you enjoy the following areas and have good luck hitting them at good water levels. The areas are sorted geographically, running south-to-north, the order you'll encounter the west-coast areas from the main road. The east coast areas (reached from Grisham Trail) appear last, south-to-north.

> We hadn't climbed for a week due to floods in southern France. They were incredible to see. Water is so powerful. I need to learn to move on the rock like water. The more I can flow on the rock like water, the more I understand and the less separation there will be between us. Climbing hard will come naturally from that point, like a flooded river wiping out a bridge without even having to think about it.
>
> *Chris Sharma*

Exit: "Maxey / Naumann"
Parking: Park in the 1st space on the right.
Approach: Walk to the cove's south bank. Walk right along a dirty ledge under a big cedar tree and do a 5.2 slab downclimb at a small Bald Cypress tree (!) and small Sycamores. It's a short swim to the north bank.
GPS: Maxey South bank: N30°26.372' W98°02.550' (30.439533 -98.0425). Back of Naumann Cove: N30°26.208' W98°02.727' (30.4368 -98.04545)

Previous guidebooks listed only a few of the popular climbing areas at PmfB. We've included all popular areas and have also thrown in seldom (never?) climbed high-water areas such as Maxey/Naumann that might be worth checking out, on the rare occasion that a season offers high water at high temperatures.

Well, the water level is fairly *low* at this writing, and so we can only sketch you a high-water adventure for later. Hope it's rad. We *can* say, Naumann is one of the prettiest coves in the park, with its spring waters running down the dome of its arroyo.

The above parking and access takes you to the first of the following areas.

1)   Maxey Cove North Bank.

Maxey Cove's north bank features several nice arêtes and a low tan featured shallow cave. It's a short swim from the south bank access.

Problems (listed right-to-left [282])	Estimated Water Level
Right side of 2nd bulge from the right; mild overhang	679'-???
Its steep left side	679'-???
Beautiful mottled tan mild overhang w/ shelf hazard	683'-???
Its left edge arête, stemming the rock island left of that	683'-???
The rock island's right side	681'-???
~5 problems on the rock island face. (left end: ledge hazard)	676'-???
~3 problems on a roof	684'-???
Roof's left side arête	687'-???
Orange face with cactus blocking the topout	687'-???
The face's crack, again with cactus blocking the topout.	687'-???
Face with two starting thin vertical cracks…still with the freaking cactus topout.	687'-???
Rounded arête with thin holds. Fuck this cactus.	687'-???
Thin face.	689'-???
More face climbing but with bad landing boulder	

(30' gap with vegetation over a boulder. The boulder is no good for DWS, but its left side looks fun for sketchpad bouldering when the cove goes dry. Which brings up the subject — *mightn't PmfB make a good general bouldering destination, whenever the water's low enough to haul pads? And not just at Duende?*)

2 problems on a magnificent 20° orange overhang with a roof sporting a nice hueco	686'
arête	686'
2 problems on a face full of slopers	686'
Thin crack	686'
2 problems on an overhang full of slopers	686'
Ivy-garnished crack problem.	684'
Overhung face painted in tans, grays, and blacks	684'
Bulge-to-bowl-to-bulge	684'

[282] We like left-to-right listings, but this guidebook gets left in the car when at PmfB, unless maybe you're climbing off a boat. So, at PmfB, we list right-to-left when you're approaching from the right, in hopes it's easier to visualize and sort of half-memorize as you swim into an area.

Thin crack-to-sidepull hueco-to-bare black face	684'
Overhung face with pockets and a ledge formed by 3 huecos	686'
Sharp arête	690'
Sharp arête's left variation, traversing roof left and up, but you'll be pulling on suspect-suspended boulders.	692'

2)   Maxey North Lake Cliff

Around the corner from problems in the previous section is a short bulge with mottled orange under black topouts, with ~5 problems good at 685'.

Continuing past them, about half way to Thrasher Cove, is a 50' wide cliff to the right of a vegetated inlet, steep and orange on the left and mild gray overhanging face on the right. Over 50 problems start here and run close to Thrasher Cove. They're described under Thrasher South Lake Cliff.

3)   Maxey South Corner and South Lake Cliff

The cove's south corner has (left-to-right) 2 face problems, 1 crack, and 1 bulge arête problem, good at about 682'. Right of that is an alcove behind a boulder island with nice looking problems but a death fall onto the island. Oh well.

After a long swim south, past various short problems over uneven landings, you reach a face with ~6 problems good at 696'.

4)   Naumann Cove, Both Banks

Drive further and park near the first picnic table (#4, but it's marked only on the backside away from the parking). Hike to the back of the cove; behold on the north bank a pretty gray and tan mild overhang with a steep left side and, left of it, a pretty choss column and bulge. Hike left on a trail wet with spring water to a beautiful bowl; hike down on its left end. Pretty spring water washed much of this bowl through August 2010, so it's likely a permanent spring.

Swim to ~6 problems on the north bank, good at about 687'.

The south bank has half a dozen short problems on three of the little protruding roof boulders. The left and right roof is good at about 679'; the middle roof good at about 683'.

Area: <u>**Thrasher South Lake Cliff**</u>

Exit: "South Thrasher"
Parking: Drive the short road and park at the cul-de-sac near picnic tables #9 & #10.
Access (to the left end of the problems): Hike along the top of the South cove bank. Dodge a little cactus near the cove's corner and take a path into the trees, staying just left of the raised tree grove at the cove's corner. Go down the gully, avoid the poison ivy on your left and do a steep Class 4 downclimb over a hackberry tree.
Alternative Access (to the middle of the problems): Hike around the big bush left of Table #9's BBQ pit and on top of the nearby fractured rock sections. Step 4' down onto a triangular shaped landing with a small oak on the left. Continue down and right on natural stairs to a crack with a big rock jammed into the top. The rock seems solid for the downclimb.
GPS at the downclimb: N30°26.503' W98°02.454' (30.441717 -98.0409)

Problems (listed left-to-right)	Estimated Water Level
The class IV access climb. This comes out 50' right of the cove's corner	???'
Slab problem	689'-???
~3 problems on a mild bulge	685'-???
Lieback edge to a crack	685'-???
Slabby face, right of a low 7' wide ledge	685'-???
Face with fractured rock	685'-???
Left facing edge over submerged boulder	688'-???
~2 problems on a pocketed bulge to a thin slabby face	685'-???
Bulge's lieback right-facing edge	685'-???
Bulge, between the two lieback edges	685'-???
Bulge's lieback left-facing edge	685'-???
Arête crack to roof	685'-???
Left of small Bald Cypress tree, starting bulge to a blank face	685'-???
Right of the Bald Cypress, right-facing edge and left facing edge or something-- sorry, notes got smudged. They form a mini-dihedral; pull to choss flakes	685'-???
Hard spraguey bulge to mini-roof topout left of the cactus	685'-???
Juggy starting edge to same mini-roof topout	685'-???
Starting jug under 5' wide mini bulge	685'-???
~4 face climbs on a slabby wave.	685'-???
At left end of an outcrop is the alternative access climb to picnic table #9.	685'-???
2 pocket face problems	685'-???
3 hard bulge pulls	685'-???
Short lieback crack	682'-???
3 easy short bulge pulls	682'-???
Easy bad-landing access climb; don't know where it comes out	684'-???
Short blank bulge pull	684'-???
2 pocket problems	684'-???
Left facing flake/edge	684'-???
Shallow bulge pull	684'-???
Starting shallow dihedral face climb	684'-???
Easy face climb	
(Land mark: low roof over a tree)	
2 hard slabby face problems	685'-???
~4 easy edge/crimp problems on a 20' wide slabby face	685'-???

The following problems are on a 50' wide cliff to the right of a vegetated inlet, steep orange rock on the left, gray mild overhanging face on the right. This is about half way to Maxey Cove.

Edge to a sidepull edge to honeycombs	685'-???
Mini-arête to pockets to a ledge	685'-???
Double roof left of a big crack	685'-???
Big crack all the way to the roof	685'-???
Thin crack	685'-???
Bare face	685'-???
Downward pointing hard flake to a big mail slot	685'-???

Pace Bend

Area: Thrasher Cove North Bank and North Lake Cliff

Exit: "North Thrasher / South Marshall"
Parking: Drive left at the dumpster and park near the first picnic table (#13).
Approach: Take the trail right of table #13 to an easy downclimb at mid-cove.

Problems on Thrasher North Bank (listed right-to-left)	Estimated Water Level
The easy downclimb at mid-cove	0'
~8 short problems and a traverse on a 15' tall tan/gray/black wave form.	686'-690'
Spot the climber over boulder on the left side. Someone should trundle those.	
Tree line.	
Easy crack with scary landing between cliff and a tree	680'-???
Slopey face left of the crack	680'-???
Tan face with starting mini-dihedral to a roof	680'-???
~5 problems on a cool honeycomb roof over small tree limbs.	695'?

Just around the corner on the main lake cliff is a probably-bare roof amphitheater with nice problems under it on a tan face to overhanging finishes under the roof:

Problems on Thrasher North Lake Cliff (listed right-to-left)	Estimated Water Level
4 distinct traverse lines on the overhangs below the main roof.	688'-???
~6 problems on the face to the ledges, finishing on a thin horizontal crack at the roof.	688'-???
Hard arête to ledge under the roof's left end.	688'-???
Start on small tan wild pocketed outcrop to short crack, onto black column at left end of the amphitheater.	688'-???
~3 face climbs left of the black column and up a roof; the leftmost starts on a snout-shaped double pocket	688'-???
Left facing fractured edge	690'-???
Diagonal right-leaning easy crack	690'-???
Smaller starting crack to old bolted route hanger	687'-???
Small honeycomb roof pull with 2(?) old bolts	687'-???

Now a slab with a massive crack on the right side emerges; it's unappealing for DWS, but perhaps trad-lead the crack at 671'and spot four (or more) old bolted routes for fun.

At the slab's left end is a dihedral with DWS on its left face.

	Estimated Water Level
2 face problems	685'-???
Arête	685'-???
Low roof right side	685'-???
Low roof left side	685'-???
Arête	682'-???
Serving-platter to hueco	682'-???
Same serving-platter, left onto mini-arête	682'-???
2 problems on tan bulge	683'-???
Fused crack	683'-???

Then landings go up 4' onto boulders and lead to the long wave formation described under Marshall South Lake Cliff.

Area: **Marshall South Lake Cliff**

Exit: "North Thrasher / South Marshall"
Parking: Drive left at the dumpster, pass 3 picnic tables (#13-15) and park near table #16 (for the rope access) or continue to the "T", bear left, and park at the dead end near table #17 (for cove-swimming access).
Approach: Access is a little more challenging than most areas. You have two choices:

    1. At table #16, take the path to a steep little gully at the cliff. It's a 10' drop. Look left and you'll see a fixed rope with knots tied to a small tree. But instead of doing the sketchy traverse over there, back up and take the easy natural stairway south of the rope.

    2. At the dead end, take the trail to the south cove bank. Exactly at the trail's end, downclimb the short (10') steep 5.6, even though it looks intimidating. Just take it slowly. Then swim the south bank to the cove's corner, where the first problems appear, and around the corner and south (upstream) to many other problems.

    3. The cove's corner has an interesting looking roof crack and a pocketed face with ~3 problems. Rounding the corner to the lake cliff, there's another cool roof crack and a plethora-pocketed bulge with ~3 problems. These problems may be climbable at about 682'.

    4. Then there's a majestic, tall long-running wave formation, starting steep, varying between 30 and 45 degrees, and working less steep, all over a raised landing, climbable at about 692'. The rock is light colored and reported to be solid with good hard problems. There may be 30 or more problems.

Area: **Marshall Cove, Both banks**

Exit: "North Thrasher / South Marshall"
Parking: Drive left at the dumpster, pass various picnic tables, bear left at the "T", and park at the dead end. The nearest picnic table is #17.
Approach: Take the trail to the south cove bank. Exactly at the trail's end, downclimb the short (10') steep 5.6, even though it looks intimidating. Just take it slowly. Then it's a short swim across to the north bank, or left to problems on the south bank.
GPS at the South bank: N30°26.714' W98°02.252' (30.445233 -98.037533)

Problems on the North bank run from mid-cove to deep-in-the-cove.

North Bank Problems (listed left-to-right)	Estimated Water Level
~4 problems on a 30° overhang with orange stone sections	685'-???
~2 problems on pockets on an overhang	685'-???
~2 problems on a roof with a hueco	685'-???

South Bank Problems (listed left-to-right)	Estimated Water Level
~7 problems and a traverse on a sweet 30' wide short roof deep in the cove.	683'-???
~6 short (8') problems on a mild overhang at mid cove.	677'-???
Many problems starting at the cove's corner, described under Marshall South Lake Cliff	682'-692'

Area: **Marshall North Lake Cliff**

Exit: "N. Marshall"
Parking: Pass tables #20-21, park at the dead end.
Approach: At table #21, take the narrow cedar-tree flanked trail to the lake cliff edge. Hike right (north) for 38 paces (btw at 29 paces you'll see an old bolted-route anchor just over the cliff). Hike down onto a low platform. You'll then see it's a rock peninsula running just 3' from the main cliff. Walk its length and you'll find old shut-anchors for (if memory serves) a very bitchin' route on its north point. Go to the middle of the peninsula and climb down (probably 5.6 with some easy stem moves). Hike the fissure floor down (south) to the water.
GPS at the peninsula: N30°26.784' W98°02.228' (30.4464 -98.037133)

Pace Bend

Kirk Holladay and Bill Gooch bolted six routes here for use in drought conditions. These bolts get submerged each year; now, perhaps, their lifetime on lead falls can be measured in milliseconds instead of years. If by chance you TR on any old anchors at PmfB, back them up. The routes are **Something** (5.11), **Mysterious White Hand** (5.9), **Baby Don't Break** (5.10), 5.10, 5.7, and 5.7.

North of the peninsula are ~6 problems on a bulge and overhang. The peninsula face has at least a couple bulge pulls and the overhanging route on the north point, good at about 687'. South of the peninsula are ~6 face climbs, good at about 680'.

Area: Thurman South Lake Cliff

Exit: "Thurman/Gracy Loop"
Parking: Bear left at the fork and park at picnic table #25 (for quick, scary downclimb access) or picnic table #27 (for mellower swim access).

Approach by downclimbing: Walk past unmarked table #26 to the cliff. Left of a shady grove on the cliff edge is an intimidating looking vertical, technical, no-pump 5.6 downclimb high over deep water. Non-climber cliff divers downclimb this all the time, usually prodding along their griped newbs. Take it down and right (south) and maybe jump in (if you know it's deep) before the landing gets bad, else keep traversing south over the bad landing to a tree atop a rock outcrop (which gets submerged probably around 682'). This downclimb has you pressed against the cliff in spots. Take it slow; find all the good holds. Perhaps tie a tow line on a tree to lower and raise floats, water, etc.

Approach by swimming: Swim along the cove's south bank and left around the corner to the nearby climbs.

This is a popular spot with tall problems and deep water.

Trevor Stanton 📷   Thurman South Lake Cliff

Problems (listed left-to-right)	Estimated Water Level
~6 face problems	678' - ???
left-facing overhanging lieback crack rated 5.10-	672' - ???
~4 hard problems on an overhang	671' - ???
Right facing lieback crack rated 5.10-	671' - ???
The intimidating 5.6 access route	
Face problem under the 5.6 access	669' - ???
~12 short problems on various blobs on the way to an enticing island full of V0- overhangs.	671'- ???
The series of blobs all slab out fast so you get a quick topout. They look good at 671' but stay good only a little higher than that. This set dwindled to 4 problems (one 5.9+, three toughies) at 668'.	
~10 V0- face and overhang problems surrounding a rock island 20' from the lake.	671' - ???
Some problems on the east side are safer at around 675'.	

Also: midway on the cove's south bank are ~2 short face problems good at maybe 676'.

Area: Thurman Cove North Bank and North Corner

Exit: "Thurman/Gracy Loop"
Parking: Bear right at the fork and park near picnic table #28.
Approach: Hike right of table #28 to the cliff edge, go right 10' to a boulder next to the cliff. Over the cliff is the nearer of two huge rock islands below

you. The south island is at Thurman Cove's north corner. Left of the boulder is a short intimidating 5.6 downclimb in the fissure between main cliff and the south island. Downclimb it and step onto the island. Walk the island south (left) close to its southern end and do a spottable, intimidating one-move 5.7 to reenter the fissure and access the water. Both downclimbs have bad landings. A mellow alternative is to park earlier at the second row of roadside boulders (or walk back to them), hike to the cove and cut left to an easy downclimb.

GPS at the rock island: N30°26.995' W98°02.072' (30.449917 -98.034533)

If you take the mellow access deep into the cove and swim out of the cove, the problems present as follows:

Problems on the North Cove Bank (listed left-to-right)	Estimated Water Level
~8 short roof pull problems and a traverse on a roof with honeycombs on its left half	689'-692'
~4 mild overhang problems	678'-???
~3 bulge pulls	676'-???
~2 bulge pulls	672'-???

This area has vestiges of a few bolted routes for low lake levels and other DWS problems named and graded long ago: **Spider Baby** (5.10a) and **Black Sunshine** (5.11) by Kirk Holladay and Alvino Pon, **Dude from Dallas** (5.8), **Heat Boat** (5.11b) by Dave Head, and James Crump did **Voyage of the Boat People** (5.12), **Bay of Pigs** (5.12d), **Plight of the Haitian Refugees** (5.10), and **Traverse from Plight** (5.10).

Voyage of the Boat People was Austin's first 5.12 ascent, in 1981. An old video does not show the start, but it shows Crump at a dihedral crack. From there, the route traverses right across an arête and up a face to a steep finish.

Continuing to the cove's corner, you come to the first of two rock islands:

Problems on the Two Rock Islands (listed left-to-right)	Estimated Water Level
~2 short problems on the southern island's southern end	678'-???
~5 short problems on its steep north end facing the lake	678'-???
A traverse on it, keeping feet high.	678'-???
Short gap between southern and northern islands	
~2 fabulous steep pumpfests squeezed together on the northern Island's southern tip	682'-690'
~4 more short high water problems on its lake-facing side	688'-???

Area: <u>Gracy Cove North Corner</u>

Exit: "North Gracy". (The "Gracy" exit leads to inconvenient parking.)
Parking: Bear right at the fork. Go to the big cul-de-sac and park at picnic table #65.
Approach: Take the trail right of table #65 to the top of a large roof. Hike right to a 15' long fissure and down the fissure. (This much is the same access as "Gracy North Lake Cliff".) Hang a left.
GPS at the cove's point: N30°27.231' W98°01.913' (30.45385 -98.031883)

The roof you just climbed off of has ~5 cool honeycomb choss pocket chaos problems and two low traverses. Beware the two submerged boulder under topouts. Eastward a ways, around mid-cove, are two little roof pulls on a small rock outcrop near the easy hike-out slabs. All these problems look good at about 685', though the honeycomb problems may be better at 680' with a spotter standing dry and solid on the boulder hazards.

Area: <u>Gracy North Lake Cliff</u>

Exit: "North Gracy". (The "Gracy" exit leads to inconvenient parking.)
Parking: Bear right at the fork. Go to the big cul-de-sac and park at picnic table #65.
Approach: Take the trail right of table #65 to the top of a large roof. Hike right to a 15' long fissure and down the fissure. (This much is the same access as "Gracy Cove North Corner".) Then swim north (right) about 40' past bad landings to the first deep-enough problems.
GPS at the cove's point: N30°27.231' W98°01.913' (30.45385 -98.031883)

This spot has quantity at 671' and quality (fewer/harder/taller problems) at 667-669'. At water levels 671-673', you shall behold the longest, most sustained monotony of short-bulge-to-slab-to-slight-overhang topout bouldering on the planet. Imagine a climbing gym with nothing but one wall shape. Gack! But good, typically jug starts to crimps or pockets, to slopers or jugs on the bulge face or top. Feet are barely edging, toeing, or dolphin-dynoing, or popping to high jug footholds. Nice training ground, and as burly as the style sounds, we found 5.8's @671'. The primary mix, @671', is 5.11's among the first 27 problems, and 5.8's through 5.11's north of there.

Problem counts drop fast and difficulty jumps fast with every foot the water level drops. And at 669', wall features emerge (roofs, mini-caves and a cool deep little tube cave), and the visual monotony disappears.

Gracy North Lake Cliff @ 667'

Problems (listed right-to-left)

	Estimated Water Levels

~27 problems @671-673', mostly 5.11 with some 5.10+, all short bulge pulls to slabs that make it too risky to topout the subsequent overhangs. This problem set dropped to ~14 @669' and ~10@667'. At 669' the first problem is 5.9 pulling to a completely detached flake, a few were 11+, and the rest harder. This set has two cool shallow dihedral/crack sloper problems.
671-673' for 27, 669' for 14, 667' for 10

1 dihedral over a submerged boulder
675'-???

~9 more short bulge pulls over a low roof. This set is easier, ranging 5.8 and up @ 671', and a few 5.10's and the rest 5.11's by 669'. At 669'-673' for 9, 667' there landings are bad on all but 2 problems.
667' for 2

~3 problems on a cool popcorn-riddled low roof. Its right side is 10a; the underside offers hard crimps and pinches. The roof isn't useful until 669' and under. Lower water expands the problems and variations. 667' sees feet-kicking-in-the-water campusing on this roof and surrounding roofs.
669' for 3, 667' for 4+ variations

A 40' span has lame non-problems and bad landings @ 669', but it ripens to ~5 hard roof problems around 667'. Left of the problems is a deep little tube cave landmark, hovering just above the 669' water level.
667'-667' for 5

5.9+ jug haul, 20' left of the tube cave and on the right end of a roof full of hard edges. The tube cave landmark is around @669' but submerged at 671'.
669'- 673'

~20 more bulge pulls @671'over the roof with hard edges, dropping to 11 problems @669'. At 669' the 11 are hard 5.11 and up, with a 5.9+. Some of these bulge pulls could be topped out on a black and brown overhanging wave formation; the bulge sticks out too far under the rest. After only a 2' drop to 667', all had bad landings, strangely, since, as the start of this chapter points out, 2' can *actually equal* 3'. Or because we screwed up our records.
671'- 673' for 20, 669' for 11

After some bad landings you'll reach problems described under Davis South Lake Cliff.

Area: Davis Cove South Corner and South Lake Cliff

Exit: "South Davis"
Parking: Park at picnic table #72.
Approach: Hike the trail left of table #72 to the cove's south bank. At low water (around 672') take the easy downclimb in the fissure near the cove's south corner. At higher water, just climb down at mid-cove. Hit the problems at the cove's corner, then swim around the corner to the nearby lake cliff problems.
GPS at the South bank: N30˚27.411' W98˚01.817' (30.45685 -98.030283)

Problems at Davis Cove South Corner (listed left-to-right)	Estimated Water Levels
2 problems on a low roof	674-676'
~4 face problems. Years ago we found two of these fun and wild.	677'-???

Problems at Davis South Lake Cliff (listed left-to-right)	Estimated Water Levels
Problems on the rock island:	
easy face problem left of rock island	680'-???
left lieback edge of island next to the main cliff	680'-???
~2 problems on island's left face, all face-to-roof.	680'-???
~2 more just like it	678'-???
Arête on rock island's left outer corner	677'-???
~6 on rock island's center face	679'-???
Arête on rock island's right outer corner	679'-???
~2 problems on bulge to mottled tan face to roof	680'-???
~7 more just like that	677'-???
Finger crack	679'-???
Slopey arête	677'-???
~6 problems on a gray bulge with a tan left section	677'-???
Shallow dihedral over a submerged boulder	681'-???
~20 hard problems on a blank slight overhang wave formation with small pockets, crimps and slopers. The formation tapers to a slabby face on the right.	677'-??? except the rightmost 10' needs a minimum of 680'
crack with a baseball in a hueco	680'-???
face problem right of the crack	680'-???
~2 problems on a big 10' wide rounded arête	679'-???
~10 mild-bulge-to-steep topout problems on white & gray rock with steep feet on the left end (from a submerged cave)	677'-???
left-facing edge	677'-???
~7 problems on a sustained gray rock face with a low white band (visible with water lower than 674'), cut with stacked edges in the middle, starts on mild bulge	674'- ???
~8 more like that	675'-???
2 problems on a roof pull	675'-???
diagonal (left-leaning) finger crack	675'-???

After that are short (at 671') problems on various protruding bulges pulling quickly to slabs you probably don't want to top out, followed by a long, sustained bulge/slab section described under Gracy North Lake Cliff.

Area: **Davis Cove North Bank**

Exit: "Mid Davis"
Parking: Bear left and park at picnic table #75.
Approach: Hike right of table #75, then right of the unmarked metal and wood picnic table to the cliff edge overlooking the cove's corner. Step onto the rock island and hike down into the roofed fissure. At the bottom, walk clockwise around the rock island. Swim right, past a poor-climbing low cave (which submerges at 674') to a slightly higher cave with wild features.

The wild cave has ~6 problems, a few requiring spotting over bad landings, climbable at about 674', until about 676'. Sadly, at that water level you won't see all the nice formations in this cave. Come back and dry boulder it.

A short distance right (to mid-cove), there's a bulge with ~5 problems starting right of a huge bowl, safe at about 677'.

Admittedly a small area, perhaps you can milk it best at 676' to work all 11 problems deeper and shallower than recommended, and also swim to the cove south bank for 6 more problems somewhat shallow at 676'.

Area: **Davis North Lake Cliff**

Exit: "N. Davis"
Parking: Go left at the fork and park at picnic tables #77 and #78.
Approach: Left of table #77, hike to the big BBQ pit right of the big oaks, go down and left in the fissure, and hike right past four choss mini-roofs to an obvious sustained face. Or, hike a steep brushy "trail" to the right of table #78 and two big oaks.
GPS at the climbs: N30°27.494' W98°01.790' (30.458233 -98.029833)

The picnic area has nice oaks, shade, and a BBQ pit.

Problems (listed left-to-right)	Estimated Water Levels
~8 slabby-face problems and a low and high traverse	685'-???
~2 problems on a chossy column	685'-???
Easy left-leaning diagonal lieback crack on the chossy column	685'-???
~4 face climbs	687'-???
~6 problems on a steep bulge	681'-???
Short pull onto easy exit slab	681'-???
overhang with a hueco to a face section	685'-???
Choss outcrop over submerged boulders	687'-???
Left facing arête	687'-???
~4 problems on a face to a roof	687'-???
2 trees	
~15 problems on orange/tan/burnt-orange(hook'em!)/gray face that steepens slightly in the middle at a thin intermittent crack. Some starting holds will be submerged — in a good way.	685'-???

Area: **Collier South Lake Cliff**

Exit: "Collier Boat Ramp / South Maugham"
Parking: Drive and park left of the boat ramp at picnic table #82.
Approach: Hike the trail left of table #82, pass table #83 and at the empty square cement slab, hike down to the water. Swim south (left) 50'.
GPS at the climbs: N30°27.630' W98°01.735' (30.4605 -98.028917)

A short and steep bulge with low horizontal mini-ledges has ~6 V0 problems. To the right (south) of it are ~5 shorter, harder, couple-move roof pulls, assuming you make the great foot-ledge off limits. These are good at about 677-679' but there's little room for lower or higher water levels. The tight tolerance and short problems make us include this area with hesitation; however, perhaps it will fill a niche. Some new DWS V0 climber may happen upon PmfB right at 677', hell bent on V0's, and eat it up like candy. This might also be a great place for child DWS.

Area: <u>Maugham Cove, Both Banks</u>

Exit: "Collier Boat Ramp / S. Maugham"
Parking: Drive right of the boat ramp, pass picnic tables 86-89, and park near the cove's south bank.
Approach: For problems good at 678', hike down and right along the cove's south bank. For problems good at 690', head left towards table #89 (near the lake cliff) and hike to its right.
GPS at the South bank: N30°27.758' W98°01.651' (30.462633 -98.027517)

The south bank has ~18 nice, short roof problems and a long traverse, good at about 678'.

Another ~12 problems are at the lake cliff south of the cove on three short roofs, good at about 690'. A short swim takes you to a few problems on the north bank:

	Estimated Water Levels
Problems on the North Bank (listed left-to-right)	
Shallow bowl	674'-674'
~2 problems in a little grotto	674'-674'
~6 problems on a wave shape	683'-???

Area: <u>Maugham North Lake Cliff (aka. "North Mom")</u>

Exit: "North Maugham / South Taylor"
Parking: Park just passed picnic table #95. Overflow parking is further north at Taylor Cove.
Approach: Just left of picnic table #95, hike to the cliff and go right to a nearby hike down to the water. Swim about 100' back south (left) to the climbs.
GPS above the climbs: N30°27.884' W98°01.652' (30.464733 -98.027533)

Blaine Burris, North Mom @ 672'

This area is an excellent set of problems between Maugham and Taylor coves. It's referred to as North Maugham in this guide, but the approach and ample parking at Taylor makes it feel more like South Taylor. The problem set is high quality with few rests, 20° to 30° overhangs and mini-roofs.

Problems (listed left-to-right)	Estimated Water Levels
Grades suggested below should drop a lot when higher water levels bury the low cruxes.	
~6 super easy short (10') problems	675'-676'
1. (5.10-) Jug haul starting between two submerged boulder stacks	676'-???
2. (5.10+/11- @673') Just right of high boulder stack	672'-???
Gap	
3. (5.11+ @673') big hueco, then left to a flake, then...???	672'-???
4. Several alternative starts: little tufa pinch, toothy wide/short matchable pocket, hueco, right sidepull, but I could not find them on the topo photo. Maybe they're out of place and really left of #3.	
5. (5.11+ @673') low horizontal slice-of-bread matchable jug, to sloper, to top of mini-arête, to thin pocket face, to the Roof With Nothing, right to slopey shelf, to plant.	672'-???
Gap	
6. (5.??) gray "right facing" incut half moon.	672'-???
7. (5.12- @673') all pockets with hard low move; left and right variations that merge at a round hole:	672'-???

Left variation: uses sidepulls to a large oval/rocky jug and then far out right to the round hole.

Right variation: starts slightly right and has a strong move to an undercling, then up to the hole.

From the round hole go upwards and rightwards using the small pockets
To the left facing ear (that is also the finish of the next problem).

8. (5.11+ @673') small left facing crimp/undercling, to a brown "left facing" incut half-moon,   672'-???
    then right to a large hueco, then up and right to a good mail slot.

    Gap

9. (5.10+/11- @673') ugly curved left-facing crack/flake/fracture, to elaborate-looking moves,   672'-???
    then a hard topout that spewed many. Ugliest crack ever, but this route is a crowd-pleaser.

Nathaniel Biggs, North Mom @ 672'

Area: **Taylor North Lake Cliff**

Exit: "North Taylor". There are two exits by that name; take the first (southern).
Parking: Drive past the bathrooms. Park at picnic table #105.
Approach: Hike down the north park fence line. Do the height-dependent-5.7 downclimb at four small oaks surrounding an old 2' wide cedar stump. Swim 140' south towards a prominent 30° overhang.
GPS at the climbs: N30°28.094' W98°01.563' (30.468233 -98.02605)

Left of the prominent 30° overhang are ~6 short (7') V0- problems, good at about 684'. At about 682' are ~10 short choss problems on the 30° overhang. AND, for your trouble coming here when the water is exactly 682', these look virgin; the low fragile choss crimps we touched suggested no one's ever climbed it. Let's see what survives, and who gets a coveted 10' First Choss Ascent.

To the right are ~3 bulge-pull problems, also at 682'. Then there's a 60' gap with easy upclimbs. Then there are ~4 V0 on a weird face with horizontal bands and an overhang on the left, good at about 680'. At the far right are ~7 taller face problems good at about 682'.

Pace Bend

Area: <u>Duende Cove</u>[283]

Exit: "S. Baldwin", off of Grisham Trail (the first right after the park entrance).
Parking: Pass a bathroom and park at the dumpster.
Approach: Walk past a picnic table and tree to the cliff edge. Heave exactly 20 sketchpads over the cliff, lower your beer on a line, then walk left to an easy downclimb.
GPS at the downclimb: N30°26.687' W98°01.360' (30.444783 -98.022667)

Duende has excellent, hard, short, steep bouldering, with a few short warmups. Some of the roof problems are pretty long.

When Lake Travis drops to about 663', Duende becomes a dry hard bouldering destination. Some landings might be tight at 663', but a few feet lower and the landings are big. The landings are sloped and rocky, so bringing a small army of boulderers, each with a sketch pad, or else Vinny with his truck full of sketch pads. Stack'em.

Erik Moore 📷   Chris "Vinny" Vinson, Duende Cove

Some locals have enjoyed dry night bouldering by head lamp and big battery powered lights, to beat the heat, late in the summer when the lake is down. Pay for a camping pass so that you're OK staying past sundown.

Duende also appears good for DWS, but only in a narrow range of water levels (roughly 674'-676'). For the most part, the problems have identical starts whether water soloing at these level or bouldering over pads at low levels. DWS should be very mellow here, compared to dry bouldering on fairly high topouts over sloped landings.

Erik Moore 📷   Andrew Oliver, Duende Cove

The topos sketch the approximate problem set, based on memory from two years back plus chalk marks. Two problems are not in the shots, starting on and next to a right-pointing horn just off camera from the right side topo.

We'll get Andrew and Vinny out to detail the problems, add them as an upload at www.AustinClimbingBook.com, and add them in later editions of the book.

Duende Cove, left end, very very approximate topo

---

[283] The word "duende" has an awesome Wiki page.

Duende Cove, right end, very very approximate topo

Brad Saylorking, Baldwin North Lake Cliff @ 672'

Area: **Baldwin Cove North Bank and North Lake Cliff**

Exit: " N. Baldwin", off of Grisham Trail (the first right after the park entrance).
Parking: Park at the big open cul-de-sac overlooking the cove's north corner.
Approach: Hike to picnic table #406 at the cove corner. Walk to the south (right) end of the island that's just 5' off the main cliff. Hike down and swim the fissure north or swim counter-clockwise around the island. To access the problems in the cove, park near the dumpster and hike right of the dumpster and recycle station to mid-cove.
GPS at the island: N30°26.654' W98°01.285' (30.444233 -98.021417)

Deep in the cove on the North Bank are ~11 short roof and overhang problems on the easy side, good at about 674'-675'.

The rock island at the cove corner near table #406 looks fun for easy traversing at about 672'. It has a steep 5.8 on the north end that was fine at 670'.

Nathaniel Biggs, Baldwin North Lake Cliff @ 672'

Roughly 40 problems start opposite the rock island's north point on cliffs ranging, at 670', 15-20' tall, with several easy exit climbs. Here's a sketch of them:

Problems (listed left-to-right)	Estimated Water Levels
North tip of the rock island	
~6 sloper-intensive face problems @670. 4 of these still had safe landings @668'. At 670' these ranged 5.9 to 5.10- and about 15-20' tall.	668' – 673'
5.7 just before the dihedral and its bad landing.	668'(or probably 662') – 673'
~33 face and overhang problems; some steep jug & pocket routes. At 670' we found a 5.9, but the rest range 5.11- and up. At 668' a hard roof pull comes into play, elevating every problem over it by exactly 2.333 V-grades.	668'(or probably 662') – 673'

After this set, you reach the access route and problems described below under "Area: Table #400". These are good from 662-672' (min level reported by www.bloodyflapper.com)

Area: **Table #400**

Exit: Grisham Trail (the first right after the park entrance), north of the N. Baldwin exit
Parking: Park at picnic table #400, right off of Grisham Trail. Table #400 parking is really close to Baldwin Cove parking as you look from the clifftop, but the swim is fairly long from Baldwin Cove's downclimb, so this access point may be worth the more difficult downclimb.

Approach: Turn right on the trail, pass an unmarked wood and metal picnic table, and cut left on a poor trail to an 8' long boulder at the cliff. Walk around the boulder and downclimb below it on the intimidating (but easy) natural stair steps to a ledge system. Traverse the ledges north until you're almost over a bad landing under a dihedral. Downclimb that (5.7ish) and jump into the water. To exit this area, climb the slimy column right of the dihedral (a 5.8-ish crux @668'), do a balancy traverse left onto the dihedral's landing, then left and up to catch the 5.7 ledges out. The difficulty of this exit is unknown below water level 668'. If this exit gives you trouble when tired at the end of the day, swim your float south (right) to Baldwin Cove.

Alternative Parking and Approach: While the parking described above gets you a shaded picnic table, the following provides you a huge parking area and puts your car near Baldwin Cove Point for the climbs at that area. Exit at N. Baldwin, park on the north end of the big Baldwin Cove parking area, and hike 50 paces from the pole at the edge of the cliff and the parking lot, along the cliff until you come to the 8' boulder and the downclimb described above.

GPS at the climbs: N30°26.708' W98°01.244' (30.445133 -98.020733)
Swimming north reaches:

Problems (listed left-to-right)	Estimated Water Levels
access route at little dihedral at 670'	
~5 hard face problems on a largely blank face	668(and lower)-672'

David Phillips, Acid Rock highball

Right-facing 5.9 lieback crack if you skip the hard roof section that's above water @668'.   668(and lower)-672'
The roof section itself offers some wildly awkward hard starts.
~25 face problems (@672') including a few 5.10's but mostly 5.11's and up.   668(and lower)-672'
By 668' the problems drop to about 20.

Swimming south reaches ~40 problems vaguely described above under "Baldwin Cove North Bank and North Lake Cliff".

Area: <u>Acid Rock & Hueco Wall</u>

Exit: Grisham Trail (the first right after the park entrance), north of the N. Baldwin exit.
Parking: Parking depends on your desired method of access. For Acid Rock and the left end of Hueco Wall, park just before picnic table #399, right off of Grisham Trail. (This table is north of Table #400.) For the right end of Hueco Wall, park at picnic table #397.

Approach: One of the most stellar climbing areas in central Texas, sporting about 26 5.8-5.10 climbs and 29 harder than that, has somewhat challenging access. It's no problem if you can brave a ghastly cliff-jump or confidently downclimb a random route. Otherwise, pick one of the following four access methods and wire your exit climb first thing, so you have a convenient exit when tired. If you (or your newbs) can't climb out, swim north to Giles Cove.

Method 1: This method is the quickest way to access the hard Acid Rock problems, the left end of Hueco Wall, and the chillacious rock island. From Table #399, hike to the cliff. Yikes! It's really far above the water, and all these soda-pop-quaffing kids are cliff diving and miraculously not dying upon impact with the water! I think I'll wimp out, use a Shermanesque excuse such as "hip inflammation" or "protecting my damaged ear" and reach the water via the following fun 5.9 (@ 672') downclimb:

Find the crack south of the video-taping cliff divers. Remember the holds you use to climb over the edge — they will be blind reaches on the way up. Bust this intimidating move down to the ledge, traverse north and downwards about 25', and downclimb to the water, opposite (or is it 20' beyond) the south end of the rock island. (Sorry—our notes got messy.) Don't jump in; downclimb the whole way to learn the route on which you'll exit the water. In past years, at lower levels, we've found a fixed line with knots helps keep the exit at 5.9. Without a fixed line, the exit will likely exceed 5.9. The 5.9 **GPS** is N30°26.768' W98°01.210' (30.446133 98.020167).

Method 2: Sometimes cliff divers will set up a knotted rope or fire ladder in the woods just north of the popular cliff dive point. (Presently, there is an intimidating fire escape ladder with its various broken rungs suggesting all rungs are suspect. You should have seen some of the drunk bubbas barely climbing this in 2010!)

Method 3: This method puts you to the right end of Hueco Wall, and the 5.8's here offer the lowest grade climbs on the wall. Hike to, or park at, picnic table #397, and walk 38 paces North (left) to a lake overlook at **GPS** N30°26.821' W98°01.176' (30.447017 -98.0196). Scramble down to a ledge, and go left to a right-facing crack dihedral spot. This short downclimb looks dangerous over a ledge, but it's 5.6 with great footholds and jugs. You're now low enough to jump about 18' @ water level 668', or do a hard-to-read 5.8 (@668') juggy downclimb below the crack.

Method 4: If the 5.8 poses a problem (or gets hard at water deeper than 668'), use the access for the Table 397 area, just north of Method 3, for a hike into the water. (How easy is it when the water is lower than 668'?)

This stellar area consists of a few problems below the popular cliff dive spot and its 5.9 downclimb, plus a lot of stellar problems at Hueco Wall, just north of the rock island. Hueco Wall is full of moderate vertical-face climbs on and between huecos and mini-caves that stretch horizontally at about the same elevation. The wall is full of happy jug finger pockets, too, and slopey ledges. The clifftop looks bare, but it has holds. At 670', a convenient shelf lies just above the water for stowing floats and drinks. At 668' there's more room, waves won't crash onto your stuff and you could even lunch there.

Problems (listed left-to-right)	Estimated Water Levels
An alternative, bad landing slab exit near table #399.	
Left-facing left-leaning diagonal overhang 5.9 crack/arête with an always-dangerous landing against the slabby main cliff. You can pump out and jump to deep water safely, but you best not slip.	668-675'
~4 overhang problems under the traverse section of the 5.9 access route. Climbing these will impress all the cliff divers. At 668' this set includes a sweet campus 5.11 semi-jug haul and a few 11's and 12's.	667 (and lower)-675'
The bottom of the 5.9 "Method 1" access route near table #399.	

Hueco Wall: these problems were graded @ 668'. 667' forces harder mantling onto the starting ledge under all problems and bumps grade on a few.

Some right-end problems recommended for higher water levels are sketchy-but-doable at lower levels, if you stay solid on the starts. If pumped just push away. Slipping means foot injury or worse.

The wall ranges about 17-22' problems @ 668'. The first seven problems are shown on the topo photo.

Laura Yero, Jann Salinas, Trip Lucas @ Hueco Wall left end @ 668'

1. 5.9 starts under the *leftmost hueco* (which is body-sized).   667(and lower)-675'
2. 5.hard problem on the face between huecos.   667(and lower)-675'

3. 5.10+ starts under the *second hueco (football sized)*.   667(and lower)-675'
4. 5.9 (tricky) under a basket-ball sized hueco with four small huecos on its right.   667(and lower)-675'
5. 10b on the 8' wide face between hueco formations.   667(and lower)-675'

6. 5.10c under an *hour-glass-shaped double stacked hueco* that forms a mini-roof on its top.   667(and lower)-675'

7. 5.11a problem up the *Evil Smirking Face triad of huecos*   667(and lower)-675'
(forming two eyes and a smirking mouth)

Problems to the right of the 1st seven:
    5.12?? up the middle of a wide shallow roof sheltering an undercling crack.   667(and lower)-675'
    5.10a up the right side of the wide shallow roof.   667(and lower)-675'

    5.10d bust a campus-y move up the low roof to an *upside down tear drop hueco* between   667(and lower)-675'
    a *softball sized hueco* on its right and a *nondescript hueco* on its left.
    5.hard on the 8' wide face between huecos.   667(and lower)-675'

    5.10a on an *flying saucer hueco* ill formed due to a triangular piece of rock.   667(and lower)-675'
    Maybe the triangle is a death ray, though.

    5.11b squeezed just right of the flying saucer; it's Wicked!   667(and lower)-675'

Pace Bend

	Estimated Water Levels
5.10d on a sea of holds 10' right of the 11b. It goes to a very mild dihedral.	667(and lower)-675'
5.10b (Easier than it looks) on a mild bulge, using a right- hand deep, sharp 2-finger-pocket. This one exceeds 10b below 668'.	667(and lower)-675'
5.10b mild rounded bulgy arête just left of a *south-pointing boulder perched on clifftop*.	672-675'
~5 problems with bad landings @ 668'. Two of them on a patch of *burnt orange rock*. (Go UT!)	672-675'
5.9 pulls a low roof to face to a bowl left of a *left-leaning diagonal roof formation*.	668(and lower)-675'
5.8+ pulls low roof to and over the upper left section of that formation.	672-675'
5.9 pulls straight up the dihedral of that formation.	672-675'
3 hard roof pull problems on the low part of that formation.	668(and lower)-675'
5.11b one-move-wonder on the right side of the roof.	668(and lower)-675'
5.8 jug haul starting where the roof peters out to just a horizontal crack, to a *basketball sized hueco*.	668(and lower)-675'
5.9 under the slopey ledge just right of the 5.8.	668(and lower)-675'
5.11a on left end of *another roof*, starting on big pockets just above the roof. Cool one-move-wonder and a beautiful left-hand sprague pocket.	668(and lower)-675'
5.10d roof pull just left of bowl in the roof's ceiling. One-move-wonder.	668(and lower)-675'
5.11? pulls the pointy bulge above the roof.	673-675'
5.10a *blank dihedral formed by a protruding left-pointing wedge*. Photo-op one-move-wonder.	677-677'
5.11? straight up the wedge's face.	674-675'
5.10a right end of the wedge.	672-675'
2 super-hard or impossible problems on a *12' wide face*	672-675'
5.10c starts just left of where the roof rounds into the cliff. Hit the low right hand 2 ½ finger pocket, climb to a small hueco, and top out on *cool massive flakes*.	670-675'
Hard problem on pockets to a sloper pocket, starting at the right third of the *roof that rounds into the cliff*.	670-675'
5.8 on left half of the column between roofs.	672-675'
5.10a just right of the column, pulling the left end of the roof to several huecos and then the crack under the topout.	672-675'
5.9+ pulls center of the low roof to the *upper roof's cave*. Climb in, rest, then pull the topout portion.	672-675'
5.10c just right of the upper roof.	672-675'
5.8 "**Method 3**" access route. Pull to the right-hand blocky hold shaped like a sideways flan, the size of a small bowling ball. Topout on the *ledge that's lower than the clifftop* and hike out.	667'(and lower)-675'

Crossing the above problems is **a massive traverse running roughly 170'**. Visit all the huecos! Left-to-right to the Evil Smirking Face is 5.10a. Continue past that to the "5.10b Easier than it looks." is 5.10d. Continue further: 5.???

Further north, after some bad landing areas, are ~8 short problems on lively looking sloper rock surface. 674'-675'

Area: Table #397

Exit: Grisham Trail (the first right after the park entrance).
Parking: Pass picnic table #397 and park on the north end of the long turnout that starts at that table. If you reach the "Giles" exit, you've gone too far.
Approach: Take the trail leading from the north end of the turnout to the water. Do the 5.8 downclimb on the south (right) end of this big rocky platform, or walk right about 50' to a shaded alcove; hike the slab to the water. (Mellow @667', this slab may become hard at lower water.)
GPS at the downclimb: N30°26.870' W98°01.129' (30.447833 -98.018817)

This is a stylin' place to pitch a shade tent, right over the water.

Problems (listed left-to-right)

Estimated
Water Levels

In the distance (south) you'll see a diagonal crack from a ledge to the clifftop. That's the 5.8 "Method 3" access described under the Acid Rock & Hueco Wall area. It's a short swim to climb that area.
Short 5.8 downclimb access

All problems in this table are about 5.11- and harder.

~7 problems pulling a rounded cave roof	670'-673'
~7 short bulge pulls	670'-673'
~3 face to short boulder-stack roof	670'-673'
1 face problem	670'-673'

80' of bad landings
Cool overhang problem left of a rounded arête, but the landing is bad. Floating sketchpad?

Hard rounded arête	670'-673'
~2 overhang problems	670'-673'

~7 roof pulls on an inverted single-stair roof low (at 670') to the water,	667'-673'

reminiscent of Exposure's inverted stair wall in Dallas. Bring shoes for heel hooks.

Area: Restroom #14

Exit: Grisham Trail (the first right after the park entrance), then turn on Giles. It's easy to miss the sign; turn around if you see the "Upper Giles Loop" sign.
Parking: Pass restroom #14 on the left. Find a small parking spot along a line of roadside boulders on the right.
Approach: At that small parking spot, start between a picnic table and BBQ pit and hike 19 paces to a water gully drop-off. Hike down it over a big oak's exposed roots. Reach the water (at 670') on class 4 ledges south of the climbs.
GPS at the downclimb: N30°26.945' W98°01.082' (30.449083 -98.018033)

Problems (listed left-to-right)	Estimated Water Levels
Class 4 access	
~3 problems on a roof over 7 chaotic ledge formations cut by a little dihedral at about 673' level. The Left problem is a steep 5.8 or so.	670-674'
Rounded arête full of ledges	670-674'
~5 problems on a left-leaning diagonal roof	678'-686'

Area: Giles Lake Cliff

Exit: Grisham Trail (the first right after the park entrance), then turn on Giles. It's easy to miss the sign; turn around if you see the "Upper Giles Loop" sign.
Parking: Pass restroom #14 and the small parking area; park at the first big parking area on the right overlooking the water.
Approach: Giles is barely a cove, and at low water levels there's no discernible cove. The climbing is south of "The Flats", the big flat area that people drive their car onto and do God knows what. Hike to the cliff and poke north (left) along it to the best walk-down. The exact spot changes a lot depending on water levels, as do the series of roof problems available to climb. The lower the water, the further the swim approach to the popular big roof — but the swim doesn't get too long. An alternative access is downclimbing a 5.8 jughaul listed below. To find the 5.8 from the clifftop, find the 12' wide limestone "patio" downhill from (and slightly north of) the metal BBQ grill. The trick will be staying on the easiest path as you climb down.
GPS at the north access: N30°26.945' W98°01.082' (30.449083 -98.018033)

This area has overhanging jug hauls on two steep roofs flanked with other problems. It's a popular cove both at high and low water; high water because of the steep moderates; low water (e.g. 653') because it's fun highballing and it's about the only available DWS left in the park.

Problems (listed left-to-right)	Estimated Water Levels
~4 mild overhang problems	668(or lower) — 674'
~5 problems on a reverse stair shaped roof (similar to the one at Table 397), full of rounded blob slopers making these one-move-wonders more fun than otherwise. These are all 1-2 move roof pulls ranging easy to hard.	668(or lower) — 670'
A traverse on the reverse stair step roof	668(or lower) — 667'

Pace Bend

Short swim between the below popular area and the above miscellany.

~4 problems on the popular roof with rebar eyesore. These are roughly 5.10 with a hard topout option on the middle of the roof.

668(or lower)-674'
(bad landings at 653' or higher)

3 mild-overhang problems on the face left of the popular big Roof (5.12?, 5.10, 5.8). The 5.8 jughaul climbs the arête flanking the roof, and it's an alternative downclimb access to the water, described above under Access.

653(or lower) — 674'

~5 moderate problems on the popular big roof.
~6 problems between and on the northernmost low pair of roof.

653 (or lower?) — 674?'
653 (or lower?) — 656'

PmfB: **History**

Pace Bend's boundaries used to be the home of Mud, Texas, named for the moist lowlands along the river. A post office was established in 1887. Population topped at around 100 in 1914.[284] The succession of land owners were the original settler J.M. **Maxey** in the 1880's, his daughter Ester **Maugham**, purchaser R.M. **Taylo**r who named it Sky Ranch, and his three sons. The current Moon River restaurant/bar was a schoolhouse[285]. A County dialogue initiative claimed Mud went under water after the Mansfield Dam brought lake levels up, and it pinpointed Mud on the lake between Marshall and Thurman Coves.[286] Yawn. Sorry…no famous gun fights, no UFO sightings, and no early DWS tournaments back in the late 1800's.

Besides all the native American DWS sends with no shoes and no stowed chalk, some of the early climbing in the area was done on the granite monoliths of the Village of Briarcliff entrance (at Pace Bend and Bee Creek), around 1977. John Sanders and Lauren Clayton put up some wild problems on them. These two and James Crump were among the earliest technical climbers to send at PmfB. Crump and others also toproped various blank home sites along Pace Bend Road.

---

[284] Spicewood Community Newsletter and www.tshaonline.org
[285] www.covesatskyranch.com/History.asp
[286] http://www.co.travis.tx.us/tnr/swtcgrowth/pdfs/final_report_050616/exhibit_G.pdf

Climbing Area: Georgetown

Also known as the Riverside Sanctuary, this convenient climbing area just north of Austin now has 16 routes (and 3 variations), on one of Austin's most beautiful, consistent-looking cliffs, over a sweet natural limestone deck. The drive is only 16 minutes from Mopac and Anderson via the toll road. Route heights compare to Hand Beyond on the left, Dead Cats for most of the routes, and tall-for-Texas on the right four routes. This spot also feels satisfyingly urban, with its hospital parking lot, chain-link fence, litter (bring a trash bag!), and the constant highway sounds of I-35. It is private property and a place of business—please keep your shirt on as you hike in and out.

Brian Derrig, "Torn Awake"

Parking Policy: The following instructions are from Ronald Weaver, Director of Risk Management and Security:
- Use the lot left (South) of the metal buildings. (This is the closest lot to I-35.)
- Do not use the nearby lot between the metal buildings and the Emergency Department entrance; it has limited space for employees.
- Do not use any spaces marked for doctors or other personnel.
- As an alternative, use the parking garage right (North) of the hospital.
- The hospital is getting busier, so try to car-pool.

Keep your dog on a leash. There's traffic in the busy parking lots, and access could be jeopardized if a patient complains about your dog.

Directions to the South parking lot: This offers the most convenient access to both the Main Wall and The Pulpit. Set your GPS for 2000 Scenic Drive, Georgetown, Texas. (Old school directions: go north from Austin/Pflugerville/Round Rock on I-35. Take exit 260 (for Leander) and look for the blue "H" (Hospital) signs the rest of the way. Turn right onto RM-2243 (Leander Road). Take the first left onto Scenic Drive. The hospital is on the left.)

Take the first hospital entrance, drive left of the hospital and park in the lot left of a big metal farm-ish building with a weathervane. Walk back towards the tall radio antenna, past a small outbuilding and you'll soon spot a fence, gate, and message board behind them. On your first visit, sign a waiver and leave it there. Take the trail down and then right, over beautiful little boulder steps to the base of the Main Wall.

If instead you want to start your day at The Pulpit, park and walk 60 paces across a field towards I-35. Walk down hill to the I-35 Bridge, then down its cement slab. Cut right and walk 50 paces. The Pulpit can also be reached from the Main Wall on a bad, poison-ivy strewn trail. Clean up that trail.

Directions to the North parking garage: If the South parking lot is full, go back to Scenic Drive and take the last entrance into the hospital and park in the multi-level parking garage. Do not park outside the garage. Walk towards the big radio antenna, past Building #1. Hike along the left end of Building #1 and cut left to the radio antenna. Pass it to reach the message board behind the fence and gate. Take the stairs down to the Main Wall.

Details: There are no sport anchors, just chains. If you do not lead, most anchors are top-accessible, but some require use of a safety rope.

A few of the newer routes have micro-crimps and footholds that break easily. Bring your sending shoes, as most of the routes require footwork. The lowest grade routes aren't juggy warmups, so use the bouldering to warm up.

The grades recorded in rockclimbing.com are stiff. Austin Rock only covered the five original main routes, and the other grades were established online by one person, with few people posting their own opinions. So, not much consensus was built online. On this shaky ground, we grabbed our axe and un-sandbagged the routes with a lot of splattered blood. For the next edition, help us fine-tune it with a scalpel.

Besides cool routes, there are two reasons to make a trek from Austin to Georgetown:
1. A Taste of Ethiopia. 1100 Grand Avenue Parkway Pflugerville, TX 78660. (512) 251-4053. Eat incredible food on the thinnest of sour-dough breads, no utensils necessary.[287]

2. Zorba Greek Restaurant. 2601 S I-35 B500 Round Rock, TX 78664. (512) 716-0100

Brian Derrig identified all the routes and contributed a lot to the following route descriptions. Luke Stollings helped with the history and polished the route and trail descriptions, and Tommy Blackwell added some history.

---

[287] Dave Phillips lived in Ethiopia until he was five. Baboons would come into the house once in a while. They'd also climb the two-story house via security bars on the windows. Dave and his twin brother did their first climbing on those bars, going up two stories and hanging on them, probably mimicking the baboons. Mom and the maid would rush out to spot them.

Brett Newman, "Use the Force Luke"

Georgetown: **Main Wall**

Sun conditions: Afternoon sun on the upper half of routes. It's climbable in the summer except from 3pm to 6pm. In the winter, sun from about 2pm-5pm keeps you warm.
Approach: 2 minutes.
GPS: N 30˚37.600' W˚97 41.371' (30.626667 -97.68952)

In addition to the routes, the face under the rightmost routes looks like a good set of traverses. There's also bouldering well left of the routes, through the brush.

1. **Good Book (aka. Short Green Dihedral)** (5.10a)* 2 bolts, Luke Stollings (TR '94). First bolted dihedral on the left. Interesting roof pull; before reading the *beta*,[288] try to solve it on your own.

2. **Howard's End** (5.10c)* 3 bolts, Brian Derrig. On the left face of the acute arête. Bolts slant up and right. Lots of different beta have been found since the breaking of a key hold.

Acute Arête / Prominent Prow

3. **Wasp Arête** (5.12b)*** 3 bolts, Brian Derrig. The most beta intensive route at the Riverside Sanctuary.

4. **La Campanita** (5.11a-b)*** 3 bolts, Brian Derrig. The boltline slants up and left at 11 o'clock. Traverse in from the right. Belay from the right to avoid a crash. *Beta*[289].

Vertical Edge Formation runs most of the cliff, with right-facing low part, left-facing high part.

---

[288] Find the only good pocket on the ledge but use it right-handed to set up a dynamic mantle left of the anchors.
[289] A planned sequence will set you up for the lunge. Continue left and up.

5. **Narthex** (5.11a)* 3 bolts, Luke Stollings (TR '94). *Beta.*[290]

15' Gap between routes; gnar cedar growing down from clifftop.

6. **Easter Uprising**[291] (5.11c)*** 3 bolts, Brian Derrig. The bolts slant up and slightly left. *Beta.*[292]

7. **Song of Myself** (5.11d)*** 4 bolts, Brian Derrig. Bolt 4 is up and left, under the anchors.

    a. underline: **Right Hand Direct** (5.11c)*** 3 bolts. Instead of going to Bolt 4, shoot up right on marginal pockets.

Big hackberry tree at cliff base.

8. **Blood Sacrifice** (5.10d)*** 4 bolts, Luke Stollings (TR, '94). Twist and turn through the dihedral and a C-shaped crack, finishing on the pocketed headwall. WARNING: loose left hand jugstone above Bolt 2, used to high-clip Bolt 3.

Rounded arête with low ledge

9. **El Machete** (5.9+)*** 3 bolts, Brian Derrig. Start on the arête to an early ledge, then a mid-cliff bulge. This line makes use of some of the Georgetown Jump territory, but is in itself a quality route. Wasps sometimes occupy this route. Without a cheat stack, the start climbs by one V-grade for every inch you are shorter than 5'8". If you don't warm up on the boulders, this is probably the best warmup in terms of hold size.

---

[290] Grit past the tendon popper to more secure holds surrounding the dihedral.
[291] This route was probably originally Holy Crow (5.11 TR), or else Song of Myself was.
[292] The dynamic finish on this route offers a good show for the peanut gallery below.

Georgetown

10. Gateway (5.10b PG)*** 4 bolts, Bryan Jacks (TR, '94). Climb the meandering crack. Runout to Bolt 3 and then it's a crux clip. Great hold mix. Gateway has some noticeably awkward clips, but remains the most traveled climb at The Sanctuary. You can skip Bolt 4. The few opinions so far split between 10b and 10c.

<u>toprope</u>: **The Georgetown Jump** (5.10a TR Aid)*, Clayton Norman, Tommy Blackwell. Possibly the most bizarre, wild, fun belay scenario ever devised. The climber stands at the stairs near Unbound. The belayer faces the climber with a tight rope. When the climber starts running towards the base of Gateway, the belayer immediately runs towards the climber, keeping a tight rope, and passing them to the right. If anyone slips or if the rope goes loose, yell "stop" and abort the mission. As they pass each other, the belayer sprints even faster to keep enough rope tension to Aid the climber in a dyno to the ledge, mantel and finish Gateway. One party interviewed had little trouble executing this maneuver.

11. Torn Awake (5.12a)*** 4 bolts, Brian Derrig. Pumpy, desperado moves up nice angles. Enjoy.

12. Use the Force Luke (5.11b-c)*** 6 bolts, Jeff Jackson (TR '94). Big holds up a steep face. This is the local lap lane. Wasps sometimes occupy this route at the roof, in which case you can evade them via the Poison Traverse.

b. variation: **Poison Traverse** (5.10d)*** 6 bolts. Start on Use the Force Luke, climb Bolts 1-4 with a long draw or 24" runner on Bolt 4, then cut right at the overhang on a mild runout to Poison Ivy's last two bolts and anchors, using a long draw after the runout. You will still likely fight rope drag topping out to the anchors; fight it with *beta*.[293]

c. <u>toprope</u>: **Pink Daisey Bunny** (5.11c-d TR)*. Start climbing the pedestal directly under the chains and go straight up the mini-roof and arête.

13. Poison Ivy (5.10b)*** 4 bolts, Brian Derrig. Traddy type balance and an abundance of sucker holds keep things interesting. Pain management *beta*.[294]

14. Unbound (5.9)* 3 bolts, Brian Derrig. Start from the last "step" of the trail, right of the bolt line. Mantle and high-step your way to the ledge (trending left). Use the same anchors as Poison Ivy. Directionals are a must if toproping.

Trail Head.

[293] Topout directly over the last bolt, not to the right. You might encounter a water puddle on one jug, but another should be dry. Going right is tempting but you might end up in a slippery beached whale fighting rope drag.

[294] Avoid the dangling leaves of pain to the left of the anchor.

Georgetown: **Sanctuary Boulders**

This 15' tall "bench" of rock is directly opposite the Main Wall. There are two sets of toprope anchors on the boulder's top.

15. **Pyramid Direct** (V1)*. Climb good holds straight up the pyramid that is found opposite Blood Sacrifice.

16. **Balcony Problems** (5.6-5.9)*. Climb anywhere on the backside. Several TR anchors make this a good kid's area.

17. **Above The Catacombs** (V0)*. Tunnel under and behind the Balcony Problems to find a short overhang. This cave area is formed by a set of boulders leaning against each other.

Georgetown: **Blocks and Comb Wall (aka. The Overlook)**

Approach: 3 minutes?
GPS: ??????

50 yards up river (towards I-35), on the left.

> toprope: **Consolidated Route** (5.9 TR)* Brian Derrig, Justin Peterson, Tim Nickels, Kiley Nickels. One crux at the top ends what is mostly 5.7-5.8 climbing. To toprope, set the anchor to the left. Cleaning is best done by the second. **??**

Georgetown: **The Pulpit**

Sun Conditions: only 1-2 hours of afternoon sun.
Approach: 3 minutes?
GPS: N30˚ 37.564' W97˚ 41.406' (30.626075 -97.690102)

Further up the river, almost to the I-35 bridge. These two routes and a variation share anchors. They would get multiple stars if there were more routes in this spot.

18. **Pulpit Center** (5.8)* 4 bolts. Climb the left boltline to the big arête at clifftop. Cut up and right on Bolt 4 to Pulpit Right's anchors.
⌶•👤•⌶?

   a. variation: **Pulpit Left** (5.6 PG)* 3 bolts. Instead of climbing to Bolt 4, climb the crack on the left side of the big arête, then traverse right to the anchors.
⌶•👤•⌶|👀?

19. **Pulpit Right** (5.6)* 3 bolts. Climb the right boltline to the right side of the big arête at clifftop and up to anchors on its right top.
⌶•👤•⌶ ≈≈👀☕▲⛺

Brett Newman, "Pulpit Right"

Georgetown: **History**

Georgetown started out as an outlaw climbing area for topropers. In 1993-4, Luke Stollings worked with Georgetown Hospital (which is now St. David's) to win toprope access for Experiential Challenge Programs (a ropes course and experiential education company). Jeff Jackson was hired to install toprope anchors. It's a little known fact that, despite all his first ascents, Jefe never owned his own drill. In 2001, Robert Kiyosaki took note of this phenomenon and soon capitalized on the wisdom that one should never own an expensive hammer drill, nor any other asset. The key to wealth isn't "it takes money to make money." It's "borrow other people's money." Robert made millions on his book "Rich Man Poor Man" and its seminars. Other people paid Robert to attend those seminars, took on debt to invest in real estate, and learned (the hard way) that with great risk comes great reward, except that great risk brings a great chance of abject failure, lasting pain, and regret.

So, yeah, we're reaching for padding material at this juncture. The book's about to go to print, we've collected very little history about Georgetown, and there's a daunting expanse of white space to consume. One would think a climbing area behind a hospital might generate some stories. The setting is perfect for missed clips, critical head injuries, 911 calls, and ambulances deployed in a rush across thirty yards of parking lot. But no; Sanctuary gurus know of no injuries. Here's what we do know.

After obtaining permission for toproping, Luke Stollings controlled access, creatively, over the phone, by testing each climber to successfully describe how to set topropes. Later, a Southwest University club obtained access too, and Tommy Blackwell coached the club at weekly outings here, from 1997-2000. Tommy started climbing around age 40, and his second outing was at this very crag. This set of routes is no material for beginners, and at the end of the day, his forearms and hands were so blown, he had trouble opening his car door. He drove home using his palms. That night at dinner, he had such trouble holding silverware that his wife asked if she needed to cut up his food for him.

In '96, Georgetown opened to the public, traffic increased, and the director of the hospital at the time became concerned with liability. He suspended access and threatened to "pour tar over the whole cliff line if I have to," to keep people out of there. CTM gained permission to bolt the routes for lead, and Tommy Blackwell bolted six of them in 1999-2000. In 2009, Gary Ellis and CTM established a waiver kiosk and solidified relations between hospital staff and the climbing community. Please do your part to keep access free and easy.

Brian Derrig took Georgetown to the next level by developing nine more lead routes, spread across the grades.

Well damn, there's no way to pad this with enough Georgetown stuff to fill the page. Let's return to Tommy. Many of you know the energy he has put into the local climbing areas, with hardware replacement, trail work, city/county communications, CTM management, and new bolted routes. His latest energetic pursuit is a cool book available on RockHoundBooks.com. It's about the wild stories of being a SWAT team commander, instructor, and the years before all that as a rookie cop around Austin. Here's an actual climbing story from the book:

> Morris Dale took his hands from behind his back and began climbing the eight-foot chain-link fence. (Officer) Vann grabbed his right leg that by now was chest high and going up the fence. I grabbed the left. Morris kept climbing. Pulling me and Vann up as he went. I couldn't believe it! Certainly I was no heavyweight. Vann and I combined had to weigh over three hundred pounds. He was pulling us up and over the fence. We fell in a pile, with chickens squawking, feathers flying, and people heaped in chicken poop.
>
> *excerpts from Tales of Travis County, by Tommy Blackwell.*

Appendix A: **Upgrades and Downgrades**

As history grinds forward, new guidebooks revise grades, always without explanation. This appendix lists the changes and their reasons. A guidebook's grades are just a written proposal in the ongoing public conversation about grades. With online forums, route databases, and mobile guidebook apps, this conversation is richer than in the past when paper guidebooks ruled alone. We'll stay tuned to the conversation and consider grade changes in future editions.

Exactly what is the grade? Some folks grade by the difficulty to onsight the route (power, endurance, and trickiness). We just grade on power ("single hardest move"), sometimes increasing the grade if a lot of endurance is needed. These grades cater to projecting (not onsighting) and ideally say how hard your project routes are, once you've found the best beta and redpointed them. Unfortunately, power requirements can depend on height and technique, technique can depend on flexibility, and climbers range widely in all three. It's impossible to assign one rating that covers power, height, and flexibility. Until you see Lipo graded 5.11c/H1/F2/E0.5 in some distant future, scratch through every grade in this book, work each route until sent, then write in your own personal grade.

We've climbed most of the routes under 5.12a, asked around, and considered online opinions. On upgrades, we may have climbed tired or missed good beta. On downgrades, we may not have talked to climbers who are less tall and less flexible. Please respond by adding grade opinions on www. rockclimbing.com or the Texas Rocks! iPhone app.

Angular Momentum (5.11d). Up from 11c. AM is comparable to Crankenstein in wall angles and the thankless task of grading endurance routes. Both have no moves harder than 11b. AM's one rest is late; Crank's is conveniently in the middle. N.H. felt the end pump was comparable to Crank.

Angel of Poets (5.10b). Up from 10a with support of online opinions averaging 10b. Someone said a hold broke.

Annie Up (5.7). Up from 5.6, comparing to routes at Zoey's Wall. This route puts some load on the forearms, whereas local 5.6 limestone routes don't seem to.

Ant Encounters (5.10d). Down from 11a on several online comments and opinions of K.V., A.P., C.S., and me. K.V. said it's been the easiest 11a, and easier than War on Rugs (10d). Comparable to Wife in the Fast Lane's 10d start. Milk this route's rest, possibly twice (after clipping), to feel it as a 10d.

Antiqua (5.11b). Up from 11a. It has an elaborate, exciting crux for the grade. The easiest beta is left-leg reachy: Skip the sucker 2-finger pocket right of Bolt 2. Both hands go on crimps left of Bolt 2, just under the roof. Left hand to a little rounded balcony (actually a finger-jug slot). Cut feet, rotate left, left foot reaches far onto the orange horn. (If you can't reach it, try a left toe-hook on the left-pointing rounded horn.) Point right knee left, bending severely for an aggressive stem against the left-pointing rounded horn. Right hand crosses to a hueco's sweet spot, bumps higher, then feet cut *yet again* (this was originally 11a? we're not talking juggy handholds here…), and the rest isn't easy but it's manageable.

Antonian (5.8). Down from 5.9. Short route, short crux, easier than Madrone.

April Fool (5.10a). Clarification. The original trad route went to the cave and that was it (5.9). It exited by walking the ledge left. The toprope anchors now allow an excellent topout over the left edge of the cave.

Beelzebubba (5.11b-c). Clarified from "5.11" on G.E.'s opinion it's slightly easier than Mother Budda. We've not yet dealt with its poison ivy to assess it.

Blood of the Dead (5.11c). Up from 11b after discussions with respected Sex Canyon regulars, in which most participants considered it 11c or 11d. The FA originally called it 11b/c.

Bloody Butt (5.10d). Up from 9+. One old timer put it this way. "If these (Bloody Butt and Skank Hole) are 5.9's, they're the hardest 5.9's on the planet!" The original grades violated federal law prohibiting sandbagging in excess of 4 letter grades.

Bolt Talk (5.11a). No change, despite a year of threatening 5.11a-b. The original grade was 11b. 11a-b was intended to show it's harder than Unnatural Selection. Certainly harder on the fingers and probably harder clips, but then Unnatural Selection presents a low reach issue. Maybe Unnatural itself is height-dependent 11a/b.

Bolted Like Mex (5.10b). Down from 5.10c. Very technical and intimidating. Take two runs on it back-to-back, and your second run will feel a lot easier.

Bolted Like Reimers (5.10c). Down from 5.10b. Heck, the first move is probably 5.10b-c. Easily "c" by the time you've toed those pockets and pulled that small stuff. I had R.D. and B.K. agreeing to "c" midway up the route! Harder than comparable Water Ballet.

Bongo Direct (5.13a). Clarified from 5.13. J.M. says it's easier than ReKleiner.

Bride of Crankenstein (5.11c). Up from 5.11b, suggested by P.B. before we got on it. Long crux felt a notch harder than Pearl.

Bulge (5.10b). Up from 5.9, though it's never clear how toprope routes run. Maybe he topped out over the arête and graded the lower 10a crimp move old-school 5.9. Grading topout mantle moves isn't easy unless you're doing mantles a lot, so please take our 5.10b with a grain of salt.

Butt Scratch (5.7). Down from 5.8; several folks online and at the crag agree with 5.7. It felt much easier than Roo Dog and hardly taxed my arms, whereas Roo Dog's first clip is a lot bigger strain. Roo Dog might feel like 5.7 on TR.

Champagne and Reefer (5.13a). Up from 5.12d, averaging inputs from J.G., J.R., C.H., and M.T.

Chicken Supreme (5.9+ / 5.10b). Sort-of-down from 5.10b. Online comments talk about the high gaston ranging from 5.9 to 5.10c, depending on how tall you are. Grades suck.

Crack Attack (5.11a). Up from 10d, but still lower than the original grade printed on Jack Lawrence's one pager back in 1992. Substantially harder than T-Roofic (10d).

Crack Smack (5.10b). Up from 5.9 on seven opinions. The route can fork but neither path felt 5.9.

Creeping Doom (5.8+). Down from 5.9+. Original grade probably had to do more with mistrusting the choss band and not having much experience at Dead Cats to compare similar 5.8 crimping.

Curious George (5.12b). Up from Mike Klein's observations of other people on it and his own feel.

Crankenstein (5.11d). Up from 11c/d. Sixteen online opinions spread evenly across 11b-c-d. But check out the math, yo. A while back, our 5'3" pal with only two 11a sends and sloppy footwork hangdogged this, strongly suggesting no 11c power is required. However, it's extremely sustained, full of hard moves except for the jug's short rest. Lots of people bag this only after Bongo Fury and about the same time as Lipo. Thus, we like 11b power + BigEnduranceFactor = 11d.

Discharge (5.12c-d). Route-redefinition. Austin Rock had 13c, up from 12c due to a hold break. But we're told that 13c means avoiding obvious holds (of Lip-o-suction) and were urged to forget the contrivance.

Diving for Rocks (5.10b/5.10d). Stretching down from 5.10d. One of the best routes depicting the often meaninglessness of grades. Good semi-short climbers have worked their ass off to get this, whereas tall newbs have TR-flashed it. Really short light climbers can find it easy, even if they aren't great jumpers, so it's not a pure tall/short slash grade. Online and offline opinions range as low as 5.10a, and two even at 5.9! (One of those is lame since he climbs 5.13 and trains on the Beast Maker.) If you worked your ass off to get this, consider it 10d. Otherwise, consider it whatever you want. In fact, ritually mark through every route grade in this book and write in the grade that matches your body type.

Faceoff (5.9+). Up from 5.9. Our buddy A.S. thought 5.10a; we figure the Greenbelt is stiff in this grade range, or else we'd listen to him.

Fearless (5.9 PG). Down from 5.10a, breaking from the 10a consensus online, figuring this route is easier than El Primero (5.9) and that people probably miss the beta footnoted under the route description. Also upgrading from negative stars to ***.

Fist Crack (5.8). Up from 5.7. There's an early 5.7 exit, but finishing the crack is substantially harder.

Flash Crack (5.7). Up from 5.6 on two opinions, and it clearly weights the arms.

Flea Circus (5.12a). Up from 5.11d. A lot of people capable of 5.11d get smacked down. J.G. initially disagreed with 12a but got back on it and sanctioned this upgrade.

Flinch (5.12c). Up from input of about six random people, though it's still considered easier than Grinch.

Get Yer Fill (5.12c). Austin Rock did not have Landfill Wall sorted out and reported this as 12a with the wrong FA, likely confusing it with Slopeamine. Rupesh said 12b-c, Mike said 12c-d (both are the FAs) and so we've averaged it to 12c.

Good Book (5.10a). Up from 5.9. JS thinks 5.10b.

Gray Streak (5.10c). Up from 5.10b. J.B. says the crux area under Bolt 2 is harder from rock breaks/changes. But mainly upgrading because several of us felt it's a lot harder than the neighboring 5.10b (Ging). Plus thin-face wizards K.V. and A.P. failed to onsight it. When asked about the 5.10b grade, B.K. said "Fuck THAT."

Gros Ventre (5.10d/11a). Half-down from 11a. (Texas Limestone II had 5.10). The crux is super hard to read, but the beta drops the power requirement a lot. We're told it requires a lot of power for shorter people, so we went with a slash grade.

Gunsmoke (5.10b/d). Up from 5.10a. N.H. is solving 5.12a's, deadpoints well and made quick work of Running Man and Iron Man. This crux took him some work, and he figured 11a. The deadpoint's power reminded us of Diving for Rocks, so why not use that route's (new) grade.

Hank's (5.9). Down from 5.10; J.S. said "everybody agrees it's 5.9," and so do we.

Hedonistic Urges (5.12b). Up from 5.12a-b on half a dozen unanimous opinions. It feels 5.12b/c to M'T.

High Anxiety (5.10b/5.10c). Half-down from 5.10c. Height-dependent.

Hissing Cloe (5.7). Down from 5.8. The route requires good technique, using 5.7 power.

Hollywood (5.7). Up from 5.6. We hear a tree used to make the start 5.6, or you could avoid the tree for 5.7. Online comments split between 5.6 and 5.7, siding mostly with 5.7 and some saying harder.

Hut Rabbit (5.11c). Up from 5.11b, since it climbs the long 5.11b portion of Girly Man, then starts a crux traverse right where Girly Man gets easy. After all that climbing, one then has to finish Buddha.

Ice Cubes, Popcorn, and Popsicles (5.9). Down from 5.10-. Online feedback averages to 5.9.

Icy Touch of a Dimensional Shambler (5.10c). Up from 5.10b. The original grade was fairer when 105% wired with Earth gravity at 2.7% below norm.

Iranian Arms Deal (5.10d). Grade clarification; three different starts are used, each at different grades (5.8, 5.9, 5.10d).

Ivy League (5.11b-d). Possible (undecided) upgrade from 5.11b. We spent enough TR time to describe the route but not grade it. The crux felt 11c for D.P. and me, and D.L. thought 11c-d. S.T. said 11b, which is pretty much a guarantee of 11c.

Jugfest (5.8). Down from the Limestoner route list.

Karen Carpenter (5.10d/5.11a). Half-down from 11a. Online comments average to 10d, with some 10c entries. We hear shorter people tend to have more trouble, so we set it as a height-dependent grade.

Left of Ferntasm (5.10a). Down from 10b.

Lonesome Dove (5.11a). Clarification. Austin Rock's 5.12a assumed a topout; most folks don't. The topout grade is listed separately.

Lord of the Dance (5.13a). Down from 13a/13c, where 13a meant using the manufactured pocket and 13c not. Half a dozen climbers advised downgrading the 13c to 13a. A few say 12c with the pocket; a few say 12d with the pocket; others say 13a either way.

Lord of the Pit (5.11b). Mrock grade change. Harder than Spider Grind. Not that the holds are similar, but both are endurance routes.

Man Hands (5.10c / 5.11a). Semi-downgraded from the online 11a entry, from comments about the crack near the anchors. If your hands are small enough, pull the crack for 5.10c. If not, deadpoint to a 3-finger pocket for 11a.

Mas Cervezas (5.11c). Up from 5.11b, from online consensus and because Pete Bishop said so.

Mai Type (5.11d-5.12b). Up from the unbelievably sandbagged "5.10". Maybe 5' of the ledge has eroded since 2005? On top of that, the huge starting dyno isn't even the crux.

Matter of Honor (5.10a). Down from 5.10.[295] Noticeably easier than neighboring Angel of Poets.

Mega Lounge (5.8+). Up from 5.8. Thin powerful face moves on bad feet. It may feel 5.8 if you're tiny and adept at face climbs. Most likely it will feel as hard as nearby Let the Wallies Loose (5.9).

Mikey Likes It (5.11a). Up from 5.10d. Everyone we've seen on this gets their ass kicked. Arguably harder than comparable Unnatural Selection.

[295] Old school 5.10 tends to mean 5.10b or 5.10c. 5.10- means 5.10a. 5.10+ means 5.10d.

More Wasabi (5.12a-5.12b). Down from 5.12c. Both FA's said 5.12a, "5.12a hard" respectively. S.I. sent it in 2005, thought it harder than other Reimers 12a's but definitely not 12c.

Natural (5.10). See the entry for "Sunday Mass".

Narthex (5.11a). Up from 5.10 on JS's call. We felt 5.11b-c but were still working off Xmas chocolate.

No Recess (5.13a). No change. A suggestion for 13a was presented to us, since rock scars suggest broken holds. However, the FA says there were fragile holds not used and a devious sequence that's likely still good (involving stemming between strong little blobs, or perhaps an actual stalactite and blob, and a dropknee deadpoint over the first roof). Please check this out and report back if a change is needed for 2nd edition.

Pay Dirt (5.11d-5.12a). Up a lot. Way up. Publishing this as 5.10c probably broke international law.

Power Snatch (5.10d). Up to the original Texas Limestone II grade (10+). Requires more power than other 10c's on the wall and more than Prototype. Online opinion followed the 10c originally entered, but the first four random people consulted agreed with an upgrade.

Prototype (5.10c / 5.10d). Half-down from 5.10d, restoring the grade published in 1992 by Jack Lawrence. Online, folks split (not evenly) between 10c and 10d. It's height-dependent. We're thinking about writing a short-person's version of this guidebook, co-authored with Neil Higa, Phil Bryant, Rachel (Harris) Bryant, Lori Bergeron, and Rona Tygress Distenfeld.

Pearl (5.11b / 5.11c). Half down from 11c. The big opening move is height-dependent (and, sadly, cheater-stack-height-dependent). This would have been my hardest ever onsight, but on the way to Bolt 3 I begrudgingly downgraded it. Damn!

Rock and Roll Highschool (5.11b). No change, but maybe next edition. Lots of strong people have trouble on this, but it's one thin move perhaps locals aren't strong at.

Rock Dog (5.11c-d). Up from 5.10+ on advice from D.W., C.B., and our own attempt.

Scary 7-11 (5.12a?). Up from 5.10, since starting hold(s) broke. 12a is suggested by one 13a type.

Schoolboys Indirect (5.9+). Up from 5.9 from some online and offline comments. Two key holds have broken off (the softball hand wrap in the crack under a bolt, and a partial break to the flake by the next bolt).

Seismic Step (5.7). Down from 5.8, based on a few online opinions.

Shower Scene From Psycho (5.11b). Mrock grade change; down from 11c. Trick beta makes it very comparable to Goblin Mutant, which is considered soft 11a.

Skank Hole (5.10d). Up from 9+. One old timer put it this way. "If these (Bloody Butt and Skank Hole) are 5.9's, they're the hardest 5.9's on the planet!"

Socks On Chicks (5.10d). Up from 5.10c. Harder than Star Belly Sneech; close to Blowing Smoke at the Monkey.

Starfish (5.12c). Clarification from "5.12". Jefe said it was considered 5.12c at the time, but 5.13a might be fairer by Reimers standards.

Stickbug (5.13c). Down from 5.13d on advice from R.C., an alleged sandbagger. (A sandbagger is an FA who routinely grades their routes too low. They're very common.) We too are accused of sandbagging, but only by short people and an overweight inflexible guy with fat fingers. Some sandbaggers do it as a prank on the public. Some are just too badass to accurately discern 10b from 10c. Some because they're humble about an FA difficulty. Some to avoid the "shame" of others' downgrading. It may take years of stealthy, letter-by-letter upgrading while no one's looking to restore sanity to certain route grades.

Stand Off (5.8 TR). Down from 5.9 on three opinions ranging 5.8, 5.8, and 5.7-5.8. Now, 3 is a horribly small sample size. Let's flash-mob this route and get a big consensus.

Sunday Mass (aka. Natural) (5.10c/d). Half up from 5.10c. It's 5.10c if you can dyno to the hueco from the cheat stack, else 5.10d. Of 5.10c, Q.G. said "everybody thinks it's harder."

Superman (5.7). 3 online opinions said 5.7, 1 said 5.6, T.B. says 5.8.

Super Yummy (5.12c). Down a little from 5.12c-d, averaging opinions of J.G., J.R., and C.H.

Swordfish (5.8+). Up from 5.8; a sustained bunch of crimps and finger jams adds up.

The Bitch Club (5.11d). Up from 11c. Harder dyno than Ralph's Route, with a harder post-crux move and an endurance run to the anchors. D.P. never got this route, back when he was sending mid 5.12. G.E. suggested 11d and says this and Tit For Tom are the hardest of the 5.11's at the wall, and we heartily agree.

The Finest and the Flyest (5.11b). Up from 11a.

The Munchies (5.12a / 5.11c / 5.11b). Clarification. Austin Rock had 11c, but the boltline serves three paths (the hardest two being eliminates of parts of the long crack system), and so it's not clear what line Austin Rock assumed. The 12a path's grade is on few opinions (D.P., K.V., N.H., me). The 11c path is an endurance route but with great holds compared to Crank and weakening, but not pumpy, by the end. The 11b path eliminates the 11c path's high power crux and has only one bad hold. All are intricate, so they'll all feel harder until worked.

Three Slackateers (5.11d). Up from 11c. We agree with Pete on this grade.

Thin Crack (5.6). Up from 5.5, though we don't know what 5.5 is. We know this route comes close to loading the forearms, which would satisfy our definition of Texas 5.7. 5.6 isn't hard here; this isn't the Gunks.

Tit For Tom (5.11d). Up from 11c. K.V. says it's a "rat bastard" of a route. The crux power is much harder than Bongo Fury's, and then it takes endurance to finish. We spent a lot of time at the wall, reviewing all the routes. Folks would come up to hit Tit, hear of our upgrade, and object, until they got back on that bastard.

Too Many Donuts (5.11b/5.10d). Semi-downgrade from "5.11". The 5.10d is a tentative grade for shorter folks; our tiny partner walked this route, probably the first crux she ever did that my big friend and I couldn't. The tall grade might be higher than 11b. Interesting route; send it and help us build a better tall & short grade consensus.

Trash Can Man (5.11b). Up from 11a, the unanimous decision of four people. Just consider how much harder it is than what you lead (Rock Retard) to set the toprope.

T-Roofic Direct (5.11a). Down from 11b, from online comments and our own runs. The crux's power felt 10d-11a but left a deliciously big pump the rest of the way up, comparable to El Presidente, Blowing Smoke at the Monkey, and Wife in the Fast Lane.

Underdog (5.11b). Up from 11a, even though we get a far left foot stem most can't reach. We imagine shorter people might be stuck campusing or making a sick dyno at three or more letter grades. If you can't stem, let us know what grade this is for you.

Unknown Route @ Hand Beyond Wall (5.10a). Down from 5.10b. Easier than Booger Boy and Freedom Fries (left path).

War On Rugs (still 5.10d). No change, but we're ounces away from saying 5.11a, the original grade printed on Jack Lawrence's one pager back in 1992. The FA and his partners felt it was 11a. Perhaps they didn't traverse left enough, to the hold shared with Teenage Parties?

Water Ballet (5.10b). Down to the original grade. Online opinions range 10b and 10c, but average to 10b.

Wowie Zowie (5.10d). Down from 11a. A handful of people say it's easier than Slate and Looking Glass. Others say it's harder. C.B. says it's balancy, not powerful. Similarly, N.H. says it's a skill 11a, not a power 11a, so he agreed with 10d. Occasionally folks will propose an upgrade (or object to a downgrade) because a route has "5.11 technique" or whatever. We don't grade on technique, since plenty of 5.9/5.10 climbers use great technique, employing all the moves of 5.11 climbers. Technique is a huge limiting factor for many, and routes vary in how tricky they are to determine what moves to use. But if we grade on technique, all the savvy climbers will think the grades are soft, and the tricky routes you wire will always feel softer than the obvious routes you wire. We like the power/endurance grade, plus the optional p or C.

Chaos, Softness & Sandbags

We're nervous about changing grades on 14% of the routes. It keeps us up some nights. Maybe we've really fucked up. Hopefully we've improved more grades then we've messed up. A lot of holds have broken or polished slick over the course of 16 years since Texas Limestone II and Austin Rock were published. Yeah…that's the ticket.

A while back, we tallied our upgrades vs. downgrades and found the counts were about equal. It was a relief that we were not on a soft-grading bent which would make us look piddly.[296] Then we reviewed a lot of the seldom-travelled ("unpopular") routes, and our upgrading increased. And, the few folks who knew these routes often suggested upgrades, never downgrades. Now the totals are roughly 3 upgrades to every 2 downgrades.

We also noticed most of these unpopular routes are good! Maybe this isn't coincidental. When climbers get sandbagged, they come away with a negative memory of the experience, and if they're chasing numbers, they have no incentive to get back on that route. As they talk about the route, the route's reputation gets tarnished, but not because of the quality of the climbing. Maybe our upgrades on unpopular routes will control expectations, improve climbers' experiences on them, and eventually get more deserved traffic on them.

Appendix B: **Other Texas Climbing Areas**

This book does not cover all of Texas, but other books and on-online sources are available. www.rockclimbing.com is pretty good; start yourself a free account, and read it as a news feed to catch new routes and changes. The following outlines some of the areas beyond Austin.

Enchanted Rock State Park

The home of early Texas climbing, and the current bread-and-butter of Texas slab and trad and rad and mad climbing (plus bouldering) on granite. A guidebook is available at www.erockonline.com.

Miller Springs (Temple/Belton)

The bolts here are likely not maintained. Rockclimbing.com describes the location but not the routes. The last route list was published in Texas Limestone II. Perhaps someone will add them to the database. Two 5.10's, one 5.11, and 20 5.12-5.13, mostly by Jack Mileski, plus Jeff Jackson, the Rands, and Paul Clark.

Morgan's Point (Temple/Belton/Lake Belton areas)

The bolts here are likely not maintained. 11 routes ranging 5.11b to 5.13a. Is this area defunct or still climbed?

"Goomba" John Sanders at Enchanted Rock with the biggest cam at the time, 7" or 8", custom made in Thailand

---

[296] Texas is already soft compared to some areas. Before venturing to Colorado, just mark through every grade in this guidebook, dropping them two letter grades until 5.9. For routes at 5.9 and under, drop them two number grades. Now you'll be emotionally ready for Colorado.

Joe Sulak 📷

"Genetic Plasm" @ Cub Cave

San Antonio: Cub Cave

Hard climbing on public (city) property. The place goes fully under water during major floods. One bolt pulled out on a climber during 2011, but the all the worthy left-end routes now have SS glue-ins. It's said you can pretty much deck at every bolt. The 3-star routes are those on pretty good stone; the rest get dirty and a bit more chossy. Climbing access is not officially allowed, but folks are working towards that. Check the Facebook fan page Climb San Antonio (or possibly www.climbsa.org) for the most recent access information. Rebolting occurred around '09. The park is just outside of the city, right off of Route 281. Find Canyon Ridge Elementary School, then spot the city park sign across the street. The cave is a one-minute walk from the parking lot. Routes:

1. **White Trash** (5.11 R)*** 3 bolts, Alex Catlin
2. **Fisher King** (5.13 R)*** 5 bolts, Mike Klein
3. **Genetic Drift** (5.12 R)*** 5 bolts, Jeb Vetters, Paul Erbe. Bolt 4 is shared with Bio Plasm, which crosses this route to form an "X" at the top of the two routes.
4. **Triple X Baby** (5.12 R)* 3 bolts, Jeb Vetters. Bolt 3 is shared with Bio Plasm, with crosses this route and Genetic Drift.
5. **Bio Plasm** (5.12 R)* 5 bolts, Jeb Vetters. Start on boulder at left end of the lower cave. Start on Subterranean's Bolt 1, traverse left, then diagonally up and left, crossing Triple X Baby and Genetic Drift. This route has two low bolts, then uses Triple X Baby's Bolt 2, then Genetic Drift's Bolt 4, then finishes on two of its own bolts left of Genetic Drift.
(bolted variation) Thieving Texan Scum (5.13)* 4 bolts, Alex Catlin. Start on Subterranean and climb Bolts 1-3, then cut up and left to another bolt.
6. **Subterranean** (5.12 R)* 6 bolts, Mike Klein.
7. **Dominion of Evil** (5.13? R) Project. Start right of Subterranean, climb just right of its Bolts 3-4, then angle slightly right and up.

San Antonio: Medicine Wall

Roughly 30 routes (and more coming), ranging 5.7 to 5.12+, on private land. Public access has not been granted.

Brian Carlisle 📷

San Antonio: Medina Lake

A bunch of DWS, though not as good as Pace Bend, accessible only by boat. Launch at Red's Cove. Probably the highest concentration of problems is on walls east of Mormon's Bluff. Lots of choss — be careful.

Lake Mineral Wells State Park

Top-rope routes ranging from easy to 5.11, plus some harder routes, on rough conglomerate, west of Fort Worth.

Camp Eagle

70' tall sport routes ranging 5.7-5.13 on a 1,400 acre Christian adventure camp. Camp Eagle hosts an annual climbing festival. Since it primarily operates as a camp, the lodgings are comfy and the food yummy. Camping is available. View a guidebook at www.campeagle.org, and contact the camp to arrange a climbing trip at: info@campeagle.org.

A *Really* Sketchy Guide to Lake mother fuckin' Whitney

More DWS! Google up the Texas Parks & Wildlife webpage. The park is Soldiers Bluff Park in Whitney, Texas, west of Hillsboro, which is between Dallas and Austin along I-35. Camping, mountain biking, and other activities are allowed. The DWS is accessible by canoe or maybe long, long swims. (Consider an inflatable dingy.) Like PmfB, the water level varies. Check the current level by googling "Lake Whitney Texas water level" (and similar for temp). That took us to a page under www.waterdata.us.gs.gov/usa/nwis, but hopefully your Google search goes straight to the Lake Whitney chart.

Ben Edwards checked it out at water level 518'. (The park says the normal level is about 533'. That's quite a difference. DWS might only be present in drought conditions.) Ben stopped at only 3 cliffs and tried over half a dozen problems, but said "there were a lot more possibilities." He thought the canoe is optional, but it's a lot of swimming to the problems. If the water level went up 10 feet, only one of the three areas would be underwater. The climbing was good, steep, but they couldn't top out what they were on.

A couple pages of Texas Limestone Bouldering covers this area and compliment its pockets, huecos and tufas.

For information on Soldiers Bluff Park, scroll down to it on www.swf-wc.usace.army.mil/whitney/recreation/parks/corpsparks.asp.

Judge Reinhardt, "Here's To Swimmin' With Bowlegged Women" @ Medicine Wall

Pecos River / Continental Ranch

Remote limestone climbing, open only a small part of the year, but now closed to individuals. Groups/guides who can demonstrate proof of insurance are still welcome. Some information on the area is on rockclimbing.com.

Hueco Tanks

Best bouldering in the universe, plus great sport routes. The sport route hardware has been rusty and suspect for years, but this winter a rebolting effort will get underway. See the article in Rock & Ice #199 (January, 2012).

El Potrero Chico

EPC is a Texas climbing area, much like Colorado is a Texas ski area. Texas climbers used to go to EPC a lot. Ritually. Every Thanksgiving *at least*. Then the drug war scared off most of us, and we muttered about the good old days for the next few years. The situation is still a topic of discussion at every seven or so ATX climbing outings. For this book, we broke out of resignation and began investigating the risks. As luck would have it, a day later, 7 deaths in Hidalgo were reported by a Facebook individual on November 8, 2011s. But, as with most things, the situation isn't black and white.

Mexico's 2010 murder rate was 3 times that of the US[297] but only slightly higher than the US for people who are not members of a drug cartel.[298] The murder rate throughout Mexico is only 14 in 100,000 (0.014%), but it varies a lot by state. The border state relevant to travel from Austin (Nuevo Leon) had an even lower rate of 0.006%[299]. If that's not good enough for you, don't ever go to New Orleans (0.064%).

But these stats are old, and the risks change as the drug war develops. The stats do not show the risk of traveling across border towns or from the Monterrey airport. Monterrey has had fire fights, road blocks, a mass-murder in a casino, and robbery of travelers. The border towns are beachheads for drug traffic into the U.S. Because you just have to smoke your weed, don't you. Because *the man* won't legalize that weed. Who's more at fault — you or *the man*? Only Jah can judge.

An entry in John Sanders' route logbook from BITD

The state department now warns about travel in Nuevo Leon and Tamaulipas,[300] and it issues general warnings about daytime and nighttime carjackings targeting all types of vehicles. It says most victims survive if they cooperate with the carjackers. If you drive, one report[301] advises always driving during the day, planning all your stops, convoying for security, and being aware that cartels keep lookouts at rest stops to spot drivers who are good targets for theft of car or money. One traveler checks several Twitter accounts for reports of cartel roadblocks. Are we there yet?

In contrast to that view of the roads, Chris Durchholz went recently and found the toll road well patrolled by federal cops (not the corrupt-prone local cops). This road's risks are likely very low compared to other Mexican roads. The toll road is pricey but is the only driving choice recommended at www. potrerochico.org/arriving/driving. That site provides detailed directions, though you should ignore the Columbia Bridge option which it suggests as an alternative. Columbia Bridge's remoteness presents risks not present in the highly populated, well-patrolled Nuevo Laredo.

Other driving tips learned over the years by Rockabout employees: Drive high-riding vehicles (not sedans) to reduce the chance of tire blowout on the many potholes. Convoy to safely deal with car trouble – a lone stranded car is a target. Drive kind of fast; it shows you know where you're going and makes you less attractive as a target. Day travel is the goal, but border delays can force you driving at night. Tell anyone you talk to (including border agents) that you are going to see friends in Mexico. That way they know someone is expecting you.

Chris Barton travels by bus (the A. Rodriguez bus line, in a building behind the IHop at Cesar Chavez and I-35), leaving late and sleeping all the way. *Beta*.[302] The only "bus jacking" hits we found are from Seattle, Kansas City, Newark, and 2 hours outside of Cancun. Chris Durchholz suggests flying into Monterrey, and having Magic Ed pick you up at the airport. He charges $50, the same as the taxis, plus you get 45 minutes of beta and stories on the ride. His auto is a beater, perhaps making it less of a target than a rental or taxi.

Is Hidalgo itself safe? On 12/10/11, www.borderlandbeat.com reported the recent "7 deaths" as 18 arrests and 1 death, when an army patrol happened upon preoccupied Zetas. (Locals say it was 7 deaths.) If it's unsettling to learn of a Zeta presence in Hidalgo, check out the gang activity regularly reported in Austin. Chris Durchholz said Hidalgo appeared safe, kids playing in the street, and the locals relaxed and wondering what the big deal is. Other locals (e.g. Lucas Johnson) went their in recent months and had no problems. Hidalgo no longer has a local police force, as Mexico has found and disbanded many corrupt police departments. Chris says the locals saw this as a positive step forward. In their place is an army station. Kita says

[297] www.economist.com/blogs/gulliver/2010/08/mexico

[298] www.bajainsider.com/baja-california-travel/mexico-travel-warning.htm

[299] www.mexicoevalua.org/descargables/d15292_Indice-de-Inseguridad-Ciudadana-y-Violencia.pdf (See the graph on page 29)

[300] www.travel.state.gov/travel/cis_pa_tw/tw/tw_5440.html

[301] An Austin American Statesman article by Alfredo Corchado, printed on 12/2/11.

[302] Conversational Spanish is advised. This bus beats Greyhound because it only stops at the border, whereas Greyhound has an additional transfer and also three stops. A. Rodriguez bus leaves 10:30pm every night, arriving in Monterrey around 6:30am. Roundtrip is around $75 plus a possible $10 bribe for the border guards. At the Monterrey bus station, show your bus ticket and ask to arrange a cab to Hidalgo's town square as part of the bus fare. At Hidalgo, ask the cabby to take you up to Posada, for a couple USD's. Chris isn't aware of a website or phone number for A. Rodriguez. Show up to get a ticket. Chris has used this line three times.

they're professional, "friendly as you can imagine" and there for your protection. Ryan Jordan fears Texas highways more than his trip to EPC.

EPC climbing season used to see 250-300 climbers. 2011 saw only about 100. That's 100 climbers who have had a great time without incident.

Conclusion: the frequently reported violence should be kept in perspective, with that violence spread over a relatively large country and heavily weighted among gang members. If you go, look and act the part of not-a-target. If you drive, take a beater car. Wear cheap clothing, and pay everything with small bills. And, perhaps, fear EPC rock-fall more than the Zetas. For now. Conditions will change, one way or the other. Do your own research and travel at your own risk.

Sodapop Wall,
~13 undeveloped routes, Pace Bend Road

Your Own Crag

Four different climbers around Austin have bought home sites, first at Monster Rock, then at Flat Creek. There are plenty of cliff home sites along Pace Bend Road, the roads on either side of Lick Creek, a side road off of Old Ferry, and likely many more areas. Pace Bend constantly has blank lots and old homes for sale. In this real estate slump, it might be possible to buy one of them and add a repossessed double-wide (where allowed), septic field, well, and hot tub for a reasonable multiple over the median price of Austin homes. Live the dream!

Other Online Sources:

www.Wideopentexas.com - a place to find anything outdoors in Texas, including climbing, mountain biking, camping, backpacking, kayaking, etc. There are entries for all the known climbing areas in Texas, including areas off the beaten path. This website will add lots of route descriptions, photos, and videos. The primary navigation is an interactive map for every combination of activity. (You can navigate a map that shows climbing and biking, or camping and kayaking, etc., to plan your multi-sport outing.) Anybody can create an account and create or edit information about areas.

www.MountainProject.com – a rock climbing route database that focuses on the classic routes in each area.

Appendix C: **Defunct Climbing Areas**

Route development is often experimental. The bolter doesn't know whether the route will stay open to the public, survive hold breaks, and be popular enough for the trouble. Bolting routes and walls is like fishing. Sometimes you catch, and sometimes you don't. In appreciation of the failed experiments inevitable for successes elsewhere, this appendix summarizes the climbing areas that, for whatever reasons (including city closure), failed to maintain traffic. The bolts on these areas are suspect. May these experiments Rust in Peace.

Greenbelt: Mopac Bridge

Access via the Twin Falls Access.

Urban Surprise (Aid), Sean O'Grady. Located on the backside of the North-bound bridge's 2nd abutment. This is a former bolted-on-plastic-holds route from the '90s, chopped by the city. It's now a tall Aid route on protruding bolts and a few drilled pockets, though the Dept. of Homeland Security might arrest you on suspicion of felony sabotage (of the bridge). Look, but stay off. The bolting by one of Austin's finest was done by a ballzzzzzzzzey solo across the underside of the bridge to install anchors. R.I.P., Urban Surprise.

Lake Ladybird: Tom Miller Dam

Access comprises terrorist activity. Don't be a terrorist. Back before 911, this 90' cement face had 3 trad routes ranging 5.9-5.10 up the cement seam cracks, with flush pipes accepting #10 hexes every 30'. Route names are lost, but John Sanders was a participant. Other routes likely went in later, during Austin's chipping phase.

Greenbelt: North Climbing Areas

The next time you tweak out or feel like some bouldering, come take a fun hike to see climbing history set in stone. Take Barton Springs Road east from Loop 1 (Mopac). Turn right into the Barton Springs parking area. Park at the south end, near the outdoor theater. Hike the big crushed-granite trail south. It passes flatlands above the banks of the creek. Reach the **Ka'nee Knee's Wall** bouldering area (described in Texas Limestone Bouldering) at N30˚ 15.764' W97˚ 46.857' (30.262733 -97.78095). It has several roofs and a traverse whose right section is in-tact, but its left section fell apart. (The three boulders at the trail's edge serve as a landmark.) The topo photos are old film shots by John Sanders plus some photo-shopping to enhance his route lines and labels.

Ka'nee Knee's Wall

Further left, 260 paces after the green "050" marker, you will reach **Rappeller's Wall** (aka. The Bluff) where there are three chest-high fence posts (chopped telephone poles) across the trail. The color roof shot shows one of the poles, but this roof is right of the known routes first toproped by John "Goomba" Sanders and friends. 3-4 anchor bolts might remain; scramble up the gully to the left. The following route lists are left-to-right, though we're presenting these various walls right-to-left, in the order you likely approach them from Zilker Park. R.I.P., Rappeller's Wall.

Roof Right of Rappeller's Wall

1. **The Sink** (V2). Start inside the small cave to the left of the wall and climb out.
2. **The Plumber** (V3). Exit "The Sink" right on thin sidepulls.

Rappeller's Wall (aka. The Bluff)

3. **The Traverse Route** (5.6)
4. **Alley Oop** (5.7)
5. **Left T Head** (5.6)
6. **Right T Head** (5.6)

Not far to the left is **Wasp Wall**, 40' tall, with branching routes forming a tree pattern (see Wasp Wall, right" topo on the next page). The wall is on private property. No house is visible, but it's up there. Land developer Sid Jagger started building his home above the cliff, chopped anchors off a route while a climber was on it, and tossed debris off the top to trash the climbing area. He installed motion-detecting sirens that went off whenever a climber topped out. He supposedly had his lot line redefined to include the cliff bottom. Bill Horton attempted civil discussions that got nowhere; someone else vandalized (or burned, depending on the account) his house that was under construction. Someone buy this house and restore the routes. Until then…R.I.P., Wasp Wall.

7. **Atomic Rush** (5.10c) Bill and Paul Horton.
8. **Rush** (5.10**)** James Crump.
   a. **Direct** (5.6). The name is deceiving. Start Wasp, cut left and arc back to Wasp's finish.
9. **Wasp** (5.8) James Crump.
10. **Mosquito** (5.9) James Crump.
11. **Grunt** (5.?)
12. **Holtzendorf Direct** (5.7) Harold Holtzendorf[303].
13. **Stretch** (5.6)
14. **Up and Back** (5.?)
15. **Classic** (5.4). This dihedral route was popular for guiding newbs.

[303] Harold died soloing Lubrication in Estes Park.

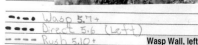
Wasp Wall, left

John Sanders
collection 📷

John Sanders' nasty 4th fall,
"The Grand Traverse"

Greenbelt: The Grand Traverse

Left of Wasp Wall is the first really sexy wall full of solution pockets on its middle band. **The Grand Traverse** (5.0-5.4, ending at 5.10) starts on the left side of the pockets and goes right about 100'. Easy trad climbing until it cruxes at 5.10. Back in the day, John "Goomba" Sanders worked it and took falls four times, the last time with a big flake breaking and pinning him and his gear, jacking him up. Goomba might have the only ascent. It's not dead—just sleeping.

Greenbelt: Balrog Wall

From The Grand Traverse, hike briefly till you see the green "075" marker on the trail. Balrog Wall is beautiful and wide, spanning well left and right of this marker, with houses (some resembling apartments) right on top of the cliff. GPS N30° 15.628' W97° 47.143' (30.260467 -97.785717). There are a lot more potential routes here than the six historical routes listed below. A coalition of climber-investors should buy all of these houses. Balrog Wall is the all-time greatest name for a climbing wall. Since the wall is defunct, let's swap bland "New Wall" with "Balrog Wall." Toproping in the Greenbelt was mainly done at this wall and Wasp Wall, in the mid-70's. R.I.P., Balrog Wall.

1. **Sanders/ McClure Traverse** (V3)*** , John Sanders, Dan McClure. Traverses the lower band. This problem appears in fine shape. Walk the ledge above the problem to clean off the holds. Dan lived in the apartments above the routes.
2. **Tit Scratch Fever** (5.11) James Crump.
3. **Head Trip** (5.11) Dave Head.
4. **Balrog** (5.11a) James Crump. James' FA was a pivotal event in Austin climbing.[304]
5. **Rocket Pocket** (5.10c) James Crump.
6. **Zipper Lounge** (5.10a) Garth McGee[305]. Climbs the dihedral.

Wasp Wall, right

Balrog Wall

[304] Back in the day, before everything was bolted out, there were rivalries on these short Texas routes, shadowing the great mountaineering rivalries of past centuries. Back in high school, James Crump and Garth McGee were rivals, competing for the FA's of Fear of Flying and Clockwerk Orange at Erock. Keith Guillory brought them together one day, at Wasp Wall and Balrog Wall. James was in the zone the whole day, flashing everything, including Garth's project, Balrog. Garth left butthurt, and they never climbed together again, and found themselves glaring at each other during workouts in a college gym-rehab class. That day of climbing and the Balrog ascent was magic for Crump, spurring his growth for the harder routes he developed later.

[305] Garth was a trip. He violently hated being photographed, observing the theory of soul-stealing, and he'd fight about it and demand your camera.

Greenbelt: Campbell's Hole

The birthplace of Austin rock climbing, on the slab boulder problems Father Clem used to teach climbing techniques to some Whole Earth employees circa 1970.

Use the Spyglass Access. Hike down the trail and turn left. Routes are on a tall wall on the other side of the creek. Or use the Directions for Balrog Wall and walk 130 more paces from Balrog Wall's left end. When the water is up, this area is a popular hangout to swim, tan, and Par Tay!! Another potential access is from behind Barton Hills Elementary School on the east bank of the creek. After climbing New Wall, come here when the water is up to chill and spot rusty bolts with binoculars. R.I.P., Campbell's Hole.

Holy Diver (5.12) Hank Caylor.
Gravity's Angel (5.11) Calvin Hiser.

Lake Austin: Frank's Meat Market

Take Highway 360 North from town. Park immediately after crossing the arching "360 Bridge" across beautiful Lake Austin. The routes are on both sides of the bridge. R.I.P., Frank's Meat Market.

East Side of the Bridge:

Left Arête (5.7)
Frank's Crack (5.9) Dave Hannah. This crack can be seen from the road. 5.9 to the roof; 5.11 pulling the roof.
Frank's Meat Market (5.11) James Crump FA (aid), Jeff Jackson FFA (first free ascent).
Franks Direct (5.12) Jeff Jackson.

West Side of the Bridge:

Hammerhead (5.12d) 4 bolts, Hank Caylor. This route starts on real rock, then climbs (climbed) the roof with four bolted-on gym holds. '94
I Do (5.11) Kirk Holladay, Brian Wann '94.
Unknown (5.11) Charlie Chapman. This route has (had?) one gym hold.
Woofin Hooters (5.11) Hank Caylor, Randy Harris. '86

North Side Road Cut

Road Pizza (5.9) Hank Caylor. As a child, I used to glance at road cuts to spot the potential lines of weakness. They looked so fun. Hank actually bolted one! '87

North-West Austin: Bull Creek (Library Wall, Bonzo Wall, Gooch Wall)

Take Loop1 (aka. Mopac) north from downtown. Take 2222 west on cool, winding roads best travelled in a bitchin' convertible. After your thrill-ride, pass the scrumptious County Line BBQ joint, then take a right on Lakewood Drive before you reach 360. (Or, when in a boring sedan, take 360 north from downtown, exit 2222, take a right, and take a left onto Lakewood Dr.)

This area is actively used for interesting (and sometimes cryptic) semi-high-ball slick-foot bouldering on an almost vertical boulder face, over sweet pea-gravel landings. All this to the right of Lakewood Drive. Thin crimps and pockets; build your tissue strength here, gradually. We used to hit it impatiently, wanting long sessions and tweaking out every time. The bouldering is covered extensively in Texas Limestone Bouldering, and the sport route descriptions on rockclimbing.com offer some details for route location.

Ryan Blenkhorn 📷

Michael Bukowski,
sick problem across the stream @ Bull Creek

The sport routes are downstream from the cool bouldering.

Rick Watson feels Surrender was about the best 5.12 around. In 2008, Tommy Blackwell said Surrender (with 5/8" stud bolts) was in great condition; it's likely fine today. The rest of Bull Creek's bolts are likely rust; Matt Twyman found it generally in ruins in 2008. Growing up, Matt's favorite routes there were Surrender, Gulliver's Travels, Lord of the Flies, Altered States, and Chemical Warfare. Pockets at Bull Creek accumulate calcification that has to be chipped out to climb them. R.I.P., Bull Creek sport routes.

***The Library Wall** – Just past the first huge overhanging section. On private land, and, more importantly, on choss and rusty bolts!*

Do the Right Thing (5.12a) Jeff Jackson. Doable in two pitches to avoid rope drag.

Blatant (5.12a) FA Dave Head, FFA Mike Head, Scott Harris, Larry Spears. Start on Do the Right Thing to Bolt 1. Cut up and right to a sovereign bolt. Continue up and right to Lord of the Flies.

Lord of the Flies (5.12) Russell Rand.
Metaphysics (5.12c) Jeff Jackson.
Kubla Kahn (5.13) Jeff Jackson.
Finnegan's Wake (5.13d).
Surrender (5.12) Jack Mileski. (His gift to Jeff and Christina Jackson on their wedding.)
Atlas Shrugged (5.12) Jeff Jackson.
Gulliver's Travels (5.12d) Jeff Jackson.
Abandoned Project.
Altered States (5.12) Greg Brooks.

***Bonzo Wall** – Downstream from The Library Wall.*
Ricks Traverse
Bronco (5.12 R) Jeff Jackson
The Green Fuse (5.12a) Jeff Jackson
Boss Bull (5.12a) Jeff Jackson
Raging Bull (5.12a) Jeff Jackson. Climbs the arête left of Bedtime for Bonzo.
Italian Route (A2) James Crump.

Bedtime for Bonzo (5.11) James Crump. Start on the left side of the leaning boulder. Traverse right and finish on Bonzo's Revenge. This and Urban Assault were trad lines but also the first bolted lines in Austin. '81 This route was named to honor President Reagan when he was shot by John Hinckley, and survived. It turns out, with 4 assassinated U.S. presidents among 56 , the Commander in Chief has a lower survival rate than the average U.S. soldier in wartime, excluding our by-far-most-deadly war, the Civil War. Presidents have only a 7% survival rate, as compared to 3.66% if you were a Marine in World War II. There have been 20 assassination attempts. No matter what party has the presidency, our presidents deserve more respect than we give them.

Bonzo's Revenge (5.13) Hank Caylor.
Head Thing (project). Starts Bonzo's Revenge, then cuts right.
Beans and Rice (5.12a) Jeff Jackson.
Chemical Warfare (5.11a) Greg Brooks
Minerva (5.11c) Elaine Catlin.

***Far Wall** – roughly 200 yards downstream.*
Gooched (5.11) Bill Gooch. The loneliest route in Austin?

North-West Austin: Mount Bonnell

The routes are at Austin's prime romantic overlook off Mount Bonnell Road, off of 2222. The bolts are not maintained, and the City banned climbing to protect the McMansion owners below the routes. You will get arrested climbing here. Jeff and Alex worked this area and Bull Creek about the time that New Wall was being bolted. They put up mixed lines, supplementing bolts with European trad techniques (jammed fabric knots), as an impact-minimizing aesthetic. Non-rock-scaring knots are way cooler than limestone-shattering tricams. Today, there's interest at CTM for regaining access here. Until then…R.I.P., Mount Bonnell.

Roof Uno
Last Picture Show (5.10) Jeff Jackson. Roof Uno (5.11 TR). Chucks (5.9) Christina Jackson.

Roof Dos
High Times (5.11) Hank Caylor. Ecbatana (5.12-) Alex Catlin. Tree of Woe (5.12-) Jefe. Torts (5.10-) Jefe.

Roof Big
Nineveh (5.12-) Alex Catlin. Aid Line (unfinished).

Eulogy

What is to be made of these obscure bygone routes? How can we benefit from the record of route names, grades, and FAs? In a pinch, one can tear out these pages for toilet paper and head downhill from your current crag location. In retrospect, each route was a mini-adventure for the FA and for anyone who subsequently climbed the route. What is left for the rest of us? Royal Robbins once said a good route name is like a short poem. Enjoy the poems.

Appendix D: **The History of Climbing**

Human climbing proceeded as follows: 1. tree climbing 2. bouldering 3. buildering (by the construction workers and thieves of early civilizations) 4. mountaineering 5. aid climbing 6 badass bouldering 7. trad 8. sport 9. gym.

Ethics squabbles over the rules of the game hit their stride in the Aid phase, where guys like Royal Robbins argued which tools were cool (e.g. rock-scarring pitons) and which weren't (e.g. expansion bolts). Recently, several hundred years into mountaineering, folks still discussed the rules of the game when considering whether Mallory or Hillary made the first ascent of Mount Everest. (Mallory died and was found close to the summit; he likely topped out and died during the descent. His son graciously sided with the opinion that a first mountain ascent is not complete until one returns alive.)

Today, sport climbing's main rule is the *send*. A *send* is leading a route, with or without pre-hung draws and tick marks, optionally stick-clipping the most commonly stick-clipped bolt, with no falls nor weighting of the rope, and clipping both anchors, after which you can be lowered and can die on the descent.[306] And you're allowed to preview the route on rappel and work any top sections prior to climbing them. The rule of sending is a little complicated, but we think we have it right. Errata will be published in 2nd edition.

John Sanders collection 📷   **Goomba, long ago**

Important milestones in sport climbing: 5.10, 5.11, 5.12, 5.13a, 5.13b, 5.13c, then 5.13d, 5.14a, 5.14b, then 5.14c, 5.14d, 5.15a, and, last but not least, 5.15b.

Along the way, climbing became as popular as softball. Every other school kid now climbs. If Mallory were asked today, "Why bolt Tree Gnome?" He'd answer, "Because it is there." Austin is a growing city, and its most popular sport-climbing walls are crowded. Crowding was seen even back in the Aid phase. Warren Harding bagged the Aid FA of the popular Nose route on El Capitan and later wrote, "It's unfortunate that great numbers of climbers bunch up the way they do at well-known climbing areas…There's still a hell of a lot of room if (they) just use some imagination — like, spread out!"[307] If Harding were alive and climbing our short Austin routes, he'd likely be at Hand Beyond, Tit For Tom, Landfill Wall, Beehive Wall, etc.

Appendix E: **The Future of Climbing**

Sport climbing is gonna progress like this: 5.15c, 5.15d, 5.16a-and-that's-fucking-IT! There actually *is* a limit to what can be climbed free, due to limits on the friction capabilities of skin on rock. The power required to pull moves approaching those limits will go up exponentially, but humans can't train power exponentially. Power increases only linearly. Humans won't have a long enough lifetime to train 5.16b power. Game over, FINALLY!

Alright…not really. There are always bigger dynos and crazier, lower-probability throws that may take 100 tries to stick. Maybe endurance and dynos will be the last frontiers for grade progression. As you proceed on your journey to 5.16b, please remember all the little people that belayed you on your way up. We all serve the elites by sharing the fun of the sport, which brings in the next generation of potential elites. Most of us know we aren't going to reach 5.16. Many of us won't reach 5.12 or 5.13. Many stay at 5.10. Since climbing is personal, the future of climbing isn't the 5.16 elites. It's you!

What's your future? Austin offers many routes under 5.11, enough to keep many of us happy for years. But many of them are crowded. Seismers and Dead Cats are overrun! Advance deep into the 5.11's, if you can, and your rewards are wilder moves, a lot more routes to climb, and more opportunities to escape the crowds. A rigorous training program can get you there, if you have the time and discipline. If not, try the following shortcuts, and have a great time climbing and growing in the sport.

---

[306] That's when most climbing accidents happen, from half-tied knots, anchor-cleaning mistakes, and rappelling off the end of your rope.
[307] From Downward Bound – A Mad Guide to Rock Climbing, Warren Harding, Menasha Ridge Press Climbing Classics Series, 1975.

How to Climb 5.11d

<u>Learn from better climbers:</u>

The most complicated sport in the world is the martial arts. Those Kung Fu guys are so *badass intricate*, they make us climbers look like we're playing checkers. But climbing is still plenty complicated, and climbing makes all other sports combined look like small-town Bingo on a hot Saturday afternoon. With this complexity, you can not progress without learning from better climbers. Watch them carefully on the routes at and slightly above your limit. Note the moves they do that you don't use. Throw those moves at your project routes. They'll fail, as you'll not try them in the right spots. But, over time, you'll build the skill to use them at the right time.

<u>Work on form:</u>

Good form boosts power *instantly*. Regularly use routes to focus on form instead of on sending. Go up the route, attempting to use one or more of the following "good forms" as much as the route allows:

1. Turn a shoulder to the wall as much as you profitably can (often set up by backstepping or stemming, and outside-edging instead of toeing). You'll feel semi-rests and higher reaches come from this. Many climbers stay faced square to the rock, ascending less efficiently than possible. (Advice courtesy of David Cardosa.)

2. Pull with both arms. Especially when one hand is lower than the other, still pull with both. If the lower hand goes up next, you'll have a timing decision about how long to keep pulling with it before releasing it to accurately hit the next hold. (Advice courtesy of Steven McReynolds.)

3. Make powerful moves by pulling first with the lats, then with the biceps. The lats pull you up only an inch — then your biceps pull far. How does the little lat pull do anything? We think it tightens the shoulder so the bicep isn't pulling on slop. And, it gets your body moving a couple miles per hour upwards, meaning your biceps kick in with momentum already going. They'll crank harder. (Advice courtesy of Rebecca Steiner.) Make this a habit on powerful moves. Your power will increase instantly. And, use it on short moves when you're pumped. You'll be less likely to pump out.

4. Weight the feet and legs as heavily as you can. (Advice courtesy of Boone Speed.) This removes weight from the arms. When the feet are bad, trust them on smears and marginal holds. Look for every foot trick: stemming, high steps, jams, rock-ons, toe hooks, heel hooks, etc. Most of us learn this basic concept early, but the trick is re-dedicating attention to it as the routes get harder.

<u>Be Strategic:</u> Practice pyramiding in selecting your current set of project routes. To reach your first 11a, work on a few 11a candidates while having sent two 10d's, four 10c's, and eight 10b's. When you've bagged that first 11a, move your entire pyramid up a letter grade: start working on a few 11b's, and fill in your second 11a, third and fourth 10d, and four more 10c's. If you take time off, refresh (re-send) the lower parts of your pyramid. Climber geeks enjoy their pyramid and the progress it expresses.

<u>Be Prepared:</u> I used to improvise my beta on every route. Improvisation is great fun, but before a project drags out and becomes frustrating, focus on execution. If you can't remember the entire dance, write it down. Not just the crux beta; the entire route (all handholds plus the key footholds), to commit to memory. On the hike out and the drive home, recall the entire route, visualizing each hold and move. Review and visualize the entire route at home, or, better yet, at work. Since climbing is so fun, this "virtual climbing" can be pretty enjoyable. Back at the crag, before every attempt, visualize every move. (This practice was motivated by watching **Russell Mayes** prepare for an FA at his limit. See the footnote under Sick Experiments.)

<u>Control Your Breathing:</u> The purpose of big, slow, relaxing breaths is to drop your heart rate. A high heart rate sends more blood to your forearms, and you pump out quicker. Pick spots on the route to chillax your breath. (Advice courtesy of **John Myrick**, coach of Team ARG.)

<u>Control Your Mind:</u> An important part of beta is your thoughts and emotions. Both your body and mind are climbing the route. If your mind says you're going to fail, your body *will*. If you get scared of pulling the crux over a runout, you *won't*. Shift your thoughts and emotions to serve you best at various spots in your beta. Identify where you want to feel relaxation, dominance, anger, and rage. Relaxation is great at the rests and semi-rests. Dominance is great on balancy moves. Rage is best as you're reaching for the crux hold. Scream! Controlled anger is productive right as you enter a runout, or right at a hard-hitting pump, to crowd out those fears and push onward. The balance of the route's feelings depends on the route; mainly it's about staying attentive to the beta and aggressive enough to eliminate defeatist thoughts and fears.

> MAYBE you need to work out more.
>
> *Ann Raber*

Appendix F: **The Dharma Gate: a rock climbing love affair**
by Rupesh Chhagan

*originally appeared in www.windhorsemedicine.com/blog
reprinted with permission*

Rock climbing is my longest relationship. Like any long-term relationship, we've gone through our ups and downs. When I first met her, my jaw dropped to the floor. I got heart palpitations. The rest of the world fell away. I dreamt of her day and night. Skipped school and worked only enough to pay for gear, gas, and park fees. She was my love. She was my obsession.

In the beginning, we were on our best behavior – always considerate and filled with wonder for each others' quirks. I was a beginner and she forgave my clumsy overtures. But slowly, over time, my happiness started to depend on how sweet she was to me that day. If there was progress on a climb or a send (completing a climb without falling), all was right with the world. I had value. She loved me. But if she spurned me…If there was regress or failure on a climbing project, I was lost. My worth creaked in the winds of our meetings, like a dead tree branch with a tenuous hold on the trunk. The torrid love affair started to fizzle. She grew tired of my lapdog fervor. Things were off and strained, but I pretended like I didn't notice. Over and over, she spit me off the rock until my shoulder was torn, my adrenaline-addled brain was mush, and my skin exploded in hives. Eventually, I got the point. She wanted a divorce.

I conceded that we needed time apart. "Let's just try being separated for awhile. We can date, try other things. Just don't give up on me baby. We used to be magic. Please?" She agreed. For a year, I wandered lonely as a cloud, trying to enjoy being single again. It was a dark time, living with my parents, working the night shift at our motel,

Rupesh Chhagan, working Clayton's 13d/14a project, Insect Wall north

and nursing an obliterated rotator cuff. But a curious thing happened. I remembered that I could read. I dabbled with Tai Chi. Saw an acupuncturist. Developed a crush on Chinese Medicine. In time, I actually fell in love with energy medicine. I dove into Chinese Medicine with the whole-hearted obsession that I once gave climbing. I actually forgot about her for awhile. I started thinking it may be over. She wasn't good for me anymore. She brought out the aggressive side of me. She callused my hands and dulled my sensitivity. So I turned my back on her. I turned my back on the incessant goal-setting, the competitive covetous side of me, the need for high stimulation to feel alive. Eventually, I broke it to her. "Sorry, I'm done with you baby."

But she would come to me in quiet moments. I'd remember the ferocious beautiful dance across horizontal roofs. The ebb and flow of muscle and tendon and kinesthetic geometry flowing through Nature. I'd remember the moment blazing with single-minded focus, karate chop explosions, followed by steady rhythmic breathing. So I'd see her every now and then. Just for kicks. Nothing serious. Something was different this time though. Rather than blame her when I got hell-bent, uptight, and possessive, the thought arose: "Maybe it's *me* who needs to change, not her…"

Which brings me here to why I chose the name, "Dharma Gate," for my latest rock climbing project. Here's the definition of dharma:

1. The essential function or nature of a thing.
2. The principle or law that orders the universe.
3. Individual conduct in conformity with this principle.

Climbing fits me like a second skin. I'm a climber. It's my dharma. Doing it feels natural. Together, we are communion – a beautiful blend of strength, flexibility, daring, meditation, puzzle-solving, exploration, and Nature expression. And it reveals my shadow side. My covetous nature, obsessive-compulsiveness, unquenchable thirst for intensity, and relentless yearning for legacy and fame. And this shadow side is my dharma as well. It's my dharma as a human being, an animal competing for resources and making meaning out of the meaningless.

If you choose to notice, a climbing project can reveal yourself to yourself just as time on a meditation cushion can. All these mental states that working on a project produces can be *mindfully observed*, becoming springboards to greater awareness. Turning your attention towards your sensations, attitudes, and thoughts is a turning towards the way the universe works. How so? We are waves in the ocean of the universe. Rising up in apparent individuality for a time, then returning back into Oneness. Often lost in self-centered absorption, we forget that we are inextricably part of it all. And when you get mindful about how you tick, you glimpse how the big picture ticks. Perhaps this is what Dogen hints at with this quote: "To study the Way is to study the self. To study the self is to forget the self. To forget the self is to be enlightened by all things of the universe."

So the shadow side teaches me about what creates suffering. Chasing after first ascents and legacy…ahhh, hello suffering mind of vanity. Fantasizing about moves instead of being with the loved ones in front of you…ahhh, hello suffering mind of distraction. Needing the euphoria of standing triumphantly on top of a rock…ahhh, hello suffering mind of craving. In this very personal way, the Way of the universe is revealed. This begets that. This cause, that effect. The dharma of the universe.

No matter the success or failure, all moments are dharma gates, entry points to an awakened mind. Hence the name, Dharma Gate. There's a line within a famous chant in the Zen tradition: "Dharma gates are boundless, I vow to enter them." So, with this climb, I took my time with the process. I went home without the prize in my hand many times, disappointed, but never crushed by the outcome. I stayed curious throughout. In the end, the send was not pretty. It was not poetry in motion as I had imagined in my mind. Yet this too, is another dharma gate. The fantasy I had and the actual reality that arose.

She's a wife now. I'm committed to her. I love spending time with her. But we also do our own things now. Give each other space. It's the dharma of relationship.

Appendix G: **The Fall**

A typical fun day at the crag. Belaying and talking. My peripheral vision catching someone taking a short, routine lead fall. The usual. The fall lasts an instant. Then longer. In less time than thought, my spine sends signals that this fall is too long, too far. By the time my mind takes notice, the horror emerges. That climber has decked.

Feet slam the ground, back clubs hard against a boulder. The face of a friend cries in agony.

A sudden hell crushes all that was.

Appendix H: **Squirrel Encounters of the Third Kind**

as told by Pete Bishop, featuring Jeff Olson[308]

originally appeared in the Austin_Climbing yahoo group
reprinted with permission

As I was walking out of the Greenbelt tonight, a blinding light flashed in the outhouse, and lo, there appeared two beings who spoke to me with this message for Jeff:

Pete Bishop on Lip-o-suction

"Hi, I'm Larry, Lord of the Squirrels. You can tell I am Lord because I have the biggest nuts. And this is my son, Bob, who, other than still believing his mother is a virgin (as if- his real father is either my brother Daryle, or my other brother Daryle), is only a little nuts. Anyhoo, I bring you a message to Jeff the Tall.

Jeff the Tall, we have your carabiner and Gri-Gri! They are, for the moment, unharmed, secreted within a dark pouch. If you wish to see them again, uncorroded, you must do one of the following. Either bring a large sack of acorns, a sack of such hugeness as to block the sun, to the large belaying rock beneath Bongo Fury in the place called Reimers, or, answer the questions three. Succeed at either one of these tests, but not both, and your items will be returned to you unharmed. Perform not more than one test, and, if it is so your choice, answer not one or two of the questions three, nor four or five. Nor bring a sack too small to block the sun, nor one so large as to hide the heavens. Neither an under achiever, nor an over achiever be, or your items will see not the light of day. Remember your previous encounter with us?

Thus I speak, Larry Thy Squirrelly Lord"

Suddenly, an implosion of light and darkness again. I was sorely afraid, not so much for me, but for what they may do to Jeff's innocent items.

Jeff the Tall soon scheduled 1 1/2 tons of acorns to be drop shipped via helicopter. The helicopter never showed up, putting my life in mortal danger as I had already negotiated with Larry, Lord of the Squirrels, to return the hostage Gri-Gri. In desperation, Jeff struggled mightily and managed to answer questions three, the difficult task being to ask himself three questions that he could then answer. After hours of pondering, and trying to send Irreverent Youth, and, failing that attempt, sending House of Pain, he had an epiphany and answered "Yes. No. I don't know." We may never know what the questions three answer were, but we must take him at his word that his answers were correct. Larry, Lord of the Squirrels, appeared to be satisfied.

> You boys goin' there ta do some ah them there rope tricks?
>
> *Old Man Stotz, at Pack Saddle*

---

[308] One day, Pete was lowering Jeff from the route "Jade." Down, down he went from this tall route...almost landing on a rattlesnake! Another time Pete was catching Jeff on Jade, Jeff forgot to tie the rest of his figure-8 and went up on a TR run, with no gear on him. Cav noticed the half-tied knot. Jeff looked at the knot, resumed climbing to a higher jug, finished the knot one-handed, and finished the climb. His on-looking wife had serious margs that evening. Pete...Jeff...these guys simply shouldn't climb together!

Appendix I: **Adventures**

The line was tall, sustained, and it scared me off. I returned, studied it harder, solved its puzzles, wired its cruxes. Trying to link it.

Twelve feet up to a sucker rest, an aggression-killer, slumped meekly under a roof. Today I skip the rest, find the crimps and attack. And gravity returns fire, blasting my arms and fingers. Feet up on crap, almost slipping. Hand arcs high to a juggy ledge, gliding barely onto it. Relief! But it's steep, so shake, chalk and go.

Foot out high on the ledge, pulls me over there, a tasty cheat past nasty handholds. Arm reaches far to teethy crimps, shoulders screaming, protesting the stretch. The crimps are briefly restful, a desert oasis surrounded by cutthroats — defeatist thoughts, beta-doubts, and fatigue. I run from them.

Aging eyes fight to find the weird footholds, and now it's time for rage. Hand high to a painful pinch. Rage kicks in. "HAAAAAAAAghgh!!!!!!!" Cut one foot loose, flying wild, freeing up the next little violence,

> a one-legged deadpoint,
> snatch a crimp in blankness,
> no aiming, just guessing,
> like shooting from the hip.

> Fingers hit it,
> body gyrates,
> hands barely hold,
> the flying leg circles,

quelling the gyrations. Brief traverse on a curvy friendly sculpture, snatch a deep pocket… Relief again! Celebrating the crux, a one-shot kill. Legs suck me into the wall, and the pocket's brief candy. A clip and short rest, but it's still steep here.

Next comes a *panic zone,* a big-time pumped-out runout, on a sea of holds, balancy footing, and two trick moves. Shut my eyes, calm for one breath. Then *rage* again, but not for power,

> for a jackboot-stomp on my inner wussy's neck,
> so he can't whine "Take,"
> right here and now,
> like every time before.

Up a tall easy reachy ladder, the rage becomes a two-edged sword.

> Now I'm shaking,
> high over the bolt,
> barely heel-hooking
> a tiny arête off right.

It crumbles a little, and my stomach drops a lot! But my heel pulls me closer to a crimpy ledge. Controlled little fall off right, and I'm on it! The trick works, just as rehearsed. My feet tip-toe nervously, back under me.

The final dance steps will work, if no mistakes are made. Uh oh… where's the rope and my leg? Will I fall inverted? No time to check. Go on!

High reach to a finger sloper, good enough to hold onto, bad to pull up on, this stretched out. I'm trapped but know my one escape. Leg stretches way out towards a dainty stem.

Am I in position to reach it again? The stretching burns, my arms are baked, the foot barely touches rock. Ahhhhh!!! The stem is pure levitation, all the way to the top.

SENT at last! Without ever taking the big plunge down. Someday, I'll watch someone else take it, and my jaw will drop to the ground.

Afterword

Afterwards comes Austin Climbing, 2nd edition!!! Watch for developments via the "Austin Climbing guidebook" fan page on Facebook or on www. AustinClimbingBook.com. Look there for downloadable errata and new route information.

For this 1st edition, I did very little market surveying to determine what to include. I wanted to have fun writing, put it out there and then listen and make changes in a later edition. (Please email me your thoughts at AustinClimbing@pobox.com.) Expect in later editions:

- Corrections to the errors you find in this edition.

- Coverage of new routes that will go up at Reimers, North Shore, the Greenbelt, and the new "South Shore" extension of Reimers bordering Crankenstein Wall (currently closed to the public).

- Coverage of San Antonio if those areas officially open to the public.

- Likely the removal of entertainment text (footnotes, appendixes, and maybe the histories) to a wiki page or other public website.

- New stories/history (that's where You come in).

- Possibly an icon revamp. Options include: total removal, retaining a few (e.g. stick clip), removing some, removing none. Another option is changing how the wall angle/shape icons work. They currently describe the routes at a micro-level. Maybe they should just show (with one or two icons) generally how steep the route is.

- Shoot better photos and give new people the opportunity to see their butts in print.

- Take feedback on grades and make adjustments.

Thanks very much for buying this book and for making Austin such a fun place to climb!

Regards,
— John

About the Author

John was voted by his peers most likely to spray and least likely to take a road trip. He retired from a software career in Dallas, and a real estate development career in Austin, and took up cedar chopping, climbing, bolting routes, and running Monster Rock. He first eyed climbing while reading history about the Matterhorn, scoping lines on road cuts as the family car sped by them on vacations, and getting nowhere on a backyard granite boulder at age 9-10 in tennis shoes. 23 years went by as a non-climber, though bagging a short dicey down-climb with his dad at Red Rocks, and a dirt/scree-pile highball in Death Valley. Then he caught plastic fever from the Dallas gyms (mostly Exposure, but also Stoneworks in the 135' tall silos).

Later he caught bolting fever from other bolters at North Shore. Among Austin's route developers, John is one of the weakest, a soft-12a wannabe, and often a total chicken on lead. Don't be surprised to see him sucking on his own routes. His biggest reason to climb is the laughs.

Route Index

Bored at the crag? Play "name the wall." One player closes their eyes to randomly select a route out of this index. Say the name, and the other players race to blurt out what wall it's on. Keep score until all but the winner concede.

S

T

All the ☐☐☐☐ check boxes are provided in case you'd like to record the different styles of ascent you manage on each route. Perhaps the first ☐ is for toproping clean or unclean, the second ☐ is for unclean leads (falls or hangdogs), the third ☐ is for redpoints, and the fourth ☐ is for onsights.

It is extremely easy to add a route and forget to mark it for inclusion in the index. If you notice a route or problem lacks an index entry, please send email to AustinClimbing@pobox.com so that it can be indexed in a later edition. Thanks!

Starters

See also page 17 for advice on taking new climbers.

5.4

5.5

5.6

5.7

Finishers

5.14

Bibliography

These recommendations are by Dmitrii Makarov, Kyle Vyoral, Chris Miller, Matt Markell, and the author. Most of these books are available on Amazon.

Serious Climbing

Cutting your teeth on well-bolted Austin sport routes is one thing, but trad climbing and multi-pitch are technical fields. They require a lot of study, practice, and different skills. Different mind sets.

You can find yourself searching for the next bolt or gear placement and spotting it 20' to your left, across blankness you cannot traverse. You can accidentally rappel past your anchors and reach the end of the rope, without anywhere to set another anchor. A placement might expand the crack enough to make the previous placement fall out. Your party can get to anchors, pull some of the rope down, but find the rest of it is caught up in some crack. And you have no other rope, traveling intentionally or ignorantly light. These books will help you decide whether you want to take on a whole level of study, practice, and risk.

Rock Climbing: Mastering Basic Skills by Craig Luebben. A comprehensive book from basic climbing moves and training to every style of climbing (e.g. multi-pitch, trad, aid, and self-rescue).

Advanced Rock Climbing by John Long & Craig Luebben. Another comprehensive book. Long's style is considered fun reading by many.

Learning to Rock Climb by Mike Loughman. Another comprehensive book. This one is out of print, but look for it on ebay.com. Dmitrii says it might be the greatest climbing book ever written.

Climbing Self-Rescue: Improvising Solutions for Serious Situations by Andy Tyson and Molly Loomis.

Climbing Anchors Second Edition by John Long. Setting anchors with gear is more complicated than setting protection on the route. A full understanding of anchoring physics not only lets you set anchors; it helps you better understand (survive) gear placements on route.

Rock Climbing Anchors by Craig Luebben. Long's book on anchors is considered classic, but this book might have the edge.

Accidents in North American Mountaineering by Jed Williamson. Annually updated, this book provides stories from all types of climbing, presenting the reasons for accidents and the ways they could have been prevented.

Climbing History

Bouldering & The Vertical Path by John Gill.

Camp 4: Recollections of a Yosemite Rockclimber by Steve Roper.

Climbing Dictionary by Matt Samet. Correctly credits Jack Mileski for "beta" and "sprague". It includes 650 (every) term from boring "crimp" to the stylish "Euroblow". Much history and amusement is recorded with these terms. Their definition of "send" is entirely imprecise, but the potential origins are amusing on "send" and other terms.

Downward Bound by Warren Harding. Amusing history of old-school and ethics squabbles, in an unusual format. This is out of print. Hound it on ebay.com.

first ascent by Stephen Venables.

Training/Performance/Rehab

9 out of 10 climbers make the same mistakes by Dave MacLeod.

Self Coached Climber by Dan Hague.

Home Climbing Gyms by Randy Leavitt.

How to Climb 5.12 by Eric Horst.

Treat Your Own Rotator Cuff by Jim Johnson, PT. The book covers *prevention* as well as rehab. We've not heard endorsements other than the glowing comments on amazon.com.